One of the greatest conundrums facing the arid western United States is the availability, use, and quality of groundwater. In large sections of the West, groundwater is the only dependable source of water for agricultural production and home consumption. Yet many of the aquifers are being depleted at a rate that will suck them dry within a century. Furthermore, dependence upon groundwater in many areas will only increase in the future. This dependence is already having serious consequences for small towns on the Great Plains. Faced with growing costs associated with deeper wells and the need for ever more advanced technology for extracting water, these towns find they lack the resources to maintain current agricultural practices.

In this timely assessment of the West's groundwater resources, the authors provide a detailed overview of groundwater management in the Western states. The authors present for each state the various management strategies, laws, and political realities that have made groundwater appropriation such a volatile subject. They also suggest possible difficulties that states and regions might face under current groundwater policies. By examining separate cases and viewing the West as a whole, the authors are able to identify not only the most pressing problems but also the most appropriate management techniques for protecting water supplies for future use.

Jeffrey S. Ashley is an assistant professor of political science at Saginaw Valley State University with published articles on risk assessment in water management and other environmental topics. Zachary A. Smith is a professor of political science and environmental and natural resource policy at Northern Arizona University. His publications include *The Environmental Policy Paradox*.

University of Nebraska Press
Lincoln NE 68588-0484
www.nebraskapress.unl.edu

GROUNDWATER MANAGEMENT IN THE WEST

Jeffrey S. Ashley and Zachary A. Smith

University of Nebraska Press   Lincoln and London

Portions of this work were previously published, in different form,
in Zachary A. Smith, *Groundwater in the West* (San Diego: Academic, 1989).
∞
Library of Congress Cataloging-in-Publication Data
Ashley, Jeffrey S., 1965–
Groundwater management in the West / Jeffrey S. Ashley and Zachary A. Smith.
p. cm.
Includes bibliographical references and index.
ISBN 0-8032-4276-x (cl.: alk. paper)
1. Groundwater—West (U.S.)—Management. 2. Water-supply—West
U.S.) 3. Groundwater—Law and legislation—West (U.S.) I. Smith,
Zachary A. (Zachary Alden), 1953-   . II. Title.
TD223.6.A86 1999 333.91'04'0978—dc21 99-21061 CIP

Contents

Groundwater Management in the West

Introduction

It is difficult to overemphasize the importance of water, yet many people take it for granted. As long as it flows out of the tap in a relatively unadulterated form and is not noticeably objectionable, most people give very little thought to where the water comes from, how it gets into their homes, or what impact changing water usage will have on their communities. One might assume that in the arid West people would be conservative in their use of water. However, for a variety of reasons—notably the development of large surface-water projects—water has been plentiful in many parts of the West, and water users have not had to think in terms of scarcity except during periods of sustained drought.

One of the greatest natural resource-management problems facing the western United States in coming decades will be that of the availability, use, and quality of groundwater. In large sections of the West groundwater is the only dependable, available source of water. Although groundwater has always been an important supply of water in the West and today provides roughly 35 percent of the water used in the nineteen western states, demands on groundwater will increase significantly in the future. Surface-water sources in the West are, for the most part, already developed or appropriated. Given federal budget deficits and the resistance of various administrations, beginning with the Carter administration, to building new surface-water delivery systems, it is unlikely that major new surface-water systems will be built in the future. Consequently, demand for and interest in groundwater will undoubtedly increase.

As dependence on groundwater rises a number of subtle shifts in local water management, economics, and usage will occur. For example, in areas where inexpensive surface water has been available, additional agricultural expansion will be possible only through pumping more expensive groundwater. In addition, water use, notably shifts in usage from farms to cities, will cause changes in land-use patterns, economic activity, and the sociopolitical composition of the area. Where groundwater supplies become depleted through overdrafting, the cost of water increases, affecting those uses for which the water had been economical. In some areas such water becomes uneconomical for agricultural use, and the lands revert to dry farming or go out of production altogether. All these shifts have social, political, and aesthetic as well as economic impacts, changing the character of communities.

This book examines groundwater on a state-by-state basis. This introduction explores the history of groundwater usage and examines how groundwater uses and the legal doctrines governing groundwater use have changed during the twentieth century. It also summarizes regional political and economic trends, paying particular attention to the role of markets or marketability of water rights and the relationship between water, economic development, and energy development in the West. In addition, the major actors in water politics and policy and the major issues and problems in the development and continued use of groundwater are covered.

The following chapters discuss the groundwater conditions in each of the nineteen western states. After a brief description of each state, the supply and current demand for groundwater are presented, along with a summary of that state's groundwater problems and the groundwater law in the state. Finally, each chapter examines the policy, politics, and future of groundwater use and the potential effects of changes in groundwater use that one might anticipate within the state. Because groundwater supply and management cannot be fully understood independent of surface water (in areas where both are a source of supply or the sources of water interconnect), surface-water conditions are, where appropriate, also summarized. Obviously some states, given their diversity and the complexity of their water environment, require more detailed treatment than others. Also, the data available for evaluating the groundwater situation in each state were not always consistent. This inconsistency was due, in part, to variances in the quality of data generated by state governments. Enough information was generated on each state, however, to provide a good summary of the groundwater situation.

Groundwater law and policy are evolving constantly, and use patterns and problems are ever changing. The sections on state demographics in this book illustrate that while the water needs of the nineteen western states have changed over the years, in many cases water law and water policy have not. The tension created between established practice and changing use patterns is a central focus of the work.

In focusing on the tension between rural use and urban growth, we have necessarily placed less emphasis on other important areas. Two such areas are Indian water rights—which will continue to be a factor in western water management for years to come—and equitable apportionment suits between states. These lawsuits arise when states cannot reach agreement over water apportionment and look to the courts for relief. Suits such as *Arizona v. California, Kansas v. Colorado,* and *Nebraska v. Wyoming* have involved surface-water apportionment, but new lawsuits are likely to focus more and more on groundwater. Although coverage of every case is beyond the scope and purpose of this work, important cases are discussed within individual chapters when the resulting decision has led to a change in that state's water management or water policy.

The Importance of Groundwater

It is estimated that in excess of 90 percent of fresh water in the United States is in the form of groundwater. The balance exists in lakes, rivers, and streams. Use of groundwater has increased dramatically in the recent past. From 1945 until 1980 groundwater use more than quadrupled, increasing from 21 billion to 88 billion gallons per day.[1] In the mid-1990s approximately one-half of all the people in the United States used groundwater as a primary source of drinking water.[2] Nationally, groundwater provides 39 percent of the water used in public supply systems, 75 percent of the water used for rural domestic consumption and livestock purposes, 37 percent of the water used for irrigated agriculture, and 2 percent of the water used for self-supplied industrial purposes.[3] In the nineteen western states 33 percent of the fresh water used comes

Table 1 Water Usage by State and Type of Use (in million gallons per day)

State	Public supply	Rural domestic and livestock	Irrigation	Self-supplied industrial	Total ground-water	Total fresh water
Alaska	34	6.3	.1	5.2	64	284
Arizona	401	58	2,060	39	2,740	6,570
California	3,260	417	10,700	125	14,600	35,100
Colorado	83	41	2,560	33	2,770	12,700
Hawaii	221	11.9	200	20	598	1,190
Idaho	173	608	6,620	170	7,590	19,700
Kansas	176	108	3,990	50	4,360	6,080
Montana	51	31	90	30	205	9,300
Nebraska	235	155	4,360	39	4,790	8,940
Nevada	104	10.6	871	9.4	1,060	3,340
New Mexico	241	42	1,370	4.6	1,760	3,480
North Dakota	32	25	78	2.1	141	2,680
Oklahoma	80	76	493	3.3	662	1,420
Oregon	105	60.2	563	31	767	8,430
South Dakota	52	25.8	141	5	251	592
Texas	1,270	186	5,590	143	7,380	20,100
Utah	305	31.6	508	77	964	4,380
Washington	434	126	754	104	1,450	7,910
Wyoming	41	22.1	237	6	384	7,580
Totals	7,298	2,041.5	41,185.1	896.6	52,536	159,776

Note: Public supply, rural and livestock, irrigation, and self-supplied industrial figures are for groundwater use only. The percentage of a state's water use that is made up of water taken from the ground can be found by dividing the total groundwater figure by the total fresh water figure. Compiled from data in U.S. Geological Survey, "Estimated Water Use in the United States, 1990," Circular 1081, (Washington DC: U.S. Government Printing Office, 1993).

from groundwater. Of this amount, 14 percent is used in public supply systems, 4 percent for rural domestic and livestock purposes, and 78 percent for irrigated agriculture (see table 1). Although these percentages vary significantly from state to state, it is clear that in the West, where agriculture is extremely important to the economy, groundwater plays and will continue to play a large role in the development and the future of that economy. And, as we might expect, shifts away from agricultural uses will have ripple effects throughout that economy.

The Resource

When rain or snow falls to the earth some precipitation seeps into the ground, where it accumulates as *soil water* and partially fills pores between soil particles and rocks in the upper layers of the earth's crust.[4] Most precipitation, however, is lost to the atmosphere through evaporation and transpiration from plants. A very small percentage of falling precipitation actually enters the ground.

Because of gravity, some infiltrating water will slowly percolate deeper into the ground through the porous layer of rock and sand. Pores and fractures in rock and sand create a spongelike, permeable layer of the earth where water can accumulate. Once all available space in this area has been filled with water, it is known as the *zone of saturation*. These water-bearing layers of saturated underground rock and sand are called *aquifers*, and the water in them is called *groundwater*. Groundwater moves very slowly: its actual speed depends on the composition of the material that holds it.

As mentioned, aquifers can be recharged or replenished naturally through precipitation. Precipitation can filter through the ground into what is called a *recharge area*. Unlike streams, which can be replenished quite quickly, the recharge process of an aquifer is generally very slow (often taking decades to hundreds of years). If the rate of withdrawal from an aquifer is allowed to exceed the natural recharge rate, the aquifer is converted from a slowly renewable resource to a nonrenewable resource. The practice of taking out more than goes in is often referred to as *overdrafting* or *groundwater mining*. Situations of overdrafting, common throughout the West, are detailed throughout the remainder of this book.

There are two types of aquifers: *confined* and *unconfined*. An unconfined aquifer, or water table aquifer, forms when groundwater collects above a layer of impermeable material such as rock or compacted clay. What is often referred to as the *water table* is the top of the saturated portion of an unconfined aquifer. Groundwater is found in the zone of saturation below the water table, while soil water is located in the earth above the water table in an area referred to as the *zone of aeration*.

Wells are drilled below the water table into the unconfined aquifer to obtain water. Pumps are used to bring the water to the surface. The height of the water table rises and falls naturally during prolonged wet periods and periods of prolonged drought. The water table also falls when overdrafting occurs. Overdrafting creates a section of waterless volume in an aquifer; this section is known as a *cone of depression*. When such conditions continue indefinitely, the water table drops, and the resource is depleted. Then, of course, pumping stops. (In such situations pumping often stops prior to total depletion because the increased cost of drawing the water from greater depths makes further use of the water uneconomical.)

Confined aquifers form when groundwater is forced between two layers of impermeable material. This type of aquifer is saturated with water under a pressure greater than that of the atmosphere. In some cases the pressure can be so great that wells drilled into the confined aquifer can draw water without the assistance of a pump. Such a well is know as a *flowing artesian well*. When the pressure is not great enough, and a pump must be used, the well is called a *nonflowing artesian well*.

One thing worth mentioning about confined aquifers is that their point of recharge is different than is that of unconfined aquifers. With confined aquifers, the point of recharge may be hundreds of miles away from wells from which water is being withdrawn. Therefore, the rate of recharge for confined aquifers may not be based on local precipitation at the point of withdrawal.

Historical Development of Groundwater

Although humans have been taking water out of the ground since ancient times, it has only been within the last century—indeed within the last few decades—that the means have been developed to withdraw large amounts of water from the ground. For most of the history of the West the major problem concerning groundwater has been how to get it out of the ground. The first successful and widely adapted device for extracting groundwater was the windmill. Although windmills took various shapes and forms, the early designs all had in common a dependence on erratic wind patterns, inefficiency, and, overall, low productivity. A windmill with a 25-foot diameter wheel (which was large) operating in a sixteen-mile-an-hour wind was capable of lifting approximately 37 gallons of water a minute from a maximum depth of 70 to 80 feet. Although such yields were sufficient for purposes of domestic use, they did not allow for widespread irrigation.[5]

After the windmill came the centrifugal pump. Early centrifugal pumps had a number of serious drawbacks. First, they had to be located within 20 feet of the water table. This sometimes required quite deep and relatively wide pits, with the pump operating at the bottom of the pit. Since these early pumps were expensive to purchase and operate, their use was limited to high-valve crops. The pumps were also often belt driven and powered by steam, which meant that they required frequent adjustments and constant care. Later, steam was replaced by low-compression oil-burning engines. The cost of such pumps in the first decade of the century was approximately $4,000 each.[6]

Pump designs improved during the 1920s. Higher-capacity centrifugal pumps were developed that allowed for operation at much greater depths. Inefficient steam and low-compression oil-burning power plants were replaced by hooking up an old car motor on a direct drive to the pump. By the 1920s the cost of a pump and power plant—including the drilling required for their use—had dropped to approximately $2,000. Further improvements in pump design in the 1930s and the availability in many areas of cheap electric power combined to rapidly increase the number of wells and the yield of these wells throughout the West and the Midwest. By the end of the decade the technological problems associated with groundwater pumping had largely been overcome, and the problem of how to access groundwater was being replaced by the problem of how to keep the water coming out.[7]

These changes in pump design increased the total amount of groundwater withdrawn for western irrigation from relatively small amounts in the early 1930s to about 10.7 million acre-feet by 1945 and up to 56 million acre-feet by 1975.[8] (An acre-foot is the amount of water that would cover one acre to a depth of one foot, or 325,851 gallons.)

Most of these expansions have taken place on the high plains. From World War II to the mid-1960s the greatest increases in groundwater use were concentrated in the southern plains. Groundwater withdrawal for irrigation in the southern plains increased from less than 1 million acre-feet in 1945 to approximately 13 million acre-feet by 1965. There has also been a substantial increase in the use of groundwater in the northern plains, although it occurred somewhat later. In 1950, 26 percent of the water used in irrigation in the northern plains came from the ground. By 1975 this had increased to 78 percent.[9]

The development of center-pivot sprinkler irrigation systems has also facilitated the expansion of groundwater use in the West. First patented in 1952, center-pivot irrigation systems are made up of a long line of sprinklers that move in a circle around a fixed pivot, like the large hand of a clock. Water is supplied from the central pivot point. Most systems are designed to irrigate a quarter of a section of land (160 acres), but because of the circular pattern of the water they dispense they irrigate less than that (130 acres). Sprinkler irrigation and center-pivot irrigation have the advantages of using less water than flood or furrow irrigation does.

Sprinklers may be used in areas with sandier soil or hillier land, where other types of irrigation is ineffective. Also, given that one person can irrigate from 10 to 15 quarter sections (1,300 to 2,000 acres), center-pivot systems can reduce labor costs significantly.[10]

Development of Law

The technological changes that facilitated rapid expansion of groundwater pumping and the development of irrigated agriculture in the West put pressure on the legal doctrines governing groundwater use and ownership. As it became possible to withdraw greater amounts of water from greater depths, competition for water developed in some areas. Legislatures in the West reacted to conflict over groundwater resources in a variety of ways. They changed their laws, or perhaps decided not to do so, depending upon the controversies involved, the participants, the interests, and the pressure lawmakers felt. As a result of early conflicts over groundwater, some states (New Mexico, for example) were quick to write relatively comprehensive groundwater-management statutes. In other states, notably Texas and California, early water law changed greatly yet retained significant parts of the law as it existed prior to the rapid development of groundwater resources. As a result, competition for and demand on the resource has sometimes led to what many feel are inefficient uses and overutilization of groundwater. Groundwater laws in each of the nineteen western states are summarized in the chapters that follow. The four major groundwater law doctrines followed in the United States, along with a general discussion of how groundwater law has changed since the turn of the century, are outlined below.

The four primary legal doctrines governing groundwater use are the English, or common law, rule of absolute ownership; the American rule of reasonable use; the correlative rights doctrine; and the doctrine of prior appropriation. Generally, groundwater law in the western states has evolved during this century from the English, or common law, rule of absolute ownership to either the American rule of reasonable use or (in most western states) the doctrine of prior appropriation.

Absolute ownership. The common law, or absolute ownership doctrine, holds that the water beneath a landowner's land is the property of that landowner and may be withdrawn, without malice, with no regard to the effect that withdrawals have on any other landowner. In theory, and in practice in many areas, this meant that landowners could pump at will the water beneath their lands as well as the water beneath the lands of their neighbors. The absolute ownership doctrine was developed in England and transferred to the relatively wet East (where it is still largely the law). The doctrine works reasonably well in areas where there is abundant water available. Following water law in other parts of the country, many courts and legislatures in the western states adopted the common law rule. Considering the small amounts of groundwater that were withdrawn in early western history, and the lack of competition for groundwater resources, the absolute ownership doctrine seemed reasonable. However, when competition for water did develop in the West it became apparent that in an arid environment there were drawbacks to this doctrine. It was shortly after competition for water developed that modifications of the rule started to be made.

American rule. One modification made by many courts in the West was the implementation of the reasonable use doctrine, or the American rule. Basically, the reasonable use doctrine limits a landowner's right to the water beneath his or her land to that amount necessary for some reasonable and beneficial purpose on the land above the water. The waste of water or the transportation of water off the land is not considered a reasonable beneficial use if such use interferes with the right of adjacent landowners to use the water beneath their own lands for the beneficial use of those lands.

Correlative rights. Some states, notably California, developed the correlative rights doctrine as an alternative to the absolute ownership doctrine. Basically, the correlative rights doctrine recognizes the landowner's right to use the water beneath his or her land but limits that right somewhat by providing that landowners overlying a common source of groundwater have equal, or correlative, rights to a reasonable amount of that water when the water is applied to a reasonable beneficial use on the land overlying the groundwater basin.

Prior appropriation. Most western states have adopted the prior appropriation doctrine. The prior appropriation doctrine simply provides that the first appropriator of water, by putting that water to beneficial use without waste, has a right to continue that use. And such rights are superior to the rights of people who appropriate water at a later date. In prior appropriation states, water rights are usually administered by a state official or office (often a state engineer) through a permit procedure.

(Chapter 11, which deals with New Mexico, provides a good example of the powers of a state engineer in administering a prior appropriation permit system.)

Although it is common in works of this nature to provide state-by-state summaries of the groundwater doctrines followed in each state, that temptation will be avoided here. In the course of doing the research for this book it became clear that, for example, what one state called the common law or prior appropriation doctrine might in practice turn out to be much more like the correlative rights doctrine. It can be said, however, that the overwhelming majority of western states found that the common law was ill suited to the arid West and changed over to one of the other doctrines, usually the prior appropriation doctrine.[11]

There are several recurring legal issues that come up in groundwater disputes in the western states. Important legal controversies that have developed in the states will be presented on a case-by-case basis in the following chapters. It might, however, be useful to discuss here a couple of terms that often present themselves.

The concept of "beneficial use" repeatedly emerges when groundwater policy and law are examined. The Utah Code is typical in its statement that beneficial use "shall be the basis, the measure and the limit of all rights to use water in this state."[12] The beneficial use concept was developed during the nineteenth century to encourage economic efficiency. Although some uses have always been considered beneficial (for example, water for domestic purposes or for irrigation, manufacturing, or stock watering), it is when we go beyond these traditional uses that a controversy over what constitutes a beneficial use sometimes arises. For example, some courts have found water needed for the protection and propagation of fish to be a beneficial use, while others have not. Courts and state legislatures have also been split on the issue of whether recreation, aesthetic, or scenic uses are beneficial uses of water.[13] This can present a problem for groundwater regulation because of the relationship between surface water and groundwater in streambeds.

Another important issue in the development of groundwater law in some states is that of whether or not water rights may be acquired by adverse possession. Basically adverse possession, or adverse use, allows for the acquisition of water rights by the open and notorious use of someone else's water for some statutory period, usually five years. The acquiring of rights by adverse use or adverse possession is not unique to water law, but, as we see in subsequent chapters, its application in water law in some states has proven problematic.

The application of legal principles in the West may vary significantly even though states may be, in theory, following the same doctrine. New Mexico, for example, follows the prior appropriation doctrine and manages groundwater quite differently than does North Dakota, which follows the same doctrine. In New Mexico, where, for all practical purposes, many groundwater basins are virtually nonrecharging, those basins are managed with the understanding that eventually they will be depleted. In contrast, in North Dakota many groundwater basins do recharge regularly, and that water is managed, for the most part, on a safe-yield basis. (*Safe yield* means that the amount of water withdrawn from the aquifer roughly equals the amount of water returning naturally or artificially to the aquifer over an extended period of time.)

It is difficult to understand the importance of groundwater law without taking into consideration the social functions that water law has served and how changes in the law have mirrored changes in water use and in society. Stability of water ownership is essential for economic growth and long-term planning. Farmers or cities are not likely to build expensive water-development facilities if their title to the resource may be called into question at some point in the future. It may have appeared to policymakers early in the history of the West that the common law doctrine, or the absolute ownership rule, would provide the stability necessary for long-term planning. In fact, in the absence of competition for water resources, the common law doctrine did provide that stability. However, when competition began to create conflict for groundwater resources it became clear that one pumper might find the use and enjoyment of his or her groundwater threatened by the pumping on adjacent lands. Converting to the doctrine of prior appropriation, as most western states did, provided the stability necessary for pumpers to understand what their rights were and to plan for the long-term use and development of their water.

This same stability, however, has tended to favor those interests that acquired their water rights early, and, to the extent that water laws prevent the transfer and change of ownership of water rights (as they do in some states), the law has favored those historical uses and has prevented change in water-use patterns and development of alternative uses. So groundwater law has provided stability necessary for economic growth and expansion. More recently that same stability has, in certain states, prevented changes in water use and, some would argue, further economic growth and development. In general the law has proven itself capable of adapting to change. Some states, as we will see, have done very little in response to changing groundwater use and conditions. This sometimes means that the resource is poorly managed, if it is managed at all. Most states, however, seem to be doing a fairly good job of managing ground-water on a statewide basis.

Politics and Economics

Groundwater law is only one part of groundwater policy. For example, in some states, who gets the water depends more on who can afford to drill the deepest hole or sustain the longest court battle than it does on the formal policy followed in the state. In other states, in spite of glowing constitutional language about beneficial uses and the prevention of waste, economic and political realities make it beneficial for farmers and others to waste a great deal of water.

The early and rapid growth of groundwater pumping and agricultural development in western states resulted in the vesting of the majority of water rights to farmers. This laid the groundwork for future conflicts over water use and development, as other users have competed with agriculture for rights to water. Often this competition has come from metropolitan areas and industrial users. When competition is between municipalities and farmers, municipal interests have a number of advantages. Water law and public opinion often favor municipal uses over competing uses for water. Also, when there is competition, municipalities have the power of eminent domain and can thereby take water or water rights whenever necessary.[14]

Energy companies, including mining companies, oil and gas interests, and coal companies, sometimes need to acquire water rights. A large part of U.S. coal reserves and most of the nation's shale oil resources are found in the West. Energy companies use water in a variety of different ways. For example, roughly equal amounts of water and coal are used in coal slurry pipelines. Coal gasification or liquefaction also requires large amounts of water. It is estimated that between 4,000 and 15,000 (depending on the BTUs produced) acre-feet of water a year are needed for a 250 million-cubic-feet per-day gasification plant. The manufacture of petroleum from oil shale uses in excess of 200 gallons of water per barrel of oil produced. Water is also necessary for the cooling of power plants, and in energy production and development it is required for, among other things, mining, processing, transportation, refining, and conversion to other forms of energy.[15]

The necessity of water for the production and extraction of energy resources insures that groundwater management will be a concern of those

interested in increased energy development. One commentator observed
that the "configuration of energy development in the West will be determined by the priorities of the governmental energies controlling the
water."[16]

To the extent that legal and institutional barriers prevent the transfer of water rights, we might anticipate conflict between water-rights
holders and other potential users. These conflicts are most likely to
present themselves in the legislative arena and to manifest themselves
as attempts to change the laws governing the transfer and ownership of
water rights. For example, in states where a groundwater right is subject
to and connected to the ownership of the land overlying the aquifer, we
might anticipate that efforts would be made to sever the right to water
from land ownership (thereby decreasing the cost of water rights and
facilitating a transfer of those rights away from a groundwater basin).
We might also anticipate conflict over statutes designed to prevent the
transfer of water outside of groundwater basins. Clearly these conflicts
are most likely to be between the primary water-rights holders (often,
agriculture) and new claimants for water rights (usually municipalities).

Many commentators have argued that the existing system of water
rights administration in most states, and the legal doctrines that under-
line those systems, prevent the efficient use of groundwater resources.
These critics (often economists or others who use economic reason-
ing) argue for increased transferability and marketability of groundwater
rights. They argue that government controls and government regulations
of water create problems of shortage and poor distribution. Terry Anderson, for example, has argued that without a price mechanism "operating
on water supply and demand, crisis situations will continue to arise."[17]
It is argued that government-mandated allocations of water necessarily
create inefficiencies and conflict among claimants for water resources.
Most important for the market advocates are the advantages to be derived in terms of conservation and the lack of scarcity that will result
from market solutions. Proponents of greater marketability and transferability argue that water-rights holders with restricted ability to transfer those rights will not consider the full cost or value of that water,
and inefficiency will result. It is for this reason, for example, that we
have seen flood irrigation in central Arizona, while municipalities a few
miles away were urging domestic consumers to cut back their water
use. Again, Terry Anderson notes that "when the government keeps fuel
prices below market clearing levels, shortages inevitably follow. . . . The
same circumstances are causing problems with water. Water prices have

been kept below market clearing levels, and the inevitable shortages have followed."[18]

Opponents to greater marketability and transferability of water resources have argued that the market ignores certain public values, third-party effects, and other externalities. Critics fear that "water will flow uphill to money," ignoring environmental concerns and long-held economic values associated with traditional water uses. Market solutions would invariably favor some uses (i.e., those associated with users who are more able to pay and for whom the water has a higher value). Those uses, it is argued, may be the ones that we should favor. Since agriculture uses most of the water in the West and since (it is often argued) it is the most marginal user, irrigators would be the ones least able to compete for water if it were allocated through a market mechanism. Farmers who benefit from artificially low prices of water subsidized by governments are likely to avoid water-management changes that will increase price competition. Furthermore, some state governments are fearful of increasing the marketability and transferability of water rights because of the impact that doing so might have on states' ability to plan (and dictate) water uses. For example, creating a market for water in eastern New Mexico might work to the benefit of El Paso, Texas, but might prevent New Mexico from saving that water for some future use (and from meanwhile allowing the water to continue being used it its existing capacity).[19]

The likelihood of change in state groundwater laws (to facilitate the transferability and marketability of water rights) will depend in large part on the relative strength in state legislatures of the various groups and actors involved. Traditionally, agricultural interests have been very influential in western legislatures. To the extent that municipalities and energy companies become more influential vis-à-vis agricultural interests, we might anticipate that farmers will lose their competitive advantage in the policy-making process in some state governments. That has happened, and we have seen increased transferability and marketability of water rights with resulting changes in uses and local economies.

A final point needs to be made concerning the role of the market as it pertains to water use. The ability to withdraw groundwater (or, more accurately, to continue withdrawing water under conditions of competition), while not directly a marketability issue, depends in many states on the economic resources of those attempting to pump the water. In some states whoever drills the deepest well or can afford to pump at greater depths is advantaged. Oftentimes in those same states (and sometimes in other states), those with the economic resources to fight protracted legal battles are also advantaged.

Issues

A number of recurring issues present themselves when one examines groundwater policy in the western states. Overdrafting (the extraction of water from an aquifer at rates that exceed natural recharge), land subsidence, pollution, saltwater intrusion, and the division of responsibility over who should manage groundwater resources are issues that often arise. The diversity among the states and differences in their hydrologic, political, and legal environments necessitates treating these issues on a state-by-state basis. However, it might be useful to discuss here, in general terms, what these groundwater issues involve.

Overdrafting

There is some controversy in the water-policy community over just how overdrafting should be defined and over whether or not it is necessarily a bad thing. The United States Geological Survey (USGS) has written that overdrafting or groundwater mining is "no more unsafe than the mining of any other mineral resource, provided it's recognized and planned."[20] Unfortunately, as becomes clear in subsequent chapters, in many areas overdrafting is not planned, and sustained pumping threatens long-term agricultural productivity.

Probably the best-known overdrafting situation in the West has occurred in the Ogallala Aquifer, a huge water source for the Great Plains area that includes portions of New Mexico, Texas, Oklahoma, Kansas, Colorado, Nebraska, Wyoming, and South Dakota. Covering an area of roughly 225,000 square miles, the Ogallala supports one-fifth of the irrigated agriculture in the United States. In some places pumping from the Ogallala has resulted in the withdrawing of water at a rate fourteen times faster than its rate of natural replenishment.[21] Again, the impact of overdrafting on the Ogallala varies significantly depending upon the region. For example, in the Texas panhandle many farmers have already converted to dryland farming (i.e., farming without irrigation), whereas Nebraska is relatively untroubled.

The USGS identified areas all over the western United States that have experienced water-level declines in excess of 40 feet. Such areas exist in almost every western state and include significant portions of California, Arizona, South Dakota, and Texas.[22]

Some state governments are powerless to prevent (or to plan for) groundwater depletion. To understand overdrafting and the reason it continues in some areas, even when it is clear that there may be long-term detrimental effects, it is necessary to understand the "common-pool" nature of the groundwater resource. When groundwater pumpers overlie the common source of water, and if no agreement for apportioning the water exists, then pumpers have little incentive to save or conserve water for future use. In fact, in such a situation one pumper has an incentive to increase pumping and to develop groundwater resources as quickly as possible, as failure to do so will only result in a loss of the resource to a neighbor's pumps. The consequences of unplanned overdrafting include economic disruption and the inability to maximize the value of the resource. Eventually all groundwater basins reach a steady state (a condition wherein the amount of withdrawal equals the amount of water returning to the basin). When a steady state is reached when groundwater levels are high, the cost of pumping water is less than it is when groundwater levels are low. (Costs are greater because of the expense of digging newer and deeper wells and because of the energy required to lift the water to the surface.)

When groundwater depletion and overdrafting is planned for, competition, overutilization, and economic disruption can be minimized. In some regions overdrafting may be the only rational way to manage the resource (e.g., in areas where aquifers are, for all practical purposes, not being naturally replenished).[23] Unfortunately, as we shall see, aquifers are sometimes managed (or, perhaps more accurately, not managed) with little thought of the future consequences and foregone opportunities.

The cost of pumping groundwater is closely tied to energy costs. In many parts of the West increased energy costs beginning in the early 1970s have significantly reduced the amount of groundwater pumping and, consequently, overdrafting.

A problem related to overdrafting is land subsidence. Prior to the lowering of the water table in a given groundwater basin, the soil is partially supported by grain-to-grain contact and partially supported by the surrounding water. The removal of the water in such a situation causes vertical and horizontal stresses and may result in the settling or subsidence of the land surface. Land subsidence has been a problem in various parts of the West, notably Arizona, California, Idaho, Nevada, Texas, and Washington.[24]

The conservation of groundwater has become an issue in some areas and promises to become one in many other parts of the West in the future. Although at first glance it might be difficult to understand why anybody would be against something as seemingly innocuous and potentially beneficial as water conservation, how conservation is achieved, what it costs, and who bears the costs are all potentially controversial issues. For example, improved irrigation practices, such as drip irrigation, may be quite expensive and may thus make little sense to a farmer who has a very low marginal cost for water. For a number of reasons conservation is closely tied to several groundwater issues, including water law, pollution (e.g., when additional water is needed to flush the soil of minerals), and the cost of energy development.

Pollution

When groundwater pollution is discussed, the sources of pollution are usually divided into point and nonpoint sources. Types of point sources (originating from a readily identifiable source) that are a threat to groundwater quality in many western states include hazardous waste sites, landfills, wastewater-disposal sites, and the leakage of refined petroleum products—notably gasoline from storage tanks. Common nonpoint sources of groundwater pollution include runoff from irrigation (which contains salts and the residue from pesticides), seepage from domestic septic tanks, storm runoff from urban areas, and salts from the salting of winter roads. The types of hazardous wastes that are most often a threat to groundwater quality are synthetic organic compounds, radioactive waste, and metallic compounds.[25]

Saltwater or seawater intrusion is an additional source of groundwater pollution in many areas. Saltwater intrusion results from the seepage of saline water into freshwater aquifers as a result of pumping the fresh water. This is a particular problem in coastal areas (notably on the Texas and California coasts) and in those inland areas where freshwater aquifers are near sources of saline water (e.g. in the Puget Sound and the Sacramento Delta).

Federal-State Relations

Although it doesn't present itself often in the state-by-state summary chapters that follow, federal-state relations have been a concern of many water managers and policymakers in the West. Basically, federal-state relations (or federalism issues) concern the division of authority and responsibility over water management and control. The federal government controls vast amounts of land in the West, including 89 percent of Alaska, 86 percent of Nevada, and 63 percent of Utah. As a result of something called the "implied reservation doctrine," the courts have found that the federal government has a right to waters (both surface and ground) that originate on federal lands. In 1976, in the Supreme Court case that extended the implied reservation doctrine to groundwater, the court halted groundwater withdrawals that had been made pursuant to permits obtained from the state of Nevada. The withdrawals were lowering water levels inside Death Valley National Monument.[26] Given the extent of federal land ownership and what in many cases has been the long-term holding of water rights based on state law, the potential in some areas for conflict over water rights between the federal and state governments is great. After the Supreme Court extended the implied reservation doctrine to groundwater, one commentator observed that these decisions would "wreak havoc upon state and private land owners' water projects. The net result of these disadvantages is to impede control by state authorities and nullify state water planning."[27]

In 1982 another U.S. Supreme Court decision found that groundwater was an article in interstate commerce and that federal government had the right to regulate its use. The court noted that "there is a significant federal interest in conservation as well as in fair allocation of this diminishing resource." The court further argued that groundwater overdrafting "is a national problem and Congress has the power to deal with it on that scale."[28]

Although the federal government has usually applied to state governments when acquiring water rights, several commentators have noted that there is the potential for increased federal activity.[29] To the extent that these observations are correct, we might anticipate future conflict over the responsibility for the management and distribution of scarce water resources in the West. A closely related issue in western water rights and federal-state relations is the question of Indian water rights. Tribes in the West often have reserved water rights that are superior to the rights of any subsequent user and, theoretically, are not subject to state control or management. (These rights were vested at the time a reservation was created and are not subject to prior appropriation.) Although the question is a bigger one in regard to surface water management than it is in terms of groundwater management, Indian water-rights issues are problematic for many water users and state management agencies. In many cases Indian water rights have not been quantified or firmly established (by court or otherwise); hence the existence of the right is a big open question.

In the chapters that follow, these and other questions of groundwater allocation, use, and management are discussed in detail as they apply to each of the nineteen western states. The reader may be tempted to jump to the chapter covering a state he or she is most concerned with (and, in fact, the chapters have been written to stand alone). To get a feel for and to appreciate the overall groundwater management situation in the region, however, one needs to study all the states in that region.

PACIFIC COAST REGION

The Pacific Coast region encompasses California, Oregon, Washington, and Alaska. For statistical purposes Hawaii is often included as well. For our purposes Hawaii is included for reasons of symmetry and because saltwater intrusion, a groundwater problem in Hawaii, is common to all the states except Alaska in the Pacific Coast region. While Alaska and Hawaii are discussed in this introduction to the region, we concentrate here primarily on the mainland coastal states—California, Oregon, and Washington. Alaska and Hawaii are discussed in detail in chapters specifically devoted to them.

The location of the Pacific mountains and the Pacific Ocean has a profound effect on the climate of the Pacific Coast region. Regionally, the mountains act as a barrier to storms coming off the ocean. The result is that the western side of these states receives more precipitation than does the eastern portion. This is especially true in the winter, when large quantities of precipitation fall on the western slope of the Pacific mountain ranges.

The fact that this region is adjacent to the ocean also presents a problem common throughout its states—that of saltwater intrusion. As more groundwater is pumped along the coast the potential for saltwater contamination increases for all of these states.

Finally, states in the Pacific Coast region (particularly California) have experienced a tremendous amount of population growth over the decades since World War II. This growth—primarily in urban areas—has resulted in a strain on water supplies and in tension between new and existing users of water. These and other problems will be discussed in detail within the chapters on each individual state.

1 Alaska

Alaska is unique among the states surveyed in this book because its economy has not developed around agriculture. While other states in the West are dealing with current and potential conflict among water users, Alaska will, for the most part, avoid such encounters. Agriculture (the primary water user in most states) accounts for only 0.002 percent of the water used in Alaska.[1] The population of the state is growing rapidly; however, this growth has yet to place any serious strain on water supplies. While there are localized cases of water contamination, the quality of Alaska's water is generally excellent, and the water is suitable for most uses. Given the lack of agriculture, the abundant supply of water, and the generally good condition of the resource, water scarcity is unlikely to inhibit social and economic growth in any way, and the state's supply of both surface and groundwater will remain adequate well into the future. Should Alaska continue its careful management of water resources, its socioeconomic future, as it relates to water, looks bright, and it is not likely to face any of the disruptions that are occurring in other states.

However, recent political pressure to cut funding for state administrative agencies and to replace the Alaska Water Use Act with a common law approach to water-resource management has to temper our optimistic outlook. It has been the success of the Alaska Water Use Act and the Alaska Department of Natural Resources (DNR) that has placed the state in its position with regard to water resources and future socioeconomic development. Should the act be replaced or the authority of the DNR be undermined, Alaska might be placing its water-related future in jeopardy.

Physical Description

Alaska covers an area of 586,412 square miles—roughly one-fifth the total area of the United States—and its topography ranges from low coastal plains of the arctic region and deltas of the major rivers to the peaks of the Alaska Range. Its climate varies from the deciduous rain forests of the southeast to the frozen desert of the Arctic, and perennially frozen ground (permafrost) is present in most geologic and climatic regions of Alaska.[2]

Alaska is the largest state in the union, with the third-smallest population. Consequently, most of its water, both groundwater and surface water, is unaffected by human influences.[3] Alaska relies heavily upon groundwater in some areas and has not been immune to problems of contamination and overdraft. The state is unique in that, because of its enormous size, its hydrological and geological characteristics vary much more than do those of most of the states discussed in this book.

Demographics

As of 1 July 1995 the resident state population of Alaska was estimated to be 603,617.[4] Between 1950 and 1995 the population of Alaska increased by 369.2 percent, which is over five times the national average for the same period.[5] Alaska's growth has occurred mostly in and around the cities of Juneau, Anchorage, and Fairbanks. Anchorage and Fairbanks are the two most heavily populated areas of Alaska; their 1992 populations stood at 245,866 and 33,221, respectively.[6] While the population of the state is gradually shifting from rural to urban dwellers, the majority of the populace resides in rural areas. In 1992, 58.2 percent of the state's population could be found living in nonmetropolitan areas.[7]

Agriculture (the largest user of water in most states) does not contribute significantly to the economy of Alaska. In fact, farms contributed a mere 0.0006 percent to the gross state product in 1992. The three largest contributors to Alaska's gross state product are mining (33.8 percent), transportation and public utilities (14.3 percent), and finance insurance and real estate (12.4 percent).[8] Aside from government employment the primary employing industries in Alaska are manufacturing, transportation and public utilities, wholesale and retail trade, and the service industry.[9]

Water Use

On a statewide basis Alaska receives 78 percent of its water from surface sources. Although the major population centers in the state depend, to varying degrees, on surface water (Ship Creek and Eklutna Lake in Anchorage and the Tanana River in Fairbanks), as we shall see below, their public supply systems are heavily dependent on groundwater.

Twenty-two percent of the fresh water used annually in Alaska comes from the ground. Of this amount, 53 percent is used in public supply systems, 10 percent for livestock and rural domestic consumption, and approximately 15 percent for mining and industry.[10]

There are four distinct climate zones in Alaska, and when assessing groundwater use and development it is necessary to understand these zones. They are: the arctic zone (roughly the area from the middle of the Brooks Range north), the continental zone (most of the interior), the transition zone (the coastal areas along western Alaska and between the maritime zone and the continental zone along the southern coast) and the maritime zone (the southern coastal areas and panhandle). Mean annual temperatures range from 45°F in the maritime zone to 10°F in the arctic zone. The continental zone has the widest seasonal temperature variation; extremes range from above 90°F to as low as –80°F.[11]

With the exception of the maritime zones of southeast and south-central Alaska, precipitation falls as snow for six to nine months of the year and often year-round on the highest peaks. This snow remains on the ground in its crystallized state for several months until it melts in the spring. What results from this seasonal storage of snow is a prolonged winter recession of streamflow in interior and northern Alaska followed by a rapid rise in water flow when the spring thaw begins. In areas where there is only a thin accumulation of snow the underlying ground often freezes to a depth of several feet during winter. This frozen ground becomes an impermeable barrier, restricting groundwater recharge and aiding runoff of snowmelt. With the initiation of runoff the ground beneath the meltwater channels thaws quickly, soon permitting groundwater recharge.[12]

Annual precipitation varies greatly throughout the state. The arctic zone receives about 5 inches in contrast to the more than 300 inches recorded at specific locations in the maritime zone. Large areas of southeast and south-central Alaska are covered by great expanses of glaciers and ice fields as a result of heavy precipitation in conjunction with low temperatures. Perennial ice covers approximately 28,100 square miles of Alaska's land, which makes it an important factor in the hydrologic areas where it occurs. Although many may think of snow as having the greatest influence on Alaska's groundwater resources, in fact permafrost has a broader and more appreciable impact.[13] Permafrost is defined as rock, soil, or any other earth material whose temperature remains at or below 32° for a continuous period of two or more years.[14]

Because of its low permeability, permafrost restricts recharge, discharge, and movement of groundwater, limits storage capacity, and isolates near-surface groundwater from the subpermafrost layer.[15] Permafrost is present throughout the state but decreases in area as one moves south from the continuous permafrost zone of the arctic and northern region.[16] There are also unfrozen zones under deep lakes, in the alluvium adjacent to major rivers, and sometimes below the base of the permafrost.[17] Unfortunately, groundwater found below permafrost is often saline.[18] In the Arctic Coastal Plain area the sediments are often frozen to depths of 2,000 feet.[19]

Icefields and glaciers also influence Alaska's groundwater hydrology. In areas where they are prevalent their effect serves to moderate and regulate streamflow, which, in turn, affects the rate of groundwater recharge. Streamflow variability is generally higher for nonglacial-fed streams and rivers than for glacial-fed ones.[20]

Since much information has been collected on groundwater near the larger urban areas of Alaska, they will be discussed separately below. Little is known of the groundwater systems in most other areas of the state. This scarcity of data, in conjunction with the known complexity and wide range of geologic and hydrologic conditions in the state, permits preparation of only a very generalized map of groundwater availability on a regional basis. (The following subregions are based on hydrologic considerations and should not be confused with the climate zones discussed earlier.)

In the arctic subregion (coterminus with the arctic climate zone north of the Brooks Range), within the continuous permafrost zone, surface water supplies most water needs. One particular water problem area within this subregion is the Prudhoe Bay Development Area. As a result of oil exploration and development on Alaska's North Slope, critical water shortages were experienced here between 1972 and 1973. Attempts to develop groundwater were unsuccessful, largely because of the omnipresent permafrost. Surface water reservoirs will necessarily be used to resolve water-supply problems in the arctic region in the foreseeable future.[21]

In the northwest subregion (southwest of the arctic region), water is derived mainly from lakes and streams.[22] Thick permafrost is extensive in the northern part and is only slightly thinner in the southern part. Although permafrost-free areas are found near the major river systems, groundwater yields to wells are usually less than 10 gallons per minute. (It is possible that much larger yields could be obtained, but there has been little incentive or need to attempt development.) Shallow wells are utilized during the summer months in some coastal areas, but winter freezing and inadequate storage prevents year-round use of such installations.[23]

Groundwater is the principal source of supply in the Yukon subregion (comprising central and west-central Alaska). Fairbanks falls within this subarea and is highly dependent on groundwater, though most of the rural villages in the area derive their water from rivers and streams. Of all the subareas in the state, the Yukon has the greatest potential for developing groundwater supplies.[24]

The water sources in the southwest subarea (southwest Alaska, including most of the Alaska Peninsula and Kodiak Island) are a combination of surface and groundwater. Many of the small villages within the subarea possess small community wells, and some areas have springs for their water. Permafrost was encountered roughly one-fourth of the time when wells were drilled in the subarea. Productive wells beneath permafrost layers derive their water from sand and gravel interbedded with glacial deposits. Future wells could yield up to 1,000 gallons per minute; however, most wells are expected to yield around 100 gallons per minute.[25]

The south-central region, which includes Anchorage, has the highest population in the state. In many of the rural areas along streams the potential for developing surface and groundwater is good. Abundant recharge from precipitation, freshwater lagoons, and streamflow create favorable conditions for the occurrence of shallow groundwater in permeable coastal sediments.[26]

Surface water is the primary source of water in most of the southeast region. Juneau, the capital city, is the exception; it relies primarily on groundwater from shallow wells in the Last Chance Basin and uses surface water as a backup. However, owing to the large amount of precipitation received and the temperateness of the region, surface-water supply is sufficient to eliminate the need for overdrafting in dry years. As of the mid-1990s it appeared that Juneau had an adequate water supply for the future.[27]

Alaska's remote cities and villages have unique water problems as well as the full range of water concerns of larger urban areas. There are over two hundred remote urban areas that range in size from those with a population of over one thousand down to those consisting of only a few families.

Most rural communities' water and waste disposal systems are inefficient, inadequate, or nonexistent, and there are serious operating problems including freeze-up, loss of power, inadequate financing, and lack of technical expertise.[28] The "water system" in some of these communities during some parts of the year may consist of no more than a bucket and a pick used to break the ice.

The lack of satisfactory disposal facilities in many rural villages results in localized pollution of surface water and groundwater and in generally unsanitary conditions. Most of these villages lack the means to construct, operate, or manage water and wastewater treatment and disposal systems without assistance from outside sources.[29]

As mentioned previously, Alaska's population increased dramatically during the 1970s, 1980s, and early 1990s. The major urban communities and their surrounding areas have borne the brunt of this boom. This rise in the population, and the subsequent commercial and industrial growth, has heightened demand on urban water sources and has increased utilization of groundwater resources. As a result, although Alaska's groundwater is generally suitable for most uses, there have been isolated problems of overdraft, saltwater intrusion, and contamination by point and nonpoint sources of pollution.

Because of Alaska's size, the diversity of its geological and hydrological environment, and the fact that much research on the state's groundwater resources has focused on Anchorage and Fairbanks (the two largest cities), these areas and their groundwater problems will be discussed individually below.

Anchorage Area

The most populous of all Alaska's cities, Anchorage is located near the head of Cook Inlet in south-central Alaska. There are two principal aquifers in the Anchorage area; an upper unconfined aquifer is separated from a lower confined aquifer by sediments of low permeability. In most of the area the upper aquifer is 10 to 50 feet below the surface and the deeper one is 70 to 300 feet below the surface.[30]

Metropolitan Anchorage is one of the fastest-growing urban centers in the United States. The population, which increased from 127,000 in 1970 to 226,338 in 1990, is expected to exceed 300,000 by the year 2000. The U.S. Bureau of the Census estimated Anchorage's population to be 245,866 as of 1992. A continuation of this rapid growth will lead to an increased demand for water.

Anchorage water consumption in the mid-1990s averaged approximately 34 million gallons per day. The city is able to supply a peak demand of 60 million gallons per day. Water needs are met through withdrawals of both groundwater and surface water. Concern over past strains on groundwater resources and the need for a long-term water supply led to development of the Eklutna Water Project in the early 1990s. This project included a pipeline built to utilize water resources at Eklutna Lake Reservoir. It is projected that the water supplied from Eklutna Lake, Ship Creek, and municipal wells will be adequate for Anchorage's needs through the year 2020 and beyond (based on a projected population of 420,000).[31] However, even with the water provided by the Eklutna Water Project, it is not uncommon for specific areas of the Anchorage Hillside and Eagle River Valley (areas not served by municipal water) to experience well failures and water shortages as a result of overuse during extended dry periods.[32] As Anchorage grows, its water-supply infrastructure will have to keep up with demand. As areas that are now dependent on wells and septic tanks experience water shortages and water-quality problems caused by overuse and septic tank failures, it will be necessary for the municipality to continue to expand its ability to provide adequate water and sewer connection to these areas.[33]

Pollution

Petroleum products are the primary contaminant affecting groundwater in Alaska. The Anchorage area is no exception. In a 1992 report to the Environmental Protection Agency (EPA), the Alaska Department of Environmental Conservation cited sixty locations where groundwater was impaired as a result of contamination by petroleum products.[34] Petroleum hydrocarbon (gasoline) contamination has forced the closure of several domestic wells in the Eagle River area.[35] In a few areas, in unconfined aquifers, bacterial and chemical pollution have been reported. The major source of this pollution is on-site disposal systems of liquid wastes.[36] Although it was not a serious problem as of 1996, additional development may increase this source of pollution if precautions are not taken. Groundwater pollution in the Anchorage area has also been a result of solid waste being disposed directly into lakes that are hydraulically connected to the groundwater sources. Also, surface disposal of solid waste has polluted groundwater where the water table is at a very shallow depth.[37] In addition, septic tanks, which are prevalent in unsewered areas of Anchorage, have caused groundwater pollution. Other sources of groundwater pollution in Anchorage and other urbanized areas are leakage of sanitary sewers and fuel tanks and infiltration from surface runoff that has been contaminated by chemicals and fertilizers.[38]

Fairbanks Area

Fairbanks and its surrounding area is situated in the Tanana River Valley in central Alaska. The presence of frozen ground in the region does not significantly reduce the storage capacity of alluvial aquifers along the major rivers, and major bodies of groundwater lie beneath the rivers. Recharge and discharge of these alluvial aquifers take place chiefly along stream channels and through lake beds and other thawed zones that perforate the permafrost.[39]

Total water consumption for the Fairbanks area was roughly 2.5 million gallons per day in the mid-1990s, which is well below the maximum projected groundwater yield for the surrounding aquifer. As of 1995, of all the areas in the state, Fairbanks and its surrounding area continued to have the greatest potential for developing groundwater supplies.[40]

Declines in groundwater levels have been observed in the upland area north of Fairbanks, where low-yielding wells produce water from fractures and small perched zones in bedrock.[41] Since 1973 well owners have reported water-level declines from 20 to 30 feet.[42] The unconfined aquifer of the Tanana Alluvium, upon which central Fairbanks is located, shows no signs of overdraft.[43]

Although there is an abundance of groundwater in and around the Fairbanks area, its quality is a major concern. Pollution caused by petroleum products is a serious problem in Fairbanks, as it is in Anchorage. According to the Alaska Department of Environmental Conservation, "Petroleum products are nearly ubiquitous in Fairbanks groundwater."[44] Most of the municipal water-supply wells in Fairbanks have been contaminated by petroleum hydrocarbons, and recently a major contamination occurred in the railroad industrial areas of Fairbanks wherein floating petroleum product was found in the water.[45] Generally, the aquifers underlying Fairbanks contain rather high levels of magnesium, bicarbonate, and sulfate, and dissolved solids concentrations average 227 (milligrams per liter).[46] The most serious groundwater contaminant in the Fairbanks area is arsenic that occurs naturally north of the city. The most common and noticeable contaminant is iron.[47] And, as it has in Anchorage, local pollution of groundwater has been caused by septic tank outflow in unsewered areas of Fairbanks.[48]

Groundwater contamination will continue to be of great concern in Anchorage, Fairbanks, and the rest of Alaska well into the future. Contaminated water will preclude groundwater's use by municipalities that are experiencing rapid growth, and some contaminants (such as petroleum hydrocarbons) will preclude its use by industry.[49] The costs involved with curbing contamination are high and the costs of cleanup even higher. Funding for monitoring, protection, and management activities is not meeting current demands, and unless this changes Alaska could face serious difficulties in the future.[50]

Law

Article 8, section 13 of the Alaska Constitution reads in part: "all surface and subsurface waters reserved to the people for common use, except mineral and medicinal waters, are subject to appropriation. Priority of appropriation shall give prior right. Except for public water supply, an appropriation of water shall be limited to stated purposes and subject to preferences among beneficial uses." This articulation of the prior appropriation doctrine has been in effect since 1959, when Alaska became a state. The statutory framework necessary to implement the principles of this constitutional provision was passed in 1966 as the Alaska Water Use Act. In 1953, prior to Alaska's becoming a state and prior to the passage of the act, a federal judge held that use of groundwater was governed by the absolute ownership doctrine.[51] The 1966 act does not distinguish between surface water and groundwater.

Alaska's appropriation system is administered via permit by the commissioner of natural resources (head of the DNR). Major provisions of the 1966 act are summarized below.

Any activity involving "diversion, impounding or withdrawal" of water, regardless of source (there is no distinction made between streams, underground streams, or percolating groundwater), is subject to the provisions of the act.[52] Individuals, corporations, and government agencies are subject to the provisions of the act.[53] No rights to water may be acquired by adverse use or possession.[54] Rights to water in Alaska may only be acquired by obtaining a permit from the commissioner of natural resources.[55]

A permit will be issued for the appropriation of water providing that four conditions are met:[56]

—the proposed use must not interfere with the rights of prior appropriations;
—the means of diversion or construction proposed must be adequate;
—the proposed use must be beneficial;
—and the proposed use must be in the public interest.

Concerning the adequacy of the proposed means of diversion or construction, water-rights expert (and an author of the act) Frank Trelease wrote, "The requirement of adequate diversion works would most often protect an appropriator from his own folly in choosing equipment that will not do his job."[57]

The beneficial use requirement is common in western water law. Alaska has codified its meaning as "a use of water for the benefit of the appropriator, other persons or the public, that is reasonable and consistent with the public interest, including, but not limited to, domestic, agricultural, irrigation, industrial, manufacturing, fish and shellfish processing, navigation and transportation, mining, power, public, sanitary, fish and wildlife, recreational uses, and maintenance of water quality."[58]

The last requirement, that the appropriation be for a use in the "public interest," is interesting given the difficulty many have with defining "public interest." Trelease found that the leading cases "give an economic interpretation to the phrase. Where sponsors of two different projects compete for the same water, the project to be chosen is the one which will produce the most benefits."[59]

In determining what is in the public interest, the natural resources commissioner is directed by section 46.15.080 of the code to consider:

1. the benefit to the applicant resulting from the proposed appropriation;
2. the effect of the economic activity resulting from the proposed appropriation;
3. the effect on fish and game resources and on public recreational opportunities;
4. the effect on public health;
5. the effect of loss of alternate uses of water that might be made within a reasonable time if not precluded or hindered by the proposed appropriation;
6. harm to other persons resulting from the proposed appropriation;
7. the intent and ability of the applicant to complete the appropriation; and
8. the effect upon access to navigable or public waters.

The commissioner may place conditions on permits including restrictions on construction, withdrawal, or other conditions he or she considers necessary to protect the public interest.[60]

The DNR, pursuant to an interpretation of section 46.15.180 (which does not explicitly grant authority for exceptions by regulation) of the water code has promulgated regulations exempting uses of less than 500 gallons per day or less than 5,000 gallons in a single day from a single source, use of water in an emergency, and the use of seawater on docks, shore establishments, and watercraft.[61] The DNR also issues temporary permits for the short-term use of water (not in excess of five years) for drilling, construction, or other temporary purposes. Temporary-use permits do not grant any rights other than those for the use of water and are subject to all current and future water rights. Temporary-use permits are governed by the same exemptions as are water-rights permits.

The act provides the commissioner with other powers typical in permit and appropriation states regarding well construction and regulation.

Politics, Policy, and the Future

In summary, it could be said that Alaska is following the words of its unofficial motto, "north to the future," because although the amount of groundwater Alaska possesses is unknown, the state seems to be tracking a course of careful control, management, and utilization of its groundwater resources. As of 1997 conflicting groundwater politics or policy within state agencies were almost if not completely absent. The state has also been fortunate to have avoided any conflict between water users.

Perhaps this is a result of the early stage of the state's development or of the abundance of water resources in most areas.

There are undoubtedly localized supply and quality problems in Alaska, but the state water agencies seem to be planning well for the future. However, fiscal cutbacks are taking their toll on agencies responsible for water management in the state. Because of inadequate staffing, enforcement of the Water Use Act is becoming a practical problem for the DNR, and quality monitoring is proving problematic for the Department of Environmental Conservation for the same reason. Political pressures to cut back state spending are the cause of this problem. Some have expressed fear that these same political pressures might generate a move to dismantle the Water Management Act and replace it with a common law, absolute ownership approach to water appropriation in the near future.[62] Because of the act, the state has been able to avoid many of the problems facing other states. Proper management of all the state's water resources has led to social and economic stability in Alaska (relative to many other states.) However, should the Water Use Act be eliminated (de jure or de facto), Alaska would be opening itself up to some of the problems it has, to date, avoided. Until the state has maintained and endorsed the act—by providing adequate funding for management—the future of Alaska's groundwater resources is unclear. If the act is kept in place, and if the agencies responsible for water management are given adequate funding to enforce it, Alaska will clearly be in good shape for the future.

2 California

California, like most states in the West, has a long tradition of agricultural water use. Agriculture is big business in the state, and many of the water-diversion projects that have been developed in California were undertaken to benefit agricultural interests. However, California is also home to many other industries that contribute to the state's economy. The large number of jobs available in California has meant a tremendous influx of people over the years. The result has been a strain on the water supply of the state because of the pressures of meeting agricultural, urban, and, more recently, environmental needs. In the past the state has avoided conflict by seeking out and developing new sources of water, allowing for use by everyone. However, it is becoming apparent that water supplies are not unlimited and that changes will need to be made in allocation and usage patterns. Given the increase in population that is expected in the future and the decreases in available supply as a result of prior allocations and redistribution for environmental concerns,

California is in a tenuous position. It is clear that currently developed supply is inadequate to meet projected needs. It is unclear where the additional needed water will come from.

Physical Description

California has more diversity in its topography than any other state in the union. The states encompasses mountain peaks rising to over 14,000 feet (the highest in the contiguous United States) and desert valleys (the lowest on the continent), California is in many ways unique. The diversity of its physical environment extends to its water resources. Surface water is abundant in many parts of Northern California, whose physiography is similar to that found in the Northwest, and scarce in the arid and—nonirrigated—largely desert south. Although groundwater can be found throughout the state, usage and supply, as well as groundwater problems, vary significantly from region to region.

Demographics

As of 1 July 1995 the resident state population of California was estimated to be 31,589,153.[1] Between 1950 and 1995 its population increased by 198.3 percent, which is well above the national average increase of 73.6 percent.[2] The population increase has been mostly urban. In 1960, 86.3 percent (over 13.5 million people) of the state's population resided in urban areas, and by 1990 the percentage of Californians living in urban areas had reached 92.6 percent (over 27.5 million people).[3] Urban growth will continue to encroach on agricultural land. Projections for growth in the state have approximately half of the new citizens locating in the South Coast region (which includes San Diego, Orange, Los Angeles, Riverside, and San Bernadino Counties). Of the remaining half, a large portion is expected to move into the San Joaquin Valley—an area that has been traditionally agricultural.[4]

While California has the highest net farm income in the nation (over $5 billion in 1991), the majority of persons living in the state earn wages through nonfarm operations. Being primarily an urban state, it is not surprising that the highest-ranking employment industries in California are industries that have traditionally been urban based. Aside from government, the industries that employ the most people in California are service industries, manufacturing, wholesale and retail trade, and finance, insurance, and real estate. Other major employment industries in California include public utilities and transportation and construction, which employ over 1 million people combined.[5]

Irrigation is the single largest user of both ground and surface water in California; however, the number of farms in the state and the total acreage devoted to agricultural use have declined over the years. In 1959 there were approximately 99,000 farms in California covering close to 37 million acres.[6] In 1993 there were 76,000 farms in California, and there were approximately 30 million agricultural acres in the state.[7] The total cash value of crops in California is staggeringly high. However, when compared to other industries operating in the state, agricultural contributions to the gross state product are put into perspective. Agriculture accounts for only 1.6 percent of California's gross state product. Other (less water-intensive) industries such as services; finance, insurance, and real estate; and manufacturing contribute 20.6 percent, 20.5 percent, and 15.1 percent, respectively, to the state's economy.[8]

Water Use

Approximately 63.5 million acre-feet of water is used each year during normal years in California. Agriculture uses approximately 44 percent, municipal and industrial uses amount to approximately 11 percent, and environmental use stands at about 45 percent. Roughly 13 percent of this use comes from the ground.[9] During drought periods, however, groundwater dependency increases dramatically. Major sources of surface water are northern California rivers, including the Sacramento Delta delivered to central and southern California via the Central Valley Project and State Water Project (discussed below).

From 1940 to 1980 irrigated acreage in California nearly doubled, increasing from approximately 5 million to over 9.5 million acres. Owing to changing economic conditions, the fact that much of the best land is already in irrigation, and the unlikelihood that major agricultural surface water impoundment and delivery systems will be built in the near future, it is not probable that agricultural activities will expand in the future. Agricultural irrigation has been declining slightly in recent years and will continue to do so. As of 1995 there were 9.4 million acres of crops being irrigated in California, and it is forecasted that the irrigated crop acreage in the state will drop another 300,000 acres by the year 2020.[10]

The ratio of agricultural water use to municipal and industrial water use can be expected to decrease in the future in California. Despite the projected 2 million acre-feet per year of water that will be saved as a result of the reduction in agricultural use and of agricultural conservation, the state's population is expected to rise from roughly 31 million in 1992 to 49 million around the year 2020, increasing urban demand by 4.5 million acre-feet per year. Municipal and industrial consumptive water demands (urban use) in California can be expected to rise from 11 percent to 17.2 percent of total use.[11] It is clear that the state's future water needs are going to increase substantially. The California Department of Water Resources is evaluating various water-management alternatives that can be implemented to meet future needs. (Long-term plans recognize that there will be shortfalls in supply.) Adding to the problem is the fact that some of the current supply may be unavailable for future municipal needs. Currently California is using roughly 5.2 million acre-feet per year of Colorado River water, despite the fact that the allotment for the state is 4.4 million acre-feet. As Arizona and Nevada begin to use their Colorado River allotments, California's supply will be reduced by some 800,000 acre-feet per year. In addition, the Central Valley Project Improvement Act of 1992 (CVPIA) reallocated some of the water diverted by the project to protecting natural habitat. This redistribution, together with actions to increase water available for environmental uses, is estimated to reduce the supply available to agricultural and urban users by 1 to 3 million acre-feet per year.[12] With the reduction of available surface water supply, groundwater may be called upon to meet future demand until additional surface water can be obtained.

Problems

Overdrafting
Many of California's groundwater problems are the result of the inability of individuals or water entities to effectively manage or control groundwater pumping. This is not to suggest that groundwater pumping in California is unmanaged. In many parts of the state effective management has occurred through litigation or through the creation of local management units (discussed below). In other parts of the state, notably in parts of the San Joaquin Valley, the cumulative uncoordinated decisions of individual groundwater pumpers constitutes a de facto groundwater-management policy (i.e., a groundwater-mining policy). Overdrafting has led to some supply problems in the San Joaquin Valley, which, coupled with drainage problems and urban encroachment, are likely to lead to agricultural acreage decreases in this region in the future.[13]

Owing in large part to the development of surface-water supplies, notably the State Water Project and Central Valley Project, overdrafting in California declined substantially from 1955 to 1995.[14] In 1955 statewide overdraft was estimated at approximately 4 million acre-feet a year. By 1990 it had been reduced to 1.3 million acre-feet a year with approximately 860,000 acre-feet of that amount occurring in the San Joaquin Valley.[15]

There are forty-two groundwater basins in California that have either been identified by studies as being overdrafted or in which there is evidence of adverse affects associated with overdrafting.[16]

The California Department of Water Resources (DWR) has identified eleven basins as "subject to critical conditions of overdraft." The definition used in this determination is: "A basin is subject to critical conditions of overdraft when continuation of present water management practices would probably result in significant adverse overdraft-related environmental, social, or economic impacts."[17] The eleven basins so designated are: Pajaro Basin, Cuyama Valley Basin, Ventura Central Basin, Eastern San Joaquin County Basin, Chowchilla Basin; Madera Basin, Kings Basin, Kaweah Basin, Tulare Lake Basin, Tule Basin, and Kern County Basin.

All except the first three of those basins are located in the agriculturally rich Central Valley. Pajaro Basin is in southern Santa Cruz County; Cuyama Valley Basin is in northern Santa Barbara County; and the Ventura Central Basin is in southern Ventura County. In most of these basins changes in management procedures could curtail overdrafting and other (usually related) problems. But given state or local governments' current lack of authority to control overdrafting, the prognosis for these areas is not good. (Legislation passed in 1992 provided authority for many local agencies to develop groundwater-management plans; however, as of 1996 no agency has implemented such a plan.)[18] Furthermore, any gains that were made in the reduction of overdrafting (particularly in the San Joaquin Valley) will likely be reversed in the near future as groundwater is needed to compensate for water diverted to environmental concerns by the CVPIA.

In addition to the declared basins subject to critical conditions of overdraft, overdrafting is occurring in many other parts of the state. Table 2 lists the major hydrologic areas of the state, along with groundwater use and average annual overdraft under 1990 conditions of development.[19]

Land Subsidence

Land subsidence in California has occurred primarily in the San Joaquin Valley in the basins subject to critical conditions of overdraft as de-

Table 2   Hydrologic Study Areas' Groundwater Safe-Yield Usage and Overdraft (1,000 acre-feet per year)

Hydrologic study area	Groundwater use	Groundwater overdraft
North Coastal	263	—
San Francisco Bay	100	—
Central Coastal	688	240
South Coastal	1,083	20
Sacramento Basin	2,496	30
San Joaquin	1,098	210
Tulare Basin	915	650
North Lahontan	121	—
South Lahontan	221	70
Colorado Desert	80	80
Totals	7,065	1,300

scribed above. Subsidence of up to 28 feet has been measured, although the amount measured is more likely to average between 2 and 5 feet.[20] Additional areas where subsidence has existed in the past include the San Jose area in the Santa Clara Valley, possibly parts of northern Los Angeles County, and central Orange County.[21]

The damage caused by land subsidence in California is similar to that generally associated with land subsidence. Many public and private facilities, particularly water facilities, which are sensitive to elevation shifts, have had to be repaired or remodeled.[22]

Pollution

Saltwater intrusion has been identified all along the California coast, from San Diego to Humboldt Counties.

In 1975 the DWR had identified fourteen known areas and fourteen suspected areas of saltwater intrusion in the state.[23] The known areas are as follows: Eel River Valley, Petaluma Valley, Napa-Sonoma Valley, Santa Clara Valley, Pajaro Valley, Elkhorn Slough Area, Salinas Valley Pressure Area, Morro Basin, Chorro Basin, Los Osos Basin, Oxnard Plain Basin, West Coast Basin (Los Angeles County), and San Luis Rey Valley–Mission Basin. The suspected areas are: Russian River Basin, Drakes Estero Basin, Bolinas Lagoon Basin, San Rafael Basin, Suisum-Fairfield Valley, Sacramento–San Joaquin Delta, Tonitas Creek Basin, Carmel Valley, Big Sur River Basin, Santa Rosa Creek Basin, and San Diego River–Mission Valley Basin. Since the time of this study, saltwater intrusion has continued to be a problem in California's coastal basins, with most of the cases of aquifer impairment (where beneficial uses of the water have been harmed or limited) being attributed to salinity or total dissolved solids (TDSs).[24]

Consistent with California water law generally, protection of groundwater basins from saltwater intrusion is the responsibility of local government. If, however, local officials fail to act, sec. 2100 of the California Water Code vests in the State Water Resources Control Board authority to file suit in Superior Court "to restrict pumping or to impose physical solution or both, to the extent necessary to prevent destruction or irreparable injury to the quality of such water."[25]

In the past it has been the policy of the board to avoid adjudication whenever possible. As concerns both saltwater intrusion and other groundwater-quality problems the board has taken the position that in administering the law it should "use it first to spur local efforts and adjudicate only as a last resort."[26] As of the mid-1990s the board had yet to file an official section 2100 action and had threatened to do so only twice. It did so most recently on 3 March 1993, when it threatened to initiate a section 2100 action if local agencies in the Salinas Valley did not appropriately address their intrusion problem.[27]

In addition to saltwater intrusion there are numerous other existing or potential groundwater-quality problems in California.

In California, regional water-quality control boards set water-quality objectives based on the beneficial uses made of a basin. The most restrictive objectives are set for basins used for drinking-water purposes. Regional boards issue waste discharge permits designed to keep water quality within the established parameters. If discharge limits are violated California law provides for various means of enforcement, including damages of up to $10,000 per day of violation.[28]

In addition, the Hazardous Waste Control Act of 1972 and subsequent amendments gave the California Department of Health Services authority to establish and enforce regulations dealing with hazardous-waste handling, processing, and disposal. Among other things, this has resulted in a toxic tracking system that requires that a manifest accompany any transportation of hazardous waste on public roads. One thing that manifests must contain is information on composition and volume. Although transportation by truck, train, or vessel is subject to the requirements, toxic wastes originating and disposed of on private property are not.[29]

Additionally, the Safe Drinking Water and Toxic Enforcement Act of 1986 prohibits the discharge of specified carcinogens or reproductive toxins into drinking-water sources. As of 1 September 1996 guidelines were in place for 420 carcinogens and 160 reproductive toxins specified by the act.[30] The state has in place a computerized tracking system that tracks violations (of which there were an average of 500 per month in 1987).[31]

In spite of these control measures, incidents of groundwater pollution from toxins as well as other substances have been identified in California with alarming regularity. For example, the pesticide DBCP, a suspected carcinogen found to cause sterility in humans, was discovered in 193 of 527 groundwater samples taken in twenty-four California counties.[32] DBCP contamination will continue to be a problem well into the future in some areas. In Hawaii DBCP applied in the 1940s was still being de-tected in the 1990s. Application of DBCP was not halted in California until 1977. According to University of California, Berkeley, toxicologist William Pease, "it just won't go away." He adds that millions of pounds of DBCP have been applied in the state and that only about half of it has degraded, leaving "millions of pounds of this stuff to contaminate after the turn of the century."[33]

Near Riverside, California, the Stringfellow dump, closed in 1972, was thought to be impenetrable. It turns out that the bedrock underlying the dump is in fact fractured. The dump accepted some 32 million gallons of industrial waste prior to closure. The resulting pollution necessitated closing private wells in the area. Various remedial measures were under-taken, including covering the site with an impervious barrier (to prevent rainfall from entering) and the drilling and operation of extraction wells. These are two examples; there are others.[34]

Prior to the passage of the various measures designed to mitigate groundwater pollution problems (discussed above), the EPA identified a number of major pollution problems in the state.[35] These include irriga-tion return flows and solid and municipal wastes.

Irrigation return flow has been identified as a major cause of ground-water pollution in many parts of California, particularly in the San Joa-quin Valley. Flushing not only results in salinization, but it can often also cause residues of nitrate fertilizers to find their way into ground-water basins.

Land disposal of solid wastes in California also poses a serious threat to water quality in many parts of the state. At many dump sites surface runoff is inadequately controlled, while at others the sites are close to or in contact with groundwater supplies.[36]

Groundwater basin pollution from the land disposal of municipal and

industrial wastes was identified in many parts of California during the
1960s and early 1970s. Among the areas identified by the EPA as suffering
from groundwater-quality degradation as a result of the land application
of municipal or industrial waste were areas in the vicinity of the cities of
Fresno, Riverside, San Bernadino, Hollister, Barstow, and Vernon.[37]

Although California has made strides to enact legislation and initiate
rules for the prevention of further groundwater contamination, the real
problem lies in the contamination already present. Pollutants that have
been introduced into the environment pose both current and potential
threats to the groundwater supplies of the state. DBCP is just one example of a contaminant that continues to pose health threats long after
its use has ceased. Even if no further pollution is allowed (an optimistic
hope given that all activity in the state cannot be monitored) state officials will have to continue to monitor water supplies for contamination
well into the future.

Law

Groundwater is managed on the local level in California. State-level
groundwater management is, among other things, limited to the collection of data on pumping in certain areas and the formulation of well
construction and abandonment guidelines. Local management has taken
three basic forms. In some parts of the state, notably the San Joaquin Valley, the cumulative uncoordinated decisions of individual groundwater
pumpers has led to overdrafting and to a de facto policy of groundwater
mining. In other parts, notably in large sections of southern California,
coordinated management of groundwater basins has taken place either
through adjudication or through the creation of a water district (as provided for in the California Code).

Water districts in California take on a variety of forms. Some are created by a specific legislative act; others are created under general acts. The
selection of district-governing bodies can be made through independent
election by all district voters, election by property owners, and various
other appointment methods. Over 900 special districts in California per-
form some water-utility functions. These districts vary significantly in
their powers, functions, and methods of creation but generally share an
authority to "levy taxes, issue both general obligation and revenue bonds,
and set rates for service."[38] (As of 1978 and the passage of proposition 13,
the property-tax limitation initiative, local governmental units in Cali-

fornia are prohibited from imposing "special taxes" unless they are approved by two-thirds of the qualified voters in the governmental unit.)[39]

The Orange County Water District (OCWD), which has been referred to as a leader "in the water district non-adjudication approach to groundwater management" provides an example of groundwater management by local district in California.[40] The OCWD has extensive powers to require data from groundwater pumpers, regulate pumping patterns, levy a pump tax, and through a "basin equity assessment" regulate the cost of groundwater in order to influence the amounts of ground versus surface water being used. A major function of the OCWD is that of recharging groundwater basins with imported surface water and natural runoff. For this purpose the district owns 1,000 acres in and adjacent to the Santa Ana River.[41]

Management by a court-appointed watermaster occurs after the adjudication of the extraction rights of pumpers in a management area. The powers of a watermaster are similar to those held by water districts. For example, the San Gabriel watermaster, a nine-member court-appointed body, can operate a groundwater-replenishment program, control basin storage, and levy a "replacement water assessment" on the amount of withdrawal in excess of a pumper's adjudicated share.[42] As reported by the California Governor's Commission to Review California Water Rights Law, nearly "all groundwater adjudications have ended with a stipulation for judgement. . . . Parties have reached agreements on allocations they believe to be fair and reasonable and have agreed to watermaster managements."[43]

Water districts and watermasters with adequate authority to manage groundwater basins are atypical forms of groundwater management. Management in some areas is often nothing more than the cumulative decisions of individual pumpers. This situation is due, for the most part, to the nature of California water law and to judicial interpretation of the law. The major cases are summarized below.

Prior to 1903 California courts had followed the English common law rule of absolute ownership in groundwater. Holding that percolating waters were part of the land and belonged to the owners of the land, the Supreme Court had found that extractions of water on one's land that interfered with extractions on adjacent lands were not actionable.[44]

In 1903 the California Supreme Court, in the landmark case *Katz v. Walinshaw*, rejected the absolute ownership doctrine and found that reasonable use should govern the rights of overlying landowners.[45] The court found that reasonable use "limits the right of others to such amount of water as may be necessary for some useful purpose in connection with the land from which it is taken."[46]

The *Katz* court also outlined what it called the "rule of correlative rights." Taken together, the rule of correlative rights and the requirement of reasonable and beneficial use provide that landowners overlying a common source of percolating groundwater have equal or correlative rights to a reasonable amount of the water when applied to a reasonable beneficial use on the land overlying the groundwater basin.

Subsequent cases have clarified and affirmed the correlative rights doctrine. In 1928, through the initiative process, a reasonable and beneficial requirement was added to the California Constitution.[47] Although the amendment was initially a response to a Supreme Court decision dealing with surface-water rights, the court in 1935 found the amendment also applied to groundwater.[48] Under the correlative rights doctrine priority in time does not give priority in right. In *Burr v. Maclay Rancho Water Co.* the Supreme Court held that overlying landowners had equal rights regardless of the fact that the defendant had not exercised his right.[49]

In the event that the underground supply is inadequate to satisfy the needs of overlying landowners, each owner is entitled to a reasonable share of the supply.[50] The courts may determine the reasonableness of extraction in such cases and may restrict overlying landowners to their reasonable share.[51]

Such extractions are subject to the doctrine of prior appropriation, and the rights so acquired are inferior to the rights of overlying landowners using the water on overlying lands.[52] Groundwater rights may also be acquired through prescription. When nonsurplus water is extracted wrongfully, and when the use is actual, open and notorious, hostile, adverse to the original owner, uninterrupted for five years, and under claim of right, a prescriptive right is created.

From 1903 until 1949 California courts applied the correlative rights doctrine and often sought "physical solutions" that would avoid waste.[53] A physical solution is fashioned when the strict application of water rights in a case will result in waste and some other appropriation of water would protect vested rights and prevent waste. (As, for example, when a senior right holder is entitled to an injunction against a junior right holder, the result of which will be a reduction in the total amount of water available to both parties.) During this period it became apparent that merely establishing and upholding the rights among parties would not protect groundwater basins from overdrafting. As one commentator noted:

> the court would enjoin pumping only if and when withdrawals di-
> rectly interfered with pumping activities of other producers who
> were prior in right. By the mid-1930's, it became apparent that steps
> had to be taken in order to control the total amount of water pumped
> from the groundwater basins of Southern California. The hit and
> miss tactics of individually oriented adjudications of groundwater
> rights were not effective in coping with the tremendous disparity be-
> tween groundwater supplies and demands. To remedy this situation,
> it was again necessary for the Supreme Court to revise the ground-
> water laws of this state.[54]

This revision came in the form of the "mutual prescription doctrine" in *City of Pasadena v. City of Alhambra.*[55] *Pasadena* involved pumpers in the Raymond Basin in Southern California. For twenty-two of the twenty-four years prior to filing the suit, the Raymond Basin had been in a condition of overdraft. The court found that appropriators that caused the overdraft were invading the rights of overlying owners and prior appropriators but that such appropriators had acquired prescriptive rights. Although it left open the question of whether or not overlying owners had obtained new prescriptive rights, the court found that by their continued pumping, overlying owners retained their rights to future extractions. The court held that "The original owners by their own acts . . . thus retained or acquired a right to continue to take some water in the future. The wrongdoers also acquired prescriptive rights to continue to take water, but their rights were limited to the extent that the original owners retained or acquired rights by their pumping."[56]

Upholding the trial court's decision, the Supreme Court limited total withdrawals to the safe yield of the basin and found all acquired prescriptive rights were of equal priority. The extractions of all parties were limited to their proportion of the safe yield based on total extractions during any five-year period from the beginning of the overdraft until the filing of the suit.[57]

After the *Pasadena* decision, one commentator noted: "Many adjudications . . . have followed a pattern of negotiation to find a physical solution, stipulation for judgment, and judgment. The first step of this stipulated judgment approach generally has been to apply the mutual prescription formula to the available pumping data. By agreeing to apply a formula, the parties have avoided adversary proceedings in many situations where determination of complex appropriative priorities might in any event been impossible because of insufficient and unreliable data."[58]

Although the *Pasadena* case protected some municipal pumpers and allowed courts to avoid "complex appropriative priorities," it had at least one serious drawback. By putting groundwater rights acquired through prescription on par with other rights, and by determining prescriptive rights on the basis of the highest level of pumping during any five-year period of the overdraft, the case provided groundwater extractors with an incentive to "race to the pumphouse . . . each party endeavoring to increase the volume of continuous use on which his prescription right will be based."[59] As one of the state's leading hydrologists noted: "More than one industry has gone into agricultural activities on lands adjacent to its plant, and has been granted pumping rights on the basis of both industrial and agricultural use, the latter sometimes of questionable economic justification."[60]

Of course municipalities had to participate in this "race to the pumphouse," and they also had to fear that their rights would be lost through prescription. Then in 1975 in the California Supreme Court case *City of Los Angeles v. City of San Fernando* several changes were made in the application of the mutual prescription doctrine that both made the doctrine more difficult to apply and gave municipalities an advantage in its application.[61]

First, the court upheld the City of Los Angeles's argument that Civil Code section 1007, prohibiting the acquisition of prescriptive rights by any person, firm, or corporation against a city, county, public utility, or other public entity prevented the courts from imposing a mutual prescription formula on a city without the city's consent.[62]

This puts private pumpers at a disadvantage vis-á-vis public pumpers. Private pumpers can lose their rights through prescription to public pumpers, but public pumpers cannot lose their rights to either private or public pumpers through prescription.

The second impact that the *San Fernando* decision had on prescription concerns the definition of overdraft as a condition in which extractions exceed safe yield.[63] The *San Fernando* court expanded this definition by interpreting safe yield to include additions and withdrawals over an extended period of time. The court noted: "Groundwater basin levels tended to vary in accordance with wide fluctuations in precipitation. Thus if a rising level of extractions were halted at the point of the safe yield based on the . . . (long-term) . . . average, ensuing heightening of groundwater levels during years of higher-than-average precipitation would cause waste."[64]

The court thus concluded that overdraft occurred only when extractions exceed safe yield plus any temporary surplus.[65]

As previously discussed, an essential element of prescription is that there be an element of adversity. Overdraft constitutes the necessary adversity. For the prescriptive right to ripen, overdraft must continue for five consecutive years. If during any one of the five years there is a surplus, the prescriptive period ceases to run. Consequently the definition of overdraft articulated by the *San Fernando* court made overdraft, and hence prescription, more difficult to establish.

San Fernando's third impact on prescription concerns the element of notice. For the prescription period to run, the holders of the original rights must be on notice that an overdraft exists. In *Pasadena* the lowering of the water table was determined to be adequate notice of an overdraft.[66] The *San Fernando* court found that the lowering of the water table alone was not adequate notice and that owners of prior rights must be on notice *in fact* that there is an overdraft.[67]

One commentator has observed: "It may be that, in order to establish notice after San Fernando, a pumper who wants to perfect his prescriptive rights will finance hydrological determinations of overdraft in a basin and, based on that data, actually notify other basin pumpers of the basin's over-draft."[68]

Another California Supreme Court case, *Niles Sand and Gravel Co. v. Alameda County Water District*, decided the year before the *San Fernando* case, aided municipalities and water districts in their efforts to manage groundwater basins through groundwater storage and conjunctive use.[69]

In the *Niles* case the Alameda County Water District had been recharging the Niles Basin by percolation for storage purposes and to prevent saltwater intrusion. The Niles Sand and Gravel Company dug pits to a depth of 120 to 125 feet below the surface elevation and 80 to 85 feet below the water table. To continue operations the company was pumping and releasing roughly 5 million gallons of water per day into San Francisco Bay.

The court found that based on the statutory powers granted to the water district by the state and on the doctrine of correlative rights, landowners in the Niles Basin had a "public servitude" that imposed "such obligations . . . limiting the use of lands lying in a particular geographical area, where an overriding public interest requires it."[70] The right to enforce the servitude is held by the district, and it limits overlying landowners' right to groundwater when such use interferes with a public groundwater-storage program. The court found that the district had a right to store water and to prevent others from extracting the water and that it was not liable for damage by flooding from such storage when water levels went no higher than their natural levels, that is, the level if there were no extractions.[71]

In summary, California groundwater law and policy developed first in response to the courts' realization that the common law absolute ownership doctrine strictly applied was not suitable to an arid environment and to full utilization of the resource and that to allow continued agricultural expansion and other water development necessitated an adjustment in the doctrine. Growth of the state's population and increasing demands on groundwater basins led to changes in the law that protected municipal interests. These court decisions and various legislation have led to groundwater management, either by adjudication or by water district, in many parts of California. But in many parts of the state, individuals are free to pump water without restriction.

Politics, Policy, and the Future

Groundwater policy in California, if it is defined as how groundwater is managed, has consisted of allowing local management through a water district or watermaster or of simply letting individual pumpers determine rates of extraction. The latter is not really management in any real sense, but it is, to reiterate, a "policy"—that is, one of groundwater mining.

In June 1981 the California State Water Resources Control Board and the Department of Water Resources issued a report entitled "Policies and Goals for California Water Management" wherein a goal for groundwater management stated in part that "groundwater overdraft is not consistent with sound water resources management practices."[72] Why, one might ask, has the State of California articulated a groundwater-management goal that is so inconsistent with current management practices? The answer lies in the fact that groundwater users have been able to prevent any significant change in California groundwater law.

The resistance of agricultural interests and other users to groundwater regulation designed to prevent overdrafting is evidence that those interests are satisfied with the status quo. Why do Californians oppose groundwater management to curtail overdrafting when a continuation of current rates of extraction will eventually make agriculture unprofitable in some areas and will possibly lead to increased pumping costs or to depletion of the resource? A group of agricultural economists at the University of California, Davis, have suggested five reasons to explain this behavior. First, farmers in many areas not being overdrafted don't want state-level regulation because they feel it is unnecessary. Many Central Valley farmers receive water either from the State Water Project or from the Central Valley Project and use that water to supplement groundwater supplies (drawing from the ground during dry years and using surface water or recharging groundwater basins during wet years). Second, the real cost of overutilization of groundwater basins may be mitigated or hidden by other cost and price trends. Third, farmers fear that groundwater regulation could shift control over allocation of resource to nonfarmers, thereby increasing the likelihood that some agricultural use will be lost to municipal, industrial, and other users. Fourth, farmers fear that regulation will necessitate cutbacks in irrigated acreage, resulting in reduced profits and reduced land values. And finally, many farmers (and local water agencies) feel that prior to reaching groundwater levels at which farming and other uses are unprofitable, new surface supplies will be made available to offset the overdraft.[73]

Why have current users been so successful at maintaining the status quo? California politics is characterized by weak political parties that are unable, for example, to exert much impact on campaign finance, to control candidate selection, or to carry out policy proposals. California politics is further characterized by strong interest groups, some of which influence candidate selection and as well as campaign finance. "The end result," as one observer noted, "is greatly to increase the role of money in politics and the role of groups which have the resources to participate in this critical aspect of political life."[74] The imposition of term limits for members of the California legislature will further increase the influence of groups in that body. Under term limits legislators will no longer be able to accumulate the years of experience with and knowledge of water policy issues that some were able to accumulate in the past.

Many irrigation and water districts in California have felt that eventually they would be able to use northern surface water from the Central Valley Project and State Water Project to "rescue" them from groundwater overdrafting before groundwater becomes too expensive to pump.[75] However, as we have seen, this seems unlikely in light of currently developed supplies. The redistribution of water for habitat maintenance in the Bay-Delta region of the state has created surface-water shortages for existing use in the surrounding area (resulting in increased groundwater use), leaving no surplus water for irrigation now or in the future.

A problem with current California groundwater management, according to many water specialists, is that absent adjudication or water-district management, groundwater users have an incentive to continue or expand groundwater pumping. Incentives for continued and/or expanded pumping are provided by both the court decisions establishing prescriptive rights and by the fact that under current law groundwater in California is a "common pool" resource.[76] In recent years the adjudication and management problems have received some attention. As of the mid-1990s thirteen groundwater basins had been adjudicated and were operating in accordance with court settlements (a fourteenth has been adjudicated in federal court, but water users are not limited in their pumping).[77] Furthermore, 1992 amendments to the California Water Code (AB 3030) provided the authority for "certain local agencies" to develop and implement groundwater-management plans. However, as of 1996 no such plans had been implemented, and it is too early to tell what the long-term impact of these amendments will be.

Projections for the future supply and demand of water in California indicate that there will be a shortfall in supply (meaning that current rates of groundwater overdraft are likely to increase if additional surface supplies are not developed). The California Department of Water Resources anticipates that even with increased conservation, projected agricultural land retirement, additional wastewater recycling, more conjunctive use programs, a solution to the problems with water delivery from the Bay-Delta area, additional storage facilities being built south of the Bay-Delta area, and water transfer, there will be shortfalls of between 2.1 and 4.1 million acre-feet per year (2.9 to 4.9 in drought years).[78] Of course if any of the activities listed above do not occur as planned the shortfalls will be even greater. In the meantime it is probable that any gap that exists between supply and demand will be met through further depletion of groundwater sources—an unsustainable solution. One can imagine the possible socioeconomic ramifications of these projected shortfalls. In addition to the obvious shifts from irrigation to municipal use and the related socioeconomic impact (such as decreasing rural populations and loss of agricultural jobs), shortfalls are likely to have a far-reaching spill-over effect. For example, strict conservation measures that will significantly change the way water is used are likely to be enacted. In some areas people may no longer be able to keep and maintain lawns (as happened in Santa Barbara during the drought of the early 1990s). This will lead to an impact on the landscaping industry, on sales of lawn mowers, on gardeners, and so on.

It is clear that given the rate of overdrafting in California and the serious environmental, economic, and social costs associated with a continuance of long-term overdrafting, some solution to the problem must be found. Perhaps it is time for the citizens of California to elect representatives who are less susceptible to the strong pull of agricultural monies and who are willing to place the state in a more active role with regard to water-resource management. At the very least, it seems that groundwater-management plans should be made mandatory rather than optional. In the future it might even become necessary for the legislature to enact provisions whereby municipalities can claim water through eminent domain. (Leasing options or water transfers can do more harm than good, as irrigators often lease surface water to municipalities and continue to irrigate with groundwater.) Such redistribution of supply from agriculture to municipalities (beyond projected levels) would not mean the end of agriculture in California, as the retirement of small amounts of irrigated acreage frees up large amounts of water. Furthermore, irrigators could be compensated for any loss.

It is apparent that severe measures might have to be taken in California in the not-so-distant future. Water is essential for both the survival of human beings and the continuance of many economic endeavors. There are simply not enough developed water supplies available at present to sustain the current socioeconomic structure of the state into the future. Increased demand and supply shortfall projections make California's future uncertain.

3 Hawaii

Hawaii is very dependent upon groundwater. The costs involved with surface-water storage and treatment, and the geographic composition of the islands, make groundwater development much more economical and feasible than storing and treating surface water is. This being the case, the long-term sustainability of groundwater resources is perhaps more important for Hawaii than it is for other states. Traditionally, agriculture has been the largest user of water in Hawaii; however, recent changes have begun to shift the bulk of water use to municipalities.

Changes in the laws of the state have improved groundwater management and have helped to decrease some of the groundwater-level declines that the state had previously been facing. In addition, the closure of many agricultural ventures in the state has helped to lessen the demand on water supplies. The potential for groundwater contamination exists, but if the state is able to effectively protect water supplies from pollution the prospects for Hawaii's water future are good.[1]

Physical Description

The Hawaiian archipelago, located more than 2,500 miles from its nearest neighbor in the central Pacific Ocean, consists of a 1,600-mile-long chain of 132 islands, shoals, and reefs. The five most populous islands are Hawaii, Maui, Oahu, Kauai, and Lanai. The island of Oahu, the location of Honolulu, holds in excess of 80 percent of the state's population. Oahu is the site of most of the state's pollution problems. Because of a lack of infrastructure to meet future demand, the most pressing supply problems are found on the islands of Molokai and Maui (Oahu is likely to face a similar situation in fifteen to twenty years).[2]

Groundwater in Hawaii falls into one of two categories: that of basal water and that of high-level or perched water. Perched waters are waters trapped above ground and resting upon some impervious body. Basal water is a lens-shaped aquifer of fresh water floating on denser sea water below the main water table. Basal water is either confined by coastal caprock and hence under artesian pressure, or, when it is found inland, is not under pressure. The principal source of fresh groundwater in most of the Hawaiian Islands, as well as on virtually all small ocean islands, is basal water, although high-level sources are becoming more attractive and are the mean source in some areas, such as on the island of Lanai.[3]

Endowed with the favorable combination of permeable basalt (i.e., dark volcanic rock) and high rainfall, groundwater recharge in each of the major islands is substantial. Average annual rainfall in the islands ranges from less than 6.5 inches to 450 inches. Groundwater recharge has been estimated at approximately 30 percent of rainfall.[4]

Demographics

As of 1 July 1995 the resident state population of Hawaii was estimated to be 1,186,815.[5] Between 1950 and 1995 the population increased by 137.4 percent, surpassing the national average growth rate of 73.6 percent.[6] The predominant growth pattern in the state has reflected an increase in urban dwelling. In 1960, 76.4 percent of Hawaiians (484,000 people) resided in urban areas.[7] By 1990 approximately 89 percent (over 1.1 million people) of the population was urban.[8]

While Hawaii is often perceived as an agricultural state because of its pineapple and sugar cane exports, a very small portion of the Hawaiian economy is based upon agriculture. Hawaii's per capita farm earnings are among the lowest in the nation. Of those people working in Hawaii,

98.2 percent earn wages through nonfarm operations. The largest employment industries in Hawaii are those often associated with tourism—services, retail trade, and public utilities and transportation.[9]

Irrigation accounts for approximately 63 percent of the fresh water withdrawn in Hawaii, with most of this water coming from surface-water sources. However, the number of farms and acreage devoted to agricultural use has declined over the years. In 1959 there were approximately 6,000 farms in Hawaii covering over 2.4 million acres.[10] In 1993 there were roughly 4,000 farms in Hawaii covering approximately 2 million acres.[11] Farming, while it accounts for most use of fresh water in the state, contributes only about 1 percent to the gross state product of Hawaii. The industries that contribute the most to Hawaii's gross state product are those that do not generally require a great deal of water—services; retail trade; and finance, insurance, and real estate. These industries contribute 21.4 percent, 13.2 percent, and 18.6 percent to the state's economy, respectively.[12]

Water Use

The most important source of fresh water in Hawaii is groundwater—particularly for drinking water. This is partly because Hawaiian stream flows are flashy, intermittent, tend to fluctuate seasonally, and are generally unreliable as a source of year-round supply. In addition, the costs involved with water treatment often preclude heavy dependence on surface water for drinking water. Exceptions are perennial streams that drain high rainfall areas along windward slopes and coasts and spring-fed streams in mountainous areas. Therefore, stream water is used primarily for agricultural purposes, and even then extensive ditch-and-tunnel systems are required to collect and convey the water from wet mountainous areas to irrigated fields at lower elevations. Groundwater provides a more constant and dependable source of water in terms of both quantity and quality and is used for most domestic and municipal water supplies.[13] Agriculture uses approximately 34 percent of the groundwater withdrawn in the state, and 93 percent of public supply water comes from the ground.[14]

Water supplies in the state as a whole exceed present and projected needs, but this is not true for individual aquifer systems. Most precipitation occurs on the windward (northeastern) side of the islands, with much less falling on the leeward areas. Consequently water often must be transported, usually via pipeline, from one part of an island to another.

The major basal aquifers on each island have been substantially developed. However, there are many aquifers that are at present undeveloped or barely developed because of lack of demand, or as a result of cost or environmental concerns. The basal lens between Hilo and Laupahoehoe on the island of Hawaii is an example of an undeveloped aquifer.[15]

The importance of groundwater is increasing steadily as community developments, requiring more and better water, spread to drier parts of the islands. The greatest demands for water use have been in the dry, sunny areas where sugar cane yields are the highest and where most people live. Development of these areas could significantly increase demand for water. This is especially true for Oahu, whose municipal water supply is totally dependent on groundwater and where water supplies are slowly being depleted because of rapid development.

The most heavily developed aquifer in the state is the Pearl Harbor Aquifer System on Oahu. In 1995 roughly 54 percent of all the reported groundwater used on Oahu was withdrawn from this source.[16] Sustainable yields for the basal lens in Honolulu and Pearl Harbor (Oahu), Lahaina-Kaanapali (Maui), and Kekaha-Mana (Kauai) have almost been reached under the present rate of extraction, and the Iao Aquifer System (on the opposite side of Maui from Lahaina) has surpassed its estimated safe yield. Other basal aquifers are not similarly stressed.

The most serious current supply problem can be found on the island of Maui in the Lahaina and Iao Aquifers. Maui is developing faster than the current water infrastructure can handle, and the island is relying on only a few aquifers without spreading out pumpage. However, because of its large population, Oahu's water situation is potentially more serious than is that of the other islands in the state. The island's water problems are further affected by an annual tourist influx of millions (approximately 5 million people per year visited Hawaii as tourists in the 1990s). On Oahu municipal water supply is virtually 100 percent consumptive.

The basal water head in Pearl Harbor wells has been declining since development began in the 1880s. A century of groundwater development on the Pearl Harbor–Honolulu Basin, and particularly the increasing withdrawals of the last two decades, have reduced the original volume of storage in the aquifer by about 30 to 40 percent. Concurrently, the water table has declined by more than 15 feet in some areas, and basal lens shrinkage has closed many of the older and deeper wells along the coast.[17] Estimates of sustainable yield range from 250 to 300 million gallons per day, while withdrawals have reached approximately 275 million gallons per day (despite reported use of only 226 million gallons per day).[18] As a result this area has been designated for water-use regulation by the State Department of Land and Natural Resources (discussed below).

Although agricultural irrigation continues to be the dominant water user in the state, domestic use is increasing rapidly as a result of increased population and tourism. Along with this increase there has been a significant decrease in agricultural use over the past few years (particularly on the islands of Hawaii and Oahu). Once one of the largest users of water in Hawaii, sugar production is no longer as profitable as it was at one time, and this has resulted in the closure of many sugar cane plantations. Two such plantations have closed on the island of Hawaii, and, to date, one has closed on Oahu. In 1995 Oahu Sugar shut down its operations—operations that had been withdrawing an estimated 60 million gallons per day of groundwater in the Pearl Harbor area. As of 1995 municipal use had surpassed agricultural use in the Pearl Harbor–Honolulu area, and it is expected to surpass agriculture on the other parts of Oahu as well. (Many more sugar cane plantations are likely to close in the near future.)[19] Overall use is increasing because of heightened industrial and domestic demands for water. These stepped-up demands have been met largely through the use of groundwater.[20]

Problems

Overview
Many of Hawaii's groundwater problems are a result of the extremely uneven distribution of rainfall, the size and shape of the islands, the varying ability of the rocks to absorb and transport water, and contamination from agriculture. Serious groundwater problems include overdrafting (primarily on Maui and Honolulu), saltwater intrusion, loss of recharge due to land development, waste disposal, and other agricultural pollution problems. The major problem areas include the entire island of Oahu, Kailua-Kona and the South Kohala coast on the island of Hawaii, the Lahaina district and Iao Aquifer system on Maui, and the Koloa and Kekaha-Mana areas of Kauai. Maui's problems are both quantity- and quality-related (Oahu is expected to face quantity problems in fifteen to twenty years), and the others' problems are mainly related to quality.[21]

Pollution
Sea water is the biggest pollutant of freshwater in the islands.[22] Sea-water encroachment effects a basal lens, but not the high-level or perched water. The basal water lens is maintained by recharge, which, if reduced,

leads to basal-lens shrinkage and, thus, to sea-water intrusion. Also, withdrawals from inland wells often increase the salinity of wells closer to the shore. In addition, an effect called localized upconing can occur when pumpage is concentrated over small areas rather than being spread out. This results in excessive pull, which draws the saltwater up through the basal lens. When encroachment does occur, as little as 2 percent of sea water renders the water unpotable. Oahu and Maui both encounter saltwater intrusion problems. The problem is most severe on Oahu in the Pearl Harbor, Honolulu, and Waialua Aquifers (the latter of which is primarily used for agriculture). (However, the Iao, Lahaina, and Kona Aquifer Systems on Maui are being increasingly subjected to saltwater intrusion resulting from localized upconing.)[23] Some of the older wells in the Pearl Harbor Aquifer have had to be abandoned because of saltwater pollution.[24]

The application of fertilizers and other surface chemicals adds soluble products—notably chloride, nitrate, and sulfate—to the groundwater bodies of Hawaii. As of 1995 none of these chemicals have been detected in excess of EPA standards for drinking water.[25] However, in 1980 wells in the Kunia area of Oahu were closed because of excessive bicarbonates. Since the closure a treatment facility has been constructed and is currently in operation.[26] Of the additive products, nitrate and sulfate have been studied most extensively. Examinations of wells on Maui and in Kahuku on Oahu found increases in nitrate and sulfate, and in silica and bicarbonate, that could be linked to irrigation and to agricultural fertilization practices.

Following national trends, liquid-waste disposal problems in the islands have grown rapidly in recent years and will likely continue to do so in the near future.[27] A significant amount of groundwater pollution is attributed to nonocean disposals of municipal, rural, industrial, and agricultural wastewater. "Although most waste waters are sewered and disposed of through ocean outfalls, a significant volume of untreated or partly treated waste water is injected into the subsurface. Most agricultural waste water is ponded. Sometimes the water is reused and the solids are spread on fields and farms. Otherwise, the waste water percolates to the water table or is channeled to sea."[28]

Because liquid waste injected into the subsurface, or leachate from waste on the surface, behaves nearly the same way as does recharge from rainwater, and easily enters the underlying groundwater bodies, disposal of liquid wastes into the Hawaiian subsurface environment has been limited to low-elevation coastal areas.

Since fresh potable groundwater is restricted primarily to lava flows and is usually not present in developable quantities in the immediate coastal areas, where most waste injection is practiced, contamination of fresh groundwater supplies was not, as of 1995, a major problem. Also, as Hawaii has become more populated and urbanized, the use of individual cesspools has diminished, and the use of centralized sewage collection systems with ocean outfalls has become the most important means of waste disposal.[29] The USGS has, however, identified wastewater injection disposal of liquid wastes as a potential threat to groundwater supplies in near-shore coastal areas.[30]

Pesticide contamination of groundwater has been a matter of increasing concern, especially on Oahu and Maui, where in the summer of 1983 nine wells were closed because their water was found to contain traces of toxic pesticides. The three major pesticide contaminants found were DBCP, TCP, and EDB. Since that time these three pesticides as well as others have continued to be detected.

DBCP (Dibromochloropropane). DBCP is a toxic chemical that causes cancer in laboratory animals and sterility in human males. In the past it was used extensively as a soil fumigant by agriculture across the contiguous forty-eight states, but in March 1981 it was banned by the EPA for all uses except for pineapple growing in Hawaii. Although they were allowed to continue DBCP application, Oahu pineapple companies had voluntarily stopped using the chemical prior to the EPA rule. It had not been commercially applied since 1977 and had been out of use for six years on Oahu, yet it was first discovered in several Mililani wells in 1984. The amounts found (at that time) were below safety levels established for DBCP by the State of California. As of 1993 DBCP has been detected in twelve monitoring wells on Oahu and in six wells on Maui (one of which contained DBCP at nine times the drinking-water standard and which has been closed).[31] DBCP breaks down slowly and is likely to be a concern well into the future. In California, for example, one toxicology expert has predicted that DBCP will continue to contaminate water in California after the turn of the century.[32]

TCP (Trichloropropane). The chemical TCP is a component of another pesticide once used on pineapple fields. It is known to reduce red blood cells and cause liver and kidney damage. It makes up less than 50 percent of the pesticide Shell DD, which was used on Oahu fields for thirty-five years. As of 1995 the highest levels of TCP detected in Hawaii have been found in Mililani wells. Other contaminated wells on Oahu include Waipahu, Hoaeae, Kunia, and the Waiawa shaft. The amount of TCP in the soil column at 40 to 60 feet indicates how persistent the substance is; while only a small amount of it was in the original pesticide, a great deal of it lingers in the soil column. Traces were also found in Kaanapali, Kuau, and Kaheka on Maui.[33]

EDB (Ethylene dibromide). EDB has been used as a substitute for DBCP. It has also been used as a fumigant against fruit flies from the island of Hawaii. Discoveries of EDB in a few California groundwater wells caught the EPA's attention, and the agency asked other states to test for the pesticide. As a result EDB was found to be a source of contamination in central Oahu's drinking water. Concentrations of EDB found in Hawaiian groundwater, at 300 parts per billion, were almost ten times the contamination levels found in California, the state with the next highest level.[34] EDB seems to be under control now, however, as 1993 monitoring revealed it in only one well on Oahu (Waipahu) and four wells on Maui. In both instances the amount of EDB found in the water was well below the level that would make the water undrinkable.

Other pesticides that might cause problems in Hawaii in the future include: atrazine (a possible carcinogen known to cause heart and liver damage and retard fetal development); TCE (a probable carcinogen known to cause nervous system and organ damage; PCE (a probable carcinogen that causes nervous system and organ damage); and Lindane (a probable carcinogen that causes nervous system and organ damage and that can lead to suppression of the immune system). All of these have been detected (currently below established standards) on Oahu, the most populous island of the state.[35]

Some of the contaminants showing up in Oahu water supplies are from pesticide treatments as far back as the 1940s. It is conceivable that even if all applications of pesticides were halted, traces would continue to be measurable in groundwater for over forty years.

A problem with pesticide contamination in Hawaii, as elsewhere, is that little is known about levels of safe exposure. Risk assessments are used to establish "safe" levels, but these assessments are fraught with uncertainty. In the absence of solid scientific standards as to what is safe, the state, to its credit, has decided to close wells used to supply drinking water when in doubt about the water's safety.

Although the pollution problems discussed in this section pose serious threats to current and future groundwater use in Hawaii, the problems—

as mentioned at the outset—are localized. Overall, groundwater quality in Hawaii is generally good. The availability of the Pacific Ocean for the deep-water disposal of wastes has allowed the state to avoid the water-pollution problems facing many other states, and continuous monitoring for pesticides and other contaminants has enabled it to act before populations were placed in jeopardy.

Law

In 1987 the Hawaii Legislature passed the Hawaii Water Code, H.R.S. 174C. The 1987 code replaced the 1959 Ground Water Use Act, which was not as comprehensive and well written and which thus resulted in many flaws that left the Board of Land and Natural Resources (replaced by the Commission on Water Resource Management) open to heavy political pressures. Under the code the Commission on Water Resource Management was created to be the governing body for water resources in the state. The commission is responsible for establishing protection programs for instream use and for establishing sustainable-yield limits for groundwater sources.[36] Sustainable-yield limits act as trigger points or threat levels for aquifers (or wells). When these levels are approached and sustainable yield is threatened, the commission has the authority to designate the area in question a water-management area "for the purpose of establishing administrative control over withdrawals and diversions of ground and surface waters in the area."[37] As of 1996 five basins had been designated as groundwater-management areas—windward Oahu, Pearl Harbor and two adjacent and hydrologically interconnected basis, and the entire island of Molokai.[38] There are no surface-water designated areas in the state. In addition, the commission has broken down these large units into thirty-four smaller administrative units (groundwater-management areas), which act as water-management areas in their own right and which deal exclusively with groundwater. All persons, except for exempted users (discussed later), wishing to extract water within a groundwater-management area must obtain a water-use permit from the commission. Hawaii Revised Statute section 48(a) reads, in part, that "no person [including county boards of water supply] may make any withdrawal, diversion, or impoundment" of any water in the management area without a permit.[39] Exempted are withdrawals made for individual domestic and rain catchment use. In addition, the 1987 laws requires construction permits for any new wells or repairs of existing wells statewide.[40] Decisions on beneficial or reasonable use as well as other permit criteria are made by the commission on a case-by-case basis. All permits except for "interim" permits are valid until the designation of the water-management area is rescinded but are subject to review every twenty years.[41] Nonuse of water granted by a permit for a period of four continuous years is grounds for permit revocation.[42]

The 1987 laws divide water-use permits into two categories: those for existing users and those for new users. Existing-rights permits are for those who can establish that they had an existing use on the effective date of a water-management area designation. The permit allows these persons to continue their use.[43] To receive an existing-use permit one must show that the existing use is reasonable, beneficial, and "allowable under the common law of the state."[44] A person must make such claims within one year of the date during which a water-management area is designated in order to qualify for an existing-use permit.[45]

Requirements for new users are stricter. In addition to showing that the proposed use is reasonable and beneficial, applicants must demonstrate that their use does not interfere with any existing legal use of the water and that the water source is able to accommodate the proposed use.[46]

Appurtenant rights are treated separately and are granted at the time of application. This special status is expressed in section 63 of the water code, which states that "appurtenant rights are preserved. Nothing in this part shall be construed to deny the exercise of an appurtenant right by the holder thereof at any time."[47] Appurtenant rights are granted for the cultivation of taro (a staple in the traditional Hawaiian diet) and domestic needs on lands in production at the time of the Great Mahele (1845–50). The amount of water granted is based on the amount necessary for such cultivation.[48]

In times of shortage the commission is granted the authority to exercise emergency powers where there is insufficient water to meet the requirements of the permit system.[49] These powers include the ability to declare a shortage and to cut back water usage of the holders of valid permits.[50] Under Hawaii Revised Statutes section 62(a), the commission is granted the authority to develop a system of permit classification and to issue orders "apportioning, rotating, limiting, or prohibiting the use of water resources" in any area, whether within a water-management area or not, if it declares an emergency condition.[51]

Politics, Policy, and the Future

The Hawaii Water Code provides the commission with adequate authority to regulate groundwater withdrawals in a manner that will prevent overdrafting and inefficient management of the resource. Since the legislation passed, overdrafting in the state has diminished somewhat. This is partially due to the fact that the requirement for reasonable use has been strictly adhered to, and much of the waste that was previously occurring has been eliminated. (Another factor is the introduction of drip-irrigation technology, which makes it cheaper to use less water because of reduced electrical costs and pumping requirements.)

The conflict between municipalities and irrigators that exists in most western states has been avoided in Hawaii. The departure of the bulk of the sugar producers has freed up large quantities of water. However, the Commission on Water Resource Management is concerned about the loss of the return irrigation component of recharge. While on the surface it appears that there is now more water available for municipal use, the available amount is smaller than one would expect. With irrigation, a fair amount of the water withdrawn seeps back into the ground, and into the aquifer. Municipal use is far more consumptive, returning little to the aquifer. In addition, if fallowed agricultural land is developed for municipal habitation there will be less surface area through which rain can enter into the ground, increasing the loss of recharge. In other words, for every acre-foot of agricultural water taken out of irrigation, there will not be one acre-foot available for new uses without increases in aquifer-level decline. Rough estimates have about half of any discontinued agricultural water actually being freed up for new uses. Existing sustainable-yield estimates therefore need to be revised to address the new recharge rates. Such revision, however, might create problems. Users are not going to want their pumping curtailed because revised figures place the area in an instant emergency situation. However, without such revisions management decisions will be made that do not reflect the true state of affairs.

Compared to many other states discussed in this book, Hawaii appears to be in a good position with regard to the future. The potential for overdraft exists, but the rigid enforcement of the recent legislation appears to be working toward avoiding any long-term problems. As we have seen, however, additional infrastructure will have to be developed to meet many future needs, especially on the islands of Maui and Oahu. Pollution, primarily from saltwater intrusion and pesticide contamination, is localized and had not, as of the mid-1990s, created any serious loss of water supply. The state is aware of the potential for increased contamination and monitors wells frequently in order to avoid any unsuspected health risks. If current quality- and quantity-management practices are continued, and if needed infrastructure is developed, the state will be able to sustain its water resources and its population for quite some time.

4 Oregon

Population growth in Oregon is slow relative to other states in the West. However, compared to national averages, the influx of people into the state is relatively high. As surface water is almost fully allocated or has been set aside for specific purposes, growth has necessarily been facilitated through groundwater withdrawals. As of the mid-1990s Oregon had conducted site studies on groundwater storage but had no comprehensive data for the state as a whole. This implies that much of the state's groundwater management occurs with incomplete information. Given the importance of groundwater for sustaining the state population, a comprehensive groundwater inventory seems necessary.

While the growth of Oregon has largely taken place in urban areas, such growth is necessarily constrained. The state has legislation in place that limits urban sprawl from encroaching on agricultural land, which means that as cities grow the need for water will be concentrated in specific areas. Groundwater has played a large part in allowing urban growth in recent years (groundwater use for public supply more than doubled between 1983 and 1993), and, as a result, some instability has developed in the resource. Thus, if the state intends to continue to provide a sustainable supply of water for agricultural, industrial, and municipal use, additional water will be needed in the future. Surface water is almost fully allocated and is not an option. Groundwater levels are declining in some areas, and this source will not be sustainable unless it is supplemented by other sources. As of the mid-1990s there were isolated supply problems—problems that are likely to expand in scope as the state grows. It is probable that increasing water shortages will lead to increasing competition between users and to a certain amount of socioeconomic disruption in the state. In Oregon, given the fact that maintaining instream flows is a high priority, surface water storage is unlikely to take place. (Storage could actually assist in maintaining instream flows but carries costs such as the loss of spawning habitat, recreational use, and aesthetic value.) Apparently the only feasible option for creating larger water supplies is that of underground storage—an option currently being examined by state officials. Short of such storage, however, Oregon will be hard-pressed to meet water needs in the twenty-first century. As urban populations grow and the state attempts to balance between municipal, industrial, and agricultural water needs, it will become clear that there is simply not enough water to go around.

Water quality is an additional area of concern. While, as of the mid-1990s, most groundwater contamination was localized, the potential for further impairment exists. Given the increasing use of groundwater for drinking water, the state must face the problem of contamination. In addition to possibly exposing people to adverse health risks, groundwater contamination often limits the types of available groundwater uses, adding to the potential supply problems.

Oregon will have to address both quality and quantity issues now if it hopes to sustain its population and its economy in the future.

Physical Description

Oregon is divided into two "climatic provinces," one lying west of the Cascades and the other lying to the east.[1] The west side receives from 25 inches of rain per year in the Willamette Valley to 180 inches in the coastal mountain areas.[2] The east side is drier, averaging only 10 inches of precipitation annually.[3]

Geologic formations in Oregon, as elsewhere, range from relatively permeable rock to impermeable rock.[4] For example, the area in the mid-eastern portion of the state is made up of tight, tuffaceous sediments, making this an area of low permeability. Most of western Oregon is also an area of low permeability.[5]

Because of the wide range in the amount of precipitation different parts of the state receive, the difference in permeability from one area to the next, and the lack of supply information, groundwater management is complex. Water levels in the state are monitored by the Observation-Well Program. The program, instituted in the early 1930s, involves the periodic measurement of water pressures and water levels in approximately 350 wells located throughout the state. Information from these wells may serve as a warning of any serious depletion problem in a given area.[6]

Demographics

As of 1 July 1995 the resident state population of Oregon was estimated to be 3,140,585.[7] Between 1950 and 1995 the state's population increased by 106.4 percent, which was above the national average of 73.6 percent.[8] Oregon's population growth has occurred mostly in urban areas. In 1960, 62 percent (1.1 million people) of Oregon's population was urban.[9] By 1990 over 70 percent (more than 2 million people) of its population resided in urban areas.[10]

The largest percentage of people living in Oregon earn wages through nonfarm occupations. Ninety percent of those working in Oregon are employed on nonfarm payrolls. The biggest employing industries in the state are those that have traditionally operated in urban settings. The biggest single categories of employment in Oregon are manufacturing, wholesale and retail trade, and service industries.[11]

While irrigation remains the largest single user of both surface and groundwater, the number of farms in the state as well as the number of acres devoted to farm use have declined over the years. In 1959 there were 43,000 farms in Oregon covering a total of 21,236,000 acres.[12] In 1993 there were 37,000 farms in the state, and the acreage devoted to agriculture had dropped to 18 million.[13] Despite using the most water, farming contributes only 2 percent to Oregon's gross state product, while urban-based industries such as finance and service industries contribute 16 percent and 17 percent, respectively.[14]

Water Use

The total supply of groundwater in Oregon is unknown. As of the mid-1990s no comprehensive groundwater inventory had been taken. Supplies have been estimated for specific areas, but not statewide.[15]

According to estimates, 73 percent of Oregon's groundwater is used in irrigation, 8 percent in livestock watering and for rural domestic purposes, and 5 percent in industrial and commercial purposes. Fourteen percent of the groundwater is used in public supply systems—more than double the amount used as recently as 1983.[16] The rapid increase of the amount of groundwater being used for public supply can be attributed to Oregon's increasing population, particularly in suburban areas around Portland and Salem.[17]

Surface water is an important source of water in Oregon, particularly for agriculture. It provides 91 percent of the water used in irrigation and 77 percent of the water used by public supply systems.[18] Major sources of surface water in the state include the Columbia, Snake, Willamette, and Deschutes Rivers.

In various parts of Oregon groundwater management is focused on correcting water-use practices that threaten the long-term beneficial use of the resource. In order to understand Oregon's groundwater-management practices, one first needs to understand the legal and institutional arrangements that govern groundwater use in the state.

Problems

Overdrafting
Six groundwater areas in Oregon have been designated as critical because of overdrafting (see discussion in the section on law in this chapter). The Cow Valley Critical Groundwater area was designated as such in 1959 because of declines in water levels of 5 to 7 feet per year. In 1976 the Ordnance area was designated as critical because of water-level declines of 7 to 8 feet per year.[19] The other designated areas are Butter Creek, Stage Gulch, Cooper Mountain–Bull Mountain, and The Dalles critical groundwater areas. As of 1995 restrictions had been placed on further groundwater development in four other areas in an effort to prevent overdraft. The areas are: Fort Rock–Christmas Valley, Ella Butte, Sandy-Boring, and Mosier.[20]

Pollution

Nitrate contamination from sewage and fertilizers is a major problem in Oregon, as is pollution from pesticides, hazardous wastes, and landfills.[21] In the north Salem area, for example, high levels of nitrates caused by fertilizers were found in test samples from 12 out of 334 residential wells, and a 1992 study found that 83 percent of the wells tested in the Canby neighborhood experienced nitrate contamination in excess of EPA standards.[22] Furthermore, 1993 monitoring revealed that nitrate contamination in over 25 percent of the wells at several testing sites exceeded the maximum EPA-established level for safe drinking water.[23] Some of these were the Prineville, La Pine, Junction City, and Ontario monitoring sites. In the rural areas of Marion County, west Stayton, Turner, and Jefferson, shallow groundwater has been found to be mixing with effluent from drain fields and septic tanks.[24] And in central Oregon near Bend and Madras, sewage has been discharged directly into wells.[25] Nitrate contamination is potentially serious for the health of Oregonians. Exposure to large quantities of nitrates is the cause of methemoglobemia (blue-baby disease), and nitrates, in high doses, are believed to be possible carcinogens.

Wood-waste disposal poses another problem for groundwater quality in Oregon, where the lumber industry is a major economic interest. Wood and bark form tannic acid leachates as they combine with water. The leachates filter down into the ground, contaminating the water. At least eleven domestic water supply wells have been rendered undrinkable because of a wood-waste site near Turner.[26] Wood treatment and the production of paper products poses a related threat to Oregon's groundwater supplies. Groundwater monitoring in 1994 revealed contamination that could be traced to these activities at about 191 sites across the state.[27]

Landfills and surface impoundments, such as the wood-waste site in Turner, also threaten quality in portions of some groundwater basins. Surface impoundments are depressions on the land surface that may hold liquids, semisolids, or solid waste. They can take the form of ponds, pits, lagoons, and pools.[28] The portions of a groundwater basin that are located beneath these impoundments are highly susceptible to contamination by impoundment contents, especially if a well is located in the shallow lowlands of alluvial deposits, as is the case in parts of Oregon.[29] Monitoring that took place in 1994 linked landfills to the contamination of 98 testing sites across the state.[30]

Leaking storage tanks, both above ground and underground, pose another serious threat to Oregon's groundwater supplies. In mid-1991 there were 15,000 known underground storage tanks. As of 1994 the Oregon Department of Environmental Quality (DEQ) was aware of 2,438 underground storage tanks that were either leaking or suspected of leaking (22 percent of the tanks were confirmed to be leaking). The primary type of contamination from these underground sources are petroleum products, which are often carcinogenic and are extremely costly and difficult to remove from an aquifer once they have been introduced.[31]

Saltwater intrusion could be a pollution problem in the future, although as yet there has been no evidence of its being so. However, there are several areas in which this possibility is a concern, including the area above Coos Bay. This area, which is monitored by the North Bend Water Board, as well as other areas are routinely monitored for groundwater contamination from saltwater and other contaminants.[32]

While widespread contamination of groundwater resources has yet to occur in Oregon, any localized instances of contamination are cause for concern. Future growth and development will probably require increasing dependence on groundwater supplies. This dependence will include increased use of groundwater for drinking water. Should aquifer degradation spread, the result will be potential health risks for the citizens of Oregon and a limit on the number of available groundwater uses.

Law

Prior to the enactment of Oregon's current groundwater code, all waters in the state in known and defined streams (including those underground) were subject to appropriation under the 1909 general surface-water laws. Percolating waters, "the course of which is unknown and unascertainable," were not subject to appropriation and could be extracted by landowners regardless of injury to others.[33] In 1927 the Oregon legislature enacted laws that applied to underground waters east of the Cascades in known and defined streams, rendering these waters subject to appropriation.[34] Years later the 1955 Groundwater Act provided that all waters, including percolating waters, belonged to the public and were subject to appropriation for beneficial use.[35]

The Oregon water resources director is the executive head of the Water Resources Department and has primary authority to manage groundwater basins under the 1955 Groundwater Act. The director is appointed by the governor of Oregon for a four-year term.[36]

The Groundwater Act of 1955 specifies that prior users are exempt from permit application requirements. Those who held water rights prior to 3 August 1955 are considered to have been granted a permit under the 1955 act.[37] Well owners who are granted water rights through this process are still required to file a registration and to provide the water resources director with information about their wells. For example, information regarding the amount of groundwater claimed, type of well, and use of the groundwater, as well as other information, must be furnished to the director.[38] Anyone wishing to appropriate groundwater after 3 August 1955 must request a permit and provide the water resources director with the same information outlined above before withdrawing or using the water.[39]

Some users are exempt from application requirements. These users are still bound by any other requirements of the 1955 act. Exempted uses include: wells drilled for stock-watering purposes, for watering a lawn or noncommercial garden not exceeding one-half acre in area, or for watering the grounds of a school not larger than 10 acres within critical groundwater areas. Further exemptions extend to wells used for a single industrial or commercial purpose not exceeding 5,000 gallons per day and to single or group domestic purposes in an amount not exceeding 15,000 gallons per day.[40]

The regulation of groundwater is different once an area is designated as critical. A groundwater area may be determined as critical by way of a motion from the Water Resources Commission, by petition from the state geologist of the State Department of Geology and Mineral Industries, or by petition from anyone in the area in question. Procedures for declaring an area as critical may be initiated when (1) there is a decline in groundwater levels, (2) the wells of two or more claimants interfere with one another, (3) available groundwater supply is overdrafted or about to be overdrawn, (4) the quality of groundwater is threatened, (5) there is interference between groundwater and geothermal production, and (6) there is substantial interference with surface water uses as a result of groundwater appropriation.[41]

A public hearing must take place before an area can be officially declared critical, and once the area has been so designated the Water Resources Commission may close it to any further appropriation and may restrict withdrawals by already existing rights.[42] Residential and livestock watering take priority over other uses, and other uses may be given relative priorities by the Water Resources Commission. As of 1995 there were six areas that had been officially designated critical: Butter Creek, Stage Gulch, the Cooper Mountain–Bull Mountain area, The Dalles, Cow Valley, and Ordnance.[43] In various other ways the water resources director regulates well drilling, construction, management, and repair; prevents waste and contamination; and develops rules for and issues licenses to drillers.[44]

Basin planning and the identification of beneficial uses may be influenced in the future by the Watershed Management Program passed in 1993.[45] With this statute, Oregon is attempting to coordinate state and local planning efforts in order to better utilize water resources and to promote "watershed health." The overall effect of this program is not yet known.

The DEQ is responsible for enforcing water-quality regulations in the state of Oregon. The Environmental Quality Commission, a five-member citizen board, is vested with policy and rulemaking authority to guide the DEQ.[46]

Politics, Policy, and the Future

In the past, one of Oregon's groundwater-management problems was that of trying to decrease pumpage once the state declared a groundwater resource critical. It took the Water Resources Commission fourteen years to effectively cut back on pumping in the Buttercreek Groundwater Area after it was designated as critical.[47] In that time orders were issued twice and both times were overturned by the courts. The first order, issued on 2 April 1976, was overturned because "nonparticipants may not have been notified." The second order, issued on 23 May 1978, was blocked pending "further action." In the meantime water levels continued to decline by as much as 10 to 20 feet per year in the 274-square-mile area.[48] The Water Resources Commission was able to begin cutting back on water use in the area in 1990.[49]

In order to address this problem a bill was introduced before the Oregon legislature in 1985. The bill would change the designation procedure from a "contested case" format to a "rule-making" format, thus giving the Water Resources Department more authority to designate critical groundwater areas.[50] The bill was opposed by agricultural interests, including the Farm Bureau, the Oregon Water Resources Congress, and the Oregon Wheat Growers League. If part or all of a groundwater resource is declared critical, permits to withdraw groundwater are no longer issued. Moreover, use under terms of existing water permits can be reduced or entirely shut off.[51] Farmers, being the primary users of groundwater in Oregon, were understandably reluctant to see the law changed. However, the bill passed, and, as a result the Water Resources Department's authority has increased and the state's groundwater management has improved. The Water Resources Department is now able to designate an area as critical by way of a "rule-making" format; however, the "contested case" format is still employed when it is attempting to reduce use by current appropriators.[52]

Budgetary constraints for the Oregon Department of Water Resources have been and continue to be a problem for groundwater management. In some groundwater areas where pumping has either increased or decreased there has not been adequate staff to assess the effectiveness of the changes in pumping practices.[53] Furthermore, the number of wells checked as a result of the Well-Monitoring Program has been reduced from a high of 830 wells in 1975, which were checked as many as four times a year, to a low of between 300 and 400 wells, some of which are checked only twice a year.[54]

The Oregon Groundwater Code also directs the director of water resources to "proceed as rapidly as possible to identify and define tentatively the location, extent, depth and other characteristics of each groundwater reservoir in this state."[55] Unfortunately, money for a statewide inventory has not been appropriated. Rather, area studies have been and continue to be conducted in lieu of such an inventory. Moreover, some studies, such as the study of the Medford area, have been abandoned because of a lack of funds.[56] The abandonment of groundwater-basin studies has been a problem for the water resources director in the past, and may be in the future. In the early 1980s water resources director James Sexson allegedly mismanaged groundwater in Oregon by failing to complete a study in the controversial Buttercreek area. Cutbacks in the geological staff of the department reportedly made it impossible to complete the necessary research. As a result, the Senate failed to reconfirm Sexton as water resources director for another term.[57] In order to deal with this situation the department was granted more funding to hire more staff. (Increasing population and related development in the state have led to a growing number of groundwater problems that the staff in 1997 seem unable to properly address.)[58]

Funding has also affected the ability of the DEQ to solve contamination problems. In 1989 Oregon passed its Groundwater Protection Act, which focuses on statewide prevention of groundwater contamination so that the resource might be maintained for present and future beneficial use.[59] While the act addresses prevention, many problems still exist. Inadequate funding might prove to be an obstacle in cleaning contaminated aquifers. The DEQ has stated that while technology is in place that will allow for the cleanup of many groundwater contaminants, at least to bring the standards of the water up to drinking-water level, rarely can the aquifer be returned to its original state of purity.[60] Without proper funding, however, even making the groundwater suitable for drinking might prove problematic. Given the increase in population and the related increase in groundwater use for drinking water, this is a major area of concern.

Effective groundwater management continues to be an issue in Oregon. Thus far, securing adequate funding for groundwater management seems to be the major problem facing the state's Water Resources Department. According to the department the demand for groundwater has doubled over the last twenty years, yet the amount of groundwater available for long-term use has not been determined.[61] With the population of Oregon rising, the state's dependence on groundwater will increase as well. Future growth and development in Oregon is dependent on appropriate management of all water resources. As we have seen, there are areas where the long-term beneficial use of this resource is threatened.

Groundwater pumpers, particularly farmers, are likely to continue to oppose increased funding for the Water Resources Department or any changes in the law that increases the regulatory authority of the department. Until the situation changes Oregon will have inadequate information, and the Water Resources Department will be hindered in its efforts to manage groundwater in a manner that will insure the long-term, beneficial use of the resource.

5 Washington

While Washington is often thought of as being abundantly supplied with water, population growth and past practices have placed significant pressures on its water resources. As of the mid-1990s the allocation of water resources was one of the state's escalating political battles. Pressures from irrigators, developers, and conservationists have drawn attention to the issue, but as of the mid-1990s the Washington legislature had not dealt with the problem adequately. Surface water is, for the most part, fully appropriated in Washington, and attention has been focused toward more groundwater use. In 1991, for example, roughly two-thirds of the applications for water permits were for groundwater withdrawals. Groundwater permit applications for municipal development exceeded surface-water permit applications by a ratio of ten to one.[1] Despite the rise in the number of applications for groundwater use, many applications are being denied because of the impact that groundwater withdrawals would have on prior surface and groundwater appropriators and on instream flows necessary to maintain salmon runs. Given the changes in Washington's economy and the changes in the population demographics of the state, water use will also have to change if the state continues to grow.

As of the mid-1990s changes in use have largely been limited to conservation measures and to the reuse of water (and even then they have been implemented on only a very limited basis). The Washington legislature is going to have to make some serious choices about the direction in which the state is going. After years of encouraging both agricultural and urban growth, state planners have come to realize that water is limited and cannot sustain all uses over time. To date, however, legislators have largely avoided the problem. Failure to address the issue has kept the state from developing as it might have otherwise. Maintaining the status quo will hinder future development in all economic sectors and will, in the long run, possibly prove impossible if groundwater is to continue being used in all its current capacities.

Physical Description

The state of Washington is divided into five natural regions. The western section of the state is part of the coastal ranges region and includes part of the Pacific Coast mountains and the Olympic mountains in the Olympic Peninsula. East of the Coastal ranges lies the Puget trough. This area runs from the Canadian border south to the Columbia River and Oregon border. Puget Sound runs through the north half of the trough and contains numerous islands. This region is a general depression topographically between the Coastal regions and the Cascade range to the east. (Maximum elevation in Puget Trough is around 500 feet.)

The Cascade range takes up roughly a fourth of the state, running down its center from the Canadian border to the Columbia River. The range is volcanic table land studded with cones such as Mount Adams and Mount St. Helens and in the northern sections contains some of the most extensive alpine glaciation in the forty-eight contiguous states. The eastern part of the state is divided between the Rocky Mountain region in the north and the Columbia Plateau in the south. The Columbia River runs through most of this region, as does the Snake River.

Like Oregon, Washington is best understood as consisting of two parts, hydrologically—the wet western part and the dry eastern part. Most of the state's urban growth is occurring in the western half of the state, and most of the agricultural activity is located in the eastern half. Annual precipitation is in excess of 100 inches in part of the Olympic and Cascade mountains in the west and is less than 16 inches throughout much of the Columbia Plateau region.

Demographics

As of 1 July 1995 the resident state population of Washington was estimated to be 5,430,940.[2] Between 1950 and 1995 the population of Washington increased by 128.2 percent, which was higher than the national average growth rate of 73.6 percent for the same period.[3] The population of Washington has been gradually shifting from rural areas to urban settings. In 1960 approximately 68 percent of the population in the state resided in urban areas.[4] In 1990, 76.4 percent of the population (4.8 million people) lived in urban settings.[5]

Although a large number of people residing in the state (approximately 84,800) rely upon agriculture for financial support, over 96 percent of Washington's employed civilian workforce earn wages through industries that are not farm related.[6] The categories of employment that are responsible for employing the most people in Washington are services, wholesale and retail trade, manufacturing, and construction.[7]

While irrigation remains the largest single use of fresh water in Washington, the number of farms and the amount of acreage devoted to agricultural use in the state have declined in recent years. In 1959 there were roughly 52,000 farms in the state, covering 18,717,000 acres.[8] In 1993 the number of farms in Washington had dropped to 36,000, and the number of acres used for farming had been reduced to approximately 16 million.[9] Despite employing a fairly large number of people, covering a significant number of acres, and using large amounts of water, agriculture, in relation to other industries, contributes very little to the gross state product of Washington. As of the mid-1990s approximately 3.7 percent of the gross state product could be attributed to farming and agricultural services. The most significant contributors to the gross state product of Washington are services, manufacturing, and the combined category of finance, insurance, and real estate, which contribute 17.5 percent, 16.8 percent, and 16.3 percent, respectively.[10]

Water Use

Groundwater supplies approximately 18 percent of the water used annually in Washington. Of this amount, roughly 30 percent is used in public supply systems, 52 percent is used in irrigation, 8 percent is used for rural domestic and livestock purposes, and 7 percent is used for industrial purposes.[11] Approximately 50 percent of the state's drinking water comes from the ground. In the eastern portion of the state it is estimated that nearly nine out of ten people are solely dependent upon groundwater for drinking water.[12] Groundwater demands have resulted in declining water levels in numerous counties within Washington. In the east the areas of greatest withdrawal are in and around Spokane and in southern Franklin County in and around Pasco. Other areas of significant withdrawal include Yakima, Grant County, and Adams County. In the Puget Trough, areas of significance in groundwater withdrawal include the Vancouver area in southern Clark County and the Tacoma and Seattle regions in metropolitan Seattle. Groundwater is the major and often the only source of water for many of the islands in counties located within Puget Sound. The magnitude of the demand has resulted in both quantity and quality problems in island and San Juan Counties.[13]

Demand for groundwater promises to increase in various parts of the state in the future. In many areas of Washington, given that surface water sources are either fully appropriated or unavailable, the only source of water for increased irrigation is groundwater. Examples include the Walla Walla area (Snake and Columbia Rivers), the Yakima River Basin and the Eastern Columbia Basin (theoretically, the second phase of the Columbia Basin Project could be developed, but costs and Endangered Species Act requirements preclude its actual viability).[14] The Washington State Department of Ecology has reported that "Proper development, use, and regulation of our groundwaters is perhaps the most important key to further economic growth and retention of a high quality of life for residents of many areas in Washington."[15]

In order to address the growing water-supply problem and rapid urban growth, the Washington legislature enacted the 1990 Growth Management Act. This legislation was largely intended to limit further municipal density to "urban growth areas." It was believed that concentrating populations in certain areas would decrease the number of problems facing the state. Instead of having to try to address supply problems statewide, the legislature reasoned, the state would only need to worry about how to meet the supply needs of these urban centers and, in some cases, about how to redirect growth to areas that had the resources to sustain it. However, the law is ambiguous and has not succeeded in limiting growth to certain areas.[16] It is difficult to regulate where people choose to live. One gets the impression that the act was passed so that the legislature would appear to be addressing the growth problem while actually doing nothing. (Many strong political interests in the state are happy with the status quo.)

Problems

Overdraft

The Washington Department of Ecology, the agency responsible for managing groundwater withdrawal, attempts to manage water resources on a steady-state basis but has allowed planned groundwater mining in some areas.[17] Population pressures have increased demand on groundwater in Island and San Juan Counties, resulting in some groundwater mining and related effects. However, the most severe groundwater overdrafting has taken place in eastern and southeastern Washington. Groundwater levels declined by as much as 20 feet on an annual basis throughout large parts of Adams, Lincoln, Franklin, and Grant Counties through the mid-1980s. Because of severe water level declines, as of the mid-1990s the pumping patterns in this area had begun to change, and the levels are beginning to increase slightly in some aquifers. Pumping has become so expensive that many irrigators have switched to dry farming or have gone out of business completely, resulting in less water being extracted from the groundwater system via agricultural interests.[18] Overdrafting is also a significant problem in Yakima, Benton, and Klickitat Counties. In addition to existing and future water availability problems, overdraft in these areas has resulted in a number of well-interference problems. Many of the aquifers in eastern Washington recharge at an extremely slow rate or, for all practical purposes, are nonrecharging.[19]

Pollution

Overall groundwater quality is generally good throughout Washington, but because of the large number of people relying upon groundwater for drinking water, and because of present contamination levels, the potential for widespread contamination is a serious concern. More than 60 percent of the population relies on groundwater for their main source of drinking water, and in rural areas the number is believed to be closer to 90 percent.[20] Despite the fact that Washington has been unable to develop a comprehensive assessment of groundwater quality in the state, site studies have revealed that groundwater pollution is a serious problem in several parts of Washington.

Agricultural activities are thought to be the single largest source of groundwater pollution in Washington. The application of both fertilizers and pesticides, and concentrated animal feedlot operations, have contributed significantly to groundwater contamination in several areas. In addition to chemical contaminants such as DCPA and atrazine, which are the result of chemical-pesticide application, high levels of nitrates resulting from biological fertilizer application and animal waste have been detected. Areas experiencing significant effects on groundwater from agricultural operations are counties in the northwest portion of the state (where the effect is primarily a result of animal waste) and the Columbia Basin (where the effect arises primarily from pesticide and fertilizer applications).

The second greatest threat to the groundwater supply in Washington comes from land applications of municipal sludge and land treatment of municipal waste water and wastes from food processing. The most common contaminants that result from these practices are nitrates and chlorides, which have been detected in aquifers throughout the state.[21]

Another serious threat to the state's groundwater supply has come about as a result of rapid population increases. The Washington State Department of Ecology has determined that use and failures of domestic and industrial septic systems have led to an increase in nitrates and chemical contamination. In addition, the increased use of landfills, which accompanies population growth, has led to groundwater contamination in several areas.[22]

Population increases have resulted in another area of concern for water managers—that of saltwater intrusion. Population increases in shore areas have led to groundwater degradation in numerous places within the state. San Juan, Island, and Pacific Counties have experienced declines in water quality severe enough that they have had to limit development. As groundwater use continues in these areas, the Department of Ecology anticipates that groundwater contamination from saltwater intrusion is likely to increase in the future.[23]

Leaking underground storage tanks pose yet another threat to Washington's groundwater supply. As of the mid-1990s it was estimated that there were over forty thousand underground storage tanks in Washington, the majority of which can be found in the three most densely populated counties in the state (King, Pierce, and Spokane). Many of the leaking tanks have been removed, but the damage has been done. Contamination from petroleum products is almost impossible to completely reverse. In addition, roughly four thousand leaking storage tanks have yet to be removed and continue to pose a threat to the groundwater supply.[24]

Finally, groundwater quality in the state is threatened in some areas by the disposal of radioactive waste and by mining operations. The area around Richland has been contaminated by radioactive materials, but the Department of Ecology believes that as of the mid-1990s contamination was confined and limited to a small area. Finally, the mining of metals has led to an increase in the amount of metals and other organic compounds found in the groundwater supply in certain areas. Mining operations can be found primarily in the northeast portion of the state.

Excessive nitrate contamination can be found in most parts of the state; however, many other types of contamination are generally site specific and are limited to small areas. In an attempt to deal with both existing and potential problems the state developed a groundwater-management strategy in 1987. Included in the strategy were the adoption of groundwater-quality standards (which were actually adopted in 1990) and plans for the implementation of these standards. The ultimate goal of the groundwater-management strategy is to "maintain high quality ground water and to protect existing and future beneficial uses."[25] As of the mid-1990s it was too early to tell what the long-term impact of the groundwater-management strategy will be.

Law

In 1913, in the case of *Patrick v. Smith*, the Washington Supreme Court adopted what it referred to as a correlative rights doctrine but which in fact was much closer to the American rule of reasonable use.[26] In 1935, in *Evans v. Seattle*, the court distinguished between definite underground streams and percolating waters and found that the latter were governed by reasonable use.[27]

In 1917 the Washington legislature passed a comprehensive water code governing the distribution and allocation of surface-water rights. The 1917 act established the prior appropriation doctrine for surface waters. In 1945 the Washington legislature passed the Groundwater Code of 1945, extending the major provisions of the earlier law to cover groundwater and establishing a permit system. The permit system is administered on a prior appropriation basis with the stipulation that "no permit shall be granted for the development or withdrawal of public groundwaters beyond the capacity of the underground bed or formation in a given basin, district, or locality to yield such water within a reasonable and feasible pumping lift in case of pumping developments, or within a reasonable or feasible reduction of pressure in the case of artisan developments."[28]

Groundwater for stock watering, for watering a lawn or a noncommercial garden that does not exceed one-half acre in area, or for domestic or industrial purposes using less than 5,000 gallons per day is exempt from the act.[29]

The 1945 code also includes provisions for allowing groundwater extractors who were pumping prior to 1945 to obtain certificates for their withdrawals upon providing satisfactory proof of the existence of a vested water right.[30] In addition, Washington law contains provisions for loss of water rights in the event of abandonment. (Abandonment is defined as continued nonuse for a period of five years, but there are exceptions.)[31] In 1967 the legislature amended the law providing that no rights to water (either appropriated or unappropriated groundwater or surface water) could be acquired by prescription or adverse use.[32]

As in most states, any water appropriated in Washington must be put to a beneficial use. In addition to the traditional beneficial uses such as domestic, industrial, commercial, agricultural, power, and mining, beneficial use in Washington also includes water for aesthetic and fish or wildlife purposes.[33] Beyond the beneficial-use requirement, statutory preferences for the allocation of water rights in Washington are somewhat confusing. For example, in 1977 the Family Farm Water Act became the law of the state through the initiative process. The act gives preference to family farms defined as "a geographic area including not more than 2,000 acres of irrigated agricultural lands, where incontiguous or noncontiguous, the controlling interest in which is held by a person having a controlling interest in no more than 2,000 acres of irrigated agricultural lands in the state of Washington which are irrigated under rights acquired after December 8, 1977."[34]

In addition, the Department of Ecology has the authority to administer water rights according to principles of highest and best use. Specifically, the Washington code directs the department to allocate water according to securing the maximum net benefits for the state using cost benefit analysis. The code states that "Allocation of water among potential uses and users shall be based generally on the securing of the maximum net benefits for the people of the state. Maximum net benefits shall constitute total benefits less costs including opportunities lost."[35]

This part of the Washington Water Code is seemingly in conflict with other sections that direct the Department of Ecology to reject water-rights application if it "threatens to prove detrimental to the public interest, having due regard to the highest feasible development of the use of waters belonging to the public."[36]

The formal requirements for receiving a permit to withdraw groundwater are straightforward. An application for a permit must contain the name of the applicant and the address and owner of the land, the location of the well, the amount of water to be withdrawn, and the depth and type of well to be constructed.[37] Although the Department of Ecology will routinely issue permits where there is no conflict over water rights, such cases are becoming increasingly rare. The department also has the authority to attach conditions to permits.[38] As is common in states with prior appropriation permit systems, the Department of Ecology has authority to license and regulate well drillers and to establish minimum construction and maintenance standards for wells.[39] The department has also adopted regulations that establish a process whereby surface or groundwater may be reserved for some public water-supply purpose in the future.

Washington's groundwater code provides the Department of Ecology with the authority to designate groundwater areas or subareas when this is necessary for individual management. As of 1996 the department had designated the Odessa, Quincy, and Duck Lake subareas for regulation and had instituted groundwater-management programs for these areas.[40] (Programs may also be developed by local governments or groundwater users in the area.) The department has a great deal of latitude in deciding when or where to identify a subarea. Among the things it is to consider when making such a decision are whether a groundwater basin is overappropriated, whether water levels are declining, and whether the basin is identified as the primarily source of water for a public water-supply system.[41] One may also petition to have a subarea established.[42]

Politics, Policy, and the Future

As of the mid-1990s Washington was not suffering from widespread contamination problems, and the amount of groundwater mining in the state was limited to certain areas. However, surface waters are fully appropriated, and attention has been focused on the increased use of groundwater. As of the mid-1990s the "hot topic" for the Department of Ecology has been "hydraulic continuity" or the interrelationship between groundwater and surface water. Because of hydraulic continuity the department has been forced to deny an increasing number of applications for groundwater withdrawals in order to maintain instream flows necessary for salmon and to avoid impairing prior appropriators of surface water. Many applications that are denied are for new development of either agricultural or municipal uses. This trend has not been well received by many in the state who are encouraging growth and feel that the Department of Ecology is perhaps too environmentally conscious.[43]

Some within the Department of Ecology fear that the Washington legislature will begin to succumb to political pressures and will start ignoring science and hydrologic continuity.[44] Elected officials are often driven by the desire to be reelected and will sometimes discount the future in order to reap short-term benefits. This can lead to a reliance on "quick fixes" for complex problems. In this case, employees of the Department of Ecology we spoke to are fearful that political pressures exerted by current and future users (developers and municipal interests, primarily) will lead to legislation that will allow for the allocation of groundwater permits separately from surface-water allocations. In other words, groundwater permits might be allowed despite their possible impact on surface-water uses.[45] Such a separation is, however, likely to be short-lived (if it happens at all), as prior appropriators will begin to feel the impact of new groundwater allocations and withdrawals. In the long run such separation would affect all interested parties. Furthermore, any groundwater pumping that has an impact on stream flow necessary for salmon is likely to be considered illegal by the courts because of tribal issues and Endangered Species Act requirements.[46]

Salmon flows have been guaranteed through treaties with some of the indigenous tribes in Washington, and therefore instream flows must be maintained.[47] The fact that extensive groundwater withdrawals will have an affect on these instream flows means that groundwater cannot be heavily relied upon for future needs. Eventually water distribution patterns will have to change if municipal growth is to continue. This means that, in addition to adopting conservation measures and encouraging the reuse of water, the legislature will have to enact legislation that will allow transfers of water rights from irrigation to municipal use and, in some cases, the termination of existing rights when such transfers are inadequate. Currently there is legal uncertainty surrounding the transfer of water rights from seasonal use (which applies to most agricultural uses) to annual use (which would apply to municipalities and industrial use).[48] Such uncertainty will have to be remedied in the future. While agricultural interests (as of this writing) are actively lobbying for legislation that would protect them from such redistribution of water rights, they are likely to lose. Agricultural interests are still important players in Washington politics, but the financial resources of municipalities and urban developers may be too much for them to overcome.

We anticipate that Washington will continue to grow and that this growth will be facilitated through a shift in water use, with municipalities receiving more water and agricultural interests receiving less and less. Such a shift will be necessary for the state to adequately sustain its growing population into the future. The question for water planners in Washington is not whether such a transition will take place, but when. If the transition is planned for and managed carefully, serious socioeconomic disruption within the agricultural sector can be avoided. If it is not, future supply shortages could result in socioeconomic disruptions in all sectors. State officials will have to act soon if they wish to make a smooth transition into a sustainable future.

ROCKY MOUNTAIN REGION

The Rockies can be broken down into three parts—the Northern, Middle, and Southern Rockies. These sections cover parts of Montana, Idaho, Wyoming, Utah, and Colorado (and a small portion of Arizona).

Precipitation in the Rockies generally increases from the southern to the northern portions, with the Northern Rockies receiving roughly three times that of the Southern Rockies. Generally speaking, the Southern Rockies tend to be the driest and receive most of their annual precipitation in the form of winter snow. The Northern Rockies tend to receive precipitation much more evenly throughout the year. Despite differences in precipitation patterns a short growing season is common to most of the Rockies.

While the Rocky Mountains is a region of water surplus (precipitation exceeds evaporation), the lands on either side of the mountains experience water deficits. Because of this, the Rocky Mountain region has been the site of many reclamation projects as people have sought to divert water for irrigation, domestic, municipal, and other uses. Where diversions have been insufficient, people have largely turned to groundwater.

The Rockies have become the site of some environmental concerns. Logging and oil exploration has led to an acceleration in slope erosion both from operations and from the construction of necessary access roads. This erosion has stripped away soil cover and caused stream siltation in some areas. Mining has resulted (to varying degrees across the states surveyed) in the release of trace quantities of harmful metals into streams and groundwater.

Finally, as in other parts of the West, some states (particularly Colorado and Utah) in the Rocky Mountain region have been forced to deal with increasing populations and changing demographics as they relate to water use. Others, such as Montana and Wyoming, have not experienced the same problem.

6 Colorado

Although ranching is historically associated with Colorado's development, the state has a long tradition of agricultural water use. Relying on prior appropriation to determine who gets title to water rights has meant that irrigators hold the rights to a great deal of Colorado's water supply. In recent years, however, agriculture has diminished in importance as a contributor to the overall economy of the state. While a large number of persons continue to depend upon agriculture as a means of support, the majority of the population lives in urban settings and draws income from nonfarm operations. Metropolitan areas are the fastest-growing areas within the state and will require more water for public supply and urban-based industries. Conflict will undoubtedly arise between prior appropriators of water and the escalating needs of new water users. As surface water is, for the most part, fully appropriated, attention will most likely focus on groundwater supplies. Groundwater has facilitated some of the current growth on the east slope of the state, but the Denver Basin is a nonrenewable source of water. Thus, while the Colorado's groundwater is sufficient for current needs, the state cannot continue to rely on it for the bulk of its municipal supply. Given the changes in population and the changes in Colorado's economy, it is apparent that changes in both groundwater and surface water use will be made. Supplies are not unlimited, and water will have to be redirected to where it will benefit the state most. Transfers of surface water have and will continue to play an important role in Colorado's growth.

Physical Description

Colorado is split into east and west slopes by the Rocky Mountains. Annual average precipitation varies from approximately 50 inches in the western mountains to around 8 inches on the High Plains and Colorado Plateau in the east. Snowfall in Colorado accounts for the largest portion of this precipitation. Melting snowpack forms the headwaters of many major western streams, most notably the Colorado River and its tributaries. Mountainous western Colorado contains only a small part of the state's cultivable land.[1]

Irrigation is by far the largest use of groundwater in Colorado. It consumes 92 percent of the groundwater withdrawn in the state. Public supply withdrawals account for 3 percent, rural domestic and livestock for 1.4 percent, and industrial withdrawals for only 1.2 percent.[2] Approximately 15 percent of the state's population depends on groundwater as a primary source of drinking water.[3]

Demographics

As of 1 July 1995 the resident state population of Colorado was estimated to be 3,746,585.[4] Between 1950 and 1995 the population of Colorado increased by 182.7 percent—far exceeding the national average increase of 73.6 percent.[5] Elbert and Douglas Counties on the eastern slope are two of the fastest growing counties in the nation, with population increases primarily supported through nontributary groundwater from the Denver Basin.[6] Colorado's population growth has occurred primarily in urban areas. In 1960, 73.7 percent (1.29 million people) of Colorado's population was urban.[7] By 1992 over 80 percent (almost 3 million people) of the state's population resided in urban areas.[8]

The largest percentage of persons living in Colorado earn wages through nonfarm occupations. Ninety-five percent of people working in Colorado are employed on nonfarm payrolls. The largest employment industries in Colorado are those that have traditionally operated in urban settings. The largest single categories of employment in Colorado are manufacturing, wholesale and retail trade, public transportation and utilities, and service industries.[9]

While irrigation remains the largest single user of both surface water and groundwater, the number of farms in the state as well as the number of acres of land devoted to farm use have declined over the years. In 1959 there were 33,000 farms in Colorado, with a total of 38,787,000 acres.[10] In 1993 there were 26,000 farms in Colorado, and there were 33 million acres of land devoted to agriculture.[11] Farming contributes only 1.7 percent to the gross state product of Colorado, while urban-based industries such as services, finance and insurance, and manufacturing contribute 19.3 percent, 16.4 percent, and 13 percent, respectively.[12] As of the mid-1990s agricultural use was continuing to decline as much of the farmland across the state was being converted for municipal use and water rights were being purchased to facilitate urban growth.[13]

Water Use

Colorado, especially the part of the state that lies west of the Rocky Mountains, is primarily dependent on surface water to meet its water needs. Groundwater provides approximately 1 percent of the irrigation water in western Colorado and approximately 33 percent of the water used in irrigation in the eastern part of the state.[14] Statewide, 87 percent of the water used in public supply systems and 78 percent of the water used for irrigation comes from surface-water sources.[15] Major sources of surface water in Colorado include the Arkansas, Colorado, La Platta, Rio Grande, and South Platte Rivers.[16] Water demands east of the Rocky mountains are met by conjunctive use of groundwater and surface water, augmented by transmountain diversions from the western slopes. However, where surface-water quality is poor, public water-supply systems tend to utilize only groundwater. Of the sixty-three counties in Colorado, twenty-nine rely solely on groundwater for public supply. In addition, for domestic purposes most rural areas depend upon groundwater almost entirely.[17]

There are five major groundwater reservoirs in the state: the South Platte Alluvial Basin in north-central and northeastern Colorado, the High Plains (Ogalalla) Sand and Gravel Aquifer of eastern Colorado, the Arkansas River Alluvial Basin in southeastern Colorado, the San Luis Valley Aquifer system in south-central Colorado, and the Denver Basin.

The South Platte Alluvial Aquifer, consisting primarily of unconsolidated sand and gravel, is hydrologically connected to the South Platte River and its major tributaries. The Arkansas Aquifer is similar to the South Platte in terms of composition. The High Plains Aquifer in Colorado is primarily unconsolidated sand and gravel. Unlike the South Platte and Arkansas Aquifers, the High Plains Aquifer's only source of recharge is precipitation. The San Luis Valley Aquifer and the Denver Basin Aquifer Systems consist primarily of confined aquifers. Because of concern over water-level declines in the High Plains and San Louis Valley Aquifers, the office of the state engineer has not granted a major permit for irrigation withdrawals in these areas since 1986.[18]

Problems

Pollution
Generally, groundwater quality in Colorado ranges from excellent in mountain areas where snowfall is heavy to poor in alluvial aquifers where surface and groundwater are used and reused for a number of purposes. Overall, the most common contaminants affecting groundwater supplies in Colorado are nitrate, fluoride, selenium, iron, manganese, alpha radiation, and uranium. Many aquifers in the eastern part of the state (the area most dependent upon groundwater for public supply and domestic use) often experience contamination from nitrate, fluoride, selenium, gross alpha, and radium in excess of EPA water-quality standards.[19]

Water-quality problems, as might be expected, have become more critical as new industries and government installments have developed around the rapidly growing metropolitan centers along the Front Range. The EPA and the Colorado Health Department have targeted several areas of particular concern. The major problem areas are discussed below.

Two hazardous waste sites in Commerce City, a suburb of Denver, are included on the EPA national priorities list. At one location organic pesticide compounds, produced by a chemical plant, were disposed of in a vacant lot. Groundwater pollution is also a concern for all supply wells in the city of Thornton, located three miles from the Commerce City site.[20]

The second priorities list site is an industrial plant in Sand Creek that has been used for petroleum and chemical production. The Colorado Department of Health found methane, sulfuric acid, pesticides, and petroleum derivatives in the soil, surface water, and groundwater.

Other pollution problems within the Denver metropolitan area are found at the Lowry and Marshall landfills. The Lowry landfill in Arapahoe County placed, between 1967 and 1980, approximately 10 to 15 million gallons of liquid industrial wastes in unlined trenches. Organic compounds have been detected in the alluvial aquifer under and adjacent to the landfill. Similarly, the Marshall landfill in Boulder County has been used for municipal and sewage-sludge landfill. Samples collected from the wells at the site indicate that the groundwater beneath the landfill contains phenols, ethylene chloride, and trichloroethylene pollutants.[21]

The production of chemical and incendiary munitions at Rocky Mountain Arsenal have resulted in the pollution of groundwater in the vicinity. Groundwater contamination there is related to the disposal of liquid industrial wastes and to industrial leaks and spills that have occurred during the forty-year history of the arsenal's operation. From 1943 to 1956 liquid wastes were discharged into unlined ponds, contaminating the underlying alluvial aquifer. Since 1956 disposal has been accomplished by discharge into an asphalt-lined reservoir, significantly reducing the amount of contaminants entering the aquifer. However, in the mid-1970s toxic organic chemicals were detected downstream of the arsenal. The Colorado Department of Health ordered a halt to the discharges and demanded cleanup and groundwater monitoring. A groundwater-containment and treatment system involving groundwater interception, treatment, and reinjection was constructed in 1978.[22]

Overdrafting

Many groundwater aquifers in Colorado (with the exception of alluvial aquifers) are being steadily drawn down, particularly in association with irrigation and rapid growth in the eastern part of the state. The most notable examples of widespread "mining" of groundwater occur in the Ogalalla formation that lies under the High Plains region and the Denver Basin. The Ogalalla formation has been called upon to facilitate part of the municipal expansion in eastern Colorado.

Water level declines of up to 40 to 50 feet in the Ogalalla have substantially increased irrigation costs.[23] Water levels have decreased by as much as 25 percent in some areas.

Another problem area is in the northeastern Rio Grande County. Water levels there have declined by 5 feet or more in an 110-square-mile area. In a 50-square-mile section, water level declines of 20 feet or more have been recorded.

In 1983 the USGS reported that there were existing or potential future groundwater availability problems in most of Phillips, Yuma, and Kit Carson Counties and substantial portions of Sedgwick, Logan, Washington, Lincoln, and Cheyenne Counties. According to the Colorado Natural Resources Department, as of 1995 this remained true, as these counties are located in eastern Colorado and are highly dependent upon groundwater from the Denver Basin Aquifer for most of their water.[24] Groundwater depletion in eastern Colorado is likely to remain a concern into the future, as this is one of the fastest-growing areas in the state. Competition between irrigators and municipalities will be eased somewhat by the availability of water transfers. However, reliance upon nonrenewable resources for sustaining populations might become problematic at some point.

Law

While Colorado was one of the first western states to develop a body of law relating to surface-water rights under the prior appropriation doctrine, it only recently enacted laws dealing with groundwater.[25]

The first legislative step toward the recognition of groundwater was taken in 1953.[26] The recognition amounted to no more than a requirement for filing well logs and the authorization of certain studies on the effect of withdrawals in given areas. The state engineer, however, took the position that he had no jurisdiction to regulate wells.[27]

By the mid-1960s a large number of wells had been drilled in the alluvial valleys of the eastern slope rivers to supply irrigation demands. It had become apparent to many that because of hydraulic connectivity these wells competed for water with the holders of surface rights. The wells were, in general, considerably junior to the surface diversions in historic order, but many had been taking water for several years. The feeling among well owners was that their rights had become "vested" even though they had never been recorded or adjudicated. The fact that well pumping did diminish streamflow in alluvial aquifers could no longer be ignored, and senior surface-right owners exerted considerable pressure.

In 1965 several canal companies in the Arkansas Valley filed a petition with the Colorado state engineer demanding that he order curtailment of groundwater withdrawals that were interfering with surface-water rights. The state engineer found that he had no jurisdiction to grant the request.[28]

Consequently, in 1965 the legislature again addressed the groundwater issue when it passed the Colorado Groundwater Management Act. The act applied the appropriation doctrine to all Colorado waters, including underground waters connected to surface water. The state engineer's duties and powers were amended to "execute and administer the laws of the state relative to distribution of surface water . . . including the underground waters tributary thereto in accordance with the right of priority of appropriation."[29]

In 1966 the state engineer attempted to curtail or shut down certain wells that were depleting the streamflow of the Arkansas River (those thought to be the worst offenders). He picked thirty-nine of the more than sixteen hundred major wells on the stream. Then in the 1968 decision of *Fellhauer v. People,* the Colorado Supreme Court upheld the general power of the state engineer to shut down a well interfering with senior rights in conformity with the 1965 act but found that the specific exercise of authority being contested had been arbitrary and capricious.[30] There had been no written regulations governing well shutdowns and no rational basis for the selection of those particular wells. The court did set forth standards that, if followed, would result in valid and constitutional regulation of groundwater pumping.[31]

Of the decision, one water-rights expert wrote that the court "seemed to reaffirm that vested surface rights, senior to the wells, must be protected, but to declare that this must be done in a systematic way . . . (and) . . . the regulatory system must be designed so as to promote the maximum utilization of water and to protect existing well users wherever possible consistent with the protection of vested rights."[32]

When the *Fellhauer* case was handed down, the Colorado Division of Natural Resources was, pursuant to legislation passed in 1967, studying the need for changes in the states' water law.[33] Incorporating the *Fellhauer* guidelines, as well as other information generated by the division's sanctioned investigations, the division made several recommendations to the legislature. These recommendations culminated in the Water Right Determination and Administration Act of 1969.[34]

The 1969 act abolished existing water districts and irrigation divisions in the state and created seven new water divisions with roughly the same boundaries as those of the former irrigation division. It authorized the appointment of an engineer for each division and the establishment of one or more field offices with a water commissioner assigned to each office.[35] The act also provided that each division will have a water judge responsible to determine "water matters."[36] Water judges have the power to appoint referees and rule in cases of conflict over water rights. (A judge may also delegate these responsibilities to the referees.)[37]

More important than the new arrangements for determining water rights was the effect that the act had on controlling well drilling and on regulating groundwater pumping that interfered with surface-water rights.

Groundwater in Colorado is classified into one of three kinds: tributary, designated, and nontributary groundwater. Tributary groundwater is water that is adjacent to and hydrologically connected with streams. In tributary groundwater basins extractions are regulated under the priority system by the state engineer to minimize the effects of groundwater withdrawals on senior surface-water rights holders. The major tributary groundwater systems are those interconnected with the South Platte, Arkansas, and Rio Grande Rivers. Designated groundwater basins are not interconnected with surface-water sources. Nontributary basins are those that are outside designated areas, that are not connected to surface water, and that are regulated by the state engineer.

Prior to 1965 and to the passage of the Colorado Groundwater Management Act, groundwater that was not tributary to a stream was not subject to appropriation.[38] The 1965 act also affirmed the prior appropriation doctrine for designated and confined groundwater basins and stipulated that the appropriation doctrine should be modified to permit the full economic development of groundwater resources.

The 1965 act also created the Colorado Groundwater Commission to regulate designated groundwater basins. The commission (a twelve-member body consisting of nine members appointed by the governor and confirmed by the Senate as well as by the executive director of the Department of Natural Resources, the state engineer, and the director of the Colorado Water Conservation Board) is responsible for establishing designated groundwater basins and holding hearings to determine the extent of such basins. In addition, the commission is responsible for the administration and the control of pumping in designated basins and has the power to limit extractions when they interfere with prior appropriators, and to establish reasonable pumping levels.[39] The commission has established the following guidelines for the use of designated basins:

1. Permits are required on wells yielding 15 gallons per minute or more.
2. Wells must be located at least one-half mile apart.
3. A well will not be permitted if it causes more than 40 percent depletion in twenty-five years of the saturated rock underlying the area within a 3-mile radius of the proposed well.[40]

The last condition has led to limitations on extraction to not more than 2.5 acre-feet annually per acre in the northern high plains and not more than 3.5 acre-feet per acre in the southern high plains.

The state engineer is generally responsible for administering the "waters of the state."[41] Whether or not to provide permits for groundwater withdrawal outside designated areas is determined by the engineer on a case-by-case basis. Applicants must provide the engineer with information on estimated amounts and proposed use of the water, the name of the landowner, and the aquifer from which the water will be removed. Such rights are granted if hydrologic and geologic proof demonstrates that the new use will not impair the rights of vested water users.[42] The state engineer is assisted by seven division engineers, one appointed to each of the seven water divisions in the state (divisions generally follow major watershed boundaries).

Politics, Policy, and the Future

Colorado, like many western states, has decided to manage its essentially nonrecharging groundwater basins in a manner that will result in the eventual depletion of the resource. This assures that the nature of agricultural groundwater use will change as water becomes more expensive to pump and as the need for water for energy development in some parts of the state increases. The urban population centers overlying the Denver Basin have already resorted to expensive surface-water diversion projects to meet their future needs for domestic and industrial water.

Since it is anticipated that the state's population and its tourism industry will grow, demands for domestic, manufacturing, and industrial water can be expected to increase in the future. In states in like or similar circumstances we might anticipate conflicts between current water users and potential future water users. However, in Colorado, this conflict will be mitigated in large part by the fact that water rights are, to a much greater extent than they are in most western states, transferable. Consequently, those in need of future groundwater rights (e.g., energy companies or municipalities) will be able to acquire those rights in the open market. Such transfers are already occurring with regard to surface-water rights wherein municipalities in the Denver metropolitan area have begun to purchase water rights from agricultural interests.[43] Stated another way, the battles that we might anticipate in other states between agricultural interests and other water users over the transferability issue and the necessity of buying land along with water are not likely to be part of the future conflict over water rights in Colorado.

What will probably be a part of Colorado's future is a shift in socioeconomic composition. The role of agriculture is likely to diminish greatly, especially in areas where farmland surrounds municipalities. Such acreage is being (and will continue to be) purchased for urban expansion. Furthermore, agricultural activity is likely to decline in areas where water is easily transported. Escalating urban needs will require such diversions. This state, which was once largely agricultural, is undergoing a social transformation, and the future sustainability of its new urban-based society will depend on water that is currently being used by agriculture.

7 Idaho

A large percentage of persons living in Idaho are dependent upon ground-water as their primary source of drinking water, and groundwater plays a major role in agricultural production in the state. Groundwater in Idaho is generally of high quality, and the state, as a whole, is not facing any serious supply problems, despite having one of the highest per capita water withdrawal rates in the nation. Those quality and supply problems that do exist or that could potentially emerge are limited to specific areas. Surface water, however, is for the most part fully appropriated. This suggests that individuals and industries will become more depen-dent on groundwater in the future. The statewide supply of groundwater, while not a problem today, may become an issue in the future. Given the changes that are occurring in the state with regard to growing urban centers, and the declining importance of agriculture versus other indus-tries, some changes in water use will have to be made in certain areas. With populations rapidly growing in the state—especially around the Boise area—municipal interests including developers and public-water suppliers are likely to push for acquiring the water rights of irrigators. Such acquisitions are currently taking place and are most likely to continue. In the future Idaho will probably sustain agricultural interests (the state's agricultural image is cherished by many); however, the amount of land and water devoted to agriculture versus other social and economic uses will likely decline.

Physical Description

Most of the northern panhandle area of Idaho is forested, while much of the central part of the state is characterized by rugged mountain wilderness. Southern Idaho contains a large desert area where most agriculture, irrigated by both groundwater and surface water, takes place. Idaho has abundant arable land but, like most of the West, is dependent on irrigation to make this land productive. Irrigation and good soil conditions have led to the production of a variety of agricultural products, including alfalfa, grain, potatoes, peas, sugar beets, and fruits.

Idaho has three primary natural regions: the Rocky Mountain area (in the north, north-central, and far eastern part of the state); the Great Basin (in the southeastern part of Idaho); and the Columbia Plateau (covering most of the area where the Snake River flows in central and southern Idaho).[1] There are five major drainage basins in the state. In the largest, the Snake River Basin, lives the majority of the state's population. Precipitation in the state varies from about 10 to over 60 inches per year and falls mostly in the form of snow. The areas of lightest precipitation are on the Snake River Plain, with the heavier amounts falling in the higher elevations. The Snake River and its tributaries provide most of the irrigation water in the desert areas.

Demographics

As of 1 July 1995 the resident state population of Idaho was estimated to be 1,163,261.[2] Between 1950 and 1995 the population of Idaho increased by 97.6 percent, which is slightly higher than the national average of 73.6 percent.[3] The state is divided fairly evenly between urban and rural dwellers; however, since 1960 the urban areas have experienced a higher level of growth than have rural areas. In 1960, 42 percent (317,000 people) of Idaho's population was urban.[4] By 1990 over 57 percent (578,000 people) of the state's population resided in urban areas.[5]

While the majority of Idaho residents are employed through nonfarm operations, approximately 9 percent (close to one hundred thousand people) of those who are employed in Idaho earn wages through agriculture. Idaho is generally thought to be a state with a primarily agriculturally based economy; however, farm income contributes less than 10 percent of the total state gross product.[6] Idaho ranked twenty-first in the nation for farm income in 1991, with earnings of $741 million.[7] Employment industries that contribute the most to the gross state product are manufacturing; finance, insurance, and real estate; and service industries. These contribute 18.1 percent, 15.9 percent, and 13.4 percent, respectively, to the state's economy.[8]

While irrigation remains the largest single user of both surface water and groundwater in Idaho, the number of farms in the state as well as the number of acres of land devoted to agriculture have declined over the years. In 1959 there were 34,000 farms in the state covering 15,232,000 acres.[9] In 1993 there were 22,000 farms in the state covering 14 million acres.[10]

Water Use

Approximately 90 percent of Idaho's population depends on groundwater as a source of drinking water (86.9 percent of the state's public supply system water comes from the ground). Irrigated agriculture is the greatest user of groundwater. In 1990, 6.6 billion gallons of water per day, or 87.2 percent of all withdrawals of groundwater, were diverted for irrigation. On a statewide basis groundwater provides approximately 35 percent of the water used for irrigation.[11] The Snake River is the primary source of surface water in the state (and is an important indirect source of groundwater). Even though a very large percentage of the state's population depends on groundwater for drinking purposes, rural domestic and livestock uses of groundwater accounted for only 3 percent of all withdrawals (surface and ground).[12] Additional withdrawals are used for commercial and industrial purposes, including aquaculture (most notably fish hatcheries).

With the exception of certain areas that have been designated as critical (discussed below), groundwater supply is not a pressing problem in Idaho. The state has the potential to irrigate considerable tracts of additional land using groundwater (with varying degrees of sustainability).[13] Some of the major aquifer systems and groundwater-use patterns are summarized below.

The Spokane Valley–Rathdrum Prairie Aquifer is the main source of water for the cities of Spokane, Washington, and Coeur d'Alene, Idaho. Wells in this aquifer are usually less than 200 feet deep, and in Idaho the water is used primarily for irrigation.

In the Weiser River Basin in western Idaho the basalt aquifers of the Columbia River group supply water for irrigation and domestic use for the cities of Council, Cambridge, and Midvale. The aquifers in the Boise Valley area provide water to Boise, Nampa, Caldwell, and other smaller cities.

The largest aquifer in Idaho is the Snake River Plain Aquifer. It is responsible for supplying more than 70 percent of the needs of about two hundred city and village systems and over one hundred industrial plants. It covers roughly 10,040 square miles. The Snake River Plain Aquifer is used primarily for irrigation. As of the mid-1990s approximately 1,785 million gallons per day were being withdrawn from the Snake River Plain Aquifer to irrigate some 2.1 million acres.[14]

There have been some significant groundwater level declines in Idaho. Declines ranging from 1 to 50 feet have been recorded at observation wells throughout the state, with the greatest declines occurring in wells along the southern part of the Snake River Plain and along the northern side of the plain (notably in Butte and Camas Counties). Irrigation is extensive in these areas.[15]

Problems

Compared to many states in the West, Idaho has few groundwater problems. For the most part, groundwater is of high quality. The majority of existing or potential pollution problems are associated with underground storage tanks, agricultural application of pesticides and fertilizers, and mining activities. Groundwater contamination can affect humans in two ways: it can cause potential health problems associated with drinking contaminated water, and it can force consumers to pay the high costs of cleaning contaminated water. As a result of human influence there are a number of sites in the state where groundwater supplies are tainted.

Idaho produces over one-third of the silver mined in the United States and is also an important source of lead, zinc, vanadium, and mercury. In addition, there is large-scale mining of sand, gravel, and stone in the state. Mining activities can affect groundwater quality in a number of ways. For example, mine wastes that pollute surface streams can percolate into groundwater supplies. Lowering water levels to allow mining in a saturated zone (i.e., mine dewatering) can lead to the formation of acids that will pollute groundwater after mining operations have stopped. Unlined tailing ponds used for the disposal of wastewater can percolate wastewater into groundwater basins. While it is estimated that there are close to two thousand abandoned metal, nonmetal, and coal mines, concerns over contamination from these sources obviously depends on the proximity of the mine to usable groundwater. While past monitoring has revealed high concentrations of arsenic and heavy metals in the water under phosphate-processing plants near Pocatello, most mines are in remote and unpopulated areas; hence pollution from mining and related activities is more of a potential problem than it is a serious immediate threat to humans.[16]

Despite its decline in importance to the gross state product in recent years, agriculture remains big business in Idaho. The state is the number one U.S. producer of potatoes and usually the number two U.S. producer of sugar beets. Heavy use of pesticides and fertilizers has accompanied the sizeable agricultural output. Nitrate contamination resulting from the use of fertilizers is common in the state, and while they usually appear in levels below those deemed to make water unfit for drinking, nitrates are an existing threat in some areas. Counties recording excessive levels of nitrate contamination include Ada, Canyon, Minidoka, Payette, Jerome, and Cassia (Ada and Canyon are the two most heavily populated counties in the state).[17] Nitrates are carcinogenic in high doses.

Volatile organic compounds (VOCs) pose a threat to groundwater supplies in Idaho. VOCs are a diverse group of chemicals commonly found in cleaning solvents, pesticides, and most notably, in petroleum products, including gasoline. There are 132 sites in Idaho where contamination by petroleum products is either suspected or confirmed. VOCs pose a threat to human health because most are thought to be carcinogenic. Benzene is one such example. VOCs do not break down under natural processes, and once they enter into groundwater supplies, cleaning them up is expensive and difficult, if not impossible. The most common source of VOC contamination in Idaho comes from leaking underground storage tanks. VOC contamination has been detected in several counties in Idaho, including Ada, the most densely populated county in the state.[18] Many VOCs have been found to cause cancer and nervous system and organ damage in laboratory situations.

Livestock feedlots and agricultural waste-disposal wells are also an existing and potential source of groundwater pollution in Idaho, as are impoundment sites containing liquid, semisolid, and waste solids. The EPA has identified four hazardous waste sites in Idaho for placement on the agency's national priorities list. These sites have been polluted by smelting wastes, solvents, lumber preservatives, and polychlorinated biphenyls (PCB). Two of the four sites are in the panhandle area (in Kootenai County and Shoshone County), one is 30 miles east of Boise (a city rapidly expanding beyond its borders), and one is near Pocatello.[19]

Instances of contaminated groundwater, although isolated, occur in populous counties such as Ada. As of the mid-1990s public supply had yet to be significantly affected; however, as urban areas continue to grow and become more dependent on groundwater as a source of drinking water, contamination is likely to become more of a concern in the future, both financially and in terms of health.

The Idaho Department of Health and Welfare, Division of the Environment, has primary responsibility for protecting Idaho's groundwater quality. The USGS, the EPA, and the Idaho Department of Water Resources (DWR) assist it with data collection.

Law

All waters in Idaho are the property of the state and are subject to prior appropriation for beneficial use. In 1951 the Idaho legislature passed the 1951 Ground Water Act confirming the prior appropriation doctrine. Although the Idaho Code states that those "first in time are first in right" (section 42-226), it also stipulates that full economic development of groundwater shall not be blocked. While recent years have seen various entities positioning themselves in battles over what should be the highest-priority use of water, the constitution of the state of Idaho establishes such a listing of economic priorities for water condemnation.[20] Beginning in 1951 the state started supervising appropriations and requiring that any appropriation be for beneficial use.[21] The state strictly adheres to the prior appropriation doctrine. The Idaho Supreme Court has found in recent years that the public trust doctrine takes precedence over even vested water rights.[22] This potential problem was addressed by the Idaho legislature in 1996, when legislation was passed stating that the public trust doctrine does not apply in Idaho.[23]

Before 1963 water rights were perfected either by diversion and application to beneficial use or by the granting of a permit and license by the state. In 1963 a law was passed requiring the filing of a water right and application for permit, subject to the approval of the director of the Idaho DWR. Wells for domestic use are exempted from the permit requirements of the act.[24] In 1968 the Idaho Supreme Court upheld the mandatory permit system.[25]

When a permit is issued, the drilling work completed, and the water put to a beneficial use, a license is issued indicating the priority date of the appropriation (which is the initial filing date). Licenses are binding on the state and conveyed with the sale of the land.[26] The director has the authority to halt additional extractions. One method of halting additional extractions is by designating critical groundwater areas. The director may designate a groundwater basin (or part thereof) as critical when it is found not to have "sufficient ground water to provide a reasonably safe supply."[27] Upon designation, the director must publish notice of the action and conduct public hearings. In critical groundwater areas no new well permits are issued unless the director finds that there is water available. Groundwater withdrawals are reduced to levels set by the director. The director is further granted the authority (not limited to critical groundwater areas) to require the use of measurement devices and the reporting of water diversions.[28]

The Idaho Code also has provisions for establishing "groundwater management areas" in those areas thought to be approaching the critical stage. In a groundwater-management area the director may require monitoring and reporting of withdrawals to insure that additional permits that might interfere with existing uses are not issued.[29] As of the mid-1990s five critical groundwater areas and five groundwater-management areas had been designated in the state, mostly within the Snake River Plain.[30]

The director also has a variety of other powers, including the authority to license well drillers; the authority to set construction standards for wells; the power to inspect wells on public or private lands; the authority to restrict pumping when a junior right holder is interfering with the withdrawals of a senior appropriator when withdrawals are in excess of natural recharge (i.e., when overdrafting is occurring), the authority to establish reasonable pumping levels to protect prior appropriators, and control of the allocation of geothermal resources.[31]

Politics, Policy, and the Future

As discussed previously, water levels have been declining in many parts of the Snake River Plain. Strict enforcement of the law prohibiting new wells and regulating pumping could force farmers to shut off irrigation pumps in some cases at some point in the future.

We will recall that although the Idaho Code provides for prior appropriation, at the same time it directs that "a reasonable exercise of this right shall not block full economic development of underground water resources."[32] This statutory language has led to conflict and controversy over who should have priority when supplies are limited. The conflict centers around four main parties: irrigators, power companies, aquaculture, and land developers. As demands on groundwater resources increase, we can anticipate competition between these interests. Given the economic resources of developers and power producers and the changing population demographics, when these interests conflict it is likely that irrigated agriculture will lose. This is not to suggest that farmers will be denied compensation. Power companies and developers may have to purchase their water rights along with farmland. Such purchases have already begun to occur around Boise—the most rapidly growing area in the state. (Idaho does have a water-banking system whereby a person can lease surplus water to another person on an annual basis without completely relinquishing his or her water right.)

Despite the decline in the economic importance of agriculture versus other industries in recent years, the public sentiment regarding water priorities is reasonably clear. In a 1992 survey conducted by Boise State University for the Idaho Resource Board, a general sample of the state's population was asked to rank priorities of water use. Sixty-eight percent of the respondents felt that irrigation should have the highest priority. Only 8 percent viewed power as a top priority, and a mere 2 percent saw maintaining instream flows for fish and wildlife as being most important.[33]

Although among those familiar with Idaho's water resources there is some disagreement over the extent of Idaho's water problems, the problems are not serious, in our estimation, on the state level.[34] Demands for groundwater will continue into the future. Given that the water in question is often hydrologically connected to fully appropriated surface water, there will undoubtedly be management problems. However, these conflicts and others discussed above will be localized and are, for the most part, manageable. We conclude, therefore, that a lack of groundwater resources in Idaho is not likely to affect growth or development in any significant way in the foreseeable future. Furthermore, those shortages that occur will be dealt with in a satisfactory manner through banking, transfer, and sales of water or land and water. Finally, given the relatively modest rate of growth in the state, conversion of water uses will tend to take place slowly over time and will not lead to the same types of economic and social disruptions we anticipate for the more rapidly growing regions of the West.

8 Montana

Montana, like most states in the upper Rocky Mountain West, is nearing full appropriation of its surface-water supplies and will depend upon groundwater for future growth and development. As of the mid-1990s, however, Montana was almost completely dependent upon surface water for its water supply. If the population of the state continues to grow, the mix of surface water and groundwater used to supply water is likely to change. It has been projected, however, that Montana will experience population declines in the near future, and the demand on groundwater supplies is likely to be slight for quite some time. Given the slow (and possibly negative) growth of the population, Montana has groundwater to provide for both current and future generations of Montanans. The primary concern facing the people of Montana in the future will be one not of groundwater supply but of groundwater quality. Current (and potential) sources of contamination have the capacity to put Montana's groundwater supply (which is generally of high quality) at risk.

Physical Description

The largest and the northernmost state in the Great Plains–Rocky Mountain region, Montana is 535 miles from east to west and 275 miles from north to south. The eastern part of the state consists primarily of rolling shortgrass plains that support most of Montana's irrigated agriculture. Vast ranges in the east are dotted with petroleum and natural gas wells and contain enormous deposits of coal. Interspersed in the livestock rangelands is extensive dryland wheat farming. Western Montana is mountainous, extending from Glacier National Park in the north to Yellowstone National Park on the southern border. The topography varies from towering mountain ranges and dense forests to fertile, river-fed agricultural valleys.

Variations in topography produce wide variations in climatic conditions. West of the Continental Divide the moderate North Pacific maritime climate prevails, and rainfall is somewhat higher than it is eastward. East of the divide cold waves of frigid arctic air hit several times during the winter. Annual precipitation ranges from around 100 inches in the higher mountains to as little as 10 inches in eastern areas. The growing season varies in length from 40 days in the highlands of the southwest to 140 days in scattered areas of the eastern plains.[1]

Demographics

As of 1 July 1995 the resident state population of Montana was estimated to be 870,281.[2] Between 1950 and 1995 the state's population increased by 47.2 percent, which was below the national average population increase of 73.6 percent for the same period.[3] The U.S. Bureau of the Census anticipates a population decline for Montana in the future and predicts that the population will drop to 794,000 in the year 2000.[4] As of the mid-1990s the state was divided evenly between urban and rural dwellers and had remained so since 1960. In 1960, 50 percent (338,000 people) of Montana's population was urban.[5] In 1990 the percentage of Montanans residing in urban settings had increased by only 2 percent, to 52 percent (420,000) of the total population.[6]

While the majority of Montanans are employed through nonfarm operations, agriculture does provide support for close to 10 percent of the civilian workforce in the state (over thirty-three thousand persons). The only industries that provide employment for more people than agriculture does are the service industry and wholesale and retail trade, which employ 21.2 percent and 21.9 percent, respectively.[7]

Despite the importance of agriculture for employing large numbers of people in Montana, farming and farm services contribute relatively little to the gross state product. Farming and agricultural services contribute approximately 6 percent to the total gross state product, while less water-intensive activities such as finance, insurance and real estate; services; transportation and public utilities; and retail trade contribute 15.6 percent, 14.6 percent, 14.2 percent, and 10.4 percent, respectively.[8]

The number of farms and total land in farms has declined only slightly in recent years. In 1959 there were approximately 29,000 farms in Montana covering in excess of 64 million acres.[9] In 1993 there were 25,000 farms in the state covering roughly 60 million acres. In the three-year period between 1990 and 1993 the acreage devoted to agriculture in Montana decreased by 1 million acres.[10] Despite these declines agriculture continues to play a major role in Montana's water economy; irrigation constitutes the largest single water user in Montana, accounting for 96 percent of total withdrawals.[11]

Water Use

Montana has a good supply of uncontaminated surface water and has yet to experience the aquifer depletion problems faced by many other western states. As of the mid-1990s an estimated 205 million acre-feet per year came from the ground—less than 3 percent of the water used in Montana.[12]

The total amount of groundwater available in Montana has not been accurately estimated. Studies have, however, revealed large quantities of groundwater beneath the western intermountain valleys and in the consolidated sedimentary rock strata found in the Kootenai, Fort Union, and Fox Hills formations that underlie much of Montana east of the Rocky Mountains.[13]

Groundwater supplies almost all of the state's rural domestic water requirements (roughly 95 percent), 38 percent of the water used by municipal systems, approximately 1 percent of the water used in irrigation, and roughly 53 percent of the water used by industrial pumpers.[14] Major sources of surface water in the state include the Yellowstone, Milk, Powder, and Missouri Rivers.

Although groundwater accounts for a small percentage of the total water used in Montana, since 1973 the rate of groundwater development for rural domestic and livestock water uses has been decreasing constantly. (Beginning in 1973 all groundwater withdrawals were required to be on file with the state.) Most of the withdrawals are small, however, as the state receives notice of approximately two thousand to three thousand new withdrawals annually that are less than 35 gallons per minute. Conversely, the state receives fewer than one hundred applications for larger groundwater withdrawals on an annual basis.[15] Although most of these appropriations involve small volumes of water for domestic and livestock use, appropriations soon may involve large amounts of water. There are several reasons for anticipating this growth. First, as more and more surface water becomes overappropriated or contaminated, municipal systems will necessarily turn to groundwater as an inexpensive alternative source of water. Second, as primary production of oil from old wells decreases, more water will be used for secondary and tertiary oil recovery. Oil firms may turn to groundwater as the least expensive and most readily available source of water. And last, overappropriation of surface-water supplies is forcing some irrigation systems to shift to groundwater.[16]

Problems

Groundwater in Montana is generally of high quality and as of the mid-1990s had not been exposed to widespread human-caused contamination. There have, however, been isolated incidents of contamination, and there is potential for groundwater degradation on a large scale. Of particular concern to the Montana Department of Health and Environmental Science are the unconsolidated alluvial aquifers used by the majority of the groundwater systems. In addressing the potential for groundwater contamination, the Department of Health and Environmental Sciences, along with the Department of Natural Resources and Conservation, has prioritized the sources of contamination in the state and is developing a comprehensive groundwater-protection plan.

The highest-priority major sources of groundwater contamination receiving the most attention in Montana include septic tanks and shallow injection wells (very high priority), storage tanks (both above and below ground), and mining and mine drainage.[17] Pesticide applications, fertilizer applications, and animal feedlots are believed to be of lesser immediate concern. However, given the amount of agricultural land in the state, it is not unreasonable to assume that these contamination sources might become more threatening in the future.

Shallow injection wells and open-bottomed drains (categorized as class V injection wells) in Montana constitute one of the greatest immediate threats to groundwater quality in the state. These contamination sources have been ranked as a very high priority because of their location relative to groundwater used as drinking water, the size of the populations at risk, the risk posed to the populations and the environment from released substances, and the hydrogeologic sensitivity of the aquifers located underneath them. The EPA has estimated that there are approximately ten thousand storm drains and four hundred industrial injection wells in Montana. The impact of this contamination has already been felt by the communities of Bozeman and Missoula (two of the larger cities in the state), which have been forced to abandon some of their public supply wells after the detection of organic solvents that originated from injection wells.[18]

Another contamination source receiving a "very high priority" status in Montana are septic tanks—a major source of nitrate and bacterial contamination in the state. In 1993 ten communities were placed under a boil order because of fecal coliform bacterial contamination. There are approximately 120,000 individual, on-site septic systems, which are used by some three hundred thousand people in the state. High priority has been given to septic tanks because of the number of sources and the location of these sources relative to groundwater used as drinking water.[19]

Storage tanks (containing a variety of potential contaminents such as petroleum products, pesticides, and industrial chemicals) present yet another threat to the groundwater supply of Montana. There are approximately 22,500 registered underground storage tanks in the state—most of which were installed ten to twenty years ago. As of 1992 there were 963 confirmed releases from registered storage tanks, and reports of other leaking tanks were being made at a rate of twenty to thirty per month. Half of the releases reached groundwater, and there were five confirmed incidents of groundwater being contaminated by benzene (a known carcinogen). Storage tanks have been ranked as a state priority because of their location in relation to drinking water supply and because of the risk that this type of contamination poses to humans. While, as of the mid-1990s, contamination from storage tanks had yet to exert a widespread impact on public groundwater systems, the potential is there. The town of Cascade, for example, was forced to abandon one of its municipal wells because of contamination from storage tanks.[20]

Mining, mine drainage, and petroleum operations also present a threat to the groundwater supplies of Montana. Cyanide is sometimes used in mining operations to process ore. Two-thirds to three-fourths of the mining operations using cyanide have resulted in documented releases of contaminants. Four of the releases affected groundwater outside the boundaries of the mine property—two contaminating nearby domestic wells. Large doses of cyanide are lethal, and in smaller doses the chemical can cause nervous-system or organ damage.

Petroleum products are among the most difficult and most expensive to clean once they have entered into an aquifer. The fluid produced from oil drilling often contains a variety of harmful contaminants including benzene, phenanthrere, barium, antimony, and high concentrations of sodium salts (which can easily migrate into groundwater supplies).

Finally, agricultural pesticide application, while not currently considered a high priority in Montana, has been detected in groundwater supplies across the state, including three wells that supply water to rural schools. As of the mid-1990s the levels of pesticide contamination were below federal drinking-water standards, but state officials are aware of the potential for increases in the levels of pesticide contamination and of the potential for adverse health impact presented by such an increase.[21]

In summary, pollution has yet to have a widespread impact on the groundwater supplies of Montana. As of the mid-1990s most cases of contamination had been localized and had not led to any serious health risk. However, because of groundwater's importance for both rural and municipal drinking supplies, state officials are tracking current and potential problems in order to insure quality water for the people of Montana.

Law

Montana initially followed the common law doctrine in groundwater. Landowners had an absolute right to use the groundwater beneath their land in any way they wished without any consideration as to whether their water use affected their neighbors.[22] Migration of settlers into Montana in the early 1900s led to increased agricultural activities and to new wells being dug for irrigation.

The first law regulating groundwater use was passed in February 1947, and it reflected the dominant influence of the farmers who were mining groundwater on their lands.[23] The law altered the common law doctrine somewhat by requiring that persons drilling wells case and cap them properly, and by prohibiting waste. The law also required well drillers to keep a log of the depth, thickness, and character of the different strata penetrated and that they file it, together with a description of the well, with the Montana state engineer. Violations of the law were treated as misdemeanors.[24]

Subsequent attempts to reform Montana's groundwater laws were led by the Montana Reclamation Association (an association of irrigators interested in attracting federally funded surface-water projects). In 1951, on the urging of the Reclamation Association, Senate Bill No. 99 was introduced.[25] The bill proposed to replace private ownership of groundwater with state or public ownership and to establish the prior appropriation doctrine. It required all would-be appropriators to submit to the state engineer a notice of appropriation and a notice of completion. An exemption was made for withdrawals for domestic livestock and irrigation where the areas to be irrigated did not exceed four acres. The farmers, ranchers, and mining companies saw the notice-filing requirements as a foot in the door for more restrictive legislation, and SB 99 was overwhelmingly opposed. An attempt was made to reintroduce the bill in 1953, but again it was defeated. In 1955 a new bill, Senate Bill No. 38, which was much the same as SB 99, was introduced.[26] Like its predecessor, it did not pass. However, the legislature agreed to appropriate $14 million to fund groundwater research.

In 1955, when SB 38 was being debated in the legislature, the USGS was conducting a survey of water resources in the state. The survey revealed abundant amounts of groundwater suitable for agricultural irrigation in Gallatin Valley. Farmers and ranchers felt that news of this discovery might be an open invitation to immigrants and that the immigration that might occur as a response to it could threaten their future water development.[27] It was this fear, in large part, that motivated the Montana Farm Bureau Federation to become involved in advocating groundwater law reform.

In 1956 the farm bureau established a committee to examine groundwater laws of other states and to make recommendations to the Montana legislature. The resultant proposals met strong opposition from mining interests, which ultimately led to most of the proposal's defeat.

In 1960 drought and poor crops in most northern parts of the state led to greatly increased usage of groundwater for irrigation. Fearing that the water would be overexploited, citizens exerted mounting pressure on the legislature to take some action to protect groundwater from overuse. In 1961 this pressure led to the passage of legislation establishing the prior appropriation doctrine in Montana.

The new groundwater law proclaimed that "all surface, underground, flood and atmospheric waters within the boundaries of the state was the property of the state for the use of its people and its administration would be vested in an administrator." The law, for the first time, defined groundwater as "any fresh water under the surface of land including water under any surface water."[28] Anyone intending to drill a well was required to file a notice of appropriation in the county clerk's and recorder's office, and within 90 days of that filing, begin drilling. Upon completion of drilling he or she would file a notice of completion.[29] The law did not require the issuance of permits. The filing of notices was a way in which the state would keep an inventory on the use of groundwater. The law also authorized the designation of controlled groundwater areas when withdrawals exceeded recharge or threatened to do so. Such areas were also to be created if significant disputes occurred regarding priority of rights, amounts of groundwater in use by an appropriator, or priority of type of use.[30] In designated groundwater areas permits are required for all new appropriations. The designation of an area as a controlled groundwater area may be initiated either by the Department of Natural Resources and Conservation or by petition signed by at least twenty or one-fourth of the users of groundwater (whichever is the lesser number) in a groundwater area. (The actual designation is made by the Board of Natural Resources and Conservation.) The administrator can limit withdrawals or forbid the drilling of any more wells in a controlled groundwater area.[31]

Unfortunately, the 1961 law did not initially function as expected. Many people continued to drill wells without filing the required notice. Then in 1972 Montana adopted a new constitution declaring that "all existing rights to the use of any waters for any useful or beneficial purpose are hereby recognized and confirmed.[32] This led the Montana Water Resources Board to recommend the enactment of "must register" legislation in 1973, when the 1973 Montana Water Use Act was passed.[33]

The Montana Water Use Act of 1973, like the constitution, recognized all water-use rights claimed up to 1973 as valid but required that any person wishing to establish a water right after 1973 must file with the state for a permit.[34] Once established, a water right may be temporarily transferred (for a period of up to ten years and renewable for an additional ten years) to other uses, places, or persons with the approval of the Department of Natural Resources and Conservation.[35]

Several laws regulate water pollution in Montana, but only two refer specifically to groundwater contamination. Public Water Supply Law (Title 69, Chapter 49, RCM 1947) prohibits pollution of groundwater that is used as a public water supply, and Montana Code Annotated (MCA) section 85.2.205 prohibits the waste and contamination of groundwater.

The former has several deficiencies that can be exploited by violators. For example, it is difficult to determine precisely what is meant by water that is used as a public water supply, and, given the mobility of groundwater resources, today's pollution of a nonpublic groundwater supply may be tomorrow's public supply pollution. The latter also does little to address Montana's overall contamination situation. The primary focus of MCA section 85.2.205 is on proper well construction for the elimination of waste and contamination from leaking casings, fittings, pipes, and pumps.

Politics, Policy, and the Future

Although conservationists have played a major role in bringing to the attention of the public the need to conserve groundwater resources, the main actors on this issue in Montana have been the farmers and mining organizations. Farmers, ranchers, and the mining industries are a strong political force in the state.

If any other parties come into conflict with the farmers, ranchers, or industry over water rights, the farmers, ranchers, and industries will more than likely prevail. For example, in a case that involved municipalities and industry in Park and Yellowstone Counties over the extension of a moratorium on new water rights applications, the Montana Board of Natural Resources refused to accept the reservation amounts put forward by the two counties on grounds of insufficient evidence and proof to support their projections. The board allowed the industries to be issued the permits for water rights they had applied for.[36]

By the mid-1990s five areas had been designated as controlled groundwater areas: the South Pine, Bitterroot Valley, Larson Creek, Hayes Creek, Warm Springs Pond, and Yellowstone controlled groundwater areas.[37]

The groundwater policy in Montana seems best understood as one of maintaining the status quo. Montana only attempts to control new appropriations and increased withdrawals. This allows the legislature to avoid, somewhat, confrontation between water users.

Nearly all the rural population in Montana relies on groundwater for domestic and, to a lesser extent, agricultural supplies. As surface water becomes overappropriated, more communities are turning to groundwater as a source of potable water. This may result in increased competition and conflicts over groundwater resources, although clearly surface water will continue to be the primary source of water used in the state.

More may need to be done to protect the quality of Montana's groundwater in the future. Very little has taken place to date to prevent ground-water pollution. Contamination cannot be easily reversed, and the problems of contamination will affect the state not for a few years but for generations. With this in mind, the legislature placed an initiative to strengthen water quality standards on the ballot in 1996. The initiative, however, came to be perceived as an attack on mining and was defeated (which is another example of the strength of mining interests in the state).[38]

This is the time for Montana to lay down the groundwork for the preservation and conservation of its groundwater resources if it is to avoid the problems that many other states are experiencing. Montana is fortunate in that—unlike many states that have been forced to deal with quality and supply problems after extreme damage has been done—as of the mid-1990s it did not have serious overdrafting or pollution problems. Montana can act now to prevent future damage.

9 Utah

Mormon settlers in Utah were among the first people to employ wide-spread use of irrigation in the West. Utah has a long tradition of agricultural water use. As the state relies upon the doctrine of prior appropriation to determine who holds title to water rights, irrigators hold title to a great deal of the state's water supply. Agricultural production was once crucial to the existence of the early settlers, but farming has declined in importance for the state as a whole. While a significant number of people continue to rely on agriculture as a means of support, the majority of the population lives in urban areas and draws income from nonfarm operations. Urban centers are the fastest-growing areas in the state and will require more water for both public supply and urban-based industries. Given the changes in Utah's economy and the changes in the population, it becomes apparent that changes in the use of water will have to be made. As surface water is, for the most part, fully appropriated, attention will likely focus on groundwater. However, as groundwater levels continue to decline (as they are in some areas), it will become apparent that water supplies are not unlimited and that water will have to be directed to where it will most benefit the people in the state. Since the majority of the population and the bulk of the state's economy is municipally based, this means that water will have to be made available for urban use. Agriculture uses the most water yet contributes the least to the state's economy and employs relatively few people. Conflict between irrigators (who tend to be the prior appropriators) and municipal water users will likely emerge. However, given the shift in economy and population over the years, it is likely that irrigators will lose. Urban centers will continue to grow and will obtain the water necessary to sustain their populations, even if this means a decline in the state's traditional means of support.

Physical Description

Utah varies considerably in terms of its hydrologic composition. The eastern two-thirds of the state is made up of the Rocky Mountains in the north and the Colorado Plateau in the south and central parts of the state. The western third of Utah is part of the Great Basin and is enclosed by mountains on the north, east, and west. The Colorado Plateau area contains most of Utah's energy resources.

Precipitation in Utah ranges from around 5 inches per year on the Great Salt Lake Desert to over 40 inches in the Uinta Mountains and the Wasatch Plateau. Groundwater recharge is less than 2 percent of precipitation in several basins in the western part of the state. Along the west side of the Wasatch Range recharge exceeds 20 percent of precipitation.[1] Major sources of surface water include the Bear, Weber, Jordan, Sevier, Colorado, San Juan, Ogden, Virgin, and Green Rivers.

Demographics

As of 1 July 1995 the resident state population of Utah was estimated to be 1,951,408.[2] Between 1950 and 1995 the population increased by 183.2 percent, which is well above the national average of 73.6 percent for the same period.[3] Utah's growth has primarily affected urban areas, as the percentage of the population residing in urban areas versus rural settings has changed significantly. In 1960 approximately 74.9 percent of the population resided in urban areas.[4] As of 1990 approximately 87 percent (some 1.5 million people) of the state's population could be found living in urban settings.[5]

While agriculture employs approximately 17,600 people in the state of Utah, over 97 percent of the civilian population employed in the state earn wages through nonfarm operations.[6] The largest single categories of employment in Utah are manufacturing, services, and wholesale and retail trade.[7]

While irrigation remains the largest single use of both surface water and groundwater in Utah, the number of farms and the acreage devoted to agriculture have declined over the years. This is mostly likely due to the urbanization of the state and to the growth of other more profitable industries. In 1959 there were approximately 18,000 farms in the state covering some 12,689,000 acres.[8] In 1990 the number of farms in the state was roughly 13,000, and the number of acres of land devoted to farming was just under 11 million.[9] Declines in the acreage devoted to agriculture are expected to continue. A tremendous amount of growth in the state is taking place in areas that have traditionally been agricultural. Urban encroachment onto agricultural land has been occurring (and will continue to occur) in Salt Lake, Davis, Weber, Box Elder, and Utah Counties.[10] Compared to other industries, the contribution that farming and farm services make to the gross state product of Utah is quite small. As of the mid-1990s agriculture contributed approximately 1.7 percent of the gross state product, the service industry contributed roughly 17.5 percent, manufacturing contributed 15.4 percent, and finance, insurance, and real estate combined contributed 14.6 percent to the gross state product.[11]

Water Use

An important source of water, particularly for domestic purposes, groundwater accounts for approximately 28 percent of the total amount of fresh water consumed in Utah on an annual basis. Of this amount approximately 31 percent is used for public supply, 52 percent is used in irrigation, roughly 3 percent is used for rural domestic consumption and livestock, and 8 percent is withdrawn by industry for its own use.[12] Many people within the state are dependent upon groundwater for their drinking water. In addition to supplying rural domestic needs, groundwater is either a primary or a supplementary source for public supply. Of the 414 community water supplies in the state, only 21 use surface water exclusively.[13] Sixty percent of the water used for public supply in Utah comes from wells or springs.

Although small quantities of groundwater may be obtained from small wells throughout much of Utah, the areas of major groundwater development and the basins capable of producing groundwater suitable both in terms of quantity and of quality for irrigation, public supply, or industrial use generally run north and south along the confluence of the Great Basin and Colorado Plateau and are associated with the river systems in the region. There are thirteen major basins in this area. Pumpage from these basins accounts for more than 85 percent of the groundwater withdrawn in Utah. In eleven of the basins irrigation is the principal use of groundwater, in some cases accounting for more than 95 percent of the total annual amount of water withdrawn. Roughly 98 percent of the wells in Utah draw their water from unconsolidated rock formations.[14]

Problems

Overdrafting

Groundwater from artesian wells has been used to irrigate in Utah since shortly after the state was settled in 1847. As in the rest of the West, however, large-scale development of groundwater resources came about in the early twentieth century and coincided with technological advances in pump design and capacity. During the late 1940s and early 1950s overdrafting of groundwater basins began in several parts of the state, and this trend has carried through to the 1990s.[15] From March 1963 to March 1993 water-level declines were measured in most parts of eleven of Utah's sixteen major groundwater areas. For example, from 1963 to 1993 declines of groundwater levels in excess of 40 feet were measured west of Ogden.[16] From 1988 to 1993 declines in excess of 20 feet were recorded in many parts of the state, with a decline of 62.4 feet being recorded north of Levan in the Juab Valley.[17] Withdrawals generally increased significantly until the early 1970s, whereupon withdrawals for irrigation began to fluctuate in response to the amount of rainfall and the availability of surface water. Restrictions have been placed on withdrawals in several groundwater basins in southwestern Utah. The negative effects associated with overdrafting include increased pumping costs (which will lead to higher prices for municipal water users), decreased water quality, and some land subsidence in southwestern Utah.[18]

Pollution

The natural leaching of dissolved salts is the most widespread groundwater-quality problem in Utah.[19] More specific groundwater pollution problems include hazardous waste sites, other waste-impoundment sites, storage tanks (both above and below ground), and animal feedlots.

Large concentrations of dissolved minerals and low-level radioactivity have been found about three miles south of Salt Lake City (the radioactivity is believed to be coming from a nearby uranium tailings–storage facility). The aquifer involved is used for both public supply and industrial purposes in Salt Lake County. In addition, an unlined sludge pit used for disposal of petroleum waste in Salt Lake City has been included for cleanup in the EPA's national priorities list of hazardous waste sites.[20] Waste tailings and smelter slag represent the areas of greatest concern for groundwater quality in the state of Utah. This is because of the number of contamination sources, the health risk presented by this type of contaminant, the contaminant's proximity to drinking-water sources, and the size of the populations that are at risk from the contamination.[21]

For a variety of reasons, including leaking and abandoned storage tanks, pollution from gasoline has been a problem in Salt Lake City. The problem is compounded by the fact that the water table beneath the city is high and mobile. In 1978 firefighters pumped gasoline out of Welfare Square in the city, and in the fall of 1977 they battled a gasoline fire on the Jordan River.[22] To date approximately twenty-one hundred leaking underground storage tanks have been identified in the state, with roughly one-third of them being linked to confirmed groundwater contamination. The majority of the leaking storage tanks have been found in Salt Lake and Utah Counties—the two most heavily populated counties in the state.[23] Petroleum products are the most common source of volatile organic chemicals (VOCs), which have often been found to be carcinogenic. In addition to the potential health problems presented by petroleum products, this type of contaminant is one of the most difficult and costly to clean up.

Finally, pollution associated with feedlots for hog and poultry farms have in some areas led to water-quality problems caused by bacteria, viruses, and nitrates.[24] While state officials view nitrates as a medium-level priority, they do pose a concern because of the areal extent of contamination and the location of pollution sources relative to drinking-water sources. Areas that could be adversely affected by nitrate contamination are, however, localized and are not a statewide problem.[25]

Overall, groundwater pollution was not a widespread problem in Utah as of the mid-1990s. This was due to precipitation and to the availability of surface water. However, many of the localized problems are in heavily populated areas. As municipalities become more dependent upon groundwater for growth and development, it will likely become a more important source of public water for these areas. What are now seen as isolated problems might have a wider impact in the future.

Law

In Utah "all waters . . . whether above or under the ground" are public property.[26] With one exception, noted below, groundwater in Utah is administered via a permit system on a prior appropriation basis by the Utah state engineer. The permit procedure for appropriating groundwater has been part of Utah water law since 1935. The exception to the prior appropriation doctrine in Utah groundwater law concerns diffused water near the surface of the soil. Such waters, if they are not held or controlled by artificial diversion or otherwise traceable to adjacent lands, are considered part of the soil and not subject to appropriation. However, if such water is taken from the soil and reapplied to the land or used for other purposes, then an appropriation right must be acquired.[27]

The procedure for acquiring a right to unappropriated water in Utah is the same regardless of the source of water involved. Applications are filed with the state engineer indicating the source of the water and the use to which it will be put.[28] In cases where there is adequate water to satisfy all claims, withdrawal permits are routinely granted. However, both surface water and groundwater have been fully allocated in many parts of Utah. The state engineer is authorized to distribute existing supply according to the priority of the rights involved and, in the same vein, to determine whether there is adequate water available to supply each existing claim (discussed below). In 1976 the state engineer was given the flexibility to issue fixed-time permits in appropriate cases. Previously, appropriation rights were nearly always granted in perpetuity.[29]

The state engineer also has the authority to halt the waste of water and to take measures to prevent groundwater pollution or contamination, to oversee and promulgate regulations for well drillers, and to issue permits for drilling (on an annual basis) to individuals or companies desiring to drill wells. The engineer also has the power to require the repair of wells and the construction of facilities.[30]

As is common in prior appropriation states, in Utah water may be appropriated only for some beneficial use. Although many court decisions in western states (including Utah) have been unclear as to what constitutes beneficial use, the state has prioritized different types of beneficial uses that are to be recognized in times of shortage.[31] The Utah Code section 73-3-21 reads in part: "in times of scarcity, while priority of appropriations shall give the better right as between those using water for the same purpose, the use for domestic purposes, without unnecessary waste, shall have preference over use for all other purposes, and [use] for agricultural purposes shall have preference over use for any other purposes except domestic use."[32]

As is common throughout the West, the waste of water is a nonbeneficial use and is prohibited.

Water rights are fully transferable in Utah. If ownership of a water right is transferred, and if it does not involve a change in the point of diversion, place, or nature of use the transfer may be accomplished without the approval of the state engineer.[33] If a modification to the water right will result from a transfer, a change application must be filed and approved by the state engineer. Generally such applications will be approved provided that the vested rights of existing appropriators are not affected and that the change in use meets the guidelines statutorily established for original applications.[34] The right to water may or may not be conveyed with the title to the land on which the water originates.[35]

Although water rights in Utah may be lost either as a result of nonuse or as a result of abandonment after the statutory five-year period, water rights may not be acquired in the state by virtue of adverse use or adverse possession.[36]

The Utah codes provide for the annual appointment of water commissioners by the state engineer. Commissioners are authorized to distribute water from sources within the state. Water commissioners are appointed when, in the judgment of the state engineer or the district court, they are necessary for the administration of Utah's water-rights system. The code also provides for the consultation of the engineer with water users within an area prior to his or her appointing the commissioner.[37] If it is decided that there is inadequate groundwater available for those claiming it, the state engineer is authorized to hold a hearing to determine whether or not there is enough water to satisfy the existing claims. Groundwater users may also petition the state engineer for a hearing. In the event that such hearings suggest that there is inadequate water to supply existing claims, the state engineer (or, at his or her direction, one or more of the water commissioners) may divide the waters available among the existing claimants in accordance with their relative priority.[38]

Politics, Policy, and the Future

It appears that as of the mid-1990s the state of Utah was aware of its groundwater supply problems, but overdrafting continues in many areas. The state will undoubtedly face groundwater-management problems in future decades. Part of the Colorado Basin in Utah contains large amounts of coal, oil shale, and tar sand. Eventually, when market conditions are right, there will certainly be pressure to develop these resources, and water will be necessary to effect that development. Furthermore, as surface water is, for the most part, fully appropriated, groundwater will be needed to facilitate the growth of urban populations and urban-based industries. As of the mid-1990s areas of rapid growth in Utah included Salt Lake, Davis, Weber, Box Elder, Utah, Washington, Summit, and Wasatch Counties.[39]

Although Utah water law does have provisions for the sale and transfer of rights, there are some questions about possible legal obstacles to interbasin exchanges in transfers of water.[40] This suggests that water-use patterns within basins with large urban populations will have to change. To the extent that interbasin transfers are not necessary, the marketability of water rights in Utah will undoubtedly, as they have in states with similar transfer guidelines, mitigate much of the conflict over future groundwater use that might otherwise develop. Irrigators will likely be pressured into accepting compensation for their rights in order to allow for urban growth and to slow the depletion of groundwater resources.

We conclude, therefore, that a lack of groundwater resources in Utah is not likely to affect growth or development in any significant way in the foreseeable future. What shortages occur will likely be satisfied through transfers or sales of water or of land and water. Given the steady decline of many aquifers and the fairly rapid population increases that are occurring in the state, conversion of water use is inevitable. Relying on the development of new groundwater supplies for supporting the growing population of the state would lead to an unsustainable future. Much of the water obtained through the purchase of agricultural land and water rights is surface water—a sustainable source. In the future we expect agricultural activity in the state to decline even further as municipalities and industries purchase the rights to water. Additional surface water will be provided by the Central Utah Project (CUP). While the project was originally designed to provide water for agriculture, plans for developing irrigation water have been abandoned. As of the mid-1990s the bulk of the water from the CUP was being diverted for municipal and industrial use (similar to the Central Arizona Project situation in Arizona). The socioeconomic composition of the state has been transformed from rural-agricultural to urban-industrial. Water distribution will undergo a similar transformation. This change in water use will have to occur if the state is to sustain its population into the future. The only questions are those of when such changes will occur and what condition aquifers will be in by the time the conversions take place.

10 Wyoming

Wyoming, like most states in the West, follows the doctrine of prior appropriation. In Wyoming prior appropriation applies to both surface water and groundwater. The state has a long history of livestock and agricultural activity, which means that irrigators hold title to much of the water currently being used. Most of the agricultural irrigation activity is located in the southeastern quarter of the state, where the majority of the municipal growth has occurred in recent years. As a result, surface water in this area is fully appropriated, and groundwater supplies are continuously being drawn down. As the cities of Laramie, Casper, and Cheyenne continue to grow, conflicts will no doubt arise between municipal water users and irrigators. Given that municipalities are dependent upon groundwater for public supply and that supplies are currently strained, irrigators will have to become more efficient in their use of both surface water and groundwater, or municipalities will have to purchase water rights from irrigators. Current needs are being met partially through overdrafting, which is not sustainable. It appears that in the long run, unless water is imported from other areas in the state or surface-water storage is developed, a shift in water distribution that will enable municipalities to adequately sustain their populations will be necessary.

Physical Description

"In recent years it has become obvious that if Wyoming is going to continue its physical and economical growth, ground water must be drawn on increasingly," a geologist in the Wyoming state engineer's office wrote in 1948. His words still hold true today.[1]

Most people who visit Wyoming remember the Rocky Mountains and particularly Grand Teton and Yellowstone National Parks. In fact, most of Wyoming is made up of the western Great Plains (comprising the eastern third of the state) and the Wyoming Basin (comprising the central and south-central third of the state). The Rocky Mountain region lies in the western and the northwestern portion of the state. Classified as a semi-arid state, Wyoming receives, on average, only 15 inches of precipitation annually. This varies from around 30 inches per year in the mountains of western Wyoming to 10 inches per year in the arid basins.

Demographics

As of 1 July 1995 the resident state population of Wyoming was estimated to be 480,184, making it the least populated state in the nation.[2] The population of the state remained small despite an increase of 65.2 percent between 1950 and 1995 (just below the national average of 73.6 percent).[3] During recent years urban areas in Wyoming have grown faster than rural ones. In 1960 roughly 56 percent of Wyoming's population resided in urban areas, while by 1990 approximately 65 percent of the population could be considered urban.[4] With 35 percent of the population residing in rural areas, the state remains one of the most rural in the nation.

While Wyoming is largely rural, the majority of people employed in the state (roughly 94 percent) earn wages through nonfarm operations. The 6 percent of the population that is dependent upon agriculture represents over twelve thousand people.[5] The primary employing industries in the state are services, wholesale and retail trade, mining, and construction.[6]

Irrigation is the largest user of both surface water and groundwater in Wyoming; however, the number of farms and the acreage devoted to agricultural use have declined over the years. In 1959 there were roughly 10,000 farms in the state covering 36,200,00 acres.[7] In 1993 there were approximately 9,000 farms in the state covering around 35 million acres.[8] Wyoming continues to have a high average number of acres per farm, ranking second in the nation behind Arizona. Despite farm size, numbers of people employed, and amount of water used, agriculture contributes only 3.6 percent of the Wyoming gross state product. Other industries such as mining; transportation and public utilities; and finance, insurance, and real estate contribute 31.4 percent, 17.6 percent, and 10.8 percent, respectively.[9]

Water Use

Much of the water originating in or flowing through Wyoming belongs to downstream users by virtue of interstate compacts or court decisions. Although in the mid-1990s groundwater provided around 5 percent of the water used in the state, the importance of groundwater is increasing, and in many parts of Wyoming dependency upon groundwater is almost total. Sixty-two percent of the groundwater used in the state is used for irrigation, 21 percent is for industrial and mining purposes, 11 percent is for public supply purposes, and 6 percent is for rural domestic and livestock purposes.[10] Surface water is employed in 96 percent of the irrigation that takes place in Wyoming (major river systems include the Green, North Platte, Powder, Snake, and Belle Fourche). These figures obscure somewhat the importance of groundwater for domestic consumption, particularly on the municipal level. The Wyoming state engineer's office estimates that 80 percent of Wyoming's population is dependent to a large degree upon groundwater for its drinking water.[11] Fifteen percent of the state's municipalities are dependent on some combination of groundwater and surface water for their supplies, and only 10 percent of municipal water suppliers use no groundwater whatsoever.

Wyoming has water for further development; however, as is the case with many states in the West, available water is not located where it is most needed. In general, available water can be found in the western part of the state, while the majority of the population resides in the eastern portion. In addition, the southeastern quarter of the state is home to most of the irrigated agriculture. Roughly two-thirds of Wyoming's 230,000 acres of land irrigated with groundwater lie in the southeast quarter of the state. One-third of the irrigated land in the state is inside three groundwater-control areas (discussed below). In the east, surface water is fully appropriated, and there is little groundwater available for further development. As of the mid-1990s there was not enough water to sustain *current* demand into the future, particularly in the southeastern quarter of the state. Should the population increase in this area (as it is likely to do given the fact that the area is one of the few in the state that is growing), water-supply problems will intensify.

As of the mid-1990s Casper's population was not rising rapidly, and growth of the state as a whole was stagnant, in large part because of the domestic energy market. Thus, past projections for growth and water needs will need to be revised. These projections do, however, illustrate the potential problems that might arise if the state were to experience rapid growth in the future. A study prepared for the Wyoming Water Development Commission in 1984 found that, given projected growth and demands, twenty-five communities in southeast Wyoming would need varying amounts of additional water over the next twenty to fifty years. The study found that by the year 2030, during drought years the southeastern communities could use somewhere between 53,000 and 67,000 acre-feet a year in additional supply. During wet years it was estimated that by 2030 the communities could use an additional 38,000 acre-feet per year in supply. It was estimated that Casper could want 26,000 acre-feet per year by 2030 during dry and wet years.[12] Once again, these figures were based on growth projections that did not materialize, and they do not reflect the current water situation. They are included to give the reader an idea of the state's growth potential, a potential that has a good chance of being realized when the domestic energy market eventually improves.

Demands for groundwater will undoubtedly increase in the future. In the mid-1990s the state engineer was processing approximately five thousand applications for groundwater permits each year.[13]

Problems

Overdrafting
The most significant groundwater overdrafting in Wyoming has occurred in the southeastern part of the state, notably in Laramie County. In this county water tables have been dropping since the 1970s and the state engineer's office estimated in 1981 that, assuming that the rate at which withdrawal was then occurring were to continue, the water table in the region would drop 40 feet in a period of twenty years.[14] In an attempt to remedy the problem, the Wyoming state engineer addresses additional groundwater development on a site-specific basis in areas of the county where heavy groundwater pumping occurs. (Water for stock watering and

domestic purposes is exempted.) Current water levels continue to decline from a few inches to as much as 3 feet per year in some parts of Laramie County.[15] Thus, though the rate of depletion has slowed, overdrafting continues. As water levels decline, pumping becomes more expensive, reducing profits for agriculture and increasing the rates municipal water users have to pay for their water.

Groundwater levels are also declining in northern Goshen and central Platte Counties. Groundwater control areas (a description of which appears below) have been created in Laramie, Platte, and Goshen Counties.[16] Given the importance of groundwater for public drinking water and for agricultural activity, serious water-level decreases are a cause for concern because water shortages could lead to socioeconomic disruption in the future.

Pollution

The groundwater in Wyoming is generally of good quality; however, there are some aquifers in the state that contain naturally high levels of fluoride, radionuclides, and selenium. For example, the Wyoming DEQ has found high levels of selenium in localized areas of Natrona, Albany, and Fremont Counties and has detected naturally occurring high levels of radionuclides in parts of Fremont County. High levels of fluoride have been detected in many counties throughout Wyoming, including Natrona, which has the second-highest population in the state.[17] In large doses, fluoride and selenium can lead to cancer or leukemia, and fluoride (in large doses) has been linked to nervous system, organ, and chromosomal damage.

Most of the localized contamination problems occurring in Wyoming groundwater are the result of human influence. As of 1994 there were sixty-five community public water supplies that had been affected and that contained one or more regulated contaminant in excess of EPA drinking water standards.[18] The most pressing contamination problems come from fertilizer applications, shallow injection wells, and underground storage tanks. The Wyoming Department of Environmental Quality (DEQ) has designated these three areas as the highest priorities because of the number of contamination sources they contain and because of the location of these sources relative to groundwater used as drinking water.[19]

Fertilizer is a major source of nitrate contamination. Exposure to high levels of nitrates can lead to cancer and is the cause of methemoglobemia (blue-baby disease). In 1988 high levels of nitrates in the town of Torrington led to the development of a contingency plan wherein bottled water would be provided for pregnant women and infants under one year of age. In 1991 Torrington became the first Wyoming recipient of an EPA grant for the development and implementation of a community wellhead protection program.[20] Underground storage tanks pose a potential threat to the groundwater supply of Wyoming because of the severity of petroleum contamination. In addition to being carcinogenic, petroleum products are among the most difficult and costly contaminants to remove from a groundwater source once they have entered an aquifer.

While fertilizer applications, injection wells, and underground storage tanks have been given priority over other sources of contamination, this does not mean that other sources will not become a problem in the future. For example, the use of pesticides associated with agricultural practices poses the potential for future groundwater contamination. As of the mid-1990s pesticides had already been detected in the groundwater of Natrona, Fremont, Goshen, Crook, Platte, Weston, and Laramie Counties.[21] Laramie County is the most populous county in the state. While most pesticide levels are currently below those determined by the EPA to make water unsafe for drinking, the potential for further groundwater degradation does exist.

Wyoming has one of the most comprehensive water-pollution management systems in the West. The Wyoming groundwater classifications system adopted in April 1982 applies "standards to protect water quality. Groundwaters of the state are classified by use, and by ambient water quality."[22]

Nonindustrial water falls into one of four classes:

1. Class I—suitable for domestic use
2. Class II—suitable for agricultural use where all other conditions (i.e., soil) are adequate
3. Class III—suitable for livestock and
4. Class special (a)—suitable for fish and aquatic life

Underground waters in Class I, Class II, Class III, or Class special (a) above should not contain biological, hazardous, or toxic waste above those amounts deemed allowable by the EPA.[23] The further breakdown of water classifications are as follows:

5. Class IV—suitable for industries; quality standards vary with the type of industry

6. Class V—groundwater closely associated with hydrocarbon deposits or other minerals or groundwater to be used for geothermal purposes and

7. Class VI—groundwater is unsuitable for any use

Discharges into Class IV groundwaters (suitable for industry) are allowed as long as the water remains fit for industrial use. Class IV groundwater basins are further subdivided into waters with less than 10,000 milligrams/l total dissolved solids, and waters with more than 10,000 milligrams/l total dissolved solids, depending on the type of industrial use. Discharges into Class V groundwater areas are allowed for the purpose of recovering the hydrocarbon or geothermal resources contained therein.

Wyoming's groundwater pollution laws are administered by the state's DEQ.[24] Discharges into groundwater basins and the application of most groundwater-quality-threatening materials to land are regulated via a permit system administered by the director of the DEQ. The director is appointed by and serves by the pleasure of the governor. The department has three divisions—an air division, a land division, and a water-quality division. The Wyoming Code gives the director a great deal of latitude in developing regulations for protecting Wyoming's groundwater quality.[25] Consistent with the classification scheme outlined above, the director has developed a permit system to regulate the type and amount of substances that are allowed in groundwater depending on the purpose for which the water will be used.

Decisions, rules, and regulations made by the DEQ may be appealed to a seven-member Wyoming Environmental Quality Council. This quasi-judicial body of seven private citizens appointed for four-year terms meets at least eight times a year in various parts of the state to hear appeals.[26]

Law

The Wyoming constitution provides the basic outlines of Wyoming water law. Article 8, section 1 reads in part "the water of all natural streams, springs, lakes or other collection of still water, within the boundaries of the state, are hereby declared to be the property of the state." Section 3 reads, "priority of appropriation for beneficial uses shall give the better right."

In 1919 the Wyoming Supreme Court in *Hunt v. Laramie* found that groundwater was owned by the owner of the land and was not subject to appropriation.[27] The court did not address the issue of a beneficial use requirement. In 1940 in *Binning v. Miller* the court reaffirmed this decision in part, finding that seepage waters were percolating waters and part of the soil.[28] The Wyoming legislature first addressed groundwater law in 1945. In 1947 the legislature largely replaced the 1945 law with more comprehensive legislation. The 1947 legislation created a prior appropriation system for groundwater that exempted domestic and stock uses and provided for registration system with the state engineer. A permit process was not part of the procedure.[29]

Then in 1957 the legislature repealed and replaced the 1945 and 1947 laws. The 1957 law added a permit requirement to the appropriation system. For wells drilled prior to 1 April 1947 one could establish the priority date by filing a statement with the state engineer on or before 31 December 1957. Individuals claiming a right acquired after 1 April 1947 had to register their well with the state engineer prior to 1 March 1958 (the effective date of the new law). For rights established after 1 March 1958 the priority of the right was set as the date on which the application for the permit to drill the well was received in the state engineer's office. The 1957 act directed the state engineer to issue a permit for any application for groundwater in areas not designated as a control area (discussed below). In 1969 an amendment provided that the state engineer may deny an application if he or she should find that the permit would not be in the "public interest." Such denial is subject to the review of the Wyoming Board of Control (discussed below).

The 1957 legislation also provided for the creation of groundwater-control areas. A control area is designated by the Wyoming Board of Control upon its receipt of information supplied by the state engineer whenever one of the following conditions is met:[30]

1. the use of underground water is approaching a use equal to the current recharge rate;
2. groundwater levels are declining or have declined excessively;
3. conflicts between users are occurring or foreseeable;
4. the waste of water is occurring or may occur; or
5. other conditions exist that may require regulation for the protection of the public interest.

The significance of the designation of a groundwater-control area is that it provides the state engineer with the authority to "without hearings or other proceedings, refuse to grant permits for the drilling of any wells within the control area." In addition, the state engineer may either on his or her own motion or after being petitioned cause hearings to be held to determine the adequacy of groundwaters within a control area for the needs of all appropriators in the area. After such a hearing the engineer may decide to (1) close the critical area for further appropriation; (2) determine the total withdrawals for every day, month, or year; (3) order junior rights holders to reduce their withdrawals; (4) require some system of rotation of withdrawal.[31] The law also provides for the creation of five-member control-area advisory boards. These boards are designed to facilitate the task of the state engineer by providing local input.[32]

As of 1996 control areas had been established for irrigated areas in Laramie and Platte Counties and at Prairie Center in northwest Goshen County.[33] In administering Wyoming's appropriation system preference is given for stock or for domestic water use (where the area to be irrigated does not exceed one acre or the flow 25 gallons per minute) regardless of the dates of priority involved.[34]

As mentioned above, the state engineer has extensive powers to develop rules and regulations to carry out his or her authority. These powers include the power to require reports from well drillers and annual reports from pumpers; the power to establish standards for well construction, spacing, and distribution (in control areas); and the power to require the capping of wells to prevent waste or the sealing of wells to prevent pollution.[35]

Beneficial uses in Wyoming are those traditionally found in most states and include waters needed for instream flows.

The Wyoming Board of Control administers water rights and distribution of water. Created by the state constitution, the board consists of the state engineer as president and the superintendents of the four water divisions in the state.[36] The board has responsibility for the supervision of the waters of the state and for their appropriation, distribution, and diversion.

Politics, Policy, and the Future

In the past in Wyoming there seemed to be a general fear of speculation in water rights. Such speculation, or the fear of it, was usually associated with energy development.[37] Often this attitude was tied to a fear that water that could be used for municipal or agricultural purposes would be taken for energy development. As of the mid-1990s, however, this fear had been partially laid to rest. The current state of the domestic energy market is such that use of major quantities of water in the widespread development of petroleum and uranium has not occurred. Additionally, the water-intensive coal conversion plants that many believed were going to enter into the state never materialized. Instead, much of the coal originating in Wyoming is exported out of state for conversion. However, should the energy market rebound, energy operations may reenter the state and compete for water.

In the meantime attention should focus on the current water situation and the very real possibility that conflict between irrigators and municipalities will arise. As of the mid-1990s such conflict had been avoided through water leasing. Irrigators who are able to make efficient use of their water can lease surplus water without having to relinquish any portion of their entitlement. The state engineer's office feels that this arrangement will allow municipal needs to be met well into the future without any significant change in the current water-rights structure.[38] However, such an assumption is based on the fact that the growth of the state has slowed in recent years. Should the economy of the state rebound, encouraging more people to migrate to Wyoming, the municipalities in question might require more than the irrigators are willing to give. If such a situation occurs the state might have to examine the possibility of transporting water from other portions of the state where supplies have not been fully utilized.

Whatever the future holds for Wyoming groundwater use, the state will be in a good position, in terms of the intelligence available, to deal with it. In the course of doing research for this book, the authors found few states that had examined their water resource problems as carefully as had Wyoming. In 1967 the Wyoming legislature authorized the state engineer to begin a state water-planning program.[39] Since that time a great deal of information has been generated. In 1981 the legislature authorized the water development commission to grant up to 3 million dollars to cities and towns for the purpose of finding groundwater sources and determining the feasibility of using these sources. As of the mid-1990s over fifty grants had been awarded under the program, and now cities are able to approach the Wyoming Water Development Commission directly for such funding.[40] Through these studies the state has been able to gather useful data regarding groundwater supply and conditions. While there is currently no long-term solution to the potential problems that exist in the southeastern portion of the state, Wyoming is in a better position with regard to water than are many other states in the West. The state has a good understanding of where supply and contamination problems exist and has yet to experience any actual conflict between existing water users. Furthermore, the population of the state is growing much more slowly than is that of many other states, which eliminates the need for immediate action. (This is not to say that no action needs to be taken at all, however.) Finally Wyoming, unlike many other states in the West, has water that has yet to be developed. While this water is not in the areas where it is needed, it exists nonetheless, making water diversion a viable option.

GREAT PLAINS REGION

Once known as the Great American Desert, the Great Plains are an immense physiographic province of North America. Parts of ten states are within the Great Plains proper; however, for our purposes we will group together North Dakota, South Dakota, Nebraska, and Kansas. Other states, such as Montana, Kansas, Colorado (Rocky Mountain region), Oklahoma, Texas, and New Mexico (Southwest) have more in common with other regions. The fact that these other states have been placed elsewhere does not diminish the importance of their linkage to the Great Plains (and to its primary aquifer — the Ogallala).

The Great Plains have cold winters, warm summers, sudden changes in temperature, and a tremendous amount of wind. They also experience low humidity and low precipitation. The major source of moisture in the Great Plains is the Gulf of Mexico. However, moisture from the gulf falls off to the north and west, leaving the plains with varying amounts of rain/snowfall. Thus the northern plains receive approximately 12 to 15 inches per year, while the southern plains receive between 15 to 25 inches. The eastern border in Nebraska receives in excess of 25 inches, while the western portion of the Great Plains in Montana often receives less than 15 inches of precipitation annually.

Much of the Great Plains has remained agricultural over the years, with eight of the leading U.S. wheat states located within or around the region. Much of this agricultural production, however, has been facilitated through overdraft in the Ogallala Aquifer. A dropping water table has increased the costs of farming in many areas, and the need for larger farms and ranches to produce viable economic units has led to heavy migration toward urban centers.

Like those of other states in this study, water managers in the Great Plains Region often have to face problems of changing demographics and the way this change conflicts with established social and political practice.

11 Kansas

Kansas has traditionally been an agricultural state, and irrigators there have always held a great deal of political clout. Past practices of allowing extensive groundwater mining have been the result of the agricultural influence on water-allocation and management decisions. As of the mid-1990s, however, many areas in the state had started moving away from the conscious depletion of groundwater resources toward managing these resources on a safe-yield basis. This change can be attributed to a shift in the economy of Kansas away from agriculture toward manufacturing and to an increase in the cost of pumping groundwater that has come about as the result of past overdrafting. Given the state's reliance on ground-water, and the increase in the number of people moving into urban areas, water rights will need to be transferred to those areas in the state where the resource will do the most social and economic good. This will mean a transfer, in some areas, from irrigation to municipal use. In areas where water levels have declined such transfers may occur naturally as pumping costs increase and municipal users become the only ones who can afford the costs of withdrawal.

Physical Description

Hydrologically and geographically Kansas is best understood as consisting of two regions. The eastern part of the state has more surface water. The western part is characterized by flat plains and rolling hills underlain by groundwater aquifers. The population of Kansas was approximately 70 percent urban as of 1990, with most of this population concentrated in the eastern part of the state and dependent upon surface water stored in reservoirs. Groundwater use is concentrated in the western part of the state, primarily in the Ogallala Aquifer. Precipitation in Kansas ranges from 16 inches per year in parts of the west to 40 inches in the east. Much of the estimated 400 million acre-feet of groundwater in storage in the state is in western Kansas.

Although the economy of Kansas has been dominated by agricultural production throughout most of the state's history, in recent years manufacturing production has outpaced agricultural production in terms of the value of goods produced. Nevertheless Kansas remains one of the leading agricultural states in the country (ranking ninth in terms of total farm receipts).[1]

Demographics

As of 1 July 1995 the resident state population of Kansas was estimated to be 2,655,328.[2] Between 1950 and 1995 the population increased by 82.8 percent, which was slightly above the national average population increase of 73.6 percent over the same period.[3] The state's urban areas have grown more than its rural ones. In 1960 approximately 60 percent of the population of Kansas resided in urban areas, while in 1990 urban dwellers made up almost 70 percent of the state's inhabitants.[4] Despite the trend toward urbanization in the state, urban encroachment of agricultural land has been limited. As of the mid-1990s the only area experiencing urban encroachment has been the one around Wichita. Such conversion from irrigated to municipal land around Wichita is likely to continue well into the twenty-first century.

While Kansas was once predominantly an agricultural state, manufacturing has surpassed farming in terms of both the number of persons employed and the economic contribution that it makes to the gross state product. However, approximately 6 percent of Kansas's population (close to sixty-one thousand people) continue to rely on agriculture for income. The primary employing industries in Kansas are manufacturing, services, and wholesale and retail trade.[5]

Agriculture is the single largest user of groundwater in Kansas despite the fact that it has lost ground vis-à-vis manufacturing and that the number of farms and total acreage devoted to farm use have declined over the years. In 1959 there were some 104,000 farms in the state covering over 50 million acres.[6] In 1993 there were 65,000 farms in Kansas, and the number of acres devoted to agricultural use was approximately 48 million.[7] As of the mid-1990s the state's agricultural production, while it employed approximately sixty-one thousand persons, contributed only about 5 percent to the gross state product. The principle industries (in terms of contribution to the gross state product) in Kansas are manufacturing, which contributes approximately 18.8 percent; finance, insurance, and real estate; which contribute roughly 14.3 percent, and service industries, which contribute about 14 percent.[8]

Water Use

Kansas is heavily dependent on groundwater. Seventy-one percent of the state's water withdrawn from all sources comes from the ground. Ninety-five percent of all water used for irrigation in Kansas comes from the ground, and 92 percent of the groundwater withdrawn is used for irrigation. Public supply systems statewide use roughly equal amounts of groundwater and surface water.[9] Overdrafting in the Ogallala groundwater basin in Kansas has been taking place for several decades and, as of the mid-1990s, had led to declines in water levels of up to 3 feet a year in some areas.[10] In some parts of Kansas the saturated thickness of the Ogallala Aquifer has decreased by as much as 50 percent from the period prior to its development to the present, resulting in reduced well yields and increased pumping costs.[11]

The number of irrigation wells in the Ogallala area in western Kansas peaked at 16,000 in 1977 and has stayed close to that level ever since. During the 1970s policymakers in the state realized that groundwater resources had to be managed. The result of water-management in the state was that existing water uses were allowed to continue, but new uses were largely curtailed in areas of widespread overdraft. In the early 1980s the Kansas Water Office projected substantial decreases in the number of irrigation wells in the Ogallala area because of the increased cost of pumping water at greater depths. The projected decrease has not occurred. As of the mid-1990s there were approximately 15,876 irrigation wells in the Ogallala area and over 30,000 irrigation wells statewide.[12]

While the number of wells in selected areas has remained constant for quite some time, many parts of the state have been closed to new appropriation. This moratorium in certain areas has actually helped strengthen Kansas's economy. While new uses might be limited, existing users are provided with a steady supply of water. The stabilization of water supplies has made banks more confident about granting agricultural loans. Declining water levels are, however, forcing some farmers in the western part of the state to make the transition from irrigated to dry farming or to install more water-efficient equipment. The challenge facing state policymakers is that of how to manage the transition from irrigated agriculture to dry farming as pumping becomes prohibitively expensive. Kansas has recognized the supply problem for a number of years, but it has only recently attempted to manage groundwater withdrawal in any comprehensive manner. (Or, more accurately, it is only recently that groundwater management has become been politically acceptable.) These efforts will be summarized in the section on Kansas groundwater law.

Problems

Groundwater contamination in Kansas is generally site-specific and, as of the mid-1990s, was not widespread. Isolated groundwater-pollution problems are occasionally attributed to natural sources but are most often the result of human influence. For example, oil-field brine contamination in western Harvey County has affected the groundwater supply in portions of the Equus Beds Aquifer to the point of making it unsuitable for most uses.[13] Nitrate contamination, which typically arises from septic tanks, fertilizer application, and animal feedlots, is the most pressing problem in Kansas. Nitrate levels in 13.4 percent of the state-monitoring wells sampled in 1992 were found to exceed EPA standards.[14]

As of the mid-1990s pesticides have not had a substantial impact on groundwater supplies in Kansas. However, because of the large amount of agriculture in the state, pesticide contamination poses a potential threat to groundwater there. In addition, the EPA has identified three hazardous waste sites in Kansas as being in need of cleanup and has placed them on its national priorities list. These are a ten-acre industrial waste-gas disposal site in Johnson County, a dump in Cowley County, and an abandoned ore-recycling site in Wichita.[15] Naturally occurring saltwater

in groundwater is a threat to municipal water supplies in several counties across Kansas, notably in McPherson, Harvey, Sedgwick, Stafford,
Pratt, and Reno Counties.[16]

In general, despite isolated incidents of nitrate contamination, the
groundwater in Kansas is of good quality. Groundwater pollution may
become a problem in the future in certain parts of the state; however,
the fact that most of the groundwater used in Kansas is used in irrigation, and given the light precipitation in the part of the state dependent
upon groundwater, pollution should not pose a serious threat to Kansas's
future groundwater use.

Law

A leading scholar on Kansas groundwater law once wrote that "[O]ur
entire water law is similar to the homesteader's house—it just grew as
demands dictated."[17] Today waters in Kansas are "dedicated to the use of
the people of the state" and subject to appropriation for beneficial use.[18]

In 1886 Kansas passed legislation providing that surface waters were
subject to prior appropriation.[19] In 1917 the Kansas legislature created the
Kansas Water Commission and vested in that body authority over the
appropriation of surface or groundwater. Then in 1927 responsibility for
administering water rights was transferred to the Division of Water Resources of the State Board of Agriculture. In 1995 the Kansas State Board
of Agriculture was abolished and replaced with the Kansas Department
of Agriculture, which retained the Division of Water Resources. Thus,
as of 1996 responsibility for administering water rights in Kansas has
rested with the chief engineer of the Division of Water Rights, Kansas
Department of Agriculture.[20]

During the late 1800s and early 1900s the Kansas legislature established the legal basis and administrative mechanism for public control
and appropriation of groundwater. In 1881 the Kansas Supreme Court followed the English common law doctrine and found groundwater to be the
private property of the owner of land overlying the groundwater basin.[21]
In 1944 the Kansas Supreme Court reaffirmed the common law doctrine
in *State ex rel. Peterson v. State Board of Agriculture* and found that the
state was without authority to hold hearings on applications to appropriate groundwater or to regulate those appropriations.[22] In response to
the *Peterson* decision, the governor appointed a committee to evaluate
Kansas water law and to make recommendations for changes.[23] The committee's recommendations later became the 1945 Water Appropriation

Act. While the 1945 act acknowledged common law rights, it established the doctrine of prior appropriation as the basis for acquiring new water rights within the state of Kansas. The 1945 act contains a beneficial-use requirement, and all uses are regulated via a permit system administered by the chief engineer of the Division of Water Resources of the Kansas State Board of Agriculture (now the Kansas Department of Agriculture). The 1945 act has withstood constitutional challenge.[24]

The 1945 legislation and subsequent amendments give the chief engineer in Kansas significant powers over the management of groundwater. (The 1945 act applies to both surface water and groundwater.) No one may appropriate water and acquire water rights in Kansas without the approval of the Kansas chief engineer, and no rights may be acquired by prescription, adverse use, or possession.[25] (Domestic uses, meaning water for household purposes, the irrigation of gardens, orchards, and lawns that do not exceed a total of two acres in area, and limited watering of livestock, poultry, and farm and domestic animals used in operating a farm are exempted from the filing requirements of the act.)[26]

Amendments made in 1957 to the 1945 act give the chief engineer the authority to require groundwater pumpers to install pump-measuring devices and to require pumpers to report the reading on such devices.[27] In 1977 the 1945 act was further amended to require pumpers to obtain a permit from the chief engineer prior to beginning any work on waterworks for the diversion, use, and storage of water, including groundwater.[28]

In addition to the aforementioned statutory powers, two sections of the Kansas Code, when read together, provide rather broad authority over water management. Section 82a-706a of the Kansas statutes allows the engineer to adopt whatever rules and regulations are necessary for him or her to carry out the duties of the office. And section 82a-711 directs the engineer to take the "public interest," among other things, into consideration when issuing permits for additional water appropriations. Included in the public interest is the safe yield of the area and the impact additional appropriations will have on prior appropriators.

In addition to the chief engineer, Groundwater Management Districts (GMDs) play a crucial role in water-resource management in Kansas.

Groundwater Management Districts (GMDs)

In 1968 the Kansas legislature found a need "for the creation of Kansas groundwater management districts for the proper management, . . . conservation, . . . [and] prevention of economic deterioration" of groundwater resources.[29] The legislation passed that year proved inadequate, reportedly because of confusion over who could take the necessary steps to establish a district.[30] The 1968 legislation was repealed and was then re-enacted in 1972 as the Kansas Groundwater Management District Act of 1972.

The Kansas legislature passed the 1972 act in part as a response to local water users and landowners who wanted management districts created to manage groundwater resources on the local level. Legislators undoubtedly also felt that by sharing authority for groundwater management with local bodies, it would relieve the state of pressure and responsibility when farmers in the western part of the state started finding groundwater too expensive to pump and were forced to convert to dry farming.

The 1972 act provides for the creation of a GMD in the following manner: first, fifteen eligible voters in the proposed district file a declaration with the chief engineer of intent to form a district.[31] (Eligible voters are owners of forty or more contiguous acres of land within the district, or one who withdraws or uses 1 acre-foot of groundwater or more per year in the district.)[32] Second, the chief engineer, in consultation with the local district organizers, makes any necessary modification he or she feels necessary to the boundaries of the proposed district in order that the area be manageable.[33] Then, within twelve months of certification by the chief engineer of the district boundaries, the local district organizers must file a petition with the secretary of state signed by the smaller amount of fifty eligible voters or 50 percent of the eligible voters in the district.[34] After the petition is circulated and approved by the secretary of state it is submitted to the chief engineer for approval. Such approval is based primarily on technical considerations but also includes the engineer's determination that the "public interest will be served by the creation of the proposed district."[35] Upon approval by the chief engineer an election is held in the proposed district.[36]

Once created, districts have extensive powers over the management of groundwater. These powers include, among others, the power of eminent domain, the power to sue and to be sued, the power to build waterworks, and the power to levy water charges and borrow money.[37] However, groundwater districts are required to submit management programs to the chief engineer for approval prior to engaging in groundwater management. Groundwater-district governing boards are required to review their programs at least annually and to submit any revisions in the program to the state engineer for his or her approval.[38] Those wishing to appropriate water in a management district must still apply to the chief engineer for a permit. However, the chief engineer, as of the mid-1990s, followed the guidelines of the district-management plan when issuing permits, and he or she rarely made any changes in management plans when they were submitted for approval, because the plans are generally written to conform with state law.

In 1973 the Kansas legislature passed the Kansas Groundwater Exploration and Protection Act "to provide for the exploration and protection of groundwater."[39] Administered by the Kansas Secretary of Health and Environment, this act provides for the licensing and regulation of well contractors. Under the statute, well contractors must be licensed by the Secretary of Health and Environment and must provide the secretary with information on well construction, well size, location, pumping tests, depth to water, and various conservation details, among other things.[40] Contractors must also provide information on abandoned wells, sealing wells, and unsuccessful drilling attempts. Violators of the act are guilty of a Class B misdemeanor.[41]

Groundwater-management districts are, for the most part, also very much involved in water quality. GMD No. Two, for example, has in place a water-quality network that consists of 334 wells at 165 groundwater-monitoring sites. Information obtained from the monitoring is used by district planners to detect and evaluate changes in water quality within district boundaries. Based on any negative change in quality, district planners initiate plans to rectify contamination problems in an effort to insure that populations served by district water supplies are not exposed to health risks.[42]

Since the passage of the 1972 act, five GMDs have been created. The GMDs existing as of 1996 are described below.

The first GMD created in Kansas was formed during the summer of 1973 and is called Western Kansas Groundwater Management District Number One. GMD No. One covers approximately 1,170,000 acres, including most of Wichita and Scott Counties and parts of Greeley, Lane, and Wallace Counties.[43]

Depletion of groundwater resources and light precipitation are the main issues facing the GMD No. One governing board. (These are also the primary issues facing the governing boards of the other two districts in western Kansas.) In some areas of GMD No. One more than 70 percent of the groundwater that was once available has been withdrawn, and as of the mid-1990s water tables in the district were declining at an average of 0.3 feet per year (down from an average decline of 1.5 feet per year in the mid-1980s). The management plan for GMD No. One calls for zero depletion of groundwater resources (a goal it has yet to reach). The governing board of GMD No. One is attempting to slow depletion of the aquifer so as to avoid any unnecessary disruption of the agricultural economy and to provide for a smooth transition for those farmers forced into dry farming. This is being accomplished in GMD No. One through a moratorium on new withdrawals of groundwater for agricultural purposes and through strict criteria for allowing withdrawals for other uses. New permits will only be issued if (1) the well falls in an area that has not been dewatered by more than 15 percent since 1950, (2) there is at least 40 feet of saturated thickness, (3) the well conforms to a one-half-mile spacing requirement, and (4) the well will not result in more than 1 percent depletion in a one-year period.[44]

The Equus Beds Groundwater Management District (or GMD No. Two) formed in May of 1975 was the second district created.[45] GMD No. Two covers approximately 900,000 acres in parts of Harvey, McPherson, Reno, and Sedgwick Counties. Roughly 100,000 acres of GMD No. Two is in irrigation. About 35 percent of the groundwater pumped in GMD No. Two is used for municipal purposes, with 50 percent being used for irrigation and the remaining 15 percent being used for industrial purposes. Groundwater is managed in GMD No. Two on a safe-yield basis. The combination of 30 inches of precipitation per year, an estimated 6 inches per year of groundwater basin recharge, and available unappropriated water makes this possible. A large population in this district, which includes the city of Wichita (which receives 50 percent of its needs from groundwater sources), makes safe-yield management a necessity.[46]

The third district, created early in 1976, is the Southwest Kansas Groundwater Management District (or GMD No. Three). This district encompasses 5,722,000 acres covering most of the southwest corner of the state. The district is attempting to manage depletion of groundwater resources in an orderly manner, planning for depletion in some areas in twenty to twenty-five years. Water levels in GMD No. Three were declining as of the mid-1990s by a rate of 1 to 5 feet per year. Groundwater development is curtailed by well-spacing requirements and a prohibition on new wells.[47]

The fourth GMD was also created in early 1976 and covers most of the northwest corner of the state. GMD No. Four, also known as the Northwest Kansas Groundwater Management District, covers 3,100,000 acres, of which approximately 425,000 acres were being irrigated in the mid-1990s. Roughly 95 percent of the water pumped in GMD No. Four is used for irrigation. The governing board of GMD No. Four has decided to manage its resources on a safe-yield basis and does not issue any new permits that would result in groundwater depletion. Most of the communities served by this district are small and have sufficient water supply for their needs (one of the largest is Colby, with a population of around six thousand). Should supply become a problem, cities do have the right to condemn water rights and claim the water through eminent domain.[48]

Finally, GMD No. Five, or the Big Bend Groundwater Management District (so named because it lies beneath the Big Bend of the Arkansas River in south-central Kansas), covers 2,500,000 acres, of which roughly 25 percent is irrigated. Rainfall averages from 20 to 27 inches per year in GMD No. Five, and the governing board of the district has adopted a management plan designed to achieve sustained yield. This is to be accomplished primarily through well-spacing requirements and through a moratorium on permits that has been in place since 1990. While roughly 97 percent of the total withdrawals in the district are for irrigation, the moratorium on new permits has forced some cities within the district to purchase water rights from prior appropriators in order to meet their needs.[49]

Politics, Policy, and the Future

State-level policymakers in Kansas have decided that most groundwater-management decisions should be made on the local level (i.e., in the GMDs) whenever local entities request that authority. Although local management plans must be approved by the chief engineer, generally he or she does not interfere in ways that would change local-level policy decisions.

Furthermore, in areas not within a GMD, the Kansas chief engineer has decided to manage groundwater either on a safe-yield basis (where groundwater basins are adequately recharged) or to mine basins (where there is little or virtually no basin recharge). In areas currently being mined, including the three western GMDs, the rate of depletion established by either the GMD governing board or by the chief engineer is from between zero (GMD No. Four) and total depletion (GMD No. Three) over a twenty-five year period.[50]

The current approach is apparently what most farmers in Kansas want. Local management bodies are, normally, dominated by groundwater pumpers themselves, and they develop management plans that they, presumably, feel are in their best interest. As we have seen, the district-management plan in one of the three western GMDs overlying the Ogallala Aquifer manages groundwater in a manner that may lead to aquifer depletion in some areas in twenty to twenty-five years. Groundwater pumpers may find this to be in their best interest (and indeed may find it necessary) in order to recover the investments they have made. The question is, however, whether the relatively short-term economic interests of the pumpers in this part of Kansas are synonymous with the long-term interests of the state as a whole. If the current value of the water used for irrigated agriculture is greater than the future value of agricultural use (or any other future use) of the water, then the current policy is in the state's best long-term interest. It does not, however, seem entirely clear that current agricultural production is the best (i.e., most valuable) use of the water. What is clear is that it would be politically difficult for Kansas policymakers to do anything other than what they are doing. The state has recognized the need for agricultural conservation of water and is working to improve conservation practices.[51] With federal help, it has been aiding some farmers in the transition to dry farming, and newspaper articles, such as the one that appeared in the 30 May 1982 *Wichita Eagle* titled "Soil, Water Conservation Keys For Western Kansas Farmers," have been conditioning others for the transition. Although manufacturing income has surpassed agricultural income in terms of value added to Kansas' economy, politically farmers are still undoubtedly one of the most powerful interests in the state. Given the nature of Kansas politics, including the importance of agriculture, and the strength of farmers (and related business) it is not likely that the Kansas legislature will enact groundwater legislation that agricultural interests feel would be detrimental to farming. That being the case, we can predict that current policy (i.e., local control and controlled groundwater depletion) will continue into the foreseeable future.

Has the 1972 act been successful? If the goal is, as the act states, for "proper management . . . conservation . . . (and) the prevention of economic deterioration," it may be too soon to tell. Clearly, district management plans (with the exception of those of GMD No. Three) reflect the importance of groundwater preservation and are attempting to slow and eventually stabilize depletion of groundwater resources. GMD No. Three, which is in the western part of the state and pumps from the Ogallala, has decided that at present the best that management can hope for is an orderly and planned depletion of the resource. Given the very low rate of natural groundwater recharge, such a position may be the only feasible way to manage the resource. On the other hand, as water tables decline and energy (i.e., water) costs increase, the economical uses for water become fewer and fewer. Already farmers are switching to crops that use less water, and the cost of pumping groundwater has forced some out of irrigated agriculture entirely. Examples of increased pumping costs and forced conversion to dry farming can be found in Scott and Finney Counties, where aquifer depletion led to supply problems and a discontinuation of irrigation. Socioeconomic effects associated with conversions to dry farming often include reduced crop size and reduced profits, sometimes leading to defaults on bank loans and closure of farms. This, in turn, puts people out of work and takes money out of local economies. As groundwater levels are allowed to decrease, more and more conversions to dry farming are likely in other parts of the state.

There is evidence that some water entities (e.g., GMD No. Four) are attempting to reach safe-yield management. As Wayne A. Bossert, manager of GMD No. Four, wrote, "the groundwater pumpers of northwest Kansas rely on the aquifer for their livelihood and are not at all interested in seeing it dewatered for short term gain."[52] It is difficult to tell what future uses (and value) the water may have; Kansas was, as of the mid-1990s, attempting to take a conservative approach (in most instances) by avoiding discounting that future value in favor of current investments. Thus, while groundwater mining continues in many areas, the state as a whole appears to be heading toward the conservation of groundwater resources and the protection of water resources for use by future generations.

12 Nebraska

Nebraska is one of the leading agricultural states in the nation. Agriculture is the major consumptive user of water in the state. The state has, however, become more urbanized in recent years. Increased municipal and agricultural water use has been facilitated largely through groundwater. Given that the rate of population growth is slow relative to that of other states and that Nebraska has a tremendous amount of groundwater in storage, it appears that both municipal and agricultural needs will be met into the future. There may be localized shortages and competition between these two entities where the two are similarly located; however, these are likely to be limited. It appears that the greatest threat to the future of Nebraska will be one not of water quantity but of water quality. The use of fertilizers and pesticides can result in aquifer contamination. Considering that much of Nebraska's population depends on groundwater for its drinking-water needs, such contamination could become a serious problem in the future.

Physical Description

Although the eastern one-fifth of the state lies in the central lowland region of the country, Nebraska is a plains state. Average annual precipitation in Nebraska ranges from approximately 13 to 17 inches in the west to 26 to 35 inches in the eastern regions.[1] However, variances from these means are common in all parts of the state.[2] Nebraska relies on groundwater and surface water almost equally; groundwater accounts for 53 percent of total withdrawals, while surface water accounts for 47 percent (much of which is used for nonconsumptive power purposes).[3] Major sources of surface water in the state include the North Platte, South Platte, Republican, Niobrara, Elkhorn, Big Blue, Little Blue, and North, South, and Middle Loup Rivers.

Demographics

As of 1 July 1995 the resident state population of Nebraska was estimated to be 1,637,112.[4] Between 1950 and 1995 the state's population increased by 23.5 percent—well below the national average increase of 73.6 percent.[5] The state has, however, experienced a slight shift from rural to urban living. In 1960 approximately 54 percent of Nebraskans were living in urban areas.[6] In 1990 the percentage of Nebraska's population living in urban areas had risen to just over 66 percent (close to 50 percent of the population resides in the four metropolitan counties of Douglas, Lancaster, Sarpy, and Washington).[7] The majority of urban dwellers can be found concentrated in the two largest cities—Lincoln and Omaha—which are located in the eastern portion of the state.

Ninety percent of Nebraskans earn wages through nonfarm operations. The remaining 10 percent (eighty-one thousand people) of the population derive their income from agriculture. Nebraska has the second-highest per capita farm earnings in the United States. Aside from government, the only industries that employ more people in Nebraska than does agriculture are manufacturing, wholesale and retail trade, and service industries.[8]

Irrigation is by far the single largest consumptive user of fresh water in Nebraska. While the number of farms in the state has decreased, the total acreage devoted to agriculture has remained fairly constant over the years. In 1959 there were approximately 90,000 farms in Nebraska covering 47.7 million acres.[9] In 1993 the number of farms had dropped to 55,000, but farms still covered over 47 million acres.[10] In order to address the national trend of family farms being replaced by large agribusiness concerns, state voters passed Initiative 300 in 1982. This initiative, known as the Family Farming Amendment, insured that the bulk of agricultural activity in the state would remain family owned. However, following national trends, increased farm size has often been necessary in order for farmers to remain competitive in the agricultural market. Thus, while farms remain largely family owned, the average farm size in Nebraska has increased. This has meant a reduction in the number of people who work in farming and farm-related activities and has contributed to a decrease in rural populations in some areas.[11] Farming contributes over 10 percent to the gross state product of Nebraska. However, urban-based industries such as finance, insurance, and real estate; services; and manufacturing have surpassed agriculture as contributors to the gross state product. These industries contribute 15.8 percent, 13.8 percent, and 13.1 percent, respectively, to the state's economy.[12]

Water Use

Groundwater supplies approximately 53 percent of the total water used in Nebraska. However, much of the surface water withdrawn is for non-consumptive power generation. Thus groundwater actually supplies a much higher percentage of the water needed for consumptive uses. Irrigation, by far the largest consumer, accounts for 91 percent of the total groundwater withdrawn annually. (Of the water used for irrigation, 85 percent comes from the ground.) Public supply constitutes about 5 percent of annual groundwater withdrawals, with rural domestic, livestock, and industrial use making up the remaining 4 percent.[13] While 5 percent seems insignificant, this is hardly the case in Nebraska, where roughly 80 percent of the state's population is dependent upon groundwater for its drinking-water needs. The vast majority of the state's municipalities and rural water districts have public supply systems that are dependent upon groundwater. The aquifer along the Platte River in eastern and central Nebraska, for example, supplies roughly 47 percent of the water used by the Omaha Metropolitan Utilities District and supplies water for a number of the state's midsized communities, which include Fremont, Grand Island, and Kearney.[14] Of the 1,412 public water-supply systems in Nebraska, only 8 use any surface water.[15]

Roughly 6.1 million of Nebraska's 6.9 million irrigated acres are irrigated with groundwater.[16] In 1993 Nebraska ranked fourth in the nation in use of groundwater for this purpose.[17] Historically, however, surface-water irrigation has been far more prominent than groundwater irrigation. Prior to 1940 there was relatively little groundwater irrigation. Acreage irrigated with groundwater did not surpass surface-water-irrigated acreage until the early 1950s.[18]

During the heyday of irrigation development in Nebraska (the five-year period between 1975 and 1980) the irrigated area of the state increased by an average of 360,000 acres per year.[19] As of the mid-1990s Nebraska had the second-highest number of irrigated acres in the nation—85 percent of which are irrigated with groundwater.[20] Primary crops in Nebraska that depend heavily on groundwater irrigation include corn, sorghum, soybeans, wheat, alfalfa, sugar beets, and dry, edible beans.[21]

Despite the growth in irrigation noted above, there has been a significant decline in new wells drilled in recent years. In the peak year of 1976 more than 5,600 new wells were registered.[22] This dropped to 770 by 1982 and to 460 by 1983. In 1985 the number of new irrigation wells had dropped to 380.[23] In the eight years between 1986 and 1994 the average number of new wells dropped to 250 per year.[24] A variety of reasons are offered for this rapid decline in drilling. The nation's farm crisis, fueled by diminishing foreign markets and a domestic glut, was certainly a contributor. Others suggest that the widespread use of irrigation scheduling and the attractiveness of federally funded surface projects have contributed to the overall decline in irrigation drilling.[25] It might simply be that many of the best areas have been developed. Reasons for the original development spurt are likely to have included the tax incentives of the 1970s and 1980s and elevated crop prices (there was a substantial spurt in the mid-1970s, largely as a result of purchases by the former Soviet Union). In addition, developments in the center pivot leading up to the 1970s are likely to have played a role. Nonetheless, as of 1994 approximately 75,000 registered irrigation wells were operating in Nebraska.[26]

Nebraska's largest aquifer, in terms of both area and volume, is the High Plains Aquifer, which includes the Ogallala system. The Nebraska portion of the High Plains Aquifer is greater than that of any other High Plains state. About 96 percent of the state's irrigation wells are found in the High Plains Aquifer.

In total, there are approximately 1.875 billion acre-feet of good-quality, recoverable groundwater underlying Nebraska.[27] There is considerable diversity, however, in the location of the resource. The majority is concentrated in north-central Nebraska, where groundwater in storage exceeds long-term requirement projections.[28] In eastern Nebraska the principal aquifer is either thin, absent, or composed primarily of material that yields water very slowly and is only suitable for low-volume uses.[29]

Problems

Overdrafting
Water-level declines of up to 50 feet have been measured in some parts of the state. The greatest amount of overdrafting in Nebraska has occurred in Buffalo County, along the Colorado border in the west, and in Box Butte County, south of the Niobrara River in the panhandle. In addition to these areas the USGS has identified significant groundwater declines in parts of Banner, Keith, Kimball, and Cheyenne Counties in western Nebraska. Significant declines have also occurred in major portions of Hamilton, York, Polk, Seward, Adams, Clay, and Fillmore Counties, all in south-central southeastern Nebraska.[30]

Recharge from surface-water infiltration has been responsible for significant water-level increases in several areas, most notably south of the Platte River in south-central Nebraska. This area is very porous and recharges very quickly. The aquifer area bordering the Platte is an important source of irrigation water, especially in central Nebraska. It is also a source of supply for some of the state's major municipalities.[31] Additional areas are likely to be artificially recharged in the future, since as of 1993 the Nebraska legislature has been authorizing municipalities to secure surface-water rights for the purpose of induced groundwater recharge that occurs subsequent to their operation of well fields in areas that are hydrologically linked to streams.[32]

Areas of concern in regard to future overdraft and potential water shortage are those small communities located in areas of high agricultural production. Limited aquifers, competitive use, and high groundwater dependency has already affected several communities in the Big Blue Basin and the Republican Basin.[33] In addition, the highly variable nature of hydrologic conditions in the eastern quarter of the state could eventually result in supply problems for some communities.[34]

Pollution
Although natural groundwater in Nebraska is generally of good quality, human influence has led to widespread water degradation. There have been hundreds of confirmed cases of contamination in the state, and more are detected each year.[35] In an effort to address the problem the Ne-

braska Department of Environmental Quality (DEQ) has prioritized the different sources of contamination according to their current and potential impact on public supply.

Major sources of groundwater contamination in the state include fertilizer application, pesticide application, unpermitted landfills, septic tanks, and underground storage tanks. All of these areas are listed as high-priority concerns because of the number of sources involved and the location of the sources relative to groundwater used as drinking water. Furthermore, all but the unpermitted landfills are considered priority areas because of the size of the population at risk from drinking contaminated water that is being polluted by these sources.[36] None of these priority concerns are considered to be limited to localized areas.

Because of the large amount of agricultural activity taking place in Nebraska, the use of fertilizers has led to elevated levels of nitrates in many parts of the state. The groundwater of some twenty-eight counties in the state is reported to have been affected by agricultural activity. The most extensive contamination has occurred in Merrick and Holt Counties, where large volumes of water exceed the drinking-water standard contamination level for nitrates.[37] In 1992 and 1993 the Nebraska Department of Health issued eight administrative orders to the operators of community water systems because these systems repeatedly exceeded the drinking-water standard for nitrates. Administrative orders require water-system owners to take the necessary steps to correct a problem and to provide alternative sources of safe water to families with infants and to pregnant women.[38]

Septic tanks, another priority area for the Department of Health, are an additional source of nitrates. Unfortunately, as of the mid-1990s the actual amount of nitrate contamination attributable to septic tanks was unknown, as there was no site-specific data on the water quality near septic systems.

The agricultural industry is also responsible for introducing large amounts of pesticides into the environment. In excess of 25 million pounds of pesticides are applied to crops in Nebraska on a yearly basis.[39] Pesticides that have been detected in Nebraska's groundwater include atrazine, alachlor, dieldrin, trifluralin, metolachor, cyanazine, heptachlor, butylate, terbufos, and many others. The most commonly found pesticide, atrazine, has been linked to organ damage, fetal damage, and child-development problems, and it is a possible carcinogen. Areas where groundwater has been impaired by pesticide contamination include parts of Dawson, Buffalo, Hall, Merrick, Phelps, Kearney, Adams, Hamilton, and Brown Counties.[40]

Finally, landfills and storage tanks are major sources of contamination by volatile organic chemicals (VOCs). There are close to three thousand underground storage tanks in Nebraska that are confirmed to be leaking. While many have been closed, hundreds remain, and there is a backlog on dealing with them. There were approximately 150 unlicensed dump sites located in the state in 1993. Most have been closed, but the contaminants that were leaking remain, and they will be a source of concern for quite some time. In excess of fifty different VOCs have been detected in Nebraska's groundwater (excluding petroleum hydrocarbons and pesticides). These include benzene, trichloroethylene (TCE), and tetracholoroethylene (PCE), which are believed to be carcinogens, and styrene, which has been linked to nervous system disorders, organ damage, and chromosomal damage.

The state is actively monitoring these problems and can act to eliminate sources such as landfills and storage tanks. Agricultural sources are being addressed by local groundwater-management areas, groundwater-management plans, and state administration of the Federal Insecticide, Fungicide and Rodenticide Act (FIFRA). Given the importance of agriculture to the state's economy and the political power that agriculture has in the state, however, it seems likely that this source of contamination will continue to pose a threat to the state's drinking water well into the future.

Law

Prior to 1975 Nebraska groundwater law evolved from a series of court decisions and limited legislative action. Several reasons have been advanced to explain the development of Nebraska's groundwater law. Some have argued that the relative abundance of the resource has postponed many of the user conflicts that served as the impetus for earlier legislative action in other western states.[41] Others suggest that the power of the irrigation lobby and Nebraska individualism have played a significant role in delaying and preventing comprehensive or centralized control of the state's groundwater.

In 1933 the Nebraska Supreme Court, in the case of *Olson v. City of Wahoo*, proclaimed what has come to be known as the Nebraska rule of reasonable use. Plaintiff Olson sued the city of Wahoo, claiming the city's withdrawals from a common pool were interfering with his own rightful use. Though the court failed to find sufficient evidence of interference, it did suggest that where such interference is proven, a combination of the American Rule and the California Rule of Correlative Rights would be followed in determining proper allocation. The court noted that "The owner of land is entitled to appropriate subterranean waters found under his land, but he cannot extract and appropriate them in excess of a reasonable and beneficial use upon the land which he owns, especially if such is injurious to others who have substantial rights to the waters, and if the natural underground supply is insufficient for all owners, each is entitled to a reasonable proportion of the whole."[42]

Although conflicts between groundwater users have been relatively common in Nebraska's history, they have generally been resolved through discussion and negotiation between the parties involved, often with the assistance of state or local agencies. Both the Nebraska Constitution and Nebraska statutes recognize preferential use of the state's waters.[43] Domestic use has preference over all other uses, and agricultural use has preference over manufacturing and industrial use.[44]

In Nebraska, as in many states, conflict has arisen between agricultural users and municipal and industrial users. For example, in 1941 the state Supreme Court was asked to review a case in which a farmer claimed that the construction of a canal by the Loup River Public Power District had drained his previously subirrigated cropland, resulting in a substantial reduction in his dryland corn production. In ruling for the farmer, the court found that subirrigation was a valuable property right, and it held the power district liable for the resulting loss in cropland value.[45]

As a result of increasing conflicts between municipal and agriculture interests over groundwater transfers, in 1963 the Nebraska legislature enacted the City, Village, and Municipal Ground Water Permit Act. Under this statute, cities, villages, and other municipalities were given the option of obtaining a permit from the director of water resources allowing the transfer of groundwater. (In 1980 the act was amended and recodified as the Municipal and Rural Domestic Ground Water Transfer Act. The new act extended its provisions to cover rural water districts, natural resource districts, reclamation districts, and sanitary improvements districts.)[46]

In 1965 the Metropolitan Utilities District of Omaha applied for and was granted a permit from the Director of Water Resources to divert water from wells on the north bank of the Platte River and from wells on an island in the river. The water was to be transferred to Omaha, which is in the Papio Creek Basin. Merrit Beach Company appealed the permit decision to the Nebraska Supreme Court, arguing that the waters involved were essentially diverted surface waters to which it had prior appropriation rights and that, in any event, an interbasin transfer was illegal. The court, relying on the fact that Nebraska's definition of groundwater does not distinguish between percolating waters and water flowing in underground streams, ruled that the water proposed to be withdrawn was groundwater and, further, that interbasin transfer was neither prohibited by statute nor by established precedent.[47]

A year later, in the case of *Burger v. City of Beatrice*, the Supreme Court was again asked to clarify the groundwater rights of a municipality. The city of Beatrice had taken action to condemn lands in order to obtain groundwater for the purpose of supplying a large fertilizer plant. In its ruling the court affirmed the authority of a city to condemn lands to obtain water to meet domestic needs. However, since the case involved a private enterprise, the court ruled the condemnation invalid.[48]

In 1978 the state high court was asked to resolve a conflict between domestic and irrigation users involving an artesian aquifer. Irrigation development in the aquifer involved reduced artesian pressure, causing the water level to fall below the domestic pump level and resulting in the pump burning out. In affirming the Nebraska Rule the court held that if users were of the same preference category, then each was entitled to proportional amounts. However, since domestic use enjoys preference over agricultural use, the irrigator was declared liable for damages caused to the domestic user.[49]

Most recently the 1981 Nebraska Supreme Court decision in *State ex rel. Douglas v. Sporhase* confirmed the essence of the Nebraska Rule, as stated in *Olson*, and further declared that groundwater in Nebraska was public property. In reaching its decision regarding the constitutionality of the Nebraska statute that requires a permit for transporting groundwater over state lines, the court held that "the public, through legislative action, may grant to private persons the right to the use of publicly owned waters for private purpose; but as the *Olson* opinion demonstrates, with its emphasis on sharing in times of shortage, the public may limit or deny the right of private parties to freely use the water when it determines that the welfare of the state and its citizens is at stake."[50]

Although the U.S. Supreme Court later overturned the Nebraska court's decision because it found that the statute in question imposed an undue burden on interstate commerce, it did not address the declaration of public ownership.[51] The court's decision suggests that groundwater remains public property even after permissive capture, indicating that the legislature could regulate use as well as withdrawals.[52]

Although the Nebraska legislature has traditionally played a limited role in groundwater management (groundwater law having developed in the courts), in 1957 the legislature created the Department of Water Resources (DWR) and assigned to it all powers and duties formerly exercised by the Bureau of Irrigation, Water, Power, and Drainage in the Department of Roads. Then in 1967 the legislature authorized the establishment of rural water districts for the purpose of regulating, to a limited extent, the storage, transportation, and use of water for rural water-supply purposes. Rural water districts could be established by petition and landowner ratification.[53] In 1969 the legislature reorganized 150 single-purpose districts, which had exercised a variety of duties relevant to the state's natural resources, into 24 natural resource districts (NRDs) concerned with the planning and management of soil, water, and wildlife resources.[54]

In 1975, in response to increasing concerns over the depletion of groundwater resources in some areas of the state, the legislature enacted the Nebraska Ground Water Management Act (amended and recodified in 1982 as the Nebraska Ground Water Management and Protection Act).[55] The act was not an attempt to establish comprehensive control under any one state agency. Rather, its purpose was to empower NRDs to request establishment of control areas if it was determined "that there is an inadequate groundwater supply to meet present or reasonably foreseeable needs of a beneficial use of such water supply."[56]

Under the act, a public hearing could be initiated by a district and would be held before the director of water resources. At the hearing the director was to consider all testimony, including reports from the Conservation and Survey Division of the University of Nebraska and the Nebraska Natural Resources Commission, in determining the need for a control-area designation.[57] If a control area was designated, any person intending to construct a well in the area must first obtain a permit for doing so from the director.[58] Under the act, NRDs were required to hold hearings to determine controls within a control area.[59] Controls adopted could include a determination and allocation of permissible total withdrawals in the designated control area; adoption and enforcement of a rotation system; adoption of well-spacing requirements more restrictive than those set by the state; adoption of well-metering requirements; and, with the approval of the director of water resources, the closing of the control area or a portion thereof, or the issuance of additional permits for a one-year period. All NRD control rules and regulations must be approved by the director of the DWR.[60] The constitutionality of the act was upheld by the Nebraska Supreme Court in 1994.[61]

As of the mid-1990s two control areas (now known as groundwater-management areas—see below) existed in Nebraska. The Republican NRD and the upper Big Blue NRD were both established in 1977. A third NRD, the Little Blue, was created in 1979 but has since been disbanded.[62]

In 1982 the state legislature granted additional power to NRDs by enabling them to establish management areas, which, unlike control areas, did not require state approval. However, any NRD that established such an area was required to develop and submit a management plan. Management plans were to include a groundwater reservoir life goal. In the same bill (LB 375), the Nebraska legislature officially adopted the Nebraska Rule of Reasonable Use as the state's standard in its pronouncement that "every landowner shall be entitled to a reasonable and beneficial use of the groundwater underlying his or her land, subject to provisions of chapter 46, article 6, and the correlative rights of other landowners when the groundwater supply is insufficient for all water users."[63]

Passed by the 1984 legislature under increasing pressure to address quantity and quality concerns, LB 1106 required all NRDs to prepare groundwater-management plans by 1 January 1986 regardless of any designation of management areas.[64] These plans were to be approved by the director of water resources and had to include a reservoir life goal. The plans were reviewed by several state agencies including the Department of Health, University of Nebraska Conservation and Survey Division, and the Department of Environmental Control (since renamed the DEQ). These agencies reviewed the plans and advised the director as to their findings. In 1992 the legislature passed LB 51, which required all NRDs to incorporate plans for addressing quality problems. These adjusted management plans were to be completed by 1 January 1996. (All NRDs were in compliance.)

Most recently the Nebraska legislature passed LB 108, which authorizes conjunctive-use management. The bill, which became effective on 19 July 1996, allows for the creation of groundwater-management areas for the sole purpose of integrated management of groundwater and surface water. These groundwater-management areas can be initiated by NRDs but will involve input from the NRD, the DWR, and surface-water users, who will develop joint plans for addressing groundwater and surface-water conflicts.[65] Groundwater-management areas can also be designated at the initiative of the DWR. However, the DWR is not granted authority to regulate groundwater use in these areas unless the applicable NRD does not develop its own action plan or if the DWR does not approve a plan submitted by the NRD.[66] In the event that the DWR should propose to take control of groundwater-management responsibilities, an Interrelated Water Review Committee consisting of the governor and two members of the NRC selected by the commission would act as a buffer between the NRD and the DWR. Any regulations proposed by the DWR would have to meet with the approval of the Interrelated Water Review Committee.[67] According to the act, any groundwater-control areas that were in place when the law became effective automatically became groundwater-management areas (this is a change in name only, as the rules and regulations remain virtually the same).[68] It is too early to tell what impact the new legislation will have on either existing or future water users.

As previously noted, no single state agency is solely responsible for groundwater management at the state level. The capacity for the management of the state's groundwaters lies with no fewer than six state-level departments.

The DWR, in addition to its duties regarding management plans, is responsible for the registration of all wells, including wells necessary for geothermal resources.[69] In addition, the DWR issues permits required for irrigation pumping occurring from wells within 50 feet of the banks of any natural streams, and it issues permits to cities, villages, and other municipalities for the purpose of transporting groundwater for public supply.[70] In 1981 the passage of the Ground Water Regulatory Act established a requirement that all new business and industry obtain a permit from the DWR to drill wells if they intend to use more than 3,000 acre-feet of groundwater a year.[71]

The NRC is responsible for state water planning. The 1978 legislature authorized several water-policy studies as a part of the state's planning and review process.[72] These studies were intended to provide the legislature, the governor, and others with a range of policy alternatives on Nebraska water problems. The commission also administers a natural-resources databank and a resources-development fund. Additionally, the NRC administers the Soil and Water Conservation Fund, which provides grants for soil and water conservation practices.[73] The University of Nebraska Conservation and Survey Division serves the state through the collection and analysis of groundwater information.

The DEQ investigates existing and potential groundwater pollution problems and monitors local groundwater quality when necessary. It also has authority to establish and enforce rules and regulations pertaining to groundwater contamination, to establish a permit system for the control of disposal wells, and, in conjunction with NRDs, to declare and regulate special water-quality protection areas (also renamed groundwater-management areas by the 1996 act discussed previously).[74]

The Department of Health is responsible for monitoring state and federal water regulations to ensure conformance with health-related contamination levels in drinking water. The department exercises control over the design and construction of water wells that provide a source for public water-supply systems.[75]

When the State of Nebraska assumed responsibility for implementation of the FIFRA, authority was given to the Nebraska Department of Agriculture. The program developed by the department will play a major role in the way pesticide problems are addressed by the state.

Finally, it is the duty of the Nebraska Oil and Gas Conservation Commission to protect water-bearing formations from contamination occurring as a result of oil and gas drilling practices. The commission enforces casing and cementing regulations for both injection and disposal wells as well as plugging requirements for dry or abandoned wells.[76]

Politics, Policy, and the Future

In order to understand groundwater politics and policy formation in Nebraska as thoroughly as possible, it is important to keep in mind the three main factors that have historically influenced the development of groundwater law in the state: (1) the relative abundance of groundwater supply, (2) the political power of agriculture, and (3) ethnosocial individualism. Throughout this century up to the 1970s, the abundance of supply was most likely the leading determinator of policy development. However, the potential for increased conflicts between cities, irrigators, and domestic users over decreasing supplies in some areas moved the legislature to enact the Ground Water Management Act of 1975. It is important to note that this act did not significantly increase the state's power to formulate a comprehensive groundwater plan. Instead, the act vested the NRDs with a strong voice in determining the course of groundwater policy. This is an important notation because many feel that agriculture is a very powerful (if not the most powerful) interest group (or, more accurately, collection of interests and groups) in the state and that NRDs are largely controlled by rural agricultural interests. This control is so strong that some have referred to NRDs as "irrigator clubs."[77]

Not surprisingly, many political battles over groundwater center around the NRDs. Much has been done to bolster the authority of the districts regarding water policy. NRDs have wide discretion as the implementors and enforcers of many of the state's adopted policies. The criticism most often levied against the state's decision to use NRDs may be that the range of financial and professional capabilities among the districts is too wide. The NRDs maintain a close relationship with the NRC, which administers soil and water conservation funds and a Nebraska Resources Development Fund and also reviews the district's management plans.

The most important political issues of the 1990s in Nebraska have been, and will continue to be, focused on water quality and conjunctive use. Given the strength of agriculture in the state, it will be difficult to enact measures (although some NRDs have been able to do so) that will curtail the use of fertilizers and pesticides that leach into groundwater. At the same time, municipalities dependent upon these same water sources will find the amount of water available for human consumption diminished or tainted. While water quantity is likely to become a serious problem in isolated areas, water-quality issues will affect the entire state. Quantity problems could be addressed through water transfers among users or through the importation of water from other areas of the state that are not similarly strained. Solving the problem of quality will not be as easy. Groundwater-management work and Nebraska Department of Agriculture FIFRA work will be important in this regard, as will a variety of educational efforts.

In the past, water policy was directed by an abundance of quality water for use by all. In the future, choices will have to be made, and conflicts are likely to arise. Because of increasing urban populations, particularly in Lincoln and Omaha, there have been cases of urban encroachment into agricultural lands. In most instances, however, the loss of land has been offset by agricultural expansion in other areas. It does not seem probable that there will be widespread decreases in agricultural acreage in the future. However, if Nebraska hopes to sustain its growing population some agricultural practices will need to be constrained. Agriculture is not likely to lose its economic or political position, but the application of pesticides and fertilizers could well come to be more strictly regulated and monitored. The resulting tradeoff of protecting water for municipal and rural domestic use in the future may be a limit to crop production, which could cause a certain amount of economic disruption. The alternative is to place the health of Nebraskans at risk by allowing them to be exposed to polluted water and to limit the number of uses for which groundwater is suitable.

13 North Dakota

North Dakota is primarily dependent upon surface water for both human consumption and economic endeavors. While the population of the state is slowly shifting from rural residence to municipal dwelling, changes in water use from irrigation to municipal use are unlikely in the near future. This is primarily because North Dakota was not facing any water shortages as of the mid-1990s and is not expected to have any severe supply problems for quite some time. Given the fact that overdrafting has not yet become a problem for North Dakota and that the state is already moving to supplement groundwater with surface water in areas with the potential for overdraft, North Dakota seems to be in a good position for maintaining water supplies for current and future generations. With the exception of isolated incidents of groundwater contamination, the water appears to be of good quality, and state officials are making strides toward insuring that water supplies do not become degraded further.

Physical Description

North Dakota is a prairie state with light precipitation. Rainfall ranges from around 13 inches per year over the northwestern part of the state to approximately 20 inches in the east. Roughly 75 percent of the precipitation falls between April and September.[1] The majority of North Dakota's water is supplied through withdrawals of surface water. Major sources of surface water include the Missouri, Sheyenne, Red, and Souris Rivers.

Demographics

As of 1 July 1995 the resident state population of North Dakota was estimated to be 641,367.[2] Between 1950 and 1990 North Dakota experienced the second-lowest growth rate in the nation (behind only West Virginia, which experienced a decline in population). North Dakota's 3.09 percent increase in population was well below the national average increase of 64.35 percent.[3] While the population as a whole has not experienced tremendous growth, the percentage of urban dwellers has increased. In 1960 only 35 percent of the population resided in urban areas.[4] In 1990 over 53 percent of North Dakotans were living in urban areas.[5] Although we might expect this shift in population to urban areas to affect groundwater management (as it has in a number of other states, such as Arizona) we do not anticipate such an impact in North Dakota. Because of the state's dependence on surface water and the relative stability of groundwater management (i.e., the largely safe yield), urbanization should not effect groundwater use and development in the foreseeable future.

The majority of persons working in North Dakota earn a living through nonfarm operations. However, close to twenty thousand persons are employed in agricultural activities, and North Dakota has the third-highest per capita farm earnings in the United States. Aside from government, the only industries that employ more people than does agriculture are the service industries and the wholesale and retail trade.[6]

The number of acres devoted to agriculture in North Dakota has declined slightly over the years. In 1959 there were 55,000 farms in the state covering over 41 million acres of land.[7] In 1993 there were approximately 33,000 farms in the state covering just over 40 million acres.[8] Despite the decrease in the number of farms and in agricultural acreage, the raising of crops plays an important part in North Dakota's economy. As of the mid-1990s agriculture ranked third in contributions to the gross state product, trailing behind only finance, insurance, and real estate, which are grouped together, and service industries. Agriculture accounts for approximately 12.7 percent of North Dakota's gross state product.[9]

Water Use

Irrigated agriculture, the largest user of groundwater in North Dakota, accounts for approximately 55 percent of total groundwater withdrawal; public supply uses approximately 23 percent; rural domestic and livestock uses approximately 18 percent; and mining and industrial uses only 4 percent.[10]

Surface water is an important source of water in North Dakota. Of the water used for irrigation, 52 percent comes from surface-water sources, and approximately 58 percent of the public supply system demand is met through surface-water diversion.[11] These numbers are likely to increase in the future, however, as there are two large surface-water diversion projects (discussed later) currently underway in the state.[12]

Groundwater is a source of drinking water for residents throughout North Dakota. As of the mid-1990s groundwater was a source of drinking water for roughly 66 percent of North Dakota's population, and 41 percent of those receiving water from a public supplier depend on it as a source of drinking water. In rural areas virtually all of the water supply comes from the ground, and the overwhelming majority of small towns in the state operate municipal water-distribution systems that, for the most part, depend on groundwater. Although the major cities and their public water-distribution systems are primarily dependent on surface water, all the state's population centers use some combination of groundwater and surface water (the exceptions being Devils Lake and Jamestown, which are solely dependent upon groundwater).[13]

Agriculture uses groundwater throughout the state. Irrigation with groundwater is concentrated most heavily in counties in the southeast quarter of North Dakota. Agricultural use of groundwater increased dramatically from 1960 to the mid-1990s. In 1960, with around sixty irrigation wells in operation, agricultural used less than 3 million gallons of groundwater per day. As of the mid-1990s the number of wells had increased to over two thousand, and they were pumping in excess of 65 million gallons a day. The USGS attributes this rise to both increased knowledge of the state's groundwater resources and to technological developments, notably the widespread use of center-pivot sprinkler-irrigation systems.[14]

Groundwater supply problems vary considerably from region to region and from city to city in North Dakota. Supply and quality are problems in the southwestern part of the state, where groundwater is of marginal quality. Supply has been a problem for the public water-supply systems using groundwater in the cities of Hettinger, Bowman, Mott, and New England. The mayor of Hettinger once remarked, "I don't believe there will be any long-term solution other than surface water. When you drill the ground you're rolling the dice quite a bit."[15] These cities have also experienced salinity problems. In the early 1980s the North Dakota legislature, responding to a request from interests in the southwestern part of the state for help in developing their surface-water supplies, approved funds for the design of a pipeline to supply water to the area from Lake Sakakawea. Funds were also appropriated to purchase the right-of-way for the pipeline. As of the mid-1990s the construction of the Southwest Pipeline Project was underway, and it was expected to be completed and in operation around the year 2003.[16] Areas in the northwest portion of the state that are currently dependent upon groundwater and surface water from the Souris River will, in the future, be receiving water from the Missouri River via the Northwest Area Water Supply Project. This project will be funded primarily through monies allocated by the U.S. Congress in the Garrison Diversion Reformulation Act of 1986, which authorized $200 million for the completion of the Garrison Project and other related projects (the Northwest Area Water Supply Project was a trade-off for reducing the irrigation supply from the Garrison Project).[17]

The North Dakota State Water Commission (SWC) and the state engineer have been managing the state's groundwater resources via a permit system in a manner designed to prevent groundwater overdrafting. Although there is no provision in the North Dakota Code that requires the state engineer to do so, the engineer has interpreted section 61-04-06 (directing that permits for water only be issued when there is unappropriated water available) as providing the authority to manage groundwater on a long-term safe-yield basis (i.e., so that extractions do not exceed recharge rates). Consequently, with one minor exception, there is very little overdrafting in the state. The exception is in the West Fargo area, where groundwater development started during the 1930s (when there was little in the way of groundwater management) and where natural recharge is slow. This is one of the growth areas within the state, and the increasing population will mean added demand on aquifers in the area. While there is adequate groundwater to meet current needs, it is anticipated that overdrafting will be reduced sometime in the future by the development of surface-water supplies. The city of West Fargo holds the rights to surface-water appropriations from the Sheyenne River, which have yet to be fully utilized. Groundwater will likely remain an important source of water for the West Fargo area, but supplemental surface-water supplies will ease the impact of the growing population on groundwater supplies.[18]

Problems

As of the mid-1990s North Dakota did not suffer from widespread contamination of its groundwater resources. There are, however, localized problems with salinity, arsenic, and nitrates. While the application of agricultural pesticides presents the potential for future groundwater contamination, state officials are currently monitoring potential problem areas and have yet to find any sites that exceed the maximum contamination level (MCL) for any agricultural chemical.

Salinity has been and continues to be a problem throughout the western part of North Dakota, where total dissolved solids (TDS) levels often exceed 1,000 milligrams per liter and sometimes are as high as 2,000 milligrams per liter.[19] Arsenic is a problem in shallow groundwater basins in various parts of southeastern North Dakota. Arsenic levels in water used in both individual domestic and municipal supplies in the area have been found to exceed North Dakota's drinking-water standards. Arsenic has also been detected in the water from a strip mine near the city of Center in Oliver County.[20] Strip mining generally presents a potential threat to water quality in North Dakota, as it is expected that mining and coal production will increase greatly in the future and will eventually cover many square miles in the state. Policymakers will, undoubtedly, have to deal with the disposal of water that is polluted as a result of mining operations.

Agriculture has traditionally been a large part of the North Dakota economy. The application of fertilizers and pesticides presents both a current (nitrates) and potential (chemicals) problem for the state's groundwater quality. Because of funding limitations, however, state officials are not fully aware of the extent to which agricultural activities have affected groundwater supplies. In an attempt to remedy the situation, the North Dakota Department of Health has prioritized aquifers for pesticide monitoring based on current use, potential for future use, and level of pesticide application. While pesticides have been detected, the level of detected chemical contaminants in North Dakota has been below the MCLs listed for those that have been found. Nitrate levels, however, continue to exceed the MCL in several of the monitoring wells. While the majority of the wells have nitrate levels below the MCL, the fact that excess levels are found on a yearly basis indicates that nitrate contamination might become more of a widespread problem in the future, especially as agricultural activities continue.

The North Dakota Department of Health is responsible for water-quality control in the state. With the assistance of the state engineer, the health department sets quality standards and monitors groundwater quality. As mentioned earlier, funding limitations restrict the health department in its monitoring activities. While there were no pressing pollution problems as of the mid-1990s, if the state continues to grow, and if groundwater supplies are affected by agricultural, mining, and municipal activities, the lack of funding for quality monitoring on a widespread scale might become problematic.

Law

Groundwater in North Dakota is subject to prior appropriation for beneficial use and is regulated via a permit system administered by the North Dakota state engineer. The North Dakota Century Code states that all waters "under the surface of the earth whether such waters flow in defined subterranean channels or are defused percolating under ground waters . . . belong to the public and are subject to appropriation for beneficial use."[21]

From 1866 to 1963 North Dakota followed the common law rule of absolute ownership of groundwater resources. In 1866 the North Dakota Territorial Legislature enacted legislation declaring that the "owner of land owns water standing thereon, or flowing over or under its surface, but not forming a definite stream."[22] In 1963 the North Dakota Supreme Court in the case of *Volkman v. Crosby* affirmed the private ownership of groundwater subject to a requirement that water be put to a beneficial use.[23] This decision was contrary to section 61-01-01 of the North Dakota Code as amended in 1955 and 1957, which declares groundwater as belonging to the public and subject to prior appropriation. The court found that the legislature could not deprive landowners of water rights merely by declaring water public without the payment of fair compensation.[24] After the *Volkman* decision the legislature repealed the Territorial Act of 1866 to clearly establish its intent that groundwater be subject to appropriation for beneficial use.[25]

Primary responsibility for water-resource development in the state rests with the SWC. The commission is a nine-member body, chaired by the governor, that meets eight to ten times a year to determine major water-policy issues in the state, including the setting of priorities and the allocation of funds for major water projects. The day-to-day direction of water policy and management, however, is the responsibility of the North Dakota state engineer, who serves at the pleasure of the commission.[26]

The state engineer's power over groundwater management stems from his or her authority to issue extraction permits when it is found that water in a groundwater basin is not appropriated, or to deny such permits when the water is fully appropriated.[27] Although the other enumerated powers of the engineer over groundwater matters as found in the North Dakota Code are not extensive, section 61-03-13 provides a great deal of discretion in determining how the engineer carries out the duties of the office. It states, in part, that the "state engineer shall make all general rules and regulations necessary to carry into effect the duties devolving upon his office, and may change the same from time to time at his discretion."[28] It is pursuant to this section that the engineer issues regulations and in other ways regulates activities associated with groundwater use.

In administering North Dakota's appropriation and permit system, whenever there is competition for groundwater resources the state engineer is directed to give preference to domestic and municipal uses over irrigation and industrial uses and preference to irrigation and industrial uses over recreational uses.[29] Permits are not necessary for domestic, livestock, or fish or wildlife purposes when the amount extracted does not exceed 12.5 acre-feet per year.[30]

The North Dakota Code provides the means for the creation of water resource districts covering all of the state. Districts are created to "provide for the management, conservation, protection, development, and control of water resources," including groundwater resources. District boundaries are approved by the state engineer and generally follow county boundaries.[31]

Water resource districts are given broad authority over the management of surface water, groundwater, and floodwater, including the ability to raise taxes and sell revenue bonds; the power of eminent domain to acquire water or property rights; the power to develop rules to prevent pollution, insure conservation, and otherwise regulate water supply use; and the authority to develop water-supply systems to store and transport water, including the authority to build culverts and bridges and other necessary structures.[32] However, the state engineer alone has the authority to appropriate water.[33] Every two years districts prepare a priorities schedule outlining projects that will be undertaken by the district in the coming two years.[34]

Water-resource districts are governed by water-resource boards, which are appointed by the boards of county commissioners of the counties making up the district.[35] The North Dakota Code makes provisions for protest by landowners within a district when landowners disagree with assessments made for public improvements.[36] Water resource districts have been created to cover all of North Dakota, and joint (or regional) boards have been created to cover major watersheds.

In addition to its provisions for the water commission, the state engineer, and water-resource districts, the North Dakota Code has provisions for the creation of irrigation districts whenever a majority of electors within an area containing eighty or more acres of land petition the state engineer for the creation of such a district.[37] Irrigation districts have powers similar to those of water-resource districts, including the power of eminent domain; the power to tax, sell bonds, and purchase property; and the power to arrange for the construction of irrigation works, canals, ditches, and other improvements.[38]

The relationship between the SWC, the water-resource districts, and irrigation districts is best understood in terms of scope of activity, with the water commission having the broadest authority (i.e., statewide), the water-resource districts having narrower authority (usually county level and sometimes regional), and irrigation districts having authority over smaller specific-use areas.

Politics, Policy, and the Future

As previously discussed, it has been the position of the North Dakota state engineer and the North Dakota State Water Conservation Commission to manage groundwater and issue extraction permits in a manner that will insure that long-term extractions do not exceed the rate of replenishment. Remarkably, the state engineer's office, in administering North Dakota's permit system from 1969 to 1996, has never had any appropriation decision challenged in court.[39] Although disagreements over appropriations have come up, apparently water users, in the face of the authority over groundwater management vested in the state engineer and the expertise available to the engineer's office to determine the safe yield of groundwater basins, have decided not to challenge the engineer's allocation decisions.

Conflict over water policy in North Dakota seems to be limited largely to ad hoc battles over the construction or financing of surface-water control systems. Major interest groups active in North Dakota water matters include the North Dakota Water Users Association (a broad-based organization representing many interests, including agriculture); the North Dakota Irrigation Association (representing irrigation districts and affiliated with the Water Users Association); the North Dakota Association of Water Resources Districts (representing those entities); and the North Dakota Association of Rural Water Districts.

Although it does not directly affect groundwater resources, one of the most controversial issues in North Dakota politics in recent years has been the Garrison Diversion Project, a surface-water delivery system designed to transport Missouri River water to farms and cities in the northern and eastern areas of the state. The Garrison Project faced stiff opposition from environmentalists because of the impact it would have on wetlands, fish and wildlife, and prairies. Controversy over the Garrison Project led to the establishment, by Congress, of a Garrison Diversion Study Commission, made up of twelve members from seven states, Canada, and Washington DC.[40] The Garrison Study Commission was given the job of deciding on changes in the project, with any recommended changes to take effect in the event that eight of the twelve members could agree on them.[41] The commission's report recommended a number of changes, including postponing construction of the proposed Lonetree Reservoir (which would have been located in central North Dakota, southwest of Harvey). The commission also recommended the deletion of other facilities which, in total, reduced the amount of irrigated acreage the project would serve by close to 50 percent. Although environmental organizations had not, as of 1996, been active in groundwater matters in North Dakota, the Garrison experience is evidence that environmental groups have the ability to mobilize politically should they decide to become active in other water areas in the future.[42]

The potential for future groundwater development in North Dakota looks promising. The state has generally good knowledge of its groundwater resources, owing in large part to a series of county-by-county groundwater studies undertaken from 1955 to 1985 by the USGS in cooperation with the SWC, the North Dakota Geological Survey, and local governments.[43] As of the mid-1990s management practices have been sound. Overdrafting has not been a major problem and will not become one if current management practices continue.

This is not to suggest that the future of groundwater development in North Dakota is without potential problems. As indicated previously, coal mining, municipal activities, and agricultural practices all present, to varying degrees, a threat to groundwater quality. However, the state has prioritized potential problem areas and has implemented, as a preventative measure, an aggressive monitoring program that officials believe will help protect groundwater resources well into the future.

Socioeconomically, shifts from agricultural dependence to municipal-based industries are occurring at a relatively slow rate (compared to similar shifts in other western states) in North Dakota, and there appears to be enough water to satisfy current patterns of use well into the future. Given the slow rate of growth in North Dakota, along with the current abundance of water, safe-yield management practices, and an awareness of the potential for groundwater contamination, North Dakota appears to be positioning itself well for the future.

14 South Dakota

South Dakota is heavily dependent on agriculture. While rapid municipal growth has occurred in the Sioux Falls area, the rest of the state remains largely rural. The strength of agricultural interests and the relatively slow municipal growth overall indicates that agricultural production and agricultural water use will continue at present levels for quite some time. Overdrafting has not been a concern in the state, but growth in the Sioux Falls area might become problematic in the future if transfers of surface water do not occur. As of the mid-1990s it appeared that groundwater contamination was the only serious difficulty that would face South Dakota in the future. While contamination is not widespread, there are a number of potential sources of contamination that might become problematic later. Many South Dakotans are dependent upon groundwater for their drinking water, and widespread contamination would likely hinder development in the state and could possibly jeopardize the health of future generations of South Dakotans.

Physical Description

The eastern half of South Dakota is relatively humid, while the western half is semiarid. The eastern third of the state lies within the central lowland region of the Midwest and is predominantly rolling glacial plains with numerous lakes and ponds. Central and western South Dakota is a part of the Great Plains, and, as a result of glacial action, those areas east of the Missouri River resemble the rolling central plains. In the far western part of the state the Black Hills rise above the plains. The Missouri River and its tributaries drain the western and central portions of South Dakota. The eastern section of the state is drained primarily by the James and Big Sioux Rivers, which flow into the Missouri.

Annual precipitation in South Dakota averages around 18 inches per year, ranging from approximately 14 inches in the northwest to 25 inches in the southeast. From 75 to 85 percent of the state's precipitation falls in the form of rain between April and September. With the exception of the Missouri River, which contains four large surface-water reservoirs managed to provide flood protection and navigation benefits for states in the Missouri Basin downstream from South Dakota, the streamflow in the state's rivers during low periods is generally undependable for continued withdrawal for major uses.[1] Given that the Missouri is the only river capable of sustaining large year-round flows, groundwater is a major source of water in the state. Groundwater use and problems can be best understood if we divide the state into two regions, the area east of the Missouri River (roughly the eastern half of the state) and the area west of the river.[2]

Demographics

As of 1 July 1995 the resident state population of South Dakota was estimated to be 729,034.[3] Between 1950 and 1995 the state's population increased by 11.6 percent, which represents the second-lowest growth rate among the nineteen western states (behind only North Dakota). South Dakota's growth rate was well below the national average of 73.6 percent.[4] The state has experienced some shifting from a rural to an urban population. In 1960 only 39 percent of South Dakotans resided in urban areas.[5] By 1990, 50 percent of the population was urban.[6] Despite the relative urban gains, the state remains primarily rural and is dependent, to a large degree, on agriculture.

The majority of people living in South Dakota earn wages through nonfarm operations. However, 12.2 percent of the population (39,270 people) depend on farming for a living.[7] South Dakota has the highest per capita farm earnings in the nation. Other industries that employ a large number of South Dakota residents are manufacturing, services, and wholesale and retail trade.[8]

Irrigation is the largest single user of both surface water and groundwater in South Dakota. While the number of farms in the state has declined over the years, there has been little, if any, change in agricultural acreage—only in the size of farms. In 1959 there were approximately 55,000 farms in South Dakota covering over 44 million acres.[9] In 1993 there were 35,000 farms in the state, and they still covered more than 44 million acres.[10] Farming and agricultural services contribute significantly to the economy of South Dakota. In addition to employing large numbers of people, agriculture contributes 14.2 percent to the gross state product. The only industry that contributes more to the gross state product of South Dakota is the combined financial category of finance, insurance, and real estate, which contributes approximately 19.6 percent annually.[11]

Water Use

On a statewide basis approximately 42 percent of the state's water comes from the ground and 58 percent from surface-water sources. However, the flow of groundwater into surface-water sources contributes in excess of 85 percent of the total volume of streamflow throughout South Dakota.[12] Of the groundwater used in the state, 56 percent is used for irrigation, 20 percent for public supply, 10 percent for rural domestic and livestock purposes, and 8 percent for mining and industrial purposes.[13] While a significant portion of the population uses surface water, over 86 percent of the public supply systems in the state rely on groundwater for a portion of their supply (approximately 85 percent of the public rely totally on groundwater). Virtually everyone not receiving water from public supply systems in South Dakota is dependent on groundwater for drinking water.[14] Groundwater contributes 68 percent of the water used in public supply, 50 percent of the water used for rural domestic and livestock purposes, 36 percent of the water used for irrigation, and 37 percent of the water used for mining and industrial purposes.[15]

The western half of the state receives approximately 73 percent of its water from surface-water sources and 27 percent from groundwater sources. In this region roughly 89 percent of the surface water is used for agriculture. If we break these numbers down further, we find that although groundwater accounts for only 27 percent of the water used by volume in the western half of the state, 80 percent of the industries and municipalities in the west rely on groundwater for approximately 71 percent of their needs.[16]

Because of glaciation, the eastern half of South Dakota has more abundant shallow aquifers than does the west. Groundwater accounts for approximately 76 percent of the water used in the east. Irrigation uses most of this, and municipalities and industry use roughly 33 percent of the water. Over 81 percent of rural domestic users in the east depend on groundwater for their supply.[17]

While overdrafting was not a problem in South Dakota as of the mid-1990s, rapid growth and development around the Sioux Falls area has led the Department of Environment and Natural Resources to place a limit on withdrawals out of the Big Sioux River Basin. The department has limited withdrawals for municipal use to 32,200 acre-feet per year. It is anticipated that this amount will meet the demands (at 1997 use levels, allowing for anticipated growth) of the Sioux Falls area through the year 2030. Plans are currently in place to divert surface water into the area by the year 2030 to supplement groundwater.[18]

Problems

There are three types of aquifers in South Dakota—glacial, alluvial, and bedrock aquifers. Most of the shallow aquifers in the state are glacial and alluvial, and most of the bedrock aquifers are found deep and often underneath glacial and alluvial aquifers. Generally the deep bedrock aquifers bear poor-quality water, and the shallow aquifers, be they glacial, alluvial, or bedrock, bear high-quality water. (There are, of course, exceptions.) Many of the bedrock aquifers are under artesian pressure. It is estimated that there are from twelve thousand to fifteen thousand artesian wells within South Dakota that are either continually flowing or leaking. When these artesian bedrock aquifers flow or leak into the high-quality aquifers that overlie them, the upper-level aquifers suffer quality degradation. The South Dakota Department of Water and Natural Resources has found that deep bedrock artesian aquifers underlie most of the state. Water flowing from these deep aquifers into the shallow ones is a potential threat to groundwater quality in the state.[19]

Aside from the naturally occurring mixing of low-quality water with high-quality water, South Dakota does not suffer from widespread groundwater contamination. There have, however, been a number of human-induced incidents of groundwater contamination in the state that have affected groundwater supplies to varying degrees. The two most serious groundwater-pollution problems in South Dakota are the contamination of public-supply wells from leaks and spills (primarily of petroleum product and agricultural chemicals) and nitrate and bacteria contamination from feedlots, fertilizer applications, and septic systems.[20] In 1994 nitrate levels in excess of EPA standards were detected in several aquifers throughout the state. For example, high levels of nitrates were detected in five observation wells in the Big Sioux Aquifer, two wells in the Bowdle Aquifer, two wells in the Delmont Aquifer, and one well in the Parker-Centerville Aquifer.[21] In addition to being considered carcinogenic in large doses, high levels of nitrates have been linked to infantile methemoglobinemia (blue-baby disease). In 1981 a six-week-old infant contracted this disease, presumably from water contaminated by nitrate. In 1986 a two-month-old infant died from the disease.[22]

Leaking storage tanks (both above and below ground) are another current and potential source of groundwater contamination. Because of the amount and the sizes of contaminated sites the Department of Environment and Natural Resources has listed leaking storage tanks (along with nitrate contamination) as warranting high-priority attention. The predominant type of contaminant that leaks from these tanks are petroleum products (although stored pesticides are also a potential health threat). In 1995, 1,669 sites in South Dakota were confirmed to be leaking, resulting in 1,372 sites whose groundwater was confirmed as contaminated.[23]

Bacterial contamination poses yet another serious threat to the groundwater supply of South Dakota and has been identified as a high priority. Bacterial contamination can come from animal feedlots and animal waste, surface impoundments, and the application of biological fertilizers. The bacteriological quality of community water supplies varies from month to month throughout the state, with approximately 83 percent of the systems being considered safe at a given time.[24] What this means for the citizens of South Dakota is that at any one time 17 percent of the public water supplies sampled are providing water that is potentially unfit for human consumption.

In summary, groundwater quality in South Dakota is generally good, although there are localized problems, and in the case of nitrates and bacterial contamination there is the potential for widespread degradation (fertilizer applications and livestock raising are not likely to decline any time soon). In 1982 Mark Steichen, then the administrator of the State Office of Drinking Water, stated, "I would say that overall health problems in the state, as far as drinking water, aren't very serious. . . . Most South Dakota problems occur in very small towns, and solutions to these problems cost a lot of money."[25] In reaction to this statement, an official with the Department of Environment and Natural Resources agreed that most problems are localized and that the number of persons affected, as of the mid-1990s, was relatively small. However, the fact that some people (no matter how few) are facing health risks and that the potential for increased degradation continues to exist led this official to state that "water quality management could be done better."[26]

Law

A 1977 article in the *South Dakota Law Review* titled "The Status of Groundwater in South Dakota" began with an introduction that stated, in part, that "an attorney embarking on groundwater litigation in South Dakota often has little idea where to begin. Statutory law pertaining to the situation may be inadequate or even nonexistent. The state's body of case law is shallow."[27]

When South Dakota became a state in 1889 the territorial law, which held that the landowner owned the percolating waters found beneath the land, was retained. In 1895 a South Dakota Supreme Court decision confirmed that percolating waters that were not flowing in defined channels were part of the property belonging to the landowner. The court distinguished the landowner's right in South Dakota as being unlike the absolute ownership doctrine and more in nature of a right to use.[28]

In 1955 the legislature passed the Ground Water Act of 1955, eliminating the distinction between percolating waters and waters flowing in defined channels and establishing a permit system for the appropriation of groundwater. Under the 1955 act those using groundwater for some beneficial purpose prior to 28 February 1955 (or who had works under construction on that date) had rights secure against appropriations that might be made after 28 February 1955. Persons wishing to appropriate water after the effective date were required to file an application with the South Dakota Water Rights Commission.

In 1972 an amendment to the 1955 act empowered the Water Rights Commission to restrict pumping of all large-capacity wells, regardless of priority of appropriation, when there is a shortage of groundwater. The amendment functions much like the correlative rights doctrine would in such situations. The commission would reduce well withdrawal "equally in the area of the shortage except that the output of wells directly contributing to a shortage of water supplies for domestic purposes may be reduced to a greater extent."[29] In 1978 the South Dakota legislature prohibited the issuing of permits in areas where appropriation would result in overdrafting (see the limitations on Sioux Falls withdrawals). The South Dakota Code states, in part, that "the board may not allow the quantity of water withdrawn annually from a groundwater source to exceed the quantity of the average estimated annual rate charge of water to the groundwater."[30] Certain exceptions are made for public distribution systems.

The state has the authority to regulate well drilling, licensing, and data collection and to issue rules and regulations governing groundwater use and development. In addition, the state reserves other powers that are similar to those found in other prior appropriation states where rights are administered via a permit system.[31]

Politics, Policy, and the Future

As of the mid-1990s there did not appear to be any serious problems surrounding the management of groundwater quantity in South Dakota. While no major political battles are being fought over this resource at the present time, this was not always the case. During the early and mid-1980s a few incidents raised the consciousness of South Dakotans regarding their water resources. One such incident was the proposed transfer of Missouri River water to Wyoming for a coal-slurry pipeline to be constructed by Energy Transportation Systems, Inc. (ETSI). The sale of up to 50,000 acre-feet of water each year over a fifty-year period would have netted South Dakota over $1.4 billion during the life of the project. This was the largest such proposed commercial diversion of water in the Midwest, and it would have had implications for the entire Missouri Basin. Opponents to the sale raised a number of concerns. A group of ranchers and Native Americans worked to block the sale, in part out of fear that future water transfers might develop as a result of this precedent. As one opponent remarked, "it is the beginning of massive exploitation of high quality water at the expense of the future."[32] It was estimated that in addition to the lost surface water and the related impact on groundwater from such diversion, South Dakota would suffer from water-level declines as high as 300 feet in some areas because of groundwater withdrawals for the pipeline on the Wyoming side of the border.[33] In part because of public outcry, and also because railroad companies were denying easements across their property for the laying of the pipeline, the sale never went through, and the issue has not come up again.[34]

In 1981 some groups discussed circulating a petition to ban the use of water from the Madison Formation Aquifer for out-of-state purposes. While the petition was never actually circulated, it points to the fact that many within the state are concerned about water transfers and about conserving water for future use. Many of the battles over South Dakota's water in the future may not occur within the state but will be with out-of-state interests who covet South Dakota's water.

Given the relatively slow rate of growth and the importance of agriculture in the state, we do not foresee many changes in South Dakota's future water use. Because of its slow growth, South Dakota is not likely to undergo the types of economic and social disruptions that are occurring in other faster-growing areas in the West. South Dakota seems to be in a good position to control competition for groundwater sources within the state and to see that groundwater resources are managed to assure maximum long-term beneficial use. In fact, South Dakota is one of the few states in the West that actually operates on a safe-yield basis (although many states are required by law to do so). As we have seen, however, there are a number of serious, although localized, pollution problems that could present a threat in the future. Given the steps the state has taken to deal with its pollution problems, there is no reason to anticipate that South Dakota will not act in a timely manner to avoid any difficulties that may arise.

SOUTHWEST REGION

Many people consider the Southwest to be made up of New Mexico, Texas, Arizona, Colorado, Utah, Nevada, and all or parts of Oklahoma. California is ordinarily excluded. Our focus in this section is on five states—Arizona, Nevada, New Mexico, Texas, and Oklahoma. (Colorado and Utah are included in the Rocky Mountain section.)

The common denominator of the Southwest is aridity. From the dry plains of Texas to the low deserts of southern Arizona, dry, warm weather is the norm. Most crops can only be grown in the Southwest with the help of irrigation. While a number of dams and diversion projects have aided Southwestern agriculture, groundwater has played a key role.

The Southwest is one of the fastest-growing regions in the nation, and most of this growth is occurring in urban areas. Increasing populations require more water for municipal purposes and for municipal-based industries. While agriculture allowed the Southwest to grow, it has been surpassed by other industries in terms of economic importance and political clout. Agriculture continues to be the dominant user of water, but it now contributes very little to the states' economies relative to other industries.

Although many feel that there is a severe shortage of water in the Southwest, others believe that there is merely a misallocation of resources. The perception of water shortages among competing needs has led to many battles over water—both between states and between diverse interests within each state. One of the major problems facing Southwestern water managers entering the twenty-first century will be that of balancing between competing interests.

15 Arizona

Arizona is one of the fastest-growing states in the nation. This state, which developed around copper, cattle, cotton, and climate (often referred to as the "four Cs") has seen its traditional economy surpassed by urban-based industries in recent years. Rapid urban expansion has, at times, led to conflict between water users as the political and economic strength of agricultural interests has declined. Given this rapid rate of urbanization, changes in water use from agriculture to municipalities was and is inevitable. The state has planned for these changes and is attempting to make the transition as smoothly as possible in order to avoid serious socioeconomic disruption. Furthermore, with legislation (passed in 1980 and amended in 1994) designed to reduce overdrafting, and with the transport of Colorado River water via the Central Arizona Project (CAP) to supplement such reductions, the state is aggressively managing its water resources. While overdrafting will likely continue for a number of years, and while there are some contamination problems, Arizona appears to have an adequate supply of water to sustain its growing population well into the twenty-first century.

Physical Description

Although the desert springs to the minds of many at the mention of Arizona, the state has considerable topographical and hydrological diversity. Arizona consists of three main geographic regions. Southwestern Arizona is made up of the Sonoran Desert or Gila Desert region consisting of broad valleys and isolated mountain ranges including the Big Horn, Castle Dome, Gila Bend, Harcuvar, and Maricopa Mountains. Northern Arizona is part of the Colorado Plateau and contains several mountains and deep gorges, and a number of level plateaus. The highest elevations are in the northeast. Between the Colorado Plateau area and the southwest, making up the central and southeast parts of Arizona, is the Mexican Highland region, consisting of a series of valleys and mountains.[1]

Major sources of surface water in Arizona include the Colorado, Gila, Salt, Agua Fria, and Verde Rivers. These surface sources are fed through a combination of rain and snow. Rainfall in Arizona is generally scarce and is concentrated in the summer and winter months. Summer storms account for approximately 43 percent of annual rainfall and contribute little to the state's usable supply because of losses that result from evaporation and from absorption into the moisture-deficient soil.[2] Snowpack runoff from winter storms is the most important factor affecting Arizona's surface-water supply.[3] Despite the renewable nature of surface water, supplies in Arizona were appropriated long ago.[4] The result has been a heavy reliance on groundwater.

Demographics

As of 1 July 1995 the resident state population of Arizona was estimated to be 4,217,940.[5] Between 1950 and 1995 the population of Arizona increased by 462.7 percent, which was the second-highest growth rate in the nation —well above the national average of 73.6 percent.[6] Arizona's population growth has occurred mostly in urban areas. In 1960, 74.5 percent (971,000 people) of Arizona's population was urban.[7] By 1990 over 87 percent (more than 3.2 million people) of the state's population resided in urban areas.[8]

The largest percentage of Arizonans earn wages through nonfarm operations. While the state has been closely associated with the "four Cs," three of these industries no longer contribute substantially to the gross state product (the exception being the climate, which is a driving force behind tourism and related municipal and economic growth). As of the mid-1990s the largest employing industries and those industries contributing the most to the gross state product were those that have traditionally operated in urban settings. The largest single categories of employment in Arizona (government aside) are service industries, manufacturing, retail trade, and public utilities and transportation.[9]

While irrigation remains the largest single use of both groundwater and surface water, the acreage devoted to agricultural use has declined over the years (the number of farms has actually risen). In 1959 there were 7,000 farms in Arizona covering some 40,203,000 acres.[10] As of 1993 there were 8,000 farms in the state covering a total of approximately 36 million acres.[11] This trend is likely to continue as municipalities grow and agricultural land decreases as a result of urban encroachment. Such encroachment is currently occurring around the cities of Gilbert, Litchfield Park, and Peoria in the Phoenix Active Management Area (AMA)—a management unit discussed below—and is likely to occur around Green Valley in the Tucson AMA. Furthermore, some municipalities might purchase agricultural land for the water even if there are no plans for urban development on the land, as the city of Tucson did in the Avra Valley, for example.[12]

Farming and agricultural services contribute only about 2 percent to the gross state product of Arizona, while urban-based industries such as service industries; finance, insurance, and real estate; manufacturing; and retail trade contribute 19 percent, 17.4 percent, 13.8 percent, and 11.8 percent, respectively.[13] Despite the relative declining importance of agriculture in recent years, approximately forty thousand Arizonans continue to support themselves through agriculture or agricultural-related activities.[14]

Water Use

Given the full appropriation of surface water, municipal and agricultural expansion has necessarily been dependent on increased groundwater pumping. It has been estimated that from 1940 to 1953 groundwater pumping for irrigation alone increased from approximately 1.5 million acre-feet per year to 4.8 million acre-feet per year.[15] In the mid-1990s total groundwater withdrawals for the state were estimated to be approximately 3.2 million acre-feet per year.[16] Of this amount approximately 1.2 million acre-feet per year represents overdrafting.[17]

Although agriculture is by far the largest user of water in Arizona, the percentage of agricultural usage vis-à-vis other uses has been declining (hence the decline in overall pumping). In 1955 it was estimated that agricultural use accounted for 95 percent of all water used in Arizona.[18] In 1975 agricultural use accounted for 89 percent of water used in the state.[19] And in the mid-1990s agriculture used approximately 80 percent of the water in the state, with public supply accounting for roughly 11 percent; commercial, industrial, and mining uses accounting for 5 percent; and rural domestic and livestock uses accounting for almost 2 percent.[20] By the year 2040 agricultural use is projected to drop to 66 percent.[21] In the mid-1990s just under 42 percent of the fresh water withdrawn annually in Arizona came from the ground. Although groundwater and surface water play roughly equal roles in meeting the needs of public supply systems and irrigation, groundwater provides virtually all of the water used for rural domestic consumption.[22] Groundwater use is projected to decline in the future as municipalities make use of more surface water and effluent (for nonpotable uses).[23]

The rapid growth of Arizona's population and economy in large part explains the increases in municipal and industrial water use and the corresponding decrease in agricultural use. These trends can be expected to continue in the future. Agricultural expansion is prohibited in AMAs, and once an irrigation water right is converted to a nonirrigation right it cannot be converted back to an irrigation right.[24] Importation of Colorado River water via CAP should further decrease agricultural dependence on groundwater. Contracts for CAP water between agricultural users and the Department of the Interior require that farmers decrease groundwater pumping by an amount equivalent to the amount of CAP water delivered.[25] Unfortunately, the level of irrigators' use of CAP water has not lived up to expectations because of the water's cost. Many irrigators have given up their CAP water entitlements in return for the Central Arizona Water Conservation District (CAWCD) offering surplus CAP water at a reduced price. This water is offered on an availability basis only, and any entitlements relinquished by farmers cannot be reclaimed in the future, nor can they revert back to groundwater use once the surplus water is no longer available.[26] In addition, groundwater pumping is likely to be reduced as developers buy up agricultural land surrounding cities such as Phoenix (where such purchases are already occurring) and turn the water rights over to the municipal government in order to continue building. Municipalities expanding into these areas are required to use CAP water rather than groundwater.[27]

To summarize, Arizona gets a large portion of its water from the ground and uses most of the groundwater and surface water in the state for irrigated agriculture. Agricultural use has, however, declined in recent years and is projected to decline even further in the future. Municipal use is expected to increase dramatically as more and more persons migrate into the state. This transformation will lead to some displaced agricultural workers and farm owners, but the economy of the state as a whole is not likely to suffer any major adverse effects. Urban-based, less water-intensive industries have already surpassed agriculture in importance and will continue to grow as the municipalities in the state do the same.

Although the exact impact of CAP on Arizona's groundwater supply is uncertain, imported water, along with the Arizona Groundwater Management Act and increased use of effluent, will, over the next several decades, significantly reduce overdrafting in the state. But as of the mid-1990s overdrafting and its related effects were still serious concerns in Arizona.

Because overdrafting figures and basin planning is done within AMAs, and because the Groundwater Management Act is crucial to Arizona's future, in this case it makes sense to discuss the water law in Arizona before discussing the problems facing water supplies in the state.

Law

In 1904 the Arizona Territorial Supreme Court in *Howard v. Perrin* adopted the common law doctrine for groundwater.[28] In 1904 overdrafting was not a concern, and adopting the common law doctrine of absolute ownership no doubt seemed the reasonable thing for the courts to do.[29]

With the exception of a brief period between January 1952 and March 1953, the Arizona Supreme Court had, consistent with *Howard*, maintained the absolute ownership doctrine for percolating groundwater.[30] Two cases handed down in 1952 and 1953, *Bristor v. Cheatham (Bristor I)* and *Bristor v. Cheatham (Bristor II)* both serve to illustrate the problems caused by application of the absolute ownership doctrine and the opposition of the agricultural community to changes in the doctrine.[31]

In the *Bristor* cases the plaintiffs had been withdrawing water from their properties since 1916 for domestic purposes. In 1948 and 1949 the defendants sank eleven wells with "powerful pumps" to "great depths" on nearby land for irrigating cotton. As a result, some of the plaintiff's wells dried up, necessitating the hauling of water from other sources at great cost. The court, in *Bristor I*, noted that "It is only in recent years that motor operated pumps capable of withdrawing thousands of gallons of water per minute from the earth have been available."[32] The court noted further that "to permit the present underground water race to continue unabated, without regulation or control, would inevitably lead to exhaustion of the underground supply and consequently to economic disaster."[33] The *Bristor I* court, by a three-to-two margin, found groundwater to be public property subject to prior appropriation.

The decision was immediately controversial and resulted in widespread predictions of calamity and inequity.[34] As historian Robert Dunbar noted: "The big pumpers were alarmed. Cutbacks in water use would mean a loss of income and investments in land, pumps, and agricultural machinery. The cotton growers were in the midst of a technological shift from harvest labor to mechanical pickers, with a consequent increase in investment."[35]

In *Bristor II*, less than a year and a half after its earlier decision, the court reversed itself and restored the common law absolute ownership doctrine tempered by reasonable use.[36]

Little changed in the state's water law to prevent overdrafting until continuing federal government pressure, among other things, resulted in the passage of the Arizona Groundwater Management Act in 1980.[37] (In 1945 and 1948 the Arizona legislature rewrote the state's groundwater laws, creating "critical groundwater basins." These, however, had little impact on overdrafting.)

The Arizona Groundwater Management Act is intended to provide "a framework for the comprehensive management and regulation of the withdrawal, transportation, use, conservation, and conveyance of rights to use the groundwater in this state."[38]

The act designated four AMAs. Most provisions of the act affect only these areas. (Significant exceptions will be noted below.)

The four AMAs are as follows:

—The Tucson area, including the upper Santa Cruz and Avra Valley subbasins.
—The Phoenix area, including the east and west Salt River Valleys, Fountain Hills, Carefree, Lake Pleasant, Rainbow Valley, and the Hassayampa subbasins.
—The Prescott area, including the Little Chino and upper Agua Fria subbasins.
—The Pinal area, including Maricopa-Stanfield, Eloy, Aguirre Valley, Santa Rosa Valley, and Vekol Valley subasins.[39]

These four areas comprise over 80 percent of the state's population and 83 percent of the state's total overdraft.[40]

After hearings, additional AMAs may be created by the director of the Department of Water Resources if he or she finds it necessary to do so to preserve the water supply, protect property or storage capacity, or prevent water-quality degradation.[41] The act also contains procedures for local formation of an AMA. Upon petition by 10 percent of the voters in a proposed AMA, all registered voters in the groundwater basin in question vote on the issue.[42]

The act created the State Department of Water Resources (DWR) and vested in it all groundwater and surface-water management responsibilities except those of water-quality control, which remained the responsibility of the Department of Health Services.[43] The director is given wide discretion in organizing and staffing the DWR and may use professionals from other state agencies and hire outside consultants.[44]

The act sets goals for management of the four AMAs. For the Tucson, Phoenix, and Prescott areas, the goal is to attain safe yield by 1 January 2025 or sooner, as determined by the director.[45] Safe yield is defined as long-term balance between annual withdrawals and natural and artificial groundwater recharge.[46] The Pinal AMA's goal is to allow development of nonirrigation uses and to allow current agricultural uses to continue "for as long as feasible, consistent with the necessity to preserve future water supplies for nonirrigation uses."[47]

The time span established for achieving safe yield in the Tucson, Phoenix, and Prescott areas, and the decision to allow current agricultural uses to continue in the Pinal AMA "for as long as feasible" were no doubt designed to minimize the impact of decreasing withdrawals on irrigated agriculture. With conservation being phased in over forty-five years, farmers are much more likely to be able to receive returns on any recently made investments in land or equipment.

To attain the goals described above for each AMA, the act provides for five management periods: 1980–90, 1990–2000, 2000–2010, 2011–20 and 2020–25. For each of these periods the director is required to promulgate management plans no later than 1 January 1983, 1 January 1988, 1 January 1998, 1 January 2008, and 1 January 2019, respectively.[48] In general terms, these management plans require the director, after public hearings, to impose increasingly stringent mandatory conservation measures on all groundwater users within the areas to meet the goals of each AMA. In the event that the management plans do not prove sufficient to meet the conservation goals of an AMA, the director is empowered, after

1 January 2006, to purchase and retire water rights.[49] Such purchases are to be financed by pump taxes on all persons withdrawing water within an AMA. (Small domestic wells are exempted from most requirements.)

Within an AMA water may be extracted only under a "grandfather right" or pursuant to a permit. Permits are discussed later in this section.

There are three types of grandfather rights designated in the act: irrigation grandfather rights, type I nonirrigation grandfather rights, and type II nonirrigation grandfather rights.[50] To claim any of these rights, an application must be filed with the DWR within fifteen months of the designation of an AMA.[51]

The three types of grandfather rights are summarized below.

Irrigation grandfather right. Land in one of the initial AMAs that was irrigated at some time during the five years prior to 1 January 1980 has an irrigation grandfather right. In subsequently designated areas, the land must have been irrigated sometime during the five years prior to the designation of the AMA.[52] (The amount of water attached to the right is discussed below.) Only lands irrigated during these periods have a right to groundwater for irrigation purposes. Irrigation grandfathered rights may be conveyed to others for farming purposes or retired for nonirrigation uses.

Type I nonirrigation grandfather right. When an individual purchases and retires from cultivation an irrigation grandfather right, the right becomes a type I nonirrigation right. Once this change is made, it is irreversible.[53] The water right so acquired is usually 3 acre-feet per year per acre of land, although if the amount of water actually used for cultivation is less or if the farm practiced crop rotation wherein some portion of the land is always unirrigated, the amount will be less than 3 acre feet.[54]

A type I right may be used for any purpose other than irrigation unless the land lies within the service area of a city, town, or private water district. In such a case the water must be used for electricity generation unless water is unavailable from the municipal or private distributor.[55] Upon approval of a development plan by the DWR, an individual may retire irrigated land, use no water, and not jeopardize his future type I nonirrigation right.[56]

Type II nonirrigation grandfather right. These are the rights established by virtue of extractions having been made for nonirrigation purposes prior to designation as an AMA. The right created is to the highest amount of extractions during any one of the five years prior to the creation of the AMA (or 1 January 1980 in the case of the four initial AMAs).[57] There is no locational limitation on the use of type II rights. Type II rights may be freely conveyed and used for any purpose except cultivation.[58] When a type II right is held by an electric utility or mining company, the right cannot be used or conveyed for any purpose other than power generation or mining, respectively.[59]

The amount of water available under an irrigation grandfather right is determined by multiplying the "irrigation water duty" by the "water duty acres." (The conservation requirements and water duties discussed herein also apply to irrigation districts.) Water duty acres are the number of acres in cultivation in any one of the five years prior to creation of the AMA. (Or 1 January 1980, in the case of the four initial AMAs.) The irrigation water duty is the amount of water the DWR finds is reasonable, given accepted conservation practices and crops historically grown, to irrigate an acre of land.[60]

The conservation aspects of the five management periods discussed above are enforced through manipulation (i.e., steady decrease) of the irrigation water duty.[61]

To illustrate the function of the water-duty acres and the irrigation-water acres, let us assume a farmer owns 600 acres, of which no more than 300 are in cultivation during any one year prior to the creation of the AMA. The farmer therefore has 300 water-duty acres. In this area cotton is the predominant crop, and given crop needs and modern conservation techniques, the director of the DWR determines that 3.8 acre-feet per year is a reasonable amount for irrigation. The irrigation water duty is 3.8. The amount of water available, then, is 1,140 acre-feet.

A farmer may withdraw less than the amount of water determined to be allowed by the director in a given year and may withdraw that "saved" water in a subsequent year, effectively establishing a credit for future years. Farmers can also extract up to 50 percent more than the allowed amount in a given year and make up the difference in a subsequent year.[62]

Under the 1948 Water Code six areas had been designated as critical groundwater areas by 1980. Of these six, four became AMAs under the act. The remaining two areas, the Douglas Critical Groundwater Area and the Joseph City Critical Groundwater Area, were designated by the act as "Irrigation Nonexpansion Areas."[63] Additional Irrigation Nonexpansion Areas (INAs) may be created by the director in the event that there is insufficient supply for irrigation and an AMA is determined to be unnecessary.[64] (As of the mid-1990s only one additional INA has been added—the Harquahala INA in west-central Arizona.)⁶⁵ The act also has provisions for local initiation, by petition, of additional irrigation non-expansion areas.⁶⁶ The director may convert an INA to an AMA if all the criteria for the creation of an AMA, as outlined above, are met.⁶⁷

Designation as an INA limits allowable acreage that may be cultivated to the highest amount cultivated during any one year of the five years prior to the creation of the nonexpansion area.⁶⁸ For lands within the Douglas or Joseph City Critical Groundwater Areas, this period was from 1 January 1975 to 1 January 1980.⁶⁹ For subsequently designated non-expansion areas, the five-year period ends when the director gives notice of designation or, in the case of locally initiated designation attempts, when the requisite petition is filed with the registrar of voters.⁷⁰

In addition to rights based on a grandfather clause or to extractions made by a municipality or private water company, the act provides for seven different types of withdrawal permits. Permits are issued by the director of the DWR. Among the uses for which permits can be issued are mine dewatering and mineral extraction and processing.

Among the other provisions of the act are various regulations on well construction and registration as well as provisions for enforcement and appeal.⁷¹

The constitutionality of the Groundwater Management Act has been upheld in numerous court decisions since its enactment in 1980. One such case, *Town of Chino Valley v. City of Prescott*, centered around the takings and due process clauses of the U.S. and Arizona Constitutions. In this case the court ruled that the transfer of groundwater control from landowner to the state did not violate either of these clauses because "there is no right of ownership of groundwater in Arizona prior to its capture and withdrawal from a common supply."⁷²

In 1996 the state legislature authorized the Arizona Water Banking Authority to further insure long-term water supplies. Currently, a portion of Arizona's allotment of Colorado River water goes unused and is being "borrowed" by California. The Arizona Water Banking Authority was created in an attempt to put the water to use and to eliminate any future claims on it that California might make. Anticipated benefits of the program are the recharge of aquifers to assist in meeting groundwater-management goals and objectives, the ability to access an additional supply of stored water to meet community water demands during drought years, the establishment of a pool of water to be used in Indian water-rights settlements, and the ability to lease unused water on a short-term basis to other states (which would be required to pay for the storage). The authority is made up of five members, including the Director of the Department of Resources (chair of the authority), the President of CAWD, and three persons appointed by the governor (of these, one will represent CAP municipal and industrial water users, one will represent the users of Colorado River water along the river, and one will be a person who has knowledge of water-resource management issues). Activities of the authority will be funded through monies deposited in the Water Bank Fund. Sources of funding include pump fees collected in the AMAs, an ad valorem tax to be levied in CAP service area, general fund appropriations, fees collected from the sale of water stored for drought protection, and money collected from the lease of water to out-of-state interests.[73]

Problems

Overdrafting
Overdrafting in Arizona is most serious within the four AMA basins. The area includes large portions of Santa Cruz, Pima, Pinal, and Maricopa Counties and the central portion of Yavapai County around Prescott. As of the 1990s overdraft in these areas was approximately 1 million acre-feet per year.[74] In some parts of the area around Tucson (Pima County) groundwater levels have declined over 150 feet since the 1940s. In the areas around Phoenix significant amounts of water have also been withdrawn and have not been replaced. Finally, the storage of groundwater of the aquifer underlying Pinal County has been reduced by 50 percent since 1949 because of extensive agricultural groundwater mining. This overdrafting has resulted in land subsidence and earth fissuring in some areas.[75] Land subsidence has caused damage to infrastructure such as roads and buildings. Subsidence also results in diminished aquifer storage capacity that can never be recovered. Fissuring has occurred near the Picacho Mountains in the Western Pinal County areas of the Lower Santa Cruz Basin. Here a fissure approximately 8 miles long and with a vertical displacement in some places of up to 1.5 feet has developed. In parts of the area the water level has declined by as much as 200 feet, resulting in land subsidence of up to 7.5 feet. Fissuring has resulted in damage to the primary highway (Interstate 10), the Picacho Reservoir, and railroads, agricultural land, wells, and streams.[76] Land subsidence has also been found in the Salt River Valley Basin and the Wilcox Basin. Fissures have been found in the San Simon Basin, the Douglas Basin, and the Harguahala Basin.[77]

In addition to fissuring and land subsidence, continued overdrafting can lead to other socioeconomic effects over time. As water levels decline it becomes more expensive to pump and extract water from greater depths. For irrigators this added cost often outweighs any economic gains from irrigating. Often the result is that farmers are forced to resort to dry farming or to go out of business altogether. Declining aquifer levels have led to farm closures around Eloy and Douglas and in the Harquahala Valley.[78] Such closures place many people out of work and contribute to declining rural populations.

The overdrafting figures presented above have to be read with an understanding of Arizona's groundwater future. Although there are, as of 1996, significant amounts of overdrafting in the areas described above, various mitigating measures—particularly the Arizona Groundwater Management Act, the delivery of CAP water, and increased water conservation and use of effluent—promise to significantly reduce levels of overdrafting in many parts of the state over the next few decades. Overdrafting is likely to continue, however, in non-AMA areas where communities have no renewable water supply and where there is no practical, affordable alternative to groundwater mining.

Pollution

Phoenix AMA. Groundwater quality within the Phoenix AMA is generally adequate for most uses. However, there are areas within this AMA that have been severely affected by human activities. The area south of Phoenix has recorded high levels of nitrates, sulfates, and pesticides. Within the Phoenix metropolitan area there are several cases of volatile organic chemical (VOC) contamination. Several federal or Water Quality Assurance Revolving Fund (WQARF, or State Superfund) sites are contained within the Phoenix AMA. The most severe instances of VOC contamination have been detected in Scottsdale (where several public supply wells had to be closed), Tempe, Goodyear, Mesa, and Phoenix.[79] Contamination in the Phoenix metropolitan area is of great concern now and will continue to be so in the future, as the area is home to almost 2 million people.[80]

Tucson AMA. Several areas of concern exist within the Tucson AMA. Elevated levels of nitrate, sulfate, and total dissolved solids (TDS) have been recorded in the Green Valley area, and high levels of nitrate have been measured around Marana. Both of these cities are areas with high residential and commercial development potential. In addition, the city of Tucson is experiencing VOC and petroleum-product contamination as a result of leaking underground storage tanks and has the potential for increased contamination because of landfills located near desert washes.[81] Tucson alone has a population of close to five hundred thousand.

Pinal AMA. Much of the groundwater contamination (such as high levels of minerals and radiochemicals) in the Pinal AMA is naturally occurring. However, human contamination is also a problem within this AMA. Many small water systems within the AMA have nitrate levels in excess of U.S. drinking-water standards. In addition, herbicide, pesticide, and VOC contamination has been found within the AMA. Most of the groundwater in the AMA is of good quality, and contamination levels do not exceed health standards for drinking water. However, the area is continuously monitored for contaminants. Groundwater will be a crucial component in the future growth of this area (more so than in the Phoenix and Tucson AMAs).[82]

Prescott AMA. The groundwater in this area is of excellent quality. As of the mid-1990s the only known contaminant affecting water quality in the Prescott AMA was naturally occurring radon, which has forced the closure of some wells in the area.[83]

Contamination outside AMAs. There are several localized cases of groundwater contamination outside the four AMAs. Most of these involve elevated levels of nitrates from septic systems. Small communities with nitrate contamination include Bullhead City, Quartzsite, St. David, and Pinetop-Lakeside.[84]

In 1986 the Arizona legislature passed the Environmental Quality Act (EQA). The act was passed in response to growing concern over increasing levels of groundwater contamination throughout the state. The EQA established the WQARF. The fund is used to identify contaminated areas and the parties responsible for the contamination, evaluate the extent of contamination, and deal with the problem.[85] In addition, the Department of Environmental Quality routinely monitors wells throughout the state to insure that drinking-water supplies meet federal and state standards. While contamination poses both a current and a future potential threat to public water supplies, if monitoring activities are continued the state should be able to address any severe problems that may arise before the growing population is exposed to serious health risks.

Politics, Policy, and the Future

The most important allocational battles over groundwater policy in Arizona seem to be over. The passage of legislation to provide the state with authority to control groundwater overdrafting took several decades and strong federal prodding, and it involved a great deal of political maneuvering between major interest groups in Arizona.[86] This is not to suggest that the politics has gone out of groundwater management and policy in Arizona. Far from it. The decisions of the director of the DWR on the allowable amount of water available or the "water duty acres" will undoubtedly spark controversy in Arizona in the future. In addition, irrigators have approached the Arizona legislature for relief from the "maximum conservation" requirements of the Groundwater Management Act. According to the irrigators this requirement is unreasonable, even though mandatory limits on pump reductions are not a part of the act; theoretically mining can continue into perpetuity. Clearly, though, the balance of power in Arizona water politics has shifted away from agriculture. During the deliberations on the Arizona Groundwater Management Act, the representatives of agriculture felt they were at a serious disadvantage vis-à-vis the representatives of municipalities and mining companies in negotiating for provisions in the act.[87] It is not likely that agriculture will ever again have the political influence that it enjoyed in the past.

The above summary of the Arizona Groundwater Management Act shows that the DWR director has the authority necessary to manage groundwater to eliminate overdrafting. The act, along with the importation of surface water via CAP, the establishment of the Arizona Water Banking Authority to recharge aquifers and store excess water, and increased use of effluent for nonpotable uses makes these authors optimistic about the future of stable long-term groundwater use and management in the state. (Groundwater overdrafting has already been reduced by approximately 1.3 million acre-feet per year since the early 1980s.)

This is not to suggest that Arizona doesn't face a number of serious groundwater issues. Overdrafting will continue to be a problem for quite a few years. To the extent that overdrafting is uncontrolled, land subsidence has been and will continue to be a major problem in certain parts of the state. There will undoubtedly be social and economic transformations in the state because of changes in water use and urbanization. Urban encroachment and increasing water prices will slowly reduce the number of people working in the agricultural sector. Those that do continue to farm are likely to change to different types of crops because of shifting needs. For example, urbanization has led to an increase in the number of dairies in the state and to an increased need for corn and alfalfa. Any change in municipal use is likely to affect several industries at once. Decreases in lawn watering, for example, would have an impact on retailers selling lawn equipment and lawn supplies, and on landscapers who might find extra work in replacing lawns with desert flora. With changes in water use and distribution, such effects and changes are inevitable. However, with careful planning the transformation can be smooth, and serious socioeconomic disruption can be avoided.

The most pressing contamination problems appear to be within the Phoenix AMA, but state planners and health officials seem aware of these areas and are acting to remedy the situation. Much of the contamination across the state can be attributed to agricultural activities, which will be decreasing in the future, and to past waste-disposal practices that have been discontinued. If officials can keep on top of the potential problems that correspond with increased industrialization, they should be able to insure quality water for future generations of Arizonans.

One final note. CAP was approved by Congress with the understanding that the water would be used for agriculture and to reduce overdrafting. There is some irony in the fact that it is now clear that most of this water will eventually be used for urban expansion—expansion that drives out farming. Arizona's population is currently one of the most urbanized in the country. As miles and miles of new subdivisions expand around Phoenix and Tucson, farming will continue its slow decline in Arizona.

16 Nevada

Nevada is one of the fastest growing states in the country, and one of the most arid. The availability of water to support growing populations and economic development is a serious concern for the state. The shortage of water available to support growth has been chronic throughout the state's history. Surface water supplies are, for the most part, fully allocated throughout the state, and many aquifers have experienced significant declines. The state's major metropolitan area is Las Vegas, which is currently exploring options for importing water into the area in order to meet both present and future needs. Currently the Las Vegas Valley has two sources of water supply—Lake Mead (which artificially stores water from the Colorado River) and the basin-fill aquifer underlying Las Vegas Valley. Colorado River water is fully allocated, and the aquifer has experienced significant declines in water level in recent years. Simply put, Las Vegas needs to find more water if the city hopes to sustain its projected growth. Given the rapid population growth and the lack of adequate water supplies—particularly in the Las Vegas area—it is likely that groundwater will be transported from other areas and thus will play a pivotal role in the future of Las Vegas and of Nevada as a whole.

Physical Description

Nevada receives an average rainfall of only 9 inches per year (ranging from 3 inches in the valleys to over 40 in the mountains).[1] Most precipitation falls in the northwestern part of the state. While it is an important source of water in Nevada, groundwater accounted for only 31 percent of total water withdrawals in 1990.[2] This percentage is likely to increase, however, as the population of the state increases and as surface water becomes fully appropriated (as it almost is). Major sources of surface water in Nevada include the Colorado, Truckee, Carson, Walker, and Humboldt Rivers.

Demographics

As of 1 July 1995 the resident state population of Nevada was estimated to be 1,530,108.[3] Between 1950 and 1995 the population increased by 855.8 percent, which was the highest rate of increase in the nation during that period (the national average was only 73.6 percent).[4] The increase in the population of Nevada has occurred primarily in urban areas such as Las Vegas and Reno. In 1960 approximately 70 percent of Nevada's population resided in urban areas, while by 1990 88.3 percent of the state's population could be found living in urban settings.[5] The largest employment industries in Nevada are those that operate primarily within the rapidly growing urban areas—services, wholesale and retail trade, construction, and, of course, casino gaming.

Despite the relatively small contribution that agriculture makes to Nevada's economy, irrigation is the largest user of both surface water and groundwater in the state. The number of farms and the acreage devoted to agriculture in Nevada have remained fairly constant since 1959. In 1959 there were approximately 2,000 farms in the state covering roughly 10 million acres.[6] In 1993 there were still approximately 2,000 farms in the state; however, the number of acres devoted to agricultural use had dropped to just over 9 million. Nevada ranks third in the nation in terms of average farm size. Farming and related activities provide employment for over ten thousand persons.[7] However, farming and agricultural services account for only 0.008 percent of the gross state product. Services are by far the largest contributor to the gross state product in Nevada, accounting for 33 percent.[8]

Water Use

Approximately 54 million acre-feet of precipitation (rain or snow) falls on Nevada in an average year, and of this amount 3.2 million acre-feet runs off from the mountains and 2.2 million acre-feet recharges groundwater reservoirs. The remainder evaporates or is transpired by vegetation. The state's current water use equals 4 million acre-feet per year. It is estimated that by the year 2020 that figure may approach 4.6 million acre-feet per year. While agriculture will likely remain the largest single use of both surface water and groundwater, the biggest increase in use will be for public supply.[9] Current public supply demand for groundwater is about 31 percent of the total amount of water used; however, approximately 40 percent of Nevada's population depends on groundwater as a source of drinking water.[10]

Nevada has used five categories for describing and prioritizing its water use: public supply, self-supplied industrial, electric power, rural, and irrigated agriculture. The first category, public supply, is "water provided by public or private systems to residential, commercial, industrial, and municipal users in urbanized areas of the state."[11] Of the total groundwater demand for diversion, 9.8 percent falls under this category.[12] As of the mid-1990s the Reno and Las Vegas areas were the two biggest areas using water under the public-use category.

The second category is self-supplied industrial, or "individually operated systems providing water primarily for commercial and industrial use." The third category, electric power, is water withdrawn for thermoelectric power generation primarily for cooling systems. Rural water, the fourth category, consists of water used by individual farms and rural home systems.[13] The fifth category, irrigated agriculture, includes water used for the irrigation of crops, pasture, or livestock watering. As of 1990 irrigated agricultural use accounted for around 82 percent of the total demand for groundwater in Nevada.[14]

Groundwater was not a primary source of water in Nevada until the early 1940s.[15] By then mining, grazing, and land developers had appropriated most major surface-water supplies. After World War II demand for water in Nevada increased significantly. Nevada's gambling, six-week divorce laws, mining activity, and military bases contributed to its population growth and heightened water demand. This demand was met in large part by an increase in groundwater pumping. It is estimated that groundwater pumpage went from 53,000 acre-feet in 1950 to about 490,000 acre-feet in 1969, an increase of 900 percent.[16] As of the mid-1990s groundwater pumpage had increased to approximately 1.2 million acre-feet per year.[17]

For management purposes, Nevada's groundwater supply is divided into 14 hydrographic regions and finally into 255 hydrographic areas and subareas. The significance of this division is that it provides the state's water department with a resource "map" for management and conservation purposes. The appropriate management of Nevada's groundwater resources is vitally important for the state's future long-term growth and prosperity. There is evidence, however, that in various parts of Nevada groundwater may not be managed in a manner that will insure long-term beneficial use of the resource.

Problems

Overdrafting
Some groundwater basins in Nevada have been designated as critical because of severe overdrafting and declines in water level. (See the section below on Nevada law for a discussion of designated groundwater basins.) These include basins in Reno, Carson City, and the Las Vegas Valley. In the Las Vegas Valley, for example, groundwater demand in the mid-1990s stood at around 68,000 acre-feet per year, and the natural recharge was estimated at around 25,000 acre-feet per year. While Colorado River water is used to artificially recharge approximately 24,500 acre-feet per year, withdrawals continue to exceed recharge by a large margin.[18]

The largest metropolitan area in Nevada, Las Vegas, is the region in the state where overdraft is most severe. Water demand is highest in the summer, when all forty-three public wells are in full operation (fewer wells are at full operation in the winter).[19] According to a 1982 report, the "Las Vegas Valley has been in a situation of basin wide overdraft since the mid-to-late 1940's."[20] As of the mid-1990s this situation meant that water levels had declined by over 100 feet in most areas since 1948.[21] Problems associated with this overdraft include increased pumping costs for private homeowners that rely on well water, the potential for eventual depletion of the resource, and land subsidence. As of 1993 there were approximately sixty-eight hundred private wells in the Las Vegas Valley area.[22]

The state engineer has the authority to issue "revocable groundwater permits" in those areas of the state where an alternative, independent source of water is (or will be) available. The only area that has qualified for the issuance of revocable permits is the Las Vegas Valley (since a portion of its allotment of Colorado River water is still available, and since there is a possibility that water will be imported into the area in the future). Once water is available from these alternative sources, the temporary permits are (or will be) revoked by the state engineer. In 1976 the engineer's authority to revoke permits was challenged by the Curtis Park Manor Water Users Association. In 1985 the Nevada Supreme Court ultimately decided the case in favor of the state engineer. By aggressively pursuing the revocation program along with forfeiture, the state engineer hopes to reduce total pumpage in the Las Vegas Valley to a goal level of 50,000 acre-feet per year. However, at the time of this writing, nonrevocable permits totaling 71,000 acre-feet per year in water rights had been issued.[23]

Land Subsidence

Not only does overdraft threaten Nevada's existing pump levels because of declining water levels, but there have also been significant problems with land subsidence. This is particularly noticeable in the Las Vegas area, where some of the valley's subsurface material consists of highly compressible fine-grain sediments, making subsidence a likely occurrence in areas of overdraft.[24] In many areas water levels have declined to the point at which there is no longer any water to support the land surface. For example, in 1965 fissuring (cracking in the soil surface) was found in the area of the Lossee well in the north Las Vegas area. The well was closed for three years. When it was reopened in 1968 the fissuring resumed. There is also a "subsidence bowl," which is the result of municipal pumping, running north and south in the Las Vegas Valley.[25]

Land subsidence and fissuring can also lead to water degradation problems. Donald Haselhoff, senior environmental engineer and project manager for URS Engineers of Las Vegas, has stated that "mining has led to problems of subsidence and reversing of groundwater gradients where lower-quality water can reduce the quality of deep aquifers."[26] A reduction in the quality of water in deep aquifers could become a problem for individuals who rely on well water for their drinking water. In addition, the Nevada Department of Conservation is aware of the potential for further water-quality problems developing as a result of debris and surface runoff that accumulates in the fissure areas near surface groundwater.

While no serious degradation resulting from runoff had been detected as of the mid-1990s, it is a potential problem that must be continually monitored.[27]

Pollution

As of the mid-1990s Nevada did not have a comprehensive resource-based method for setting priorities for the prevention or remediation of groundwater contamination.[28] However, the Nevada Department of Conservation is aware of several current and potential pollution problem areas in the state.

Nitrate contamination is one of the most pressing problems in Nevada. Excessive levels of nitrates have been detected in Carson City, Douglas County, and Humboldt County, as well as in a nitrate "zone" in the northern part of Las Vegas Valley. The department has traced the majority of the nitrate contamination to septic tanks located in these areas.[29]

Underground storage tanks pose another existing and potential threat to groundwater quality in Nevada. There are over nine thousand underground storage tanks in the state that are registered with the Nevada Division of Environmental Protection. Of these, approximately thirty-three hundred have been identified as leaking.[30] One major contaminant that is typically contained in such tanks are petroleum products, which are a common source of volatile organic chemicals (VOCs) (a known carcinogen). Once petroleum products enter into a groundwater aquifer they are difficult to remove, and the process is very expensive. Groundwater basins have also been contaminated by synthetic chemicals. For example, the USGS found leakage into shallow groundwater of chemicals that had been produced and stored from 1940 to 1970 in the southeastern corner of Las Vegas Valley. These chemicals included benzene, pesticides, nitrate, chloride, and a variety of heavy metals.[31] These contaminants have been linked to a variety of adverse health effects including cancer, organ damage, and chromosomal damage.

Mercury is a localized concern in the Carson River Basin area. Excessive levels of mercury have been traced to the historic Comstock Lode mills, which used mercury to process silver and gold. In August 1990 the EPA listed the Carson River Mercury Site on its Superfund list because of the potential threat to human health presented by the mercury contamination.[32] This contamination could affect aquifers that are hydrologically connected to the Carson River in the contamination area. Mercury poisoning has been linked to nervous system disorders and organ damage.

Yet another localized problem is that of hydrocarbon products in the

East Sparks area. Operations of several companies, including those of the Southern Pacific Railroad, are responsible for the release of these products. The result of hydrocarbon releases has been the detection of free-floating diesel and jet fuel (measuring up to 2 feet in some areas) in the groundwater in this area. The spread of this contamination was limited because of dewatering by the Helms Construction Company (which discontinued dewatering activities in 1990).[33] A suit filed by the Department of Conservation against the Helms Construction Company and other polluters in the area has been one of the most successful actions in the history of the agency. Not only were several companies forced to pay for the cleanup costs in the area, they were fined a combined total of $10 million (which the department has redirected toward cleaning up other problem areas in the state). Nonetheless, current as well as future contamination is and will continue to be of great concern in Nevada as the population increases and as people become more dependent on groundwater for drinking water.

Law

Prior to the passage of the 1939 Nevada Groundwater Law, Nevada followed the common law doctrine of absolute ownership of groundwater. In 1872 the Nevada Supreme Court found that groundwater that percolates to the surface in "no known or defined course" belonged to the owner of the land above the water and could be used regardless of injury caused to others.[34] Later, in 1881, the court distinguished between definite underground streams and percolating groundwater, finding the former governed by the laws of surface waters.[35]

In 1939 the Nevada legislature enacted a groundwater-use statute that declared all groundwater within the state as belonging to the public and subject to appropriation for beneficial use (or the only recognized legitimate use).[36] The act exempted wells drilled prior to 25 March 1939 and the drilling of a well for "domestic" use, which includes water for "culinary and household purposes" in a single-family dwelling. No more than 1,800 gallons a day can be withdrawn from a domestic-use well.[37]

There are two forms of groundwater regulation in Nevada under the 1939 legislation—regulation of groundwater in designated groundwater basins and regulation in nondesignated basins. A basin is changed from nondesignated to designated status either by the declaration of the Nevada state engineer or upon petition to the engineer by 40 percent of the appropriators on record in the office of the state engineer.[38]

The state engineer, who is the executive head of the Division of Water Resources within the Nevada Department of Conservation and Natural Resources, has the authority to manage groundwater basins in Nevada. The state engineer can designate groundwater basins (to decide that the basin is in need of administration for groundwater-conservation purposes), establish preferred uses of water within designated basins, and limit withdrawals.[39] As of the mid-1990s 116 of Nevada's 232 groundwater basins had been designated, including virtually all of the most heavily used basins in the state.[40]

The essential differences in management practices as they affect designated versus nondesignated basins concerns the authority of the state engineer. In a designated basin a permit to sink a well must be obtained from the engineer prior to the commencement of any drilling. In a nondesignated basin no application or permit to appropriate water is required until after the well is drilled and water diverted and put to beneficial use. However, if the intent of the well driller is to divert the water from his or her well off the land, a permit to appropriate the water is required.[41] All appropriated groundwaters in Nevada must be put to a beneficial use, whether the waters be from undesignated or designated basins; however, in nondesignated basins the state engineer does not prioritize among uses.[42] A right to withdraw groundwater is forfeited after five successive years of nonuse.[43]

In designated basins the state engineer has the authority to prioritize among those who may use the water, and he or she may issue and revoke temporary permits to appropriate groundwater.[44] In nondesignated basins the engineer's authority is basically limited to determining when there is unappropriated water within the basin and issuing a permit for the extraction of that water. In either designated or nondesignated basins the state engineer will not issue a permit for the extraction of groundwater unless it is determined that there is unappropriated water in the basin, that the proposed use will not conflict with existing rights, and that the use will not prove detrimental to the public interest.[45]

In the case of designated basins located within the boundaries of a county having three or more incorporated cities, the state engineer may order the establishment of a groundwater board. Local groundwater boards, which serve in an advisory capacity to the state engineer, are made up of seven area residents appointed by the governor. The engineer cannot issue drilling, extraction, or use permits until he or she has conferred with the board and obtained its written advice and recommendations. However, the ultimate authority lies with the state engineer.

The groundwater board may be dissolved following determination that it is no longer needed, as was the case with the Las Vegas Valley Ground Water Board, which was dissolved in July 1973.[46]

The engineer also regulates well drilling, extraction, and management in various other ways. For example, he or she can limit the depth of or can prohibit the drilling of domestic wells if there is an alternate supplier of water. The engineer has the power to require well repairs, prevent waste, require pumping and other data, and develop rules for and issue licenses to drillers.[47]

Despite regulation since 1939, overall management of Nevada's groundwater supply has not been as successful as it could be—an observation that is substantiated by the fact that the majority of the state's groundwater basins are overappropriated.[48]

Politics, Policy, and the Future

Water quantity seems to be the primary determining factor that the state engineer uses in deciding who gets how much water and for what purpose. However, as we have seen, overappropriation does occur. In Las Vegas, for example, the Nevada state engineer has appropriated 91,257 acre-feet per year in groundwater rights—71,000 of which are permanent rights.[49] Recharge is estimated at 25,000 acre-feet per year. Temporary permits are issued, according to one water-planning report, to "allow temporary use, even overuse, of a system so that sufficient users become available to develop the economic base necessary to finance more permanent solutions."[50] One solution being discussed is the Cooperative Water Project (CWP), which is designed to meet the future needs of the Las Vegas area. Water projections have estimated that the region's current water resources will not be able to support anticipated development past the year 2002. It is felt that even if an aggressive conservation program is implemented, the available water will only be adequate through the year 2006. CWP is a project wherein about 250,000 acre-feet of water will be delivered to the Las Vegas area via the Virgin River and groundwater sources. The project will be quite expensive to develop, as plans call for over 1,000 miles of pipeline, two hundred or more groundwater production wells, monitoring wells, numerous pumping plants, and associated electrical facilities.[51] It has been projected that the project will meet the needs of Southern Nevada through the year 2030 (if it is undertaken in conjunction with conservation programs); after that time the state will still have to find alternative sources of water for the region.

Clearly, Nevada policymakers recognize the potential problems of long-term overdraft, but many seem to have concluded that the immediate economic benefits possible from using water now and the possibility that additional supplies may be available in the future mitigate current overdrafting problems.

As discussed earlier, the state engineer would like to lower Las Vegas groundwater appropriations to 50,000 acre-feet per year. However, as David Haselhoff mildly put it, "achieving this reduction is politically uncertain."[52] Current water-rights holders are not likely to willingly concede their holdings. As the state engineer is forced to deny more and more water permits because of the lack of sufficient groundwater supply, conflict will increase. As competition and conflict over groundwater resources increase in the future, it seems reasonable to anticipate that groups with agricultural, mining, or other interests concerning groundwater will increasingly feel a need to better organize on a state level so that they can more forcefully present their demands to the Nevada legislature. No matter how well the interests organize, however, water-use patterns in the state will have to change at some point in the future, and the losers in any battles will most likely be the agricultural interests. The relatively small amount of money that agriculture brings into the state, as compared to the amounts contributed by other, less water-intensive industries, makes irrigators a likely target for water redistribution.

The CWP is only a temporary fix for a long-term problem. Given the fact that agriculture contributes less than 1 percent to the economy of the state (while comprising well over half of the total water used) and the fact that the population is rapidly growing in urban areas, we conclude that shifts in water allocation are inevitable. These shifts are likely to benefit municipal interests at the expense of rural areas and agriculture. Much of the redistribution will be facilitated through the purchase of existing water rights as Nevada allows the purchasing of water rights for change in use. Reno is already purchasing agricultural water rights in the area to increase stream flow because of water-quality problems. Las Vegas is looking into transporting water from rural counties to meet its growing needs. While these counties are opposed to such diversion, given the monetary and political clout of Las Vegas, they will likely lose. Growth patterns in the state, and the related economic shifts, have dictated that the future of Nevada will center around its municipalities. Water supplies in Nevada are not unlimited, and water will have to be directed to the places where it will most benefit people within the state.

17 New Mexico

Like the majority of the states in the Southwest, most of New Mexico's recent growth has taken place in its urban areas. Throughout this century groundwater has been a very important source of water for both agriculture and municipal growth in the state. Over 88 percent of the population of New Mexico is totally dependent upon groundwater for their water needs.[1]

As of 1996 roughly equal amounts of surface water and groundwater were being withdrawn from New Mexico annually (53.3 percent of New Mexico's supply came from surface sources and 46.7 percent came from the ground).[2] However, surface water has almost all been appropriated or reserved; hence significant increased water use in New Mexico will, barring additional surface-water storage projects, be from groundwater resources. Groundwater is currently being mined in many parts of the state. Given the fact that urban populations are increasing, water supplies are limited, and agriculture is declining in importance for the overall state economy, it seems likely that there will be an increasing redistribution of both surface water and groundwater from agricultural to municipal uses.

Physical Description

New Mexico is a topographically diverse state. The area south of the Canadian River constitutes the eastern third of the state and is part of the High Plains and Pecos River Basin. The Rocky Mountains extend down through the central part of the state. The southwestern and central parts of New Mexico consist of a series of mountain ranges, valleys, and desert basins.

Average annual precipitation in New Mexico is approximately 13 inches. Regionally, precipitation varies significantly; some desert valleys receive less than 6 inches per year and some mountainous areas receive over 20 inches. Over half of the rainfall in New Mexico occurs during the months of July, August, and September.[3] Major surface-water sources in New Mexico include the San Juan, Canadian, Gila, San Francisco, and Pecos Rivers, and the Rio Grande.

Demographics

As of 1 July 1995 the resident state population of New Mexico was estimated to be 1,685,401.[4] Between 1950 and 1995 the population increased by 147.4 percent—well above the national average of 73.6 percent for the same period.[5] The greatest population increases have occurred in urban areas; however, over 25 percent of the state continues to reside in rural settings. In 1960 approximately 65 percent of New Mexico's population was urban.[6] By 1990 over 73 percent of the population (1,106,000 people) could be considered urban dwellers.[7]

Most New Mexicans (roughly 88 percent) earn wages through nonfarm operations. The largest industries, in terms of the numbers of persons employed, in New Mexico are service industries and wholesale and retail trade. However, the 3.3 percent of the population that is dependent upon agriculture for income represents approximately fifty thousand persons.[8] Despite the large number of people employed in agriculture, and the large portion of the state devoted to farm use (including ranching and grazing), farming and farm services contribute only about 2 percent to the gross state product, which is very little compared to other industries.[9] The largest contributors to New Mexico's gross state product are services (15.7 percent), manufacturing (13.8 percent), and finance, insurance, and real estate (13.3 percent).[10]

New Mexico ranks in the top five states nationally in terms of both the total number of acres devoted to farm use and in terms of average farm size. Over the years the number of farms in the state and the number of acres devoted to agricultural use have been declining, but the number of irrigated acres has not. In 1959 there were approximately 16,000 farms in New Mexico, with a land area in excess of 46 million acres.[11] In 1993 the number of farms in the state had dropped to 14,000, and approximately 44 million acres were devoted to farm use (with irrigated acreage comprising only a fraction of this total).[12]

Water Use

Annually, approximately 4.1 million acre-feet of water is withdrawn in New Mexico from all sources. Groundwater supplies 46.7 percent and surface water 53.3 percent of this total. Agriculture and livestock accounts for approximately 80 percent of the total water used in the state. Roughly 54 percent of agricultural water comes from surface water sources, and 46 percent comes from the ground.[13] Municipalities are the second-largest users of water in the state. Groundwater provides approximately 88 percent of New Mexico's municipal water supply. Groundwater also plays an important role for mining operations by supplying 67 percent of the mining industry demand.[14]

Given the limited supply and assuming continued population growth, shifts in use from agriculture to municipalities and industry can be anticipated. As of the mid-1990s municipalities and industry were already beginning to purchase agricultural water rights—a practice certain to be continued in the future.[15]

Although agriculture uses the bulk of the water available in the state, only about 3.3 percent of New Mexico's land is devoted to crops (only 1.8 percent of it is irrigable, and only 67 percent of that is actually irrigated).[16] Grazing accounts for roughly 82 percent of the state's land use, and slightly more than 1 percent (1.25) goes toward urban use (i.e., is subdivided for residential or industrial use).[17]

Problems

Overdrafting

Because New Mexico's surface water has been fully appropriated, the use of groundwater in the state has increased. Although rates vary, declining water levels are not unusual in most parts of the state. Areas of significant overdraft include the Estancia Basin, Portales Basin, Curry County Basin, Lea County Basin, Mimbres Basin, and portions of the Rio Grande Basin.[18]

In many parts of New Mexico annual rates of groundwater recharge are low or, for all intents and purposes, recharging does not occur at all. Because of this, overdrafting or groundwater mining may be the only feasible way to utilize the resource. As former New Mexico state engineer S. E. Reynolds has written, "It is New Mexico's position that it is not intrinsically evil to deplete groundwater resources at a rate greater than the rate of recharge (groundwater mining) where the quantity in storage is far greater than the annual recharge and there is no intimate relationship to fully appropriated stream flows."[19]

As of the mid-1990s the policy regarding overdrafting in nonconjunctive basins has remained unchanged.[20] This policy has been upheld by the New Mexico courts.

The New Mexico Supreme Court in *Mathers v. Texaco, Inc.* rejected a challenge to the state engineer's decision to allow groundwater mining as part of the basin's plan in the Lea County Basin, which, for all practical purposes, is nonrechargeable.[21] In 1952 the state engineer estimated the amount of water that could be withdrawn from the basin over a forty-year period to leave approximately one-third of the basin's water remaining. On the basis of this calculation he granted Texaco a permit to extract 350 acre-feet a year to Texaco.[22]

When a request is made for a groundwater appropriation in a declared groundwater basin (the only area where the state engineer has permit-issuing authority, as is discussed below), the state engineer determines the amount of unappropriated water in the basin. The amount of unappropriated water equals total water supply (down to a depth of around 230 feet; the depth may vary, and there may be water available at greater depth) less the amount farmers need for irrigation and the amount municipalities need to maintain a reasonable rate of growth for forty years. When there is unappropriated water in the basin, each year's pumping for existing municipal and farming uses is, effectively, taken out of the unappropriated amount. (If, or when, the basin becomes fully appropriated, at that time existing rights holders can, theoretically, count on a forty-year use period.)[23]

Pollution

Responsibility for monitoring and protecting groundwater quality in New Mexico is vested primarily in the Water Quality Control Commission. One of the duties of the commission is to adopt a comprehensive water-quality program that includes water-quality standards and regulations designed to prevent or abate pollution of surface water or groundwater.[24]

Since monitoring for contamination began in the 1920s it has been found that over eighteen hundred water-supply wells (both public and private) across the state are contaminated. Four hundred and ninety-one cases of groundwater contamination have been recorded in Bernalillo County, home to Albuquerque, the state's most populous city. Of these, 154 sites (49 of which are in Bernalillo County) had initiated cleanup efforts as of the mid-1990s.[25]

The commission has identified several groundwater pollution sources that are or have the potential for becoming serious threats to groundwater quality. These sources include saline intrusion, nonpoint source contamination from agricultural activity and septic systems and cesspools, and point source contamination from oil field sources, storage tanks, and mining activities.[26]

Saltwater intrusion is a threat to fresh groundwater supplies in many parts of New Mexico. The USGS has estimated that approximately 75 percent of New Mexico's groundwater is too saline for most uses.[27] (Almost all aquifers in the state contain both fresh and saline water.)[28] The major cause of saltwater pollution in New Mexico is the underground movement of saline water into freshwater areas as a result of overdrafting. The commission anticipates that this will be a future problem in the Tularosa and Estancia Basins.[29] In the Roswell Basin, saltwater encroachment, which is occurring as a result of extensive irrigation pumping, has been a problem since the 1950s. In addition, because saline water is heavier, improperly constructed or abandoned wells may facilitate intrusion when a saline aquifer overlies a freshwater aquifer.

Agricultural activity can be the source of nitrate contamination (from fertilizers) and pesticide pollution. While as of the mid-1990s the commission was not attributing much of the nitrate contamination in the state to agriculture, the potential for further aquifer degradation from fertilizer application exists. Similarly, in the 1990s pesticide contamination poses more of a potential threat than an actual problem. For example, aldicarb and carbofuran have been used extensively in some parts of the state, which means that these chemicals are present in the soil and have the potential to leach into groundwater.[30]

Septic systems and cesspools constitute the largest known source of groundwater contamination in New Mexico. There are over 162,000 septic tanks and cesspools in the state, and they discharge approximately 32 million gallons of wastewater into the ground every day. This waste is a leading cause of nitrate contamination and contamination by organic chemicals, which are contained in many household cleaning agents. One common organic chemical contained in household cleaners is trichloroethylene (TCE), a possible carcinogen known to cause nervous system and organ damage. Nitrates are also possibly carcinogenic in large doses and are the cause of methemoglobemia (blue-baby disease). Widespread nitrate contamination—sometimes at up to three times the U.S. public health standard—has been detected in parts of Chamita, Espanola, Tesuque, Santa Fe, Bernalillo, Corrales, Albuquerque, Carnuel, Bosque Farms, Los Lunas, Belen, Carlsbad, Nara Vista, Lovington, and Hobbs.[31]

Oil field operations and leaking storage tanks (both above and below ground) are believed to be the leading cause of aromatic hydrocarbon contamination in the state. (They are also responsible, to a degree, for some of the inorganic chemical contamination.) Up to one-third of the estimated sixty-five hundred underground storage tanks in the state are believed to be leaking. Oil field activities can lead to contamination through spills, secondary recovery (where water is injected into the well in order to force oil to the top), and improper disposal of waste water. Petroleum contamination was once limited to the southeastern portion of the state, but documented instances of contamination for other parts of the state have been recorded in recent years.[32] Aromatic hydrocarbons (a petroleum byproduct) are among the most costly and difficult contaminants to clean up once they have entered a water supply. Aromatic hydrocarbons have been linked to genetic and chromosomal defects and to leukemia.

Water from mines can contain a number of undesirable potential pollutants, including uranium, radium-226, vanadium, selenium, molybdenum, sulfates, iron, and total dissolved solids (TDS).[33] Mines usually must be dewatered; that is, the groundwater has to be pumped out so that the minerals can be extracted. As of the mid-1990s much of the mining activity in the state had been suspended, and dewatering has decreased over the years. For example, the Quivira Mine (uranium) is currently dewatering in an attempt to clean up its operations, which have been suspended. Other mining operations have closed without having had to clean up sites through further dewatering. However, mining interests in the state have for the most part kept their water rights and could continue to dewater in the future, should it once again become profitable to mine.[34] In the cases of mines that have suspended operations, damage to water resources may have already been done. In other words, even though dewatering has decreased, minerals and other mining-related contaminants have already been released and could potentially leach into aquifer systems.

The wastewater from ore processing contains many of the same pollutants found in water as a result of dewatering. This water is typically disposed of in tailing ponds and spoils spills, which for economic reasons and engineering convenience are often located in alluvial valleys close to the mill. The location of the tailings ponds often causes groundwater contamination, which remains even after operations have been discontinued. As of the mid-1990s pollution-control measures had failed to address this historic source of contamination.[35]

To date, water-quality control measures in New Mexico have been effective in controlling new pollution but have not yet had a significant impact on old sources. There are two primary reasons for this. First, the cleanup of existing problems is extremely expensive, and second, many of the existing problems (contamination by pesticides, for example) are in the form of potential health risks rather than in forms that would constitute actual or immediate risks. With continued monitoring, however, the Water Quality Control Commission should be able to spot potential problems when they become real problems.

Law

Absent conflicts over groundwater use, early New Mexico policymakers borrowed the absolute ownership doctrine from English common law. In 1910 the Territorial New Mexico Supreme Court found that "the water was a part of the land, and that each landowner could do with it as he chose."[36] As in other arid states, policymakers subsequently found the need to modify the doctrine. What distinguishes the development of New Mexico's groundwater law from that of most other states is that early in New Mexico's history of groundwater utilization the state legislature realized that changes were needed. These changes were brought about because of conflicts, in the 1920s, over groundwater use in the Roswell Basin.

During the 1920s technological developments and cheap energy led to increases in groundwater pumping throughout New Mexico. In the 125,000-acre Roswell Basin, wells were affecting artesian pressures. Many farmers, unable to make their mortgage payments, were being put out of business. In 1927 the legislature responded to their demands for assistance with New Mexico's first groundwater-appropriation statute.[37] The 1927 act gave the state engineer supervision and control of groundwater and declared groundwater to "belong to the public, and subject to appropriation to beneficial uses."[38] In 1930 the New Mexico Supreme Court found the 1927 act unconstitutional because of a technical error, but upheld its principles and intent.[39] To correct the act's technical defects the New Mexico legislature passed a similar law in 1931.[40] In 1950 the constitutionality of the 1931 act was upheld.[41] Although there have been various amendments and additions to the 1931 act, it provides the basis for current groundwater law in New Mexico. Section 72-12-1 of the New Mexico Statutes is similar to parts of the 1927 and 1931 acts. It reads in part: "The water of underground streams, channels, artesian basins, reservoirs or lakes, having reasonably ascertainable boundaries, are hereby declared to be public waters and to belong to the public and to be subject to appropriation for beneficial use."[42]

In 1985 the legislature added a provision for the conservation of water within the state for the protection of public welfare. The legislature amended the state's water code, prohibiting the issuance of a permit to extract groundwater if it is found to be contrary to the conservation of water or detrimental to the public welfare of the state.[43]

Only water within declared groundwater basins is subject to the control of the state engineer. No permit or license is required to appropriate waters in basins not declared by the state engineer. Where there is not a declared basin, the state engineer has no jurisdiction over groundwater use. In these areas individuals claiming that new appropriations will impair their water rights (i.e., senior rights holders) must sue in district court. In such actions the burden of proof is on the senior appropriator to establish an impairment of his or her water right. As of 1991 designated basins covered the majority of the state. Almost the entire western half of the state has been declared, and many portions of the eastern half (including the basins supporting Taos, Mora, Eddy, Lea, and Curry Counties) have been declared as well.[44]

Once an application has been filed for an appropriation in a declared basin, the state engineer is required to publish notice in a newspaper of general circulation in the county of the proposed appropriation for no less than three consecutive weeks. Such notice must indicate that objections to the application may be filed with the state engineer within ten days after the last date of publication.[45]

If no objections are filed and the state engineer finds that there is unappropriated water in the basin or that the proposed appropriation would not impair the water rights of prior appropriators, and if the appropriation is not found to be detrimental to the public welfare of the state, the application is approved and a permit is issued.[46] The burden of proof is on the person seeking the appropriation to show that the appropriation will not impair existing water rights.[47]

If objections have been filed to an application or if the state engineer is of the opinion that the permit should be denied, the application may be denied with or without a hearing.[48] On occasion the state engineer will hold administrative conferences prior to hearings to determine the issues between parties.[49] All decisions of the state engineer may be appealed to the district court. Such a proceeding is a trial de novo,[50] and the district court is limited in its review to the evidence that was before the state engineer.[51]

Section 72-12-1 of the New Mexico Statutes directs the state engineer to routinely grant permits for all applications for watering livestock and for domestic purposes including irrigation of one acre or less of noncommercial trees, lawn, or garden irrigation or other household domestic uses not to exceed 3 acre-feet. The engineer is also directed to issue permits for the extraction of up to 3 acre-feet per year for a period of one year or less for prospecting, mining, constructing public works and roads, or drilling to discover or develop mineral resources. Such applications need not follow the ordinary permit procedure (outlined above) if they do not permanently impair any existing rights.[52]

Section 72-12-8 of the New Mexico Statutes provides for the revocation of a permit issued by the state engineer and for the loss of the appropriator's water right. The section stipulates that when for a period of four years the owner of a water right or the holder of a permit does not put the water to the use for which the permit was granted or the right vested, and if one year after receiving notice and declaration from the state engineer the nonuse continues, the permit shall be revoked, and the right to the water reverts to the public and is subject to further appropriation. Section 72-1-9 exempts municipalities, counties, and public utilities supplying water to municipalities and counties from the four-year forfeiture provision. These entities may hold water rights without using them for up to forty years.

The way in which artesian waters and groundwaters in general are governed in New Mexico water law differs. Defined as a well that "derives its water supply from any artesian stratum or basin,"[53] an artesian well is under the supervision and control of the state engineer unless an artesian conservancy district has been formed, in which case the district has authority similar to that of the state engineer. The owner of land on which an artesian well is located must obtain a permit from the state engineer prior to any drilling, repairing, abandoning, or plugging of the well.[54] Contractors drilling within an artesian basin or through an artesian stratum are required to keep records of the work and to file the records with the state engineer upon completion of the drilling.[55]

The waste of artesian water is considered a misdemeanor and a public nuisance. Ten days after giving notice to the well owner of such a nuisance, the state engineer or an artesian conservancy district may correct the nuisance and recoup the costs of the correction by attaching a lien on the property.[56] Any transport of artesian water by ditch or conduit that results in a loss of more than 20 percent of the water prior to delivery is unlawful.[57]

In summary, the state engineer has the power to issue drilling permits in declared groundwater basins for further extractions when there is unappropriated water *or* if the proposed appropriation would not impair the rights of prior appropriators (provided the permits are not contrary to the conservation of water within the state and are not detrimental to the "public welfare" of the state). Extraction permits are routinely granted for livestock and domestic purposes, and rights may be lost if the water is not put to use. Special provisions protect artesian basins.

Politics, Policy, and the Future

It has been the state engineer's position, at least since the early 1950s, that additional extractions in excess of natural recharge will not always impair existing groundwater rights and that, given the physical limitations on groundwater recharge in areas where recharge is for all practical purposes nonexistent, such extractions should be allowed. This position has been ruled constitutional by the New Mexico courts.

By administering the state's laws in a way that permits groundwater mining the state engineer has been able to accommodate agricultural expansion and municipal growth as well as other uses of groundwater, such as industry and mining (although economic factors have led to a reduction in mining in recent years). Additional rights have not been granted, however, when they would impair existing surface water rights. (This is partly because New Mexico has entered into several interstate compacts that require it to deliver certain amounts of water to other states.)

Managing groundwater in a manner that allows for the controlled mining and eventual depletion of groundwater resources in some areas may lead to social and economic disruptions and to conflicts over preferred uses. Nevertheless, New Mexico is in a good position to avoid these disruptions by planning groundwater depletion. As of the mid-1990s such planning was underway, and regional and state plans are being developed.[58]

In New Mexico, as in most of the Southwest, to the extent that conflicts over future groundwater involve agricultural users in competition with municipalities and industrial users (including extractive industries), we can anticipate that agricultural users will see a decrease in their share of the available supply of water. This is currently taking place as municipal and industrial users are purchasing land and water rights from irrigators. Should irrigators become unwilling to sell in the future, the courts have held that water may be claimed through eminent domain.[59] Such takings, however, are often political and would require strong support for the municipality in question. Although the shift in political power from agricultural-rural areas to urban-industrial areas in New Mexico is not as pronounced as it is, for example, in Arizona, there has been a shift nonetheless, and it can be expected to continue as the state becomes more urbanized. New Mexico will undergo a shift in water distribution in the future. Eventually municipal and industrial use will surpass agricultural use. Furthermore, given the rapid population growth that has been and will be occurring in the state, such a redistribution will be necessary if New Mexico wishes to sustain its growing population into the future. This shift will be accompanied by a loss of the rural flavor of the state (as the population becomes more cosmopolitan) and by a decrease in the influence of farmers and ranchers on state politics and policy. To date these shifts have been gradual, allowing for the assimilation of displaced agricultural workers into the urban economy. But, like its neighbor Arizona, New Mexico will, in the not-too-distant future, become much more urbanized and will experience all the advantages and disadvantages that implies.

18 Oklahoma

Oklahoma has experienced substantial socioeconomic upheaval in recent years. This state, which depends heavily upon oil/gas production and on agriculture, was hurt badly by the collapse of the world oil market in the mid-1980s and by the instability that has affected the domestic agricultural market since then. On the positive side, however, these things did substantially reduce groundwater use in Oklahoma. In addition, recent economic developments and a growth rate that is below the national average have eased somewhat the stress placed on groundwater supplies in the state. Given the decline in Oklahoma's growth rate and the decline (in recent years) of irrigated agriculture, the state appears to have adequate groundwater supplies to sustain its population well into the future. Furthermore, the water is generally of good quality and does not, in most cases, threaten the health of Oklahomans. There are isolated instances of excessive contamination, but the state is making strides toward ensuring that the people of Oklahoma are provided with healthy drinking water.

Physical Description

Oklahoma is a plains state with two climatic regions, the humid east and the semiarid west. Accordingly, precipitation ranges from approximately 16 inches annually in the western panhandle to about 54 inches annually in southeastern Oklahoma.[1] Maximum precipitation occurs in the spring, with rainfall decreasing throughout the summer until fall, the second-wettest season.[2] Oklahoma receives approximately 53 percent of its fresh water supply from surface water.[3] The major sources of surface water in Oklahoma include the Arkansas River, which provides water in the northern part of the state, and the Red River in the southern Oklahoma.

Demographics

As of 1 July 1995 the resident state population of Oklahoma was estimated to be 3,277,687.[4] Between 1950 and 1995 Oklahoma's 46.7 percent rate of population growth was below the 73.6 percent national average.[5] Growth in Oklahoma's urban areas has occurred at a slightly higher rate than it has in the state's rural areas. In 1960 roughly 63 percent of the population resided in urban areas.[6] In 1990 it was estimated that 67.7 percent (1,015,000 persons) of Oklahomans were living in urban settings, with the largest concentrations being found around the two major cities in Oklahoma—Oklahoma City and Tulsa.[7] Despite the relative growth of urban areas, Oklahoma remains largely rural.

The largest percentage of Oklahomans earn wages through nonfarm operations. Approximately 96 percent of the employed civilian workforce in Oklahoma is nonagricultural. There are, however, over fifty thousand people residing in Oklahoma who depend upon agriculture.[8] Industries such as services, manufacturing, wholesale and retail trade, and financially related industries are the largest employing industries in the state. In addition, Oklahoma ranks third nationally for the number of people (some thirty-five thousand) employed through mining operations.[9]

Over the years the number of farms in Oklahoma and the acreage devoted to agricultural production have declined slightly. In 1959 there were roughly 95,000 farms in the state covering 35,801,000 acres.[10] In 1993 the number of farms in the state had fallen to 71,000 covering just over 34 million acres.[11] Irrigation is the largest single use of groundwater in Oklahoma, but farming contributes only 3.2 percent to the overall state gross product—a relatively small contribution. Manufacturing represents the largest single contributor, at 16.1 percent of the total. Other industries that contribute significantly to the gross state product of Oklahoma are services, and finance, insurance, and real estate, both of which contribute 14.2 percent.[12]

Water Use

Of all the water reportedly used in Oklahoma, over half comes from the ground.[13] Groundwater serves the drinking-water needs of over three hundred mostly rural communities throughout the state. The major metropolitan areas of Tulsa, Oklahoma City, and Lawton depend on surface water as the primary supply.[14] The most highly groundwater-dependent areas in Oklahoma are the northwest and the panhandle in the High Plains Region, home to the biggest single source of groundwater in the state and nation, the Ogallala Aquifer.

Irrigation, the largest user of groundwater in Oklahoma, accounts for 74 percent of total groundwater withdrawal; public supply accounts for approximately 12 percent; and rural domestic and livestock accounts for about 11 percent.[15] Groundwater use is most prevalent in the western half of the state, where irrigation withdrawals account for almost 90 percent of the total irrigation water use in the state.[16] While counties in the western portion of the state are generally lacking in surface water supply, groundwater use has allowed them to develop socially and economically. For example, Texas County, located in the panhandle, is almost completely dependent upon groundwater and is the largest single user of water among Oklahoma's seventy-seven counties.[17]

Over four hundred thousand acres of croplands are irrigated each year, primarily in the western region of the state.[18] Crops that depend significantly on this source include wheat, grain sorghum, alfalfa, cotton, and peanuts. In addition, groundwater use could become important for the oil industry for secondary and tertiary oil recovery methods if, or when, the domestic energy market improves.

As of the mid-1990s the western part of the state was using groundwater at a rate that exceeds recharge, but the rate of withdrawal has leveled off in recent years. Agricultural use of groundwater increased significantly from 1960 to the mid-1980s, particularly in the panhandle counties of the High Plains. In 1960 there were approximately four hundred groundwater wells in the panhandle. By 1981 the number had increased to just over twenty-six hundred. As of the mid-1990s the number of groundwater wells remained the same—the end of the growth period being marked by the 1980s depression in the domestic energy market.[19]

Problems

Groundwater contamination in Oklahoma is generally site specific and tends to arise from human influence. Because groundwater plays an important part in supplying water for municipal needs in many areas of Oklahoma, the quality of the water supply is necessarily a concern. While groundwater is generally of good quality in the state, contamination has led to the closure of some public supply wells and will continue to be a concern well into the future.

In assessing the relative priority of groundwater contamination sources in Oklahoma, the state's Department of Environmental Quality (DEQ) has determined that agricultural activities pose the most immediate threat to the quality of groundwater. The most common types of contaminants that arise from agricultural practices are nitrates and pesticides—usually in the form of volatile organic chemicals (VOCs). Nitrates in excess of EPA drinking-water standards have been detected in nineteen counties in Oklahoma, including Cleveland and Comanche Counties (two of the state's most populous counties).[20]

According to the DEQ's priority ranking, injection wells, both deep and shallow, pose the second-greatest threat to groundwater quality in Oklahoma. Septic tanks (a source of nitrates) rank third, followed by surface impoundments and industrial spills.[21] Industrial spills and surface impoundments containing oil and gas brine, combined with pesticide use, hold the potential for VOC contamination of groundwater resources. Many VOCs are believed to be carcinogenic, and when they come in the form of petroleum product, as is the case with gas and oil brine, they are among the most difficult and costly of all contaminants to remove from a water supply. As of the mid-1990s there were eight confirmed cases of VOC contamination of groundwater used in public supply in Oklahoma. The result of this contamination is that many of the public supply wells have been closed, and the affected communities are being forced to look for a new source of water. For example, those served by the Jack Griffin MHP public water supply system (Garber Wellington Aquifer) are using bottled water until an alternative water supply is found.[22]

Law

Beginning with the passage of the Oklahoma Territorial Statutes in 1890 and continuing until 1937, Oklahoma followed the common law or absolute ownership doctrine.[23] In 1937 the Oklahoma Supreme Court, in the case of *Canada v. City of Shawnee,* adopted the reasonable-use doctrine (or American rule). The court recognized the need to adopt the rule when it exposed "the futility of attempting to justify the complete exhaustion of a common supply of water on the ground that the landowner who has taken it all 'owned' that part thereof underlying his land when the operations commenced. His neighbor likewise had an ownership."[24] Oklahoma law does not distinguish between percolating groundwater and water flowing in underground streams (if it flows outside the cut bank of the stream).

The state codified its first groundwater law twelve years after the *Canada* decision in 1949. The Oklahoma Ground Water Law of 1949 declared a policy of conservation of groundwater resources based on a permit system that required the Oklahoma Water Resources Board (OWRB) to make "a determination of annual yield of each basin measured by the average annual recharge of such basin." Section 1013 essentially prohibited the issuance of permits that would authorize overdrafting. The 1949 law recognized the existence of prior rights and established a method of court adjudication of these rights.[25] The Ground Water Law of 1949 remained in effect until its repeal in 1972 and the subsequent adoption of new groundwater legislation.[26]

Under the 1972 legislation currently in effect the OWRB is required to make hydrologic surveys and investigations of each fresh groundwater basin or subbasin for the purpose of determining a maximum annual yield of fresh water to be produced from each basin based upon a minimum life of twenty years (from 1 July 1973, the effective date of the legislation).[27] This determination is utilized by the OWRB in approving permits and making allocations. Excepting that a "landowner has a right to take groundwater from land owned by him for domestic use without a permit," all other drilling and taking of groundwater are subject to the permit requirements of the 1972 legislation as amended.[28] Subsequent to application, a hearing is held. Section 1020.9 provides the instructions for the determination of permit issuance and allocation and reads, in part:

> At the hearing, the Board shall determine from the evidence presented by the parties interested, from hydrologic surveys and from other relevant data . . . whether the lands owned or leased by the applicant overlie the fresh groundwater basin or subbasin and whether the use to which the applicant intends to put the water is a beneficial use. If so, and if the Board finds that waste will not occur, the Board shall approve the application by issuing a regular permit. A

regular permit shall allocate to the applicant his proportionate part of the maximum yields . . . [being] that percentage of the total annual yield . . . which is equal to the percentage of the land overlying the fresh groundwater basin or subbasin which he owns or issues.[29]

If a hydrologic survey has yet to be completed for a particular basin or subbasin, the OWRB may issue temporary permits. Special permits, allotting water in excess of that allotted under a regular or temporary permit, are issued for periods not to exceed six months.[30] (These permits may, however, be renewed three times.) As the 1949 law does, the 1972 legislation recognizes the existence of prior rights.[31]

As is evident from the foregoing synopsis, the primary responsibility for the management of groundwater, as well as of all other waters in Oklahoma, lies with the OWRB. In addition to its duties with regard to allocations, the OWRB has statutory power to develop programs and to adopt and enforce standards protecting waters from pollution, and it is charged with adopting and enforcing water-well drilling regulations.[32] Section 905.1 of the board's *Rules, Regulations and Modes of Procedure 1982*, as amended in 1983, requires "all persons who drill in connection with a business, trade or occupation or for compensation in any manner [to] make application to and be licensed by the board." Requirements for licensing include residency in the state for a period of ninety days prior to application, two years' drilling or related experience, posting of a five-thousand-dollar bond payable to the OWRB, and a passing mark on a written examination.[33]

Oklahoma statutes also provide for the organization of irrigation districts "wherever ten, or a majority of the holders of title to lands susceptible to irrigation from a common source or combined sources petition for such organization."[34] The law provides the irrigation districts with broad powers, including the ability to establish equitable rules and regulations for the distribution and use of water among landowners within the district, the authority to collect tolls and charges for water used, and the power to sell property. The irrigation districts' business is conducted by boards of directors selected by members of the districts.[35]

Conservancy districts enjoy similar powers that cover a wide variety of purposes, including the provision of irrigation and the development and provision of water supplies for domestic, industrial, and agricultural requirements. Master conservancy districts are established where a need exists for intergovernmental coordination of water facilities development.[36]

The relationship between the OWRB and the irrigation districts has been strained at times. The relationship between the board and the conservancy districts, which is considerably more cooperative, concentrates almost exclusively on planning and implementation of surface-water delivery and treatment projects. Despite the existence of local governmental water-policy units in Oklahoma, the vast majority of substantive decision making regarding groundwater management rests with the OWRB.

A better understanding of the role of local and state governmental units, the clientele they serve, and the roles each plays in the development and application of groundwater policy in Oklahoma can be gained through an examination of the 1985 Oklahoma Supreme Court decision in *Oklahoma Water Resources Board, et al. v. Texas County Irrigation and Water Resources Association, Inc.*[37] In February 1979 Mobil Oil Company filed an application to mine fresh groundwater for use in secondary and tertiary oil recovery. The OWRB conducted a hearing on the application in August 1979 and issued a temporary permit on 8 January 1980. The Texas County Irrigation and Water Resources Association, which had protested Mobil's application at the administrative hearing, sought judicial review of the board's ruling in the Texas County District Court. The association argued that the use of fresh groundwater for secondary and tertiary oil recovery constituted waste (and was, thus, unlawful use) because the water was not continued in the natural cycle but was polluted and lost permanently. The district court, relying on previous Oklahoma Supreme Court rulings on the issues of fresh groundwater use for secondary enhanced recovery, ruled that Mobil's intended use of the water was beneficial. However, in a finding that took all parties by surprise, the district court held that "Mobil's proposed use of fresh groundwater off the lands from which it was produced constitutes an unreasonable use of water from a critical groundwater source."

In rejecting the district court's finding, the Oklahoma Supreme Court found that "in addition to not recognizing 'critical groundwater areas,' the 1972 Act neither recognizes nor mentions preferences between beneficial uses. The concept of conflicting beneficial uses in a critical groundwater area has no application in the current groundwater law." The court further rejected the finding that transfer of water for use off the premises from which it was withdrawn was contrary to the legislative intent of the 1972 legislation, stating that "The only substantive limitation on use per se, whether on or off the place of origin, is that it be a reasonable use."

The significance for present-day policy, however, is found in the court's consideration of the issue of waste. It is particularly interesting to note that the issue was never considered or argued by either side at the administrative hearing or the trial court level. The Oklahoma Supreme Court, applying the doctrine of publici juris, and determining the issue to be an integral part of the relevant and applicable law, opened the issue for examination at the review level, an uncommon occurrence.[38] Rules of the OWRB define waste of water as "any act permitting or causing the pollution of fresh water or the use of such water in an inefficient manner or any manner that is not beneficial."[39] The court's primary concern was that waste "by pollution" was not even considered in the administrative ruling. No evidence was presented by Mobil that would have served to insure that such waste would not occur. This, the court suggested, was of particular importance in examining tertiary recovery, whereby "detergent additives and polymers will be mixed with the fresh water to reduce the waters' surface tension so that more oil can be recovered." The court further admonished Mobil for its failure to supply evidence that waste by depletion would not occur, thus enlarging the concept of waste even further. The court noted that "Mobil presently has no program to monitor on a regular basis the drop in the Ogallala water level, resulting from Mobil's mining activities."

In conclusion, the court remanded the case to the OWRB for further hearing, "to receive evidence and make essential findings of fact to determine whether waste by pollution, as well as waste by depletion, will not occur." In short, the court ruled that the use of fresh water for secondary and tertiary oil recovery might constitute waste and has given the OWRB the authority to decide about each proposed project on an individual basis. However, such authority was partially undermined in the 1991 case of *Oklahoma v. Texas County Irrigation and Water Resources Association*, 818 P.2d 449, 455 (Okla. 1991). In this case the court held that the Oklahoma Corporation Commission may grant recovery permits for enhanced recovery using fresh water even though the users have yet to receive a fresh groundwater appropriation from the OWRB. In addition, the court held that owners of groundwater that might be affected by such recovery are not entitled to personal notice that the recovery activities are taking place, and that published notice of the recovery activities need not state that fresh water is being utilized.[40]

Based on the court's interpretation of the 1972 groundwater law expressed in the Mobil case (the only limitation on withdrawal is that the use be "reasonable"), it appears that the Oklahoma legislature, by enacting the 1972 groundwater law, has sanctioned the eventual depletion of the Ogallala in Oklahoma. Through adoption of a permit allocations based on a minimum twenty-year life for each aquifer, the legislature has opted for an orderly exhaustion of the state's groundwater resources.

Politics, Policy, and the Future

In the past, the largest single source of conflict over water policy in Oklahoma centered on a multidecade battle over the issue of interbasin transfer. Plans had involved a two-phase construction of conveyance systems to transport water from eastern Oklahoma to central and western Oklahoma. The 1980 Oklahoma Comprehensive Water Plan supported the proposed project as the option that "potentially allows the greatest expansion of irrigated acreage, utilizes the greatest amount of water, and results in the highest levels of production and returns."[41] Alternative options were believed to be inadequate. For example, the OWRB once wrote that, "[A]n assessment of non-transfer alternatives indicates they can provide only supplemental water supplies and cannot be relied upon to provide the quantities of water required to meet Oklahoma's future needs."[42] The emphasis on interbasin transfer was driven, in part, by powerful political interests who were unsuccessful.[43] The push came primarily from irrigators who wanted to expand agricultural activity in the western part of the state.

Interbasin transfer is no longer a priority item for the state of Oklahoma, nor is it likely to become one in the foreseeable future. The reasons for this are many. One is the successful resistance of a powerful though informal coalition of eastern and central Oklahomans. An eastern member of the OWRB may have expressed the coalition's feelings when he stated that "They not only want to move our water to western Oklahoma, they want us to pay for it."[44] (Regionalism was undoubtedly partially responsible for this sentiment.) Other, perhaps more important concerns that helped kill the appeal of interbasin transfer were the economic feasibility of the project and a serious socioeconomic transformation in the state. Early projections on the cost of the project estimated that cost as ranging from $11 to $20 billion.[45] A decline in the state economy, coupled with an increasing reluctance on the part of the federal government to fund new water projects, has left the state without the resources necessary to fund such an enormous undertaking. Furthermore, the major push for the transfer of water came before the unexpected collapse of the world oil market and the U.S. agricultural industry in the mid-1980s. This collapse "devastated Oklahoma's economy, significantly reducing projected growth patterns of population, industry, water use and virtually all other factors related to economic well-being."[46] In other words, socioeconomic changes meant that water use would decline in the areas to be served by the project, making such transfers unnecessary and unfeasible in the near future.

Furthermore, state water planners believe that no major water conveyance should occur until local supplies are fully developed. While overdrafting continues to be the norm in many parts of the state, additional water supply would do nothing to promote conservation or more efficient use of the resource. In addition, declining agricultural use has led to groundwater increases in some areas, and current projections indicate that if conservation measures are implemented, present supplies are adequate to meet both current and projected needs in all areas of the state through the year 2050 (with a few localized exceptions) with few implications.[47] There might, however, continue to be localized problems with contamination (discussed previously). It appears, at least for now, that Oklahoma is knowledgeable about both the quality and the quantity of its water resources and that it is looking toward the future. The irony of the situation is that the rapid deterioration of two of the state's leading industries might have been the savior of its water resources.

19 Texas

Texas is undergoing a transformation in its orientation toward water planning. While the state developed under an assumption of unlimited water supply, state planners now realize that future growth and development will have to occur within the boundaries of a fixed supply. Decades of relatively unlimited water use have begun to take their toll on the state. Increasing urbanization, declining crop prices, and a heightened awareness of environmental water needs have led to changes in the state's water requirements. Given the past history of Texas water use, some serious contamination problems, and the optimistic assumptions that are a part of the state's long-term water plan, the outlook for the state's future as it relates to water is uncertain.

Physical Description

With 691,027 square kilometers (266,807 square miles), Texas is a geographically, climatologically, and hydrologically diverse state. The western part of the state, much of central Texas, and the Texas panhandle are the driest regions, with precipitation increasing as one moves east. Average annual precipitation ranges from a low of 8 inches per year in west Texas to a high of around 56 inches in the southeast.[1] Surface water contributes heavily to the fresh-water supply of Texas, providing approximately 55 percent of the fresh-water withdrawals in the state.[2] Major surface-water sources in the state include the Canadian, Red, Brazos, Colorado, Sulphur, Cypress, Sabine, Neches, Trinity, Lavaca, Guadalupe, San Antonio, San Jacinto, and Rio Grande River Basins.

Demographics

As of 1 July 1995 the resident state population of Texas was estimated to be 18,723,991.[3] Between 1950 and 1995 the population increased by 142.8 percent, which was almost double the national average growth of 73.6 percent for the same period.[4] Texas's urban areas have experienced greater growth than have its rural ones. In 1960 approximately 75 percent of the population resided in urban areas.[5] In 1990 the urban areas of Texas contained 80.3 percent of the state's population.[6]

While over 97 percent of the people living in Texas earn wages through nonfarm-related occupations, a large number are dependent upon agriculture. Over 200,000 people (213,759 by the latest estimates) rely on farming as a means of support. The biggest employing industries in Texas are manufacturing, services, and wholesale and retail trade.[7]

Irrigation is the largest user of groundwater in Texas. However, as populations have shifted to urban areas, and as other industries have grown in relation to agriculture, the number of farms in the state and the acreage devoted to agriculture have declined. In 1959 there were approximately 227,000 farms in the state covering in excess of 143 million acres.[8] In 1993 there were around 185,000 farms covering just over 130 million acres. In the three years between 1990 and 1993 the number of farms dropped by 1,000, and the number of acres they occupied fell by approximately 2 million.[9] Despite the numbers of people employed through agriculture and the vast amount of acreage devoted to raising crops, farming and farm-related services actually contribute a small amount to the gross state product of Texas in relation to other industries. Farming and farm-related services contribute approximately 1.9 percent to the gross state product. The largest economic contributors to the gross state product of Texas are services and manufacturing, which contribute approximately 16.2 percent and 15.9 percent, respectively.[10]

Water Use

As of the mid-1990s Texas was using a total of 20.1 million acre-feet of fresh water per year.[11] Roughly 40 percent of that supply (7.4 million acre-feet) comes from the ground.[12] About half of the state's population is served by groundwater. It supplies municipalities (to some degree) in all areas of Texas and in practically every county.[13]

Although it plays a smaller role in Texas irrigation, surface water is an important source of water for public supply systems in the state. Roughly 60 percent of public supply water comes from surface sources, which include twenty-three river and coastal basins in the state. However, if groundwater sources continue to experience widespread contamination (which will be discussed in a later section), surface water will necessarily gain in importance for public supply.

Groundwater supply comes from some two dozen major and minor aquifers that underlie more than half of Texas. Annual recharge is about 5.3 million acre-feet, or just about 70 percent of the current level of groundwater use. In many areas of the state, notably in the northern High Plains, the long-term use of groundwater from the Ogallala Aquifer (and other aquifers) is lowering water levels and resulting in current shortages or in what will become shortages in the foreseeable future.[14]

These problems have not gone unnoticed. In 1966 the Texas Water Development Fund was expanded to $400 million by voter approval of a constitutional amendment. In 1968 the Texas Water Development Board revised its Preliminary Texas Water Plan and called for sixty-seven new reservoirs and two saltwater intrusion barriers. It included plans for storage, regulation, and distribution of up to 13 million acre-feet of imported water, if such were to become available.[15]

However, in the 1981 general election, Proposition 4, which would have provided bonds to fund state water projects, was defeated. This defeat led to a broad-based public involvement program conducted by the Texas DWR and to a successful bond election in 1984.[16] Since that time there have been water plan updates in 1984, 1990, and 1992. Current plans call for fourteen new reservoirs and five chlorine-control projects.[17]

Texas groundwater supply and other problems are closely related to the state's groundwater law (wherein there is little state regulation, and wherein most management decision-making power is held by decentralized water districts or individual property owners). Although the same is true to varying degrees in the other states examined in this book, in Texas the law is so closely associated with some of the state's major groundwater problems that here it makes sense to discuss those problems after the following summary of Texas groundwater law.

Law

History

Texas is a good example of a state that is experiencing problems with adapting the English common law doctrine to the realities of the physical environment in the West. While the state was part of Mexico, Texas water practice was naturally influenced by Spanish water tradition. However, after Texas separated from Mexico in 1836, Spanish and Mexican law prevailed in the state until 1840, when the Texas legislature, "in its wisdom," adopted the English common law.[18] According to John Teutsch, four factors are believed to have influenced the Texas court decisions on groundwater law: (1) the court's understanding of hydrology, (2) the relationship of pumping technology to the problem caused by the pumping, (3) the importance of groundwater in the jurisdiction of the dispute, and (4) the court's willingness to become involved in groundwater disputes.[19]

In 1904 the Texas Supreme Court decided *Houston and Texas Central Railroad v. East,* the leading case establishing the absolute ownership doctrine in Texas groundwater law.[20] In *East,* lower courts had found that pumping 25,000 gallons of water per day from a railroad well dried up the plaintiff's well and that the railroad company's use was unreasonable. The court thereby briefly established the "rule of reasonable use."

However, the Texas Supreme Court overturned the earlier *East* decision, arguing that the law recognized no correlative rights involving underground water movement because of the unknown nature of any such movement. The *East* decision established the rule by which landowners could claim undisputed ownership of groundwaters pumped from their property. (Surface water and groundwater flowing in definite underground streams are governed by surface-water law and are subject to prior appropriation.)

Various attempts have been made to overturn or modify the absolute ownership doctrine in Texas. In 1948, in the case *Cantwell v. Zinser,* the plaintiff was unable to claim that a depleted spring was a watercourse and thereby enjoy the protection of surface-water (i.e., prior appropriation) rights.[21]

In the 1954 case of *Pecos County Water Control and Improvement District No. 1 v. Williams* (popularly referred to as the "Comanche Springs" case), the plaintiff's wells, serving thousands of acres of agricultural land, were dried up by the Pecos water district's pumping.[22] The plaintiff asked that either the water in question be classified as a subsurface stream, giving him the protection of surface-water laws, or that the absolute ownership rule be rejected by overturning *East*. The lower court rejected the plaintiff's arguments and reaffirmed *East*. Subsequently the Texas Supreme Court declined to overturn the lower court's decision. The resulting situation was later characterized by one water rights expert who said, "you can steal your neighbor's water, but you can't pollute his well."[23]

Efforts to limit the absolute ownership rule have also been based on arguments against waste. In 1955, in *City of Corpus Christi v. City of Pleasanton*, plaintiffs argued that the water in transit via open channels (a dry streamcourse) was being wasted because of evaporation of as much as three-quarters of the original amount.[24] The plaintiff's argument was accepted by the trial court and affirmed by the court of civil appeals, but rejected by the Texas Supreme Court. The justices urged the state legislature to correct the situation, noting advances in the science of hydrology since the 1904 *East* decision.

More recently, in 1974, the Texas Supreme Court declined to overturn a lower court's use of the absolute ownership rule in *Bartley v. Stone*.[25] The owner of a spring was held to be entitled to use all of the water from the spring regardless of the effect on downstream users.

In another recent decision, *Friendswood Development Co. v. Smith-Southwest Industries, Inc.* (1977), the plaintiffs sought to restrict groundwater pumping on the basis of damage done to surface structures.[26] Landowners in the case sued for subsidence damage done to their land as a result of the pumping of groundwater for industrial use. The court carried on the tradition of *East* and ruled that since no waste of water was involved there was no liability from the use of the water nor damage resulting from its use. However, the court warned that in the future another rule would be applied that would impose liability for pumping that negligently causes subsidence.

One of the few restrictions to be placed on pumping groundwater in Texas occurred in 1981 in the case of *Public Utilities Commission v. City of Sherman*.[27] In this instance the Texas Court of Civil Appeals was willing to restrict pumping because it interfered with service provided by another public utility. The rationale offered was that the public utility commission's action constituted regulation of utility service, not groundwater, despite the significant impact of the order upon groundwater.

Thus we see that from 1904 to the early 1990s the Texas Supreme

Court steadfastly refused to impose meaningful restrictions on ground-water withdrawal, leaving the absolute ownership rule in force.[28] However, *In re Adjudication of Edwards Aquifer*, filed on 15 June 1989, Hayes County District Court, Twenty-second Judicial District, might be an indication that the court is shifting its stance somewhat. The case was an attempt by the Texas Water Commission to restrict pumping in the Edwards Aquifer and to make the waters of the aquifer subject to appropriation. The case hinged on two issues—the taking of private property (restricting the pumping of overlying land owners) and whether subterranean streams are considered surface water subject to appropriation. (The latter had never been directly addressed by any Texas court, although it has been implied in dictum that the rules governing surface water can be applied to underground streams.)[29] In the fall of 1996 the court upheld bill 1477, which established the Edwards Aquifer Authority and allowed for the regulation of pumping. The takings issue may reappear, however, once the level of pumping restrictions are established by the authority.[30]

Groundwater Administration

Local government entities are important in the management of ground-water resources in Texas. Although their activity has been limited and their success at controlling groundwater overdrafting even more limited, what control there is in Texas is mainly exercised on the local level.

In 1949 the Texas legislature authorized the voluntary creation of underground water conservation districts (UWCDs) with discretionary power to regulate groundwater withdrawals as long as landowners did not lose their "ownership" of groundwater.[31] UWCDs have the power to "provide for the spacing of water wells" and to "regulate the production of wells"; they also have other powers that enable them "to minimize as far as practical the drawdown of the water table."[32] Although forty-three UWCDs had been created by 1995 they have not, for the most part, been effective managers of groundwater (partly because only one—the Harris-Galveston Coastal Subsidence District—has directly regulated pumping). Well spacing requirements undertaken by some districts have slowed groundwater development and depletion in some areas, but no attempts (exception noted) have been made to control groundwater production and thereby extend the life of the aquifer.[33] This failure (which it may or may not be, depending on one's perspective; clearly many ground-water pumpers are happy with the status quo) is due to the fact that a landowner's absolute right to the water beneath his or her land cannot be abrogated by a UWCD and has not been limited by the courts or the

Texas legislature. Another problem related to the extent of a UWCD's control over groundwater concerns the ability of any county to exclude itself from a district's jurisdiction. With that option available to local pumpers, UWCDs are not likely to pursue management practices (assuming they had the desire to do so) that threaten the economic activities of groundwater extractors within their borders.

Two of the groundwater-management bodies created by the Texas legislature are the Edwards Underground Water District (now the revamped Edwards Aquifer Authority) and the Harris-Galveston Coastal Subsidence District. The former was created in 1959 to "conserve, protect, and increase the recharge of" groundwater in the San Antonio area. However, the powers necessary to carry out this mandate were not conferred on the district, and the district's activities, as of the mid-1990s, have been largely limited to gathering and disseminating data and to encouraging conservation measures in times of drought.[34] The other district, the Harris-Galveston Coastal Subsidence District, was created in 1975 to regulate groundwater withdrawals in an effort to decrease land subsidence and associated flooding. The district has successfully used permit requirements and pumping fees to curtail withdrawals, and the Texas courts have upheld its authority to do so.[35]

Other local entities with responsibility over water use and management in Texas include 1,092 public municipal water systems, 800 rural water-supply corporations, and 750 investor-owned public water-supply systems.[36] Few of these organizations are actively involved in groundwater management to prevent overdrafting. This is due in large part to the nature of Texas groundwater law. One notable exception (along with the Harris-Galveston UWCD) is the water-short city of El Paso, which has taken various "measures to conserve groundwater including in-well blending of fresh water and saline water, use of municipal wastewater to recharge the aquifer, and a public education campaign."[37]

On the state level, Texas is not directly involved in the regulation of groundwater withdrawals except for the creation of water districts, some of which have (as we have seen) the power to regulate groundwater extraction.[38]

In 1990 the Texas Water Development Board published an extensive report entitled *Water for Texas*, which included the state's fifty-year water plan. The report contains recommendations for water conservation, water-quality protection, water-supply development, and public education. In addition, it describes a variety of groundwater problems usually associated with overdrafting. While the report does recommend amending the Texas Water Code to allow the water commission more authority for working with local districts in implementing management plans, it is interesting that it does not recommend any change in the common law rule. In fact the report clearly states that "the policy discussions and recommendations presented in this Plan are not intended to subvert the current State laws pertaining to a landowner's rights to the groundwater occurring beneath that landowner's property."[39]

Texas groundwater law is both unique and archaic. As Roger Tyler wrote in the *Texas Bar Journal,* Texas "is probably the only state in the United States following the early English or common-law rule without qualification"; others have called the Texas law a rule that is "one of anarchy rather than law."[40] The absolute ownership doctrine has led to competition over water resources with bordering states and with Mexico and to various other problems including land subsidence, saltwater intrusion, and other forms of pollution.[41]

Problems

Pollution
Much of the contamination in Texas groundwater comes from natural sources such as salt-water intrusion, mineralization, and naturally occurring high levels of metals, nitrate, and radioactivity. It has been estimated that natural contamination of aquifers affects the quality of more groundwater than do all other sources of contamination combined.[42] For example, widespread overdrafting, which has resulted in lowered water tables and to drilling through aquifers of good quality into aquifers of poor quality, has led to instances of saltwater intrusion statewide. Examples of saltwater or brackish water intrusion affecting groundwater quality can be found in the areas of El Paso–Ciudad Juarez, Texas City–Galveston, areas of the northern High Plains, and the area south of Corpus Christi.

While there is a great deal of naturally occurring contamination in some areas, this does not suggest that Texas faces no contamination problems at the hands of humans. Humans' impact on the groundwater supplies of Texas is significant. The Texas Water Development Board has identified several areas of concern for state water supplies, including septic tanks, storage tanks, improperly completed or abandoned wells, holes drilled for oil- and gas-related activities, injection wells, and fertilizer and pesticide application.[43]

Improperly constructed or abandoned wells are thought to be a significant source of contamination because they provide direct access from the surface to groundwater supplies and vertical access from one aquifer to another through vertical leakage. It is believed that most pesticide contamination in Texas can be attributed to this source. Of the more than 600,000 wells in Texas (a conservative estimate) approximately 150,000 are abandoned.[44]

Over 1.5 million oil- and gas-activity related holes, many of which have not had the casing treated and are either currently leaking or have the potential to leak in the future, have been drilled in Texas over the past eighty years. These holes, along with leaking storage tanks, are the leading cause of petroleum contamination in the state. Over five thousand storage tanks in Texas have been confirmed to be currently leaking, and close to forty thousand have the potential to leak. As of the mid-1990s the Texas Water Commission had been receiving notices of about 50 confirmed leaks per month.[45] Recent testing conducted by the Texas Natural Resource Conservation Commission has revealed contamination from gasoline, oil, or diesel fuel in virtually every county in the state.[46] Many petroleum-based contaminants are believed to be carcinogenic, and once these contaminants enter into an aquifer they are among the most difficult and costly of all contaminants to remove.

While there has yet to be a confirmed case of potable water being contaminated by industrial waste from injection wells, the Texas Water Development Board is aware of the potential for such contamination. Roughly 5 billion gallons of industrial waste are disposed of in this manner every year. Over half of the industrial waste disposed of in the state each year is injected into disposal wells, creating the potential for widespread problems in the future, should leaks develop in any of these underground dumpsites.

Finally, fertilizer and pesticide applications have led to excessively high levels of nitrates and pesticides in the water found in several parts of the state. The potential for both current and future health risks has led the Texas Natural Resource Conservation Commission and others to address the situation through the development of a statewide agricultural chemical groundwater strategy.

Overdrafting
Overdrafting is the rule rather than the exception in much of Texas. Water levels have declined by as much as 200 feet in northwest Texas since groundwater development began after the turn of the century. The total volume of water in the High Plains of Texas has decreased by ap-

proximately 23 percent—the highest percentage of depletion of any state underlying the Ogallala.[47] Overdrafting of the Ogallala Aquifer carries possible serious social consequences.

As the water level drops it becomes more expensive to pump, which makes it unprofitable for many farmers to continue pumping. If agricultural interests go out of business, people lose jobs. Municipalities are also forced to pay more for withdrawals, resulting in higher prices for water consumers. Long-run depletion could result in water shortages and in competition between water users, as well as in changes to the state's existing socioeconomic structure as it relates to water. However, while declines of up to 15 feet have been recorded since 1980 in parts of the Ogallala, water levels have risen by the same amount in other portions of the aquifer.[48]

Groundwater pumping in many parts of Texas slowed in the 1980s, allowing aquifers to recover somewhat. The decrease has been attributed to several factors, including increased precipitation, declining crop values, and a drop in the domestic oil market. Economic conditions in the 1980s forced many farmers to resort to dry farming because the prices they were receiving for their crops did not keep up with the increased cost of pumping water from deeper depths. As a result, many acres of agricultural land were taken out of irrigation or out of farming altogether during this period. However, if oil prices go up and it becomes profitable to develop Texas petroleum once more, the demand for Texas's groundwater could rise.[49] (Water is pumped into oil wells to force oil to the surface, a practice that will only become profitable when oil prices rise above current levels.)

If groundwater pumping continues unabated in the Ogallala, there is a possibility that the social disruptions mentioned previously could develop. However, if projections included in the Texas Water Plan prove correct, the Ogallala will have enough water to meet the area's water needs for the next one hundred to two hundred years.[50] (The plan includes conservation measures, supply augmentation, and the anticipation of a significant drop in irrigation, which would mean a change in the area's economy.)[51]

Other areas of serious overdrafting include El Paso, San Antonio, areas south of San Antonio, areas just to the west of Interstate 35, Houston, and Galveston (although groundwater development has been restricted in these areas to prevent further land subsidence).[52] Overdrafting in the Edwards Aquifer area has led to habitat destruction of some endangered species. The impact on habitat has forced the federal government to step in and regulate the amount of pumping. The result could potentially be a nearly 40 percent reduction in the amount of water available for municipal supply during drought periods.[53] The area affected is home to approximately 1.3 million persons. The major city affected is San Antonio, whose population is 1.2 million. San Antonio is currently attempting to purchase agricultural rights surrounding the city in order to meet the needs of its population.[54]

In the past, overdrafting in the Houston area has led to severe subsidence. The primary problem is that once the aquifer was lowered, the clay particles compacted and the aquifer was less amenable to recharge. This has meant that the groundwater underlying the city could no longer be counted upon for public supply. In order to meet the needs of its population, the city is laying plans for the diversion of water from the Sabine and Neches Basins. Such diversion will, of course, be expensive, and the costs are likely to be passed on to the citizens of the community. In order to sustain their future, they will be paying for the past practice of overdrafting.

In summary, overdrafting has created some socioeconomic disruption in certain parts of the state and has the potential to affect others. In the heavily populated areas of San Antonio and Houston, overdrafting has resulted in uncertainty over the source from which the growing populations are to get their water. These populations have been forced to enact emergency conservation measures until they are able to determine from where more water can be obtained. The purchase of agricultural water and the development of water-diversion projects appear to be a solution, but these attempts to augment public supply are, as of the mid-1990s, not guaranteed to adequately fill the void left by depleted groundwater.

Subsidence

The southeast and upper Gulf Coast regions of Texas have suffered significant land subsidence.[55] Subsidence south of Houston began as early as 1917 as a result of fluid withdrawal from an oil field. In the entire United States, the Houston area is one of the places most affected by land subsidence. The water table has been lowered some 350 feet since the 1940s, with a resulting land subsidence of as much as 10 feet.[56] The Texas DWR notes the impact subsidence can have and has had on coastal areas in the state in its 1984 report *Water for Texas*.

These changes affect drainage patterns, which aggravate flooding problems in coastal areas and increase the risk of hurricane, tidal surges, and flooding of such areas. Increased fault activity damages structures such as homes and commercial buildings, highways, airport runways, pipelines, and railroad tracks, in addition to allowing the entry of poorer-quality water into groundwater resources.

The Harris-Galveston Coastal Subsidence District, formed in 1975, mandated detailed pumping and subsidence monitoring, with production controls and legal tools to enforce the programs. As noted above, the district has been successful in curtailing withdrawals and in substantially lessening the damage caused by subsidence.[57] Alternative sources of water are being planned for the Houston area; they include conservation, reuse, and the development of new surface-water supplies. However, there is an abundance of water underlying the Houston area, and decision makers might decide to live with the consequences of subsidence in order to obtain municipal water should supplies become scarce in the future. (This is not likely in the near future given current attitudes and supply, but one never knows what the distant future might hold.)

Politics, Policy, and the Future

To date, Texas law and policy have refrained from limiting the absolute ownership doctrine. Continued pumping of groundwater beyond recharge rates has resulted in several problems. Saltwater intrusion into aquifers has occurred, ruining portions of some aquifers as a freshwater source. Naturally and human-introduced pollutants have rendered some groundwater supplies unfit for drinking. Subsidence has resulted in extensive damage and loss, especially in the greater Houston area. In spite of these problems, there seems to be little willingness on the part of the Texas legislature or courts to provide agencies with statewide authority to limit groundwater pumping. While management plans are being developed by a number of UWCDs, some of which will attempt to eliminate overdrafting in these areas, the long-term impact of these plans won't be known for years and, given the past record of groundwater mining in the state, might be too late.

Without effective conservation measures and further water development, water shortages could occur in the state within the next two decades. Such shortages would affect municipal water supplies and could lead to wholesale loss of agriculture and to difficulties with power generation, sewage systems, and industrial water demands. It is fairly easy to generalize about who some of the winners and losers are in a situation such as that faced by Texas. Clearly those with the resources necessary to sink deeper wells or to purchase whatever land is necessary to provide needed water will benefit. Energy companies and municipalities are two such beneficiaries.

In Texas, as in other western states, policymakers are either intentionally, or by default, allowing current use of groundwater preference over potential future uses of that resource. It may be that the political and economic influence of those benefiting from the status quo is such that Texas groundwater law will not change (except to prevent land subsidence in cities and to end pollution). Then again, it may be that the current generation would rather live a quality life (based on a water-intensive lifestyle) today rather than cut back on water use for the benefit of future generations. In either case the losers would be the not-too-distant future generations that might have applied the water to some longer-term and perhaps more beneficial use.

The current state water plan has been developed to provide water for projected needs through the year 2040. The plan, however, hinges on three projections that have yet to occur—a large reduction in irrigation use, aggressive conservation measures, and the costly development of more storage, reclamation, and delivery infrastructure. The plan has contingencies for additional development should conservation measures prove inadequate but does not have any contingencies in place for irrigation use (which is projected to decrease by 37 percent over the next fifty years).[58] The plan has allocated 1.3 million acre-feet per year of water from reduced irrigation to other uses, yet it does not specify how this reduction will occur—whether the lands will be voluntarily taken out of agriculture or whether they will have to be purchased. Furthermore, the plan centers around the development of surface-water supply storage and delivery, allowing for a projected decline in groundwater reliance. However, should the additional infrastructure fail to materialize or should it prove inadequate, groundwater would be more important to the socioeconomic future of Texas than it is at present. Given current overdrafting and pollution problems, however, it seems unlikely that groundwater can be drawn on to a greater extent than it is being drawn on now. Should surface-water development and reclamation plans fail, Texas will face a challenging future as it relates to water.

Conclusion

Examinations of environmental policy and natural resource issues frequently conclude on a sour note. Often it seems that—because of their complexity, persistence, pervasiveness, and politics—far-reaching resource-related problems are beyond our control. But optimism seems warranted in evaluating groundwater policy in the western states. As we have seen, many states in the West have been active in collecting data and examining their water resources. Many have also been closely involved with groundwater pumpers and water users in disseminating information and helping water users plan for long-term use. Data gathering and information dissemination provide the basis for intelligent decision making in water-resources planning, whether decisions are made by the individual on the local level, on the state level, or by the federal government.

There are a number of future problem areas that we might anticipate in groundwater use and development. Major problems will inevitably present themselves in states that have little incentive or opportunity to control the development of their groundwater resources. Such situations come up where there are common-pool incentives to develop ground-water resources. Within a state, the state government may decide to limit groundwater withdrawals or to apportion existing groundwater and to plan for eventual depletion of groundwater (if an aquifer is virtually nonrechargeable). However, where state governments either lack legal authority (under existing law) or share water resources with entities over which they have no control (e.g., when states compete for water along common borders), we can anticipate that there will be poor planning and possibly eventual depletion (for all practical purposes) of groundwater resources.

In the western states there is competition for groundwater somewhere on the borders of all states except Oregon.[1] Individual pumpers in these states (and their state governments) have little incentive to unilaterally restrict withdrawals of groundwater. Saving of water on one side of the border will only result in the loss of the resource to pumpers on the other side at some point in the future. This is a potential problem area that, some commentators have noted, may provide incentives for the federal government to become involved in groundwater management.[2]

Although federalism is the cause of one possible negative groundwater-management situation, in the future federalism may provide one of the more positive aspects of current and future groundwater policy and management. As we have seen, the states have taken many different paths in their efforts to control and manage their groundwater resources. Centralized administrative agencies issuing permits have been popular in many states, other states use decentralized groundwater-management districts, and combinations of management entities are used in many states. Studies comparing different types of administrative structures have found that the users of groundwater had very little preference for the type of structure (i.e., highly centralized or decentralized) but rather that preferences for groundwater management depend upon the attitudes and the policies of the people manning those administrative structures.[3]

Farmers and other water users know that groundwater, in most instances, is a limited resource. If dealt with fairly and equitably these users, understanding the diminishing nature of their resource, will in many cases consent to restrictions on its use and its future development. The perception of inequity and arbitrariness has led, in some states, to strict opposition to controls or management of groundwater resources. The loss of water rights is much easier to take if it is understood to be part of an overall plan designed to balance the equities and to insure a reasonable payment (when that is appropriate) for rights that are forgone. For example, in Arizona, during negotiations that led up to the creation of the Arizona Groundwater Management Act, agricultural interests were willing to concede that they were going to lose something. They complained because of the perception, at one point in the negotiations, that municipal and mining interests were combining to support legislation that would be unfairly detrimental to agricultural interest.[4]

We can anticipate more market solutions and the use of market mechanisms in the allocation and administration of water and groundwater in the future. In states where there has been opposition to increased marketability, the opposition has usually been due to the perception that the controls in the market mechanism (it is unlikely that there will ever be a free market in water) put an undue burden on and work to the disadvantage of agricultural interests. Furthermore, it is likely that in the absence of that perception, market solutions would be more attractive to agricultural interests in the future.

It is clear from an examination of water policy in the nineteen western states that in many states more planning for existing and future groundwater use is needed. In many of our endeavors, we have a tendency to discount (sometimes quite heavily) the future (or the value of future uses). Put another way, the value of a good today is often much higher than is the potential value of that good at some point in the future. Clearly, most states are heavily discounting the future value of water consumed. This may be either intentional (i.e., it occurs under state water-use plans) or unintentional (i.e., it occurs because of the individual or unregulated pumping of groundwater). In some cases it may be justified (e.g., when the water is being used for domestic consumption and there are a limited number of alternative uses); in other cases it seems somewhat foolish (e.g., when water-intensive crops are being grown in an area where there is little natural water available and where that water might have a future value for domestic consumption). Perhaps it is the responsibility of governing bodies to make sure that individuals have enough of an incentive not to value the present at the expense of the future to an extent that they will one day regret.

There are agricultural communities in New Mexico, Arizona, and Texas, for example, that in thirty, forty, fifty, or more years may want to be something other than low-productivity dry-farming areas. When groundwater is the only source of water, it would seem prudent for states that have the capacity to undertake such planning to reserve a certain amount of water for some future use and/or development. Some states are doing that, but many are not, preferring instead the current value of development. (Of course, in fairness to irrigators, some find it necessary to continue pumping to pay off their debts for improvements made on the land.)

It is frightening to think that we may wake up some day and discover that because of our unplanned and uncoordinated behavior we have bequeathed to ourselves a future of water use in some states and in parts of other states that we did not anticipate and do not want.

Notes

Introduction

1   Wendy Gordon, *A Citizen's Handbook on Groundwater Protection* (New York: Natural Resources Defense Council, 1984), p. 10, 11. Although estimates of total groundwater storage in the United States are problematic at best, they range from 90 percent to over 98 percent of fresh water.

2   National Resource Council, *Groundwater Recharge Using Waters of Impaired Quality* (Washington DC: National Academy Press, 1994), p. 1.

3   Wayne B. Solley, Robert R. Pierce, and Howard A. Perlman, "Estimated Water Use in the United States, 1990," Circular 1081, (Washington DC: U.S. Government Printing Office, 1993), pp. 13–17.

4   The discussion of the nature of the resource is found in G. Tyler Miller Jr., *Living in the Environment: An Introduction to Environmental Science*, 6th ed. (Belmont CA: Wadsworth, 1990).

5   Charles Bowden, *Killing the Hidden Waters* (Austin: University of Texas Press, 1977), pp. 82–119.

6   Bowden, *Killing the Hidden Waters*, pp. 82–119.

7   Zachary A. Smith, *Interest Group Interaction and Groundwater Policy Formation in the Southwest* (Lanham MD: University Press of America, 1985), chap. 10.

8   Kenneth D. Frederick and James C. Hanson, *Water for Western Agriculture* (Washington DC: Resources for the Future, 1982), p. 73.

9   Frederick and Hanson, *Water for Western Agriculture*, p. 73.

10 Frederick and Hanson, *Water for Western Agriculture*, p. 163.

11 For a general discussion of the legal doctrines and their applicability in the West, see Zachary A. Smith, "Centralized Decisionmaking in the Administration of Groundwater Rights: The Experience of Arizona, California and New Mexico and Suggestions for the Future," *Natural Resources Journal* 24 (July 1984), p. 641, nn.2–8.

12 Utah Code sec. 77-1-3.

13 Robert W. Swenson, "A Primer of Utah Water Law: Part I," *Journal of Energy and Policy* 5 (1984), p. 178.

14 Z. Smith, *Interest Group Interaction*, chaps. 7–9.

15 A. Didrick Castberg, "Water and the Future of Energy Development in the Southwest," in *Water and the Future of the Southwest*, ed. Zachary A. Smith (Albuquerque: University of New Mexico Press, 1989).

16 Mel Horwitch, "Coal: Constrained Abundance," in *Energy Future*, ed. Robert Stobaugh and Daniel Yergin, 3d ed. (New York: Vintage, 1983), pp. 100–133.

17 Terry L. Anderson, *Water Crisis: Ending the Policy Drought* (Baltimore: Johns Hopkins University Press, 1983), p. 5.

18 Anderson, *Water Crisis*, p. 5.

19 Ann Rodgers, interview by Z. Smith, New Mexico School of Law Natural Resources Center, 8 October 1986.

20 U.S. Geological Survey, *National Water Summary 1983: Hydrologic Events and Issues*, Water-Supply Paper 2250 (Washington DC: U.S. Government Printing Office, 1984), p. 36.

21 Dick Russell, "Ogallala: Half Full or Half Empty?" *The Amicus Journal* 7, no. 2 (fall 1985), p. 13.

22 U.S. Geological Survey, *National Water Summary 1983*, p. 40.

23 In this case "rational" assumes that the water must be utilized (a common assumption in the West) and that depletion is merely an unfortunate consequence of resource use. Therefore, it is rational to use the water rather than to let it "go to waste," despite the fact that use will eventually lead to depletion.

24 U.S. Geological Survey, *National Water Summary 1983*, p. 66.

25 U.S. Geological Survey, *National Water Summary 1983*, p. 75.

26 Zachary A. Smith, "Federal Intervention in the Management of Groundwater Resources: Past Efforts and Future Prospects," *Publius: The Journal of Federalism*, 15 (winter 1985), pp. 145–59.

27 "Cappaert v. United States: A Dehydration of Private Groundwater Use?" *California Western Law Review* 14 (1978), pp. 383–414, 388.

28 *Sporhase v. Nebraska*, 102 Sup. Ct. 3456 (1982).

29 See Zachary A. Smith, "Stability amid Change in Federal-State Water Relations," *Capital University Law Review* 15, no. 3 (spring 1986), p. 479, n.1.

1 Alaska

1   Solley, Pierce, and Perlman, "Estimated Water Use," p. 13.

2   Gary S. Anderson and Chester Zenone, *Summary Appraisals of the Nation's*

Groundwater Resources—Alaska (Washington DC: U.S. Government Printing Office, 1984), p. 2.

3 Alaska Department of Environmental Conservation, Water Programs Division, *Alaska Water Quality Management Study—Initial Phase,* Executive Summary (May 1979), p. 1, and Alaska Department of Natural Resources, telephone conversation with J. Ashley, 1 November 1995.

4 U.S. Bureau of the Census, Internet site, <<www.census.gov>>, 15 December 1996.

5 U.S. Bureau of the Census, "Press Release CB 91-07," (7 January 1991), and <<www. census.gov>>, 15 December 1996.

6 U.S. Bureau of the Census, *County and City Data Book,* 12th ed., 1994, p. 710.

7 U.S. Bureau of the Census, *Statistical Abstract of the United States,* 1994, p. 38.

8 U.S. Department of Commerce, *Survey of Current Business,* 1995, p. 54.

9 U.S. Department of Labor, Bureau of Labor Statistics, unpublished data, quoted in Kathleen O'Leary Morgan, et al., *State Rankings 1993: A Statistical View of the Fifty United States* (Lawrence KS: Morgan Quinto Corp, 1993), pp. 150–73.

10 Solley, Pierce, and Perlman, "Estimated Water Use," pp. 13–17.

11 Anderson and Zenone, *Summary Appraisals,* p. 2.

12 D. J. Cederstrom, "Groundwater Resources of the Fairbanks Area," Water-Supply Paper 1590 (Alaska: U.S. Geological Survey, 1963), p. 25.

13 Anderson and Zenone, *Summary Appraisals,* p. 2.

14 G. O. Balding, *Water Availability, Quality, and Use in Alaska,* (Washington DC: U.S. Department of the Interior, Geological Survey, August 1976), p. 16.

15 Gary S. Anderson, "Hydrologic Reconnaissance of Tanana Basin, Central Alaska," U.S. Geological Survey Hydrologic Atlas, HA-319, 1970.

16 Balding, *Water Availability,* p. 16.

17 David M. Hopkins et al., "Surface Geology of Alaska," U.S. Geological Survey Professional Paper 264-F (Washington DC), pp. F113–F146.

18 U.S. Geological Survey, *National Water Summary 1983,* p. 82. Subpermafrost water is brackish or salty in the arctic coastal plain, the Copper River Basin lowlands, and along the western coast. In most other areas it is often fresh.

19 Anderson and Zenone, *Summary Appraisals,* p. 12.

20 Stephanie Hoag and Lynne Minton, *Surface Impoundment Assessment—Alaska* (Anchorage: Environment Services Limited, 1979), p. 35.

21 Hoag and Minton, *Surface Impoundment,* p. 35.

22 Hoag and Minton, *Surface Impoundment,* p. 39.

23 Balding, *Water Availability,* p. 72.

24 Hoag and Minton, *Surface Impoundment,* p. 39.

25 Hoag and Minton, *Surface Impoundment,* pp. 39, 43.

26 Hoag and Minton, *Surface Impoundment,* p. 43.

27 Gary Prokosch, Alaska Department of Natural Resources, telephone conversation with J. Ashley, 29 August 1996.

28 Alaska Water Study Committee, *Alaska Water Assessment—Problem Identification* (Juneau: State of Alaska, August 1975), p. 10.

29 Alaska Department of Environmental Conservation, Executive Summary, p. 1.

30 U.S. Army Corps of Engineers, in conjunction with the Municipality of Anchorage, Alaska, *Metropolitan Anchorage Urban Study—Summary Report,* vol. 2 (Washington DC: U.S. Army Corps of Engineers, August 1979), p. 18.

31 Gary Prokosch, Alaska Department of Natural Resources, letter to J. Ashley, 18 September 1996.

32 Alaska Department of Natural Resources, letter to J. Ashley, 21 September 1995.

33 Alaska Department of Natural Resources, letter to J. Ashley, 21 September 1995.

34 Alaska Department of Environmental Conservation, "Water Quality Assessment, 1992" (July), appendix 1, pp. 1–2.

35 Alaska Department of Natural Resources, telephone conversation with J. Ashley, 8 November 1995.

36 R. O. Straughn, "The Sanitary Landfill in the Sub-Arctic," *Arctic* 25, no. 1 (1972) pp. 40–48, and letter from Alaska Department of Natural Resources to J. Ashley, 21 September 1995.

37 C. L. Dearborn and W. W. Barnwell, "Hydrology of Land-Use Planning—The Hillside Area, Anchorage, Alaska," U.S. Geological Survey open file report 75-105, p. 46.

38 Anderson and Zenone, *Summary Appraisals*, p. 21, and letter from Alaska Department of Natural Resources to J. Ashley, 21 September 1995.

39 Anderson and Zenone, *Summary Appraisals*, p. 6.

40 Hoag and Minton, *Surface Impoundment*, p. 39, confirmed through Alaska Department of Natural Resources, letter to J. Ashley, 21 September 1995.

41 Alaska Department of Natural Resources, letter to J. Ashley, 21 September 1995.

42 Anderson and Zenone, *Summary Appraisals*, p. 19. This information was reviewed recently by employees with the Alaska Department of Natural Resources and was unchallenged, leading the authors to believe that declines in this area are continuing.

43 Alaska Department of Natural Resources, letter to authors, 21 September 1995.

44 Alaska Department of Environmental Conservation, "Water Quality Assessment, 1992," p. 35.

45 Alaska Department of Environmental Conservation, "Water Quality Assessment, 1992," p. 35., and Alaska Department of Natural Resources, letter to J. Ashley, 21 September 1995.

46 Lawrence Casper and Daniel W. Smith, *Groundwater Quality Effects on Domestic Water Utilization* (Fairbanks: Institute of Water Resources, University of Alaska at Fairbanks, March 1974), pp. 14–15.

47 U.S. Geological Survey (Alaska), letter to J. Ashley, November 1986, confirmed through Alaska Department of Natural Resources, letter to J. Ashley, 21 September 1995.

48 Straughn, "Sanitary Landfill," pp. 40–48.

49 Alaska Department of Natural Resources, telephone conversation with J. Ashley, 8 November 1995.

50 Alaska Department of Environmental Conservation, "Water Quality Assessment, 1992," pp. 32–33.

51 *Trillingham v. Alaska Housing Authority*, 109 F. Sup. Ct. 924 (D. Alaska 1953).

52 Alaska Statutes, sec. 46.15.260(1) (2).

53 Alaska Statutes, sec. 46.15.160(8).

54 Alaska Statutes, sec. 46.15.040(a).

55 Alaska Statutes, sec. 46.15.040(a).

56 Alaska Statutes, sec. 46.15.080(a) (1–4).

57 Frank J. Trelease, "Alaska's New Water Use Act," *Land and Water Review* 2, no. 1 (1967), p. 22.
58 Alaska Statutes, sec. 46.15.260(3).
59 Trelease, "Alaska's New Water Use Act," p. 24.
60 Alaska Statutes, sec. 46.15.100.
61 Wells A. Hutchins, *Water Rights Laws in the Nineteen Western States* (Washington DC: U.S. Government Printing Office, 1974), 3:158; and Alaska Department of Natural Resources, letter to J. Ashley, 21 September 1995.
62 Alaska Department of Natural Resources, telephone conversation with J. Ashley, 2 November 1995.

2 California

1 <<www.census.gov>>, 15 December 1996.
2 U.S. Bureau of the Census, "Press Release CB 91-07," (11 March 1991), and <<www.census.gov>>, 15 December 1996.
3 U.S. Bureau of the Census, *1960 U.S. Census of the Population*, vol. 1, part A; and U.S. Bureau of the Census, "1990 Census of the Population and Housing, Population and Housing Counts," (1990 cph-2).
4 Naser Bateni, California Department of Water Resources, State Planning Branch, telephone conversation with J. Ashley, 3 September 1996.
5 U.S. Department of Labor, Bureau of Labor Statistics, unpublished data, pp. 150–73.
6 U.S. Bureau of the Census, *U.S. Census of Agriculture: 1964 and 1969*, vol. 2.
7 U.S. Department of Agriculture, National Agricultural Statistics Service, "Farm Numbers, and Land in Farms," (July 1994 release). As they are for other states, these numbers are provided to show the decline in the relative importance of agriculture (which includes ranching) versus municipal growth and other industries. Land in farm numbers include nonirrigated acreage. The number of irrigated acres are somewhat smaller—approximately 9.5 million acres in 1993.
8 U.S. Department of Commerce, *Survey of Current Business*, p. 56.
9 California Department of Water Resources, Division of Planning, *California Water Plan Update 1994*, Bulletin 160-93, Executive Summary (November 1994); and Naser Bateni, Statewide Planning Branch, letter to J. Ashley, 17 November 1996.
10 Naser Bateni, telephone conversation with J. Ashley, 22 August 1996.
11 Naser Bateni, telephone conversation with J. Ashley, 22 August 1996.
12 California Department of Water Resources, *California Water Plan Update 1994*.
13 Naser Bateni, telephone interview with J. Ashley, 3 September 1996.
14 John Fielden, California Department of Water Resources, telephone conversation with J. Ashley, 22 August 1996.
15 California Department of Water Resources, *California Water Plan Update 1994*, and Naser Bateni, telephone conversation with J. Ashley, 22 August 1996.
16 California Department of Water Resources, *Groundwater Basins in California* (January 1980), p. 3.
17 California Department of Water Resources, *Groundwater Basins in California*, p. 13. Confirmed through the California Department of Water Resources, telephone conversations with J. Ashley, 22 August 1996.

18 Assembly Bill 3030 was signed into law in 1993 and codified as section 10750 of the California Water Code. The legislation grants authority for a large number of local agencies to develop and implement groundwater-management plans but does not require any such action. As of January 1997 no agency in the state has implemented a groundwater-management program under the authority granted by the legislation.

19 California Department of Water Resources, *California Water Plan Update 1994*, table ES-1.

20 California Governor's Commission to Review California Water Rights Law, *Final Report* (Sacramento: The Commission, 1978), p. 137. See also California Department of Water Resources, *California Water Plan Update 1994*.

21 California Department of Water Resources, "California's Ground Water Bulletin No. 118" (September 1975), and "Analysis of Aquifer-Systems Compaction in the Orange County Ground Water Basin" (June 1980).

22 California Department of Water Resources, "California's Ground Water Bulletin No. 118," p. 119.

23 California Department of Water Resources, "Sea-Water Intrusion in California," Bulletin No. 63-5 (October, 1975), p. XII.

24 California State Water Resources Control Board, Division of Water Quality, "California's Ground Water Profile," (April 1994), p. 3.

25 California Water Code 2100 (Deering 1977).

26 Carla M. Bard, "The California Approach to Ground Water Quality Protection," in *Proceedings of the Thirteenth Biennial Conference on Groundwater*, (Davis: Water Resource Center, University of California, 1981), p. 43.

27 California State Water Resources Control Board, Division of Water Quality, "California's Ground Water Profile," pp. 44–45.

28 See Porter-Cologne Water Quality Control Act, chaps. 4 and 5 (revised 1977). The $10,000 fine can be imposed as a result of California Superior Court action. The nine regional water-quality control boards may issue fines of up to $1,000 a day for permit violations or $10 per gallon of effluent discharged per day (e.g., a 1-million-gallon discharge could result in a $1 million fine). The frequency of fines levied varies significantly from board to board and over time. For example, the Los Angeles–Ventura County Regional Water Quality Control Board reportedly issues fines "relatively frequently," described as six to eleven times a year, "although we sometimes have four a month." (Telephone interview with Z. Smith, 6 November 1987.)

29 Hal Rubin, "The Toxic Chemical Storm Over California," *California Environment and Energy* (Sacramento: California Journal Press, 1980), p. 84.

30 California Office of Environmental Health and Hazards Assessment, telephone conversation with J. Ashley, 3 September 1996.

31 California State Water Resources Control Board, Division of Water Quality, "California's Ground Water Profile," p. 45.

32 Rubin, "Toxic Chemical Storm," p. 81.

33 *Los Angeles Times*, 12 June 1995, p. A18.

34 Rubin, "Toxic Chemical Storm," p. 81; Bard, "California Approach," pp. 40–41; and California State Water Resources Control Board, Division of Water Quality, "California's Ground Water Profile," pp. 32–45.

35 U.S. Environmental Protection Agency, *Ground Water Pollution in Arizona, California, Nevada, and Utah*, (Washington DC: Government Printing Office, December 1971).

36 U.S. Environmental Protection Agency, *Ground Water Pollution*, p. 93.

37 U.S. Environmental Protection Agency, *Ground Water Pollution*, p. 105.

38 Merrill R. Goodall, John D. Sullivan, and Tim De Young, *Water Districts in California: An Analysis by Type of Enabling Act and Political Decision Process* (Sacramento: California Department of Water Resources, 1977), p. 2.

39 "Ballot Proposition Analysis," *California Journal* (May 1978), p. 153.

40 California Governor's Commission, *Final Report*, p. 146. For a more detailed summary of the Orange County Water District's management see Preston K. Allen and Gordon L. Elser, "They Said It Couldn't Be Done—The Orange County California Experience," *Desalinization* 30 (1979), pp. 23-28.

41 Allen and Elser, "They Said It Couldn't Be Done," pp. 27-28.

42 *Upper San Gabriel Valley Municipal Water District v. City of Alhambra*, Civil No. 924128, California Superior Court, Los Angeles County, 4 January 1973. For a more detailed summary of the San Gabriel situation see California Governor's Commission, *Final Report*, p. 147.

43 California Governor's Commission, *Final Report*, p. 148.

44 *Vineland Irrigation District v. Azusa Irrigation Co.*, 126 Cal. 486, 58 P. 1057 (1899).

45 *Katz v. Walkinshaw*, 141 Cal. 116, 74 P. 766 (1903).

46 *Katz v. Walkinshaw*, 141 Cal. 134, 74 P. 771.

47 California Constitution, art. 10, sec. 2 (originally art. 14, sec. 3). See Marybelle D. Archibald, *Appropriative Water Rights in California*, (Sacramento: Governor's Commission to Review California Water Rights Law, 1977), p. 13.

48 *Herminghaus v. Southern California Edison Company*, 200 Cal. 81, 252 P. 607 (1926); *Peabody v. City of Vallejo*, 2 Cal. 2d 351, 40 P.2d 486 (1935).

49 *Burr v. Maclay Rancho Water Company*, 160 Cal. 268, 116 P. 715 (1911).

50 *Cohen v. LaCanada Land and Water Company*, 142 Cal. 437, 76 P. 47 (1904).

51 *San Bernadino v. Riverside*, 186 Cal. 7, 198 P. 784 (1921).

52 *Katz v. Walkinshaw*, 141 Cal. 116, 135, 74 P. 766, 772 (1903); *Los Angeles v. San Fernando*, 141 Cal. 3d 199, 293, 537 P.2d 1250, 1318, 123 Cal. Rptr. 1, 69 (1975).

53 Anne J. Schneider, *Groundwater Rights in California* (Sacramento: Governor's Commission to Review California Water Rights Law, 1977), p. 19.

54 Robert I. Reis, "Legal Planning for Ground Water Production," *Southern California Law Review* 38 (1965), pp. 484 and 487.

55 33 Cal. 2d 908, 207, P.2d 17 (1949). Most commentators have seen *Pasadena* as adopting the mutual prescription doctrine in California (see, e.g., Reis, "Legal Planning," p. 488; Archibald, *Appropriative Water Rights*, p. 19). For a contrasting view, see Hutchins, *Water Rights Laws*, 2:677-78. Hutchins notes that the *Pasadena* court did not use the term "mutual prescription" and argues instead that the court decided the case "on the basis of the concept of prescriptive rights in the classical sense and on the doctrine of correlative rights as developed in California" (p. 678). Regardless of whether or not the *Pasadena* court intended to adopt the mutual prescription doctrine, the practical result (i.e., the remedy) was the same.

56 *City of Pasadena v. City of Alhambra*, 33 Cal. 2d 908, 933, 207 P.2d 17, 21 (1949).

57 *City of Pasadena v. City of Alhambra*, 33 Cal. 2d 908, 933, 207 P.2d 26. (1949).

58 Archibald, *Appropriative Water Rights*, pp. 23–24. The author cites several cases
that have followed this approach, including *California Water Service Company v.
Sidebottom and Son*, 224 Cal. App.2d 715, 37 Cal. Rptr. 1 (1964) and *Tehachapi-
Cummings County Water District v. Armstrong*, 49 Cal. App.3d 992, 122 Cal. Rptr.
918 (1975).

59 *Los Angeles v. San Fernando*, 14 Cal. 3d 199, 265, 537 P.2d 1250, 1298. (1975)

60 John F. Mann Jr., "The San Fernando Case—Its Impact on Future Groundwater
Management," *Proceedings of the Tenth Biennial Conference on Ground Water*
(Davis: Water Resources Center, University of California, 1975), p. 212.

61 14 Cal. 3d 199, 537 P.2d 1250, 123 Cal. Rptr. 1, (1975).

62 Cal. Civil Code (1007) was amended in 1935 to read, in pertinent part, "no possession by any person, firm, or corporation no matter how long continued of any . . .
water, water right . . . owned by any county, city and county, city irrigation district, public or municipal corporation or any department or agency thereof, shall
ever ripen into any title, interest or right against such county, city, and county." In
1968 the section was amended to read, "but no possession by any person, firm or
corporation no matter how long continued of any . . . water right . . . dedicated to
or owned by the state of any public entity, shall ever ripen into any title, interest
or right against the owner thereof." The *San Fernando* court found "any person,
firm or corporation" to include municipal entities. 14 Cal. 3d 199, 278, 537 P.2d
1250, 1307, 123 Cal. Rptr. 1, 58 (1975); *Los Angeles v. San Fernando*, 14 Cal. 3d 199,
208, 537, P.2d 1250, 1301, 123 Cal. Rptr. 1, 52 (1975).

63 *Pasadena v. Alhambra*, 33 Cal. 2d 908, 929, 207 P.2d 17, 30 (1949).

64 *Los Angeles v. San Fernando*, 14 Cal. 3d 199, 208, 537 P.2d 1250, 1309, 123 Cal Rptr.
1, 59 (1975).

65 *Los Angeles v. San Fernando*, 14 Cal. 3d 199, 280, 537 P.2d 1250, 1309, 123 Cal.
Rptr. 1, 60 (1975).

66 *Pasadena v. Alhambra*, 33 Cal. 2d 908, 930, 207 P.2d 17, 31 (1949).

67 *Los Angeles v. San Fernando*, 14 Cal. 3d 199, 283, 537 P.2d 1250, 1311, 123 Cal. Rptr.
1, 62 (1975).

68 Archibald, *Appropriative Water Rights*, p. 34.

69 37 Cal. App.3d 924, 112 Cal Rptr. 846 (1974) cert. denied, 419 U.S. 869 (1975).

70 37 Cal. App.3d 924, 112 Cal. Rptr. 846, 853, (1974). See also Archibald, *Appropriative Water Rights*, pp. 67–68.

71 37 Cal. App.3d 924, 935, 112 Cal Rptr. 846, 849, 854, (1974). See also Archibald, *Appropriative Water Rights*, pp. 67–68.

72 "Policies and Goals for California Water Management," California Water Resources
Control Board and California Department of Water Resources (June 1980).

73 B. Delworth Gardner, Richard E. Howitt, and Carole Frank Nucton, "The Case for
Regional Groundwater Management," *California Agriculture* 35 (1981), pp. 1–2, 9–
10. As of the mid-1990s farmers' sentiments remained much the same as they had
been at the time this article was written. The basic belief held by many farmers
is that the state has provided water for agricultural need in the past and that it
will continue to do so into the future. John Fielden, telephone conversation with
J. Ashley, 22 August 1996.

74 Eugene C. Lee and Harrison C. Dunning, "Political Dynamics and Decision Making," in *California Western Law Review*, 20 (1984), p. 223.

75 John Fielden, telephone conversation with J. Ashley, 22 August 1996.
76 *City of Pasadena v. City of Alhambra*, 33 Cal. 2d 908, 207 P.2d 17 (1949); *City of Los Angeles v. City of San Fernando*, 14 Cal. 3d 199, 537 P.2d 1250, 123 Cal. Rptr. 1 (1975).
77 California Department of Water Resources, *California Water Plan Update 1994*, vol. 1.
78 California Department of Water Resources, *California Water Plan Update 1994*, vol. 1.

3 Hawaii

1 State and city officials are generally optimistic about the availability of water for future demand. There is, however, fear among some Hawaiians that while water is available for certain uses, it will become scarce for some uses that have been a part of Hawaii's culture. See, e.g., Robbie Dingleman, "State's Future Depends on a Limited Resource," *The Honolulu Advertiser*, 16 December 1996, p. A1.
2 Roy Hardy staff, Commission on Water Resource Management, Hawaii Department of Land and Natural Resources (DLNR), letter to J. Ashley, 29 November 1996.
3 Roy Hardy staff, letter to J. Ashley, 29 November 1996.
4 U.S. Geological Survey, "Summary Appraisals of the Nations Groundwater Resources—Hawaii Region," Professional Paper 813-M, by K. J. Takasaki, (Washington DC: U.S. Government Printing Office, 1978), p. 1.
5 <<www.census.gov>>, 15 December 1996.
6 U.S. Bureau of the Census, "Press Release CB 91-07," and <<www.census.gov>>.
7 U.S. Bureau of the Census, *1960 U.S. Census of the Population*, vol. 1, part A.
8 U.S. Bureau of the Census, "1990 Census of Population and Housing, Population and Housing Counts," (1990 cph-2).
9 U.S. Department of Labor, Bureau of Labor Statistics, unpublished data, pp. 150–73.
10 U.S. Bureau of the Census, *U.S. Census of Agriculture: 1964 and 1969*, vol. 2.
11 U.S. Department of Agriculture, "Farm Numbers and Land in Farms."
12 U.S. Department of Commerce, *Survey of Current Business*, p. 56.
13 Gordon A. MacDonald and Agatin Abbott, *Volcanoes in the Sea: The Geology of Hawaii* (Honolulu: University of Hawaii Press, 1983), pp. 201–2.
14 Solley, Pierce, and Perlman, "Estimated Water Use," pp. 13–15.
15 According to Roy Hardy of the DLNR, there has been discussion of piping water from this aquifer to the developing Kona (leeward) area of the island but transmission costs are prohibitive. Geothermal projects were to have supplied the energy to make such a diversion possible but have yet to be developed.
16 Roy Hardy staff, telephone conversation with J. Ashley, 19 August 1996. During the course of the conversation, Hardy stressed that these are rough figures because actual use on the island is probably slightly higher than what is reported to the CWRM.
17 Roy Hardy staff, telephone conversation with J. Ashley, 19 August 1996.
18 Thomas W. Giambelluca, "Water Balance of the Pearl Harbor–Honolulu Basin 1946–1975," Hawaii Water Resources Research Technical Report No. 115, Honolulu (1983), p. 1; and CWRM, telephone conversation with J. Ashley, 19 August 1996.
19 Roy Hardy staff, telephone conversation with J. Ashley, 19 August 1996.
20 James J. Jacobs, *Hawaii's Water Resources: Sources, Demands, and Issues* (Manoa:

Hawaii Institute of Tropical Agriculture and Human Resources, University of Hawaii, 1983), p. 6.

21 Roy Hardy, telephone conversation with J. Ashley, 19 August 1996.

22 U.S. Geological Survey, "Summary Appraisals," p. 1.

23 Roy Hardy, telephone conversation with J. Ashley, 19 August 1996.

24 U.S. Geological Survey, *National Water Summary 1983*, p. 113.

25 Hawaii Department of Health, telephone conversation with J. Ashley, 22 August 1996.

26 Roy Hardy staff, telephone conversation with J. Ashley, 19 August 1996.

27 Michael J. Chun, H. F. Reginald, Arthur S. Kowatache, and Paul R. Bolduc, "Groundwater Pollution from Sanitary Landfill Leachate," Hawaii Water Resources Research Center, Technical Report No. 87, Honolulu (1975), p. 1.

28 U.S. Geological Survey in cooperation with Hawaii Department of Health, "Elements Needed in Design of a Groundwater-Quality Monitoring Network in the Hawaiian Islands" Report 79-263, by K. J. Takasaki (Washington DC: U.S. Government Printing Office, 1976), p. 10.

29 Stephen Wheatcraft, F. Patterson, and D. Heutmaker, "Water Injection into the Hawaiian Ghyben-Herzberg Aquifer," Technical Report No. 96 (Honolulu: Hawaii Water Resources Research Center, 1976), pp. 2–3.

30 U.S. Geological Survey, *National Water Summary 1983*, p. 113.

31 State of Hawaii, Department of Health, "Updated Groundwater Contamination Maps for the State of Hawaii" (October 1993).

32 *Los Angeles Times*, 12 June 1995, p. A18.

33 Hawaii Department of Health, "Groundwater Contamination Maps."

34 Veronica I. Pye, Ruth Patrick, and John Quarles, *Groundwater Contamination in the United States* (Philadelphia: University of Pennsylvania Press, 1983), p. 107.

35 Hawaii Department of Health, "Groundwater Contamination Maps."

36 Hawaii Revised Statutes, 174C sec. 31(f).

37 Hawaii Revised Statutes, 174C sec. 41(a).

38 Roy Hardy staff, telephone conversation with J. Ashley, 19 August 1996.

39 Hawaii Revised Statutes, 174C sec. 48(a).

40 Hawaii Revised Statutes, 174C sec. 84.

41 Hawaii Revised Statutes, 174C sec. 55 and sec. 56.

42 Hawaii Revised Statutes, 174C sec. 58.

43 Hawaii Revised Statutes, 174C sec. 50(a)(b).

44 Hawaii Revised Statutes, 174C sec. 50(b).

45 Hawaii Revised Statutes, 174C sec. 50(c).

46 Hawaii Revised Statutes, 174C sec. 49.

47 Hawaii Revised Statutes, 174C sec. 63.

48 David H. Getches, *Water Law*, (St. Paul MN: West, 1990), pp. 207–8.

49 Hawaii Revised Statutes, 174C sec. 62(b).

50 Hawaii Revised Statutes, 174C sec. 62(c).

51 Hawaii Revised Statutes, 174C sec. 62(g).

4 Oregon

1　Oregon Department of Water Resources, "Groundwater Levels 1967–1968," (1970), p. 4.

2　Oregon Department of Water Resources, "Groundwater Resources of Dallas-Monmouth Area, Polk, Benton, and Marion Counties, Oregon," Groundwater Report No. 28, (1983), p. 1; and Oregon Department of Environmental Quality, letter to Z. Smith.

3　U.S. Geological Survey, *National Water Summary 1984*, p. 194.

4　Oregon Department of Water Resources, "Groundwater Levels," p. 5.

5　Oregon Department of Water Resources, "Groundwater Levels," p. 7.

6　Oregon Department of Water Resources, "Report for January 1981 to December 1982," p. 29; and Water Resources Department, telephone interview with J. Ashley, 6 October 1995.

7　<<www.census.gov>>, 15 December 1996.

8　U.S. Bureau of the Census, "Press Release CB 91-07," and <<www.census.gov>>, 15 December 1996.

9　U.S. Bureau of the Census, *1960 U.S. Census of the Population*, vol. 1, part A.

10　U.S. Bureau of the Census, "1990 Census of Population and Housing, Population and Housing Counts," (1990 cph-2).

11　U.S. Department of Labor, Bureau of Labor Statistics, unpublished data, pp. 150–73.

12　U.S. Bureau of the Census, *U.S. Census of Agriculture: 1964 and 1969*, vol. 2.

13　U.S. Department of Agriculture, "Farm Numbers and Land in Farms."

14　U.S. Department of Commerce, *Survey of Current Business*.

15　Oregon Department of Water Resources, telephone conversation with Z. Smith.

16　Figures for 1983 were obtained from U.S. Geological Survey, *National Water Summary 1984*, p. 195. Recent figures were obtained from Solley, Pierce, and Perlman, "Estimated Water Use," p. 17.

17　Oregon Department of Water Resources, telephone conversation with Z. Smith.

18　U.S. Geological Survey, *National Water Summary 1984*, pp. 13–17.

19　Oregon Department of Water Resources, letter to J. Ashley, 1 September 1995.

20　Oregon Department of Water Resources, letter to J. Ashley, 1 September 1995.

21　Oregon Department of Environmental Quality, "Oregon's 1994 Water Quality Status Assessment Report," (1994), p. 4:10.

22　Dan Postrel, "Nitrate in Water North of Salem Brings Warning," *Oregon Statesman Journal*, 4 November 1980; Oregon Department of Environmental Quality, "1994 Water Quality Status," p. 4:15.

23　Oregon Department of Environmental Quality, "1994 Water Quality Status," pp. 4:5–4:8.

24　Sue Hill, "Water Purity Problems Growing Worse," *Oregon Statesman Journal*, 4 November 1980.

25　Oregon Department of Water Resources, "Report for January 1981 to December 1982," p. 8.

26　H. R. Sweet and R. H. Fetrow, "Groundwater Pollution by Wood Waste Disposal," *Groundwater* (March–April 1975), pp. 227–31.

27　Oregon Department of Environmental Quality, "1994 Water Quality Status," p. 4:13.

28　Pye, Patrick, and Quarles, *Groundwater Contamination*, p. 68.

29 Pye, Patrick, and Quarles, *Groundwater Contamination*, p. 63.
30 Oregon Department of Environmental Quality, "1994 Water Quality Status," p. 4:13.
31 Oregon Department of Environmental Quality, "1994 Water Quality Status," p. 4:13.
32 Oregon Department of Water Resources, letter to J. Ashley, 1 September 1995.
33 *Hays v. Adams* 109 Oregon 51, 58–61, (1923). The decision was reaffirmed in *Bull v. Siegrist* 169 Oregon 180, 186 (1942).
34 Gen. Laws of Oregon 1927, chap. 410 sec.1.
35 Oregon Revised Statutes, sec. 537.505 to 537.795.
36 Oregon Revised Statutes, sec. 536.032 and sec. 537.780.
37 Oregon Revised Statutes, sec. 537.575.
38 Oregon Revised Statutes, sec. 537.605.
39 Oregon Revised Statutes, sec. 537.615.
40 Oregon Revised Statutes, sec. 537.545.
41 Oregon Revised Statutes, sec. 537.730, and Oregon Department of Water Resources, letter to Z. Smith.
42 Oregon Revised Statues, sec. 537.730 (2).
43 Oregon Department of Water Resources, letter to Z. Smith.
44 Oregon Revised Statutes, sec. 537.630 and sec. 537.775; Oregon Revised Statutes, sec. 537.525 (3) and sec. 537.525 (8); Oregon Revised Statutes, sec. 537.747. to 537.753.
45 Oregon Revised Statutes, sec. 536.600, and Oregon Laws 1993, chap. 601, sec. 1 to 5.
46 Oregon Revised Statutes, sec. 468.010 to 368.030.
47 Oregon Department of Water Resources, telephone conversation with Z. Smith, 6 October 1995.
48 Oregon Department of Water Resources, "Report for January 1981 to December 1982," p. 34.
49 Frederick G. Lissner, Oregon Department of Water Resources, letter to J. Ashley, 18 October 1996.
50 Oregon Department of Water Resources, telephone conversation with Z. Smith, 23 April 1985.
51 Frederick G. Lissner, letter to J. Ashley, 18 October 1996.
52 Oregon Department of Water Resources, telephone conversation with J. Ashley, 6 October 1995.
53 Oregon Department of Water Resources, telephone conversation with J. Ashley, 6 October 1995.
54 Oregon Department of Water Resources, telephone conversation with J. Ashley, 6 October 1995.
55 Oregon Revised Statutes, sec. 537.665.
56 Oregon Department of Water Resources, telephone conversation with J. Ashley, 23 April 1985.
57 Oregon Department of Water Resources, telephone conversation with Z. Smith, 2 May 1985.
58 Oregon Department of Water Resources, telephone conversation with J. Ashley, 6 October 1995.
59 Oregon Department of Environmental Quality, "1994 Water Quality Status," p. 4:2.
60 Oregon Department of Environmental Quality, "1994 Water Quality Status," p. 4:2.
61 Oregon Department of Environmental Quality, "1994 Water Quality Status," p. 4:1.

5 Washington

1 Washington State Department of Ecology, "Hydraulic Continuity Policy," draft, 9 September 1992, p. 3.

2 <<www.census.gov>>, 15 December 1996.

3 U.S. Bureau of the Census, "Press Release CB 91-07," and <<www.census.gov>>, 15 December 1996.

4 U.S. Bureau of the Census, *1960 U.S. Census of the Population*, vol. 1, part A.

5 U.S. Bureau of the Census, "1990 Census of Population and Housing, Population and Housing Counts," (1990 cph-2).

6 U.S. Bureau of the Census, *County and City Data Book*, 1994.

7 U.S. Department of Labor, Bureau of Labor Statistics, unpublished data, pp. 150–73.

8 U.S. Bureau of the Census, *U.S. Census of Agriculture: 1964 and 1969*, vol. 2.

9 U.S. Department of Agriculture, "Farm Numbers and Land in Farms."

10 U.S. Department of Commerce, *Survey of Current Business*, p. 56.

11 Solley, Pierce, and Perlman, "Estimated Water Use," pp. 15–17.

12 John K. Wiley, "Eastern Washington May Face New Controls on Water," *Sea Times*, 3 February 1995.

13 Washington Department of Ecology, telephone conversation with J. Ashley, 5 January 1996.

14 Washington State Department of Ecology, *Washington's Water Resources Program: Sixth Biennial Report to the Legislature*, (draft) (Olympia: Washington State Department of Ecology, 1983), p. 43. A telephone conversation between the Department of Ecology and J. Ashley confirmed that this remained true as of the mid-1990s.

15 Washington State Department of Ecology, *Washington's Water Resources Program*.

16 Washington State Department of Ecology, personal interview by J. Ashley.

17 Doug McChesney of the Washington State Department of Ecology, letter to J. Ashley, 26 October 1996.

18 Doug McChesney, letter to J. Ashley, 26 October 1996.

19 Doug McChesney, letter to J. Ashley, 26 October 1996.

20 Washington State Department of Ecology, "1994 EPA 305(b) Report" (draft).

21 Washington State Department of Ecology, "1992 EPA 305(b) Report."

22 Washington State Department of Ecology, "1994 EPA 305(b) Report."

23 Washington State Department of Ecology, "1994 EPA 305(b) Report."

24 Washington State Department of Ecology, "1994 EPA 305(b) Report."

25 Washington State Department of Ecology, "1994 EPA 305(b) Report."

26 75 Washington 407, 134 P.1076 (1913).

27 182 Washington 450, 453 P.2d 984 (1935).

28 Washington Revised Code, sec. 90-44-070.

29 Washington Revised Code, sec. 90-44-050.

30 Washington Revised Code, sec. 90-44-090.

31 Washington Revised Code, sec. 90-14-160.

32 Washington Revised Code, sec. 90-14-220.

33 Washington Revised Code, sec. 90-54-020.

34 Washington Revised Code, sec. 90-66-040.

35 Washington Revised Code, sec. 90-54-020.

36 Washington Revised Code, sec. 90-03-290.

37 Washington Revised Code, sec. 90-44-060.
38 State of Washington Water Research Center, *Washington State's Water* (Pullman: Washington State University and University of Washington, 1984), p. 26.
39 Washington Revised Code, sec. 18-104.
40 Washington Department of Ecology, telephone conversation with J. Ashley, 5 January 1996.
41 Washington Revised Code, sec. 90-44-400.
42 Washington Revised Code, sec. 90-44-130.
43 Department of Ecology employee, telephone conversation with J. Ashley, not for attribution.
44 Department of Ecology employee, telephone conversation with J. Ashley, not for attribution.
45 Washington Department of Ecology, telephone conversation with J. Ashley, 5 January 1996. The legislature has, in recent years, tinkered with existing laws in order to allow for more groundwater permits. Whether the legislature will go so far as to enact laws that will ignore hydrologic continuity is uncertain.
46 While on the surface tribal rights and Endangered Species Act requirements appear to be clear, these issues have yet to be fully resolved by the courts.
47 While this case has been made generally, and specifically in some cases, the question of tribal rights to maintaining instream flows for salmon is not fully resolved. However, cases such as *United States v. Adair*, supra 723 F.2d 1409; *Colville Confederated Tribes v. Walton*, supra 647 F.2d 48; and *United States v. State of Washington*, 506 F. Supp. 187 (1980) give these authors every indication that should the issue arise, the tribes will win.
48 Washington Department of Ecology, telephone conversation with J. Ashley, 29 August 1996.

6 Colorado

1   Ted Arnow and Don Price, "Summary Appraisal of the Nation's Groundwater Resources—Upper Colorado Region," Geological Survey Paper No. 813-C, (U.S. Government Printing Office: Washington DC 1974), p. 9.
2   Solley, Pierce, and Perlman, "Estimated Water Use," p. 17.
3   Colorado state engineer's office, telephone conversation with J. Ashley, 27 December 1995.
4   <<www.census.gov>>, 15 December 1996.
5   <<www.census.gov>>, 15 December 1996.
6   Colorado Division of Water Resources, telephone interview with J. Ashley, 29 August 1996.
7   U.S. Bureau of the Census, *Statistical Abstract of the United States*, 1975, p. 20.
8   U.S. Bureau of the Census, *Statistical Abstract of the United States*, 1994, p. 38.
9   U.S. Department of Labor, Bureau of Labor Statistics, unpublished data, pp. 150–73.
10 U.S. Bureau of the Census, *U.S. Census of Agriculture: 1964 and 1969*, vol. 2.
11 U.S. Department of Agriculture, "Farm Numbers and Land in Farms."
12 U.S. Department of Commerce, *Survey of Current Business*, p. 6.
13 Colorado Division of Water Resources, telephone interview with J. Ashley, 29 August 1996.

14 Colorado Department of Natural Resources, telephone conversation with J. Ashley, 27 December 1995.

15 Solley, Pierce, and Perlman, "Estimated Water Use," pp. 15–17.

16 Colorado state engineer's office, telephone conversation with J. Ashley, 27 December 1995.

17 Colorado Department of Public Health and Environment, "Status of Water Quality in Colorado, 1994," November 1994, p. 101.

18 Colorado state engineer's office, telephone conversation with J. Ashley, 27 December 1995. While no permits for major irrigation projects have been granted, the department of records for the engineer's office receives approximately twelve thousand applications for various types of well permits each year. Of the twelve thousand, a very small number (about three hundred) are denied.

19 Colorado Department of Public Health and Environment, "Status of Water Quality in Colorado, 1994," p. 98.

20 U.S. Geological Survey, *National Water Summary 1983*, p. 96.

21 U.S. Geological Survey, *National Water Summary 1983*, p. 96.

22 Geophysics Study Committee, National Research Council, *Groundwater Contamination* (Washington DC, 1984), p. 93.

23 U.S. Geological Survey, *National Water Summary 1983*, p. 96.

24 Jody Grantham, special assistant to the Colorado state engineer, letter to J. Ashley, 25 October 1996.

25 Art. 16, section 6, of the Colorado Constitution reads: "The rights to divert the unappropriated waters of any natural stream to beneficial uses shall never be denied. Priority of appropriation shall give the better as between those using the water for the same purpose; but when service of all those desiring the use of the same, those using the water for domestic purposes shall have the preference over those using the water for agricultural purposes, and preference over those using the same for manufacturing purposes."

26 Colorado Revised Statutes, 147-18-1 (1953) (Underground Water).

27 David L. Harrison and Gustave Sanstrom Jr., "The Groundwater Surface Water Conflict and Recent Colorado Water Legislation," *University of Colorado Law Review* 43 (1971), p. 9.

28 William A. Hillhouse, "Integrating Ground and Surface Water in an Appropriation State," *Rocky Mountain Mineral Law Institute* 20 (1975), p. 691.

29 Colorado Revised Statutes, *Annotated*, 148-18-1 and 148-11-22.

30 157 Colorado 320, 447 P.2d 986 (1968).

31 Hillhouse, "Integrating Ground and Surface Water," p. 702.

32 Hillhouse, "Integrating Ground and Surface Water," p. 702.

33 Colorado Revised Statutes, *Annotated*, 148-2-9 (Supp. 1967). Both engineering and legal research was conducted for the division by various entities. See Hillhouse, "Integrating Ground and Surface Water," p. 700.

34 Colorado Revised Statutes, chap. 148, art. 21 (1969 Supp.).

35 Colorado Revised Statutes, *Annotated*, 37-92-201, 202.

36 Colorado Revised Statutes, *Annotated*, 37-92-203.

37 Colorado Revised Statutes, *Annotated*, 37-92-203.

38 *Whitten v. Coit*, 153 Colorado 157, 385 P.2d 137 (163).

39 Colorado Revised Statutes, *Annotated*, sec. 37-90-111.

40 Gina Wickersham, "Groundwater Management in the High Plains," *Groundwater* 18, no. 3 (May/June 1980), p. 286.
41 Colorado Revised Statutes, *Annotated*, sec. 37-92-301 (1).
42 Colorado Revised Statutes, *Annotated*, sec. 37-90-137.
43 Colorado Department of Natural Resources, telephone conversation with J. Ashley, 27 December 1995.

7 Idaho

1   U.S. Geological Survey, *National Water Summary 1984*, p. 193.
2   <<www.census.gov>>, 15 December 1996.
3   U.S. Bureau of the Census, "Press Release CB 91-07," and <<www.census.gov>>, 15 December 1996.
4   U.S. Bureau of the Census, *1960 U.S. Census of the Population*, vol. 1, part A.
5   U.S. Bureau of the Census, "1990 Census of Population and Housing, Population and Housing Unit Counts," (1990 cph-2).
6   U.S. Department of Commerce, *Survey of Current Business*, p. 56.
7   U.S. Department of Agriculture, "Rankings of States and Commodities by Cash Receipts," Report SB-848 (1991). This statistic alone might be somewhat misleading. When the net farm income of Idaho is divided by the population of the state, one finds that Idaho actually has the fifth-highest per capita farm income in the nation, behind only Nebraska, Iowa, North Dakota, and South Dakota.
8   U.S. Department of Commerce, *Survey of Current Business*, p. 56.
9   U.S. Bureau of the Census, *U.S. Census of Agriculture: 1964 and 1969*, vol. 2.
10 U.S. Department of Agriculture, "Farm Numbers and Land in Farms."
11 Solley, Pierce, and Perlman, "Estimated Water Use," pp. 15–17.
12 Solley, Pierce, and Perlman, "Estimated Water Use," p. 17.
13 Gary Spackman of the Idaho Department of Water Resources, telephone conversation with J. Ashley, 10 January 1995.
14 Gary Spackman, telephone conversation with J. Ashley, 10 January 1995.
15 Gary Spackman, telephone conversation with J. Ashley, 10 January 1995.
16 U.S. Geological Survey, *National Water Summary 1983*.
17 Idaho Department of Health and Welfare and Idaho Department of Water Resources, "Annual Ground Water Contamination Report, State Fiscal Year 1991," pp. 6–7.
18 Idaho Department of Health and Welfare, "Annual Ground Water Contamination Report," pp. 9–10. As of 1991 Ada County had not recorded any contamination of public drinking water supplies by petroleum products. However, several less populated counties such as Bannock, Cassia, Custer, and Power have recorded contamination of drinking-water supplies.
19 U.S. Geological Survey, *National Water Summary 1983*, p. 117.
20 Idaho Department of Water Resources, letter to J. Ashley 9 November 1995.
21 Idaho Code, sec. 42-226.
22 *Kootenai Environmental Alliance, Inc. v. Panhandle Yacht Club, Inc.*, 105 Idaho 622 (1983).
23 Gary Spackman, letter to J. Ashley, 1 November 1996.
24 Idaho Code, sec. 42-227

25 *State ex rel. Tappan v. Smith*, 92 Idaho 451, 444 P.2d, 412 (1968).
26 Idaho Code, sec. 42-219.
27 Idaho Code, sec. 42-233a.
28 Idaho Code, sec. 42-701, and Idaho Department of Water Resources, letter to J. Ashley, 9 November 1995.
29 Idaho Code, sec. 42-233b.
30 Gary Spackman, telephone conversation with J. Ashley, 2 November 1995.
31 Idaho Code, sec. 42-237a-g.
32 Idaho Code, sec. 42-226.
33 Gary Spackman, telephone conversation with J. Ashley, 2 November 1995.
34 The U.S. Geological Survey reported in 1985 that Idaho's "groundwater resources have barely been tapped" (U.S. Geological Survey, *National Water Summary 1983*, p. 193). This suggests an abundance, and idea with which Idaho water officials are cautiously in disagreement. While officials agree that there is an abundance of groundwater in the state, they also understand the interrelationship between groundwater and surface water. Although groundwater may be largely untapped, this is because significant groundwater withdrawals will have an adverse impact on surface water uses, which are generally the senior appropriators in the state.

8 Montana

1 Compton's Encyclopedia and Atlas, CD-Rom edition, 1991.
2 <<www.census.gov>>, 15 December 1996.
3 U.S. Bureau of the Census, "Press Release CB 91-07," and <<www.census.gov>>, 15 December 1996.
4 U.S. Bureau of the Census, "Current Population Reports," (series P-25, No. 1017).
5 U.S. Bureau of the Census, *1960 U.S. Census of the Population*, vol. 1, part A.
6 U.S. Bureau of the Census, "1990 Census of Population and Housing, Population and Housing Unit Counts," (1990 cph-2).
7 U.S. Department of Labor, Bureau of Labor Statistics, unpublished data, pp. 150–73.
8 U.S. Department of Commerce, *Survey of Current Business*, p. 56.
9 U.S. Bureau of the Census, *U.S. Census of Agriculture: 1964 and 1969*, vol. 2.
10 U.S. Department of Agriculture, "Farm Numbers and Land in Farms."
11 Solley, Pierce, and Perlman, "Estimated Water Use," p. 13.
12 Solley, Pierce, and Perlman, "Estimated Water Use," pp. 13–15.
13 Robert G. Dunbar, *Property Rights and Controversies in Montana Completion Report* (Bozeman: Montana University Joint Water Resources Research Center, Montana State University, 1976), p. 1. According to the Montana Department of Natural Resources, as of the mid-1990s no comprehensive study of state groundwater supplies had been undertaken. However, the fact that groundwater is used to a limited degree in the state implies that the quantities of groundwater found in the 1976 study are still in place.
14 Solley, Pierce, and Perlman, "Estimated Water Use," pp. 13–15.
15 Kim Overcast of the Montana Department of Natural Resources and Conservation, Water Rights Division, telephone conversation with J. Ashley, 14 November 1996.
16 Jim Kindle of the Montana Department of Natural Resources, telephone conversation with J. Ashley, 14 March 1996. While some irrigation systems are shifting to

groundwater, it is not likely that there will be widespread conversion. Most of the groundwater in Montana is located in the western part of the state, while most of the irrigation occurs in the eastern half. In addition, much of the groundwater, in the Milk River area for example, is too deep (and thus too expensive) to pump for agricultural purposes.

17 Montana Department of Health and Environmental Science, "Montana Water Quality 1994," p. 41.

18 Montana Department of Health and Environmental Science, "Montana Water Quality 1994," p. 40.

19 Montana Department of Health and Environmental Science, "Montana Water Quality 1994," pp. 40–41.

20 Montana Department of Health and Environmental Science, "Montana Water Quality 1994," pp. 40–41.

21 Montana Department of Health and Environmental Science, "Montana Water Quality 1994," pp. 40–41.

22 Dunbar, *Property Rights and Controversies*, p. 2.

23 House Bill No. 205, 30th Montana Legislative Assembly, 1947, quoted in Dunbar, *Property Rights and Controversies*, p. 6.

24 House Bill No. 205, 30th Montana Legislative Assembly, 1947, quoted in Dunbar, *Property Rights and Controversies*, p. 6.

25 Senate Bill No. 99, 32nd Montana Legislative Assembly, 1951.

26 Senate Bill No. 38, 34th Montana Legislative Assembly, 1955.

27 Montana, Session Laws 1961 656, p. 37.

28 Montana Revised Codes, *Annotated*, sec. 89-2911 (a) (Supp. 1965), in Hutchins, *Water Rights Laws*, 3:643.

29 Montana Revised Codes, *Annotated*, sec. 89-2926 (1964), p. 656.

30 Montana Revised Codes, *Annotated*, sec. 89-2914 (1964), p. 661.

31 Montana Revised Codes, *Annotated*, sec. 89-2915.

32 Montana Constitution, art. 93(1), quoted in Albert W. Stone, "Montana Water Rights, a New Opportunity," *Montana Law Review* 32 (winter 1973), p. 57.

33 Montana Constitution, art. (4).

34 Mars Charlier, "Laws and Red Tape Restore Our Water," *Billings (Montana) Gazette*, 18 December 1983, 100: c10.

35 Montana Code *Annotated*, sec. 85-2-407 (1991).

36 "Billings Needs Central as Water Decision Nears," *Billings (Montana) Gazette*, 22 September 1978, 15:69.

37 Montana Department of Natural Resources and Conservation, telephone conversation with J. Ashley, 14 March 1996.

38 Kim Overcast, telephone conversation with J. Ashley, 14 November 1996.

9 Utah

1 U.S. Geological Survey, *National Water Summary 1984*, p. 18.

2 <<www.census.gov>>, 15 December 1996.

3 U.S. Bureau of the Census, "Press Release CB 91-07," and <<www.census.gov>>, 15 December 1996.

4 U.S. Bureau of the Census, *1960 U.S. Census of the Population*, vol. 1, part A.

5   U.S. Bureau of the Census, "1990 Census of Population and Housing, Population and Housing Counts," (1990 cph-2).

6   U.S. Bureau of the Census, *County and City Data Book*, 1994.

7   U.S. Department of Labor, Bureau of Labor Statistics, unpublished data, pp. 150-73.

8   U.S. Bureau of the Census, *U.S. Census of Agriculture: 1964 and 1969*, vol. 2.

9   U.S. Department of Agriculture, "Farm Numbers and Land in Farms." Note, however, that land in farm numbers include range land. Irrigated acreage, as of late 1996, was approximately 1.5 to 2 million acres. The figures are given to demonstrate the decreasing importance of agriculture as a whole in the state.

10 Bob Morgan, state engineer with the Utah Division of Water Rights, telephone conversation with J. Ashley, 29 August 1996.

11 U.S. Department of Commerce, *Survey of Current Business*, p. 56.

12 Solley, Pierce, and Perlman, "Estimated Water Use," pp. 15-17.

13 Utah Department of Environmental Quality, "EPA 305(b) Report 1994," p. 163.

14 Utah Department of Natural Resources and U.S. Geological Survey, "Ground-Water Conditions in Utah," Cooperative Investigations Report No. 34, (spring 1994), pp. 1-6.

15 U.S. Geological Survey, *National Water Summary 1984*, p. 415.

16 Utah Department of Natural Resources, "Ground-Water Conditions," p. 21.

17 Utah Department of Natural Resources, "Ground-Water Conditions," pp. 42-43.

18 U.S. Geological Survey, *National Water Summary 1983*, p. 218.

19 Pye, Patrick, and Quarles, *Groundwater Contamination*, p. 52.

20 U.S. Geological Survey, *National Water Summary 1983*, p. 218.

21 Utah Department of Environmental Quality, "EPA 305(b) Report 1994," p. 158.

22 Hal Spencer, "Monitoring Examined on Underground Gas," *Salt Lake Tribune*, 20 March 1978.

23 Utah Department of Environmental Quality, "EPA 305(b) Report 1994," p. 156.

24 U.S. Geological Survey, *National Water Summary 1983*, p. 218.

25 Utah Department of Environmental Quality, "EPA 305(b) Report 1994," p. 159.

26 Utah Code, *Annotated*, 73-1-1.

27 *Riordan v. Westwood*, 115 Utah 215 203, P.2d 922 (1949). The last sentence in the paragraph is based on Utah state engineer's office, letter to the authors.

28 Utah Code, *Annotated*, 73-3-2.

29 Utah Code, *Annotated*, 73-3-8.

30 Utah Code, *Annotated*, 73-5-9.

31 Robert W. Swenson, "A Primer of Utah Water Law, Part I," *Journal of Energy Law and Policy* 5 (1984), p. 178.

32 Utah Code, *Annotated*, 73-3-21.

33 Utah Code, *Annotated*, 73-3-3.

34 *Bohnam v. Morgan*, 788 P.3d (Utah 1989).

35 Swenson, "A Primer," p. 186.

36 Utah Code, *Annotated*, 73-1-14; Swenson, "A Primer," p. 190.

37 Utah Code, *Annotated*, 73-5-1.

38 Utah Department of Natural Resources, *State of Utah Water*, 1985.

39 Bob Morgan, Utah Division of Water Rights, telephone conversation with J. Ashley, 29 August 1996.

40 Utah Department of Natural Resources, *State of Utah Water*, p. 3.

10 Wyoming

1 Donald A. Warner, "Ground Water in Wyoming," *Journal of the American Water Works Association* 41, no. 3 (March 1949), p. 253.

2 <<www.census.gov>>, 15 December 1996.

3 U.S. Bureau of the Census, "Press Release CB 91-07," and <<www.census.gov>>, 15 December 1996.

4 U.S. Bureau of the Census, *1960 Census of the Population*, vol. 1, part A, and U.S. Bureau of the Census, "1990 Census of Population and Housing, Population and Housing Counts," (1990 cph-2).

5 U.S. Bureau of the Census, *County and City Data Book*, 1994.

6 U.S. Department of Labor, Bureau of Labor Statistics, unpublished data, pp. 150–73.

7 U.S. Bureau of the Census, *U.S. Census of Agriculture: 1964 and 1969*, vol. 2.

8 U.S. Department of Agriculture, "Farm Numbers and Land in Farms."

9 U.S. Department of Commerce, *Survey of Current Business*, p. 56.

10 Solley, Pierce, and Perlman, "Estimated Water Use," p. 17.

11 Richard Stockdale, Wyoming state engineer's office, telephone conversation with J. Ashley, 8 April 1996.

12 Anne MacKinnon, "Study Spurs Interest in Water Projects," *Casper Star-Tribune*, 19 July 1984. As of the 1990s these numbers might be high, because populations have not increased to projected levels. However, according to Richard Stockdale of the Wyoming state engineer's office (telephone conversation with J. Ashley, 8 April 1996) the numbers are "in the ballpark," because this area continues to draw the most surface and groundwater in the state, and because it continues to experience some municipal growth while other portions of the state are experiencing population decline.

13 Richard Stockdale, telephone conversation with J. Ashley, 8 April 1996.

14 Richard Stockdale, telephone conversation with J. Ashley, 8 April 1996; Wyoming state engineer's office, telephone conversation with Z. Smith, 31 October 1986. Others have reported more serious declines. See "Groundwater Level Continues to Drop," *Wyoming Star Tribune*, 24 December 1981, where water table declines averaging 4 feet were reported. As of the mid-1990s these projections appeared to be accurate, as there had been no change in water use according to Richard Stockdale of the state engineer's office (telephone conversation with J. Ashely, 8 April 1996.)

15 Richard Stockdale, telephone conversation with J. Ashley, 8 April 1996.

16 Richard Stockdale, telephone conversation with J. Ashley, 8 April 1996.

17 Wyoming Department of Environmental Quality, Water Quality Division, "1994 Wyoming Water Quality Assessment," p. 298.

18 Wyoming Department of Environmental Quality, "1994 Wyoming Water Quality Assessment," p. 306.

19 Wyoming Department of Environmental Quality, "1994 Wyoming Water Quality Assessment," pp. 299–300.

20 Wyoming Department of Environmental Quality, "1994 Wyoming Water Quality Assessment," p. 303.

21 Wyoming Department of Environmental Quality, "1994 Wyoming Water Quality Assessment."

22 Pye, Patrick, and Quarles, *Groundwater Contamination*, p. 216.

23 Wyoming Department of Environmental Quality, "Water Quality Rules and Regulations—Chapter VIII," 1980, p. 5.

24 Wyoming Statutes, sec. 35-11-101-1207. The statute, passed in 1973, was known as the Wyoming Environmental Quality Act, under which the Department of Environmental Quality was created.

25 Wyoming Statutes, sec. 35-11-101-1104.

26 Wyoming Department of Environmental Quality, "1983 Annual Report." p. 3.

27 26 Wyoming 161, 181 P. 137 (1919).

28 55 Wyoming 451, 102 P.2d 54 (1940).

29 "Rights of Wyoming Appropriators in Underground Water" (case note) 1, *Wyoming Law Journal II* (1947).

30 Wyoming Statutes, sec. 41-3-912.

31 Wyoming Statutes, sec. 41-3-915.

32 Wyoming Statutes, sec. 41-3-313.

33 Richard Stockdale, telephone conversation with J. Ashley, 8 April 1996.

34 Wyoming Statutes, sec. 41-3-97.

35 Wyoming Statutes, sec. 41-3-909.

36 Wyoming Constitution, art. 8, sec. 002.

37 See, e.g., Anne MacKinnon, "Possible Changes in State Water Law Divides Officials," *Casper Star-Tribune*, 15 February 1984.

38 Richard Stockdale, telephone conversation with J. Ashley, 8 April 1996.

39 Wyoming, state engineer's office, "A Water Development Program for Wyoming" (October 1974), p. 1.

40 Richard Stockdale, telephone conversation with J. Ashley, 8 April 1996.

11 Kansas

1 U.S. Department of Commerce, *Survey of Current Business*, p. 55.

2 <<www.census.gov>>, 15 December 1996.

3 U.S. Bureau of the Census, "Press Release CB 91-07," and <<www.census.gov>>, 15 December 1996.

4 U.S. Bureau of the Census, *1960 Census of the population*, vol. 1, part A, and U.S. Bureau of the Census, *1990 Census of Population and Housing, Population and Housing Counts* (1990 cph-2).

5 U.S. Department of Labor, Bureau of Labor Statistics, unpublished data, pp. 150–73.

6 U.S. Bureau of the Census, *U.S. Census of Agriculture: 1964 and 1969*, vol. 2.

7 U.S. Department of Agriculture, "Farm Numbers and Land in Farms."

8 U.S. Department of Commerce, *Survey of Current Business*, p. 55.

9 Solley, Pierce, and Perlman, "Estimated Water Use," pp. 15–17.

10 Kansas Conservation Commission, telephone conversation with J. Ashley, 3 April 1996. The conversation revealed that while major declines are still occurring in certain areas, they are leveling off in others. This is mostly because of the costs involved with pumping water from greater depths. Many irrigators have been forced to discontinue groundwater withdrawal and to move toward dry farming because of the costs of pumping. This has decreased the demand on aquifers in those areas.

11 Kansas State Board of Agriculture, Kansas Agriculture Ogallala Task Force, "Report of the Kansas Agriculture Ogallala Task Force," September 1993, p. 9.

12 Kansas Conservation Commission, telephone conversations with J. Ashley, and Kansas Water Resource Division, telephone conversation with J. Ashley, 29 April 1996.

13 Kansas, Equus Beds Groundwater Management District No. 2, "Management Program," 1 May 1995, p. 20.

14 Kansas Department of Health and Environment, "Groundwater Quality Monitoring Network 1992 Annual Report," December 1994, p. 15.

15 U.S. Geological Survey, *National Water Summary 1983*, p. 129.

16 Laura Palmer, Kansas Department of Agriculture, letter to J. Ashley, 6 December 1996.

17 Arno Windscheffel, "Kansas Water Rights: More Recent Developments," *Journal of the Kansas Bar Association* (fall 1978), p. 298.

18 Kansas Statutes, *Annotated*, sec. 82a-702.

19 Kansas Laws 1886, chap. 115.

20 Kansas Statutes, *Annotated*, sec. 82a-706.

21 *Emporia v. Soden*, 25 Kansas 558 (1881).

22 158 Kansas 603, 149 P.2d 604 (1944).

23 Hutchins, *Water Law in the Nineteen Western States*, vol. 3, p. 298.

24 Hutchins, *Water Law in the Nineteen Western States*, vol. 3, p. 642.

25 Kansas Statutes, *Annotated*, sec. 82a-705.

26 Kansas Statutes, *Annotated*, sec. 82a-701(c).

27 Kansas Statutes, *Annotated*, sec. 82a-706(c). Please note that the original language of this statute was somewhat generic. Kansas Statutes, *Annotated*, sec. 82a-732, enacted in 1988, addresses the problem by specifically mandating water right/permit owners to file an annual water-use report.

28 Kansas Statutes, *Annotated*, sec. 82a-709.

29 "Administrative Action in the Processing of Ground Water Appropriation Permits: Where is Kansas?" *Washburn Law Journal* 2 (1972), p. 251, n.5.

30 John C. Peck, *Legal Questions and Problems of Kansas Groundwater Management Districts* (Topeka: Kansas Water Resources Research Institute, 1980), p. 1.

31 Kansas Statutes, *Annotated*, sec. 82a-1022.

32 Kansas Statutes, *Annotated*, sec. 82a-1021.

33 Kansas Statutes, *Annotated*, sec. 82a-1002.

34 Kansas Statutes, *Annotated*, sec. 82a-1023.

35 Kansas Statutes, *Annotated*, sec. 82a-1024(b).

36 Kansas Statutes, *Annotated*, sec. 82a-1025.

37 Kansas Statutes, *Annotated*, sec. 82a-1028.

38 Kansas Statutes, *Annotated*, sec. 82a-1029.

39 Kansas Statutes, *Annotated*, sec. 82a-1202.

40 Kansas Statutes, *Annotated*, sec. 82a-1212.

41 Kansas Statutes, *Annotated*, sec. 82a-1213 82a-1214.

42 Kansas Equus Beds, "Management Program," pp. 43–45.

43 Peck, *Legal Questions and Problems*, p. 3.

44 GMD No. One, telephone conversation with J. Ashley, 10 April 1996.

45 Richard F. Sloan, "Groundwater Resource Management in Kansas," *Kansas Water News* 22, nos. 1, 2 (winter 1979), p. 3.

46 Mike Dealy, GMD No. Two, telephone conversation with J. Ashley, 11 April 1996.

47 GMD No. Three, telephone conversation with J. Ashley, 11 April 1996.
48 GMD No. Four, telephone conversation with J. Ashley, 11 April 1996.
49 GMD No. Five, telephone conversation with J. Ashley, 11 April 1996.
50 GMD Nos. One through Five, and Kansas Conservation Commission, telephone conversations with J. Ashley, 3–11 April 1996.
51 See Kansas Water Office, "Irrigation Water Conservation Program for the State of Kansas," November 1993.
52 Wayne A. Bossert, letter to Z. Smith, 20 November 1986.

12 Nebraska

1 U.S. Geological Survey, *National Water Summary 1984*, p. 291.
2 Carl A. P. Fricke and Darryll T. Pederson, "Ground-Water Resource Management in Nebraska," *Ground Water* 17 (November–December 1979), p. 545.
3 Solley, Pierce, and Perlman, "Estimated Water Use," pp. 15–17.
4 <<www.census.gov>>, 15 December 1996.
5 U.S. Bureau of the Census, "Press Release CB 91-07," and <<www.census.gov>>, 15 December 1996.
6 U.S. Bureau of the Census, 1960 U.S. Census of the Population, vol. 1, part A.
7 U.S. Bureau of the Census, 1990 Census of Population and Housing, Population and Housing Counts, (1990 cph-2).
8 U.S. Department of Labor, Bureau of Labor Statistics, unpublished data, pp. 150–73.
9 U.S. Bureau of the Census, *U.S. Census of Agriculture: 1964 and 1969*, vol. 2.
10 U.S. Department of Agriculture, "Farm Numbers and Land in Farms."
11 Steve Gaul, Nebraska Natural Resources Commission, letter to J. Ashely, 3 September 1996.
12 U.S. Department of Commerce, *Survey of Current Business*, p. 55.
13 Solley, Pierce, and Perlman, "Estimated Water Use," pp. 15–17.
14 Steve Gaul, Nebraska Natural Resources Commission, telephone conversation with J. Ashley, 5 April 1996.
15 Nebraska Department of Environmental Quality, "1994 Nebraska Ground Water Quality Report," p. 32.
16 Nebraska Department of Environmental Quality, "1994 Nebraska Ground Water Quality Report," p. 32.
17 Solley, Pierce, and Perlman, "Estimated Water Use," p. 17.
18 Steve Gaul, Nebraska Natural Resources Commission, letter to J. Ashley, 23 September 1996.
19 High Plains Study Council and Nebraska Natural Resources Commission, "Summary of the Nebraska Research for the Six-State High Plains Ogallala Aquifer Study," December 1981, p. 15.
20 Steve Gaul, letter to J. Ashley, 23 September 1996.
21 Nebraska Natural Resources Commission, "Estimated Water Use in Nebraska 1990," (December 1994), p. 20. Note that among these crops, the overwhelming majority of the irrigated acreage is devoted to corn. In 1994, for example, approximately 79 percent of the irrigated acreage (5,450,000 acres) in the state was used for corn.

22 Fred Thomas, "1982 Ruling Fails to Trigger Rush to Divert State Water," *Omaha World-Herald*, 12 November 1984.

23 Martin S. Johnson and Darryll T. Pederson, "Groundwater Levels in Nebraska 1983," Nebraska Water Survey Paper Number 57 (Conservation and Survey Division, Institute of Agriculture and Natural Resources, University of Nebraska–Lincoln), p. 62; and Nebraska state engineer's office, letter to Z. Smith, 12 March 1985.

24 In 1986 there were 73,001 irrigation wells in the state according to the state engineer, and 1994 figures provided by the U.S. Geological Survey, "Open File Report 94-92" (1994), indicate that there were approximately 75,000 irrigation wells in the state. The average was obtained through the use of these figures.

25 "Falling Aquifer Raises Water Worries," *Omaha World-Herald*, 10 March 1980. See also Jim Auction, "Well Drilling Slows Across Nebraska," *Lincoln Journal Star*, 17 October 1982. It appears that the domestic glut had ended by the mid-1990s, and since then new federally funded surface projects have been minimal.

26 U.S. Geological Survey, "Open File Report 94-92," p. 6.

27 Nebraska Department of Environmental Quality, "1994 Nebraska Ground Water Quality Report," p. 1.

28 Nebraska Department of Environmental Quality, "1994 Nebraska Ground Water Quality Report," p. 1. At the time of this writing the estimate was for a two-hundred-year supply.

29 Nebraska Department of Environmental Quality, "1994 Nebraska Ground Water Quality Report," p. 27.

30 U.S. Geological Survey, *National Water Summary 1984*, p. 294. Given the fact that agricultural use has not declined and that the municipal use has increased, 1984 figures remain accurate.

31 Steve Gaul, letter to J. Ashley, 23 September 1996.

32 Nebraska Revised Statutes, 46-613.

33 High Plains Study Council, "High Plains Ogallala Aquifer Study," pp. 6–7.

34 Steve Gaul, letter to J. Ashley, 23 September 1996.

35 Nebraska Department of Environmental Quality, "1994 Nebraska Ground Water Quality Report," p. 1.

36 Nebraska Department of Environmental Quality, "1994 Nebraska Ground Water Quality Report," p. 18.

37 Nebraska Department of Environmental Quality, "1994 Nebraska Ground Water Quality Report," p. 29.

38 Nebraska Department of Environmental Quality, "1994 Nebraska Ground Water Quality Report," p. 29.

39 Nebraska Department of Environmental Quality, "1994 Nebraska Ground Water Quality Report," p. 36.

40 Nebraska Department of Environmental Quality, "1994 Nebraska Ground Water Quality Report," pp. 29–30.

41 J. David Aiken, "Nebraska Ground Water Law and Administration," *Nebraska Law Review* 59, no. 317 (1980), p. 919. This article contains an excellent and exhaustive review of the evolution of Nebraska's groundwater law. It served as a reference for much of the historical discussion on the topic that we present here.

42 *Olson v. City of Wahoo*, 124 Nebraska 802, 248 N.W. 304 (1933).

43 The Nebraska Constitution provides the preference; however, the state engineer's office contends that it applies only to surface water. Letter to Z. Smith, mid-1980s. The application of preferences in groundwater rights is established through Nebraska Revised Statutes, sec. 46-233.

44 Nebraska Revised Statutes, sec. 46-613. For discussion, see Paul H. Gessaman, *Groundwater Rights, Part 1 — Property Right, Preferences, and Conflict Resolution*, (Lincoln: Cooperative Extension Service, University of Nebraska–Lincoln, 1984) p. 3.

45 *Luchsinger v. Loup River Public Power District*, 140 Nebraska 179, 299 N.W. 549 (1941).

46 Jim Cook, Nebraska Natural Resources Commission, letter to J. Ashley, 23 September 1996.

47 *Metropolitan Utilities District of Omaha v. Merrit Beach Co.*, 179 Nebraska 783, 140 N.W.2d 626 (1966).

48 *Burger v. City of Beatrice*, 181 Nebraska 213, 147 N.W.2d 766 (1967).

49 *Prather v. Eisenmann*, 200 Nebraska 1, 261 N.W.2d 766 (1978).

50 *State ex rel. Douglas v. Sporhase*, 208 Nebraska 708, 305 N.W.2d 618 (1981).

51 *State ex rel. Douglas v. Sporhase*, 50 U.S.L.W. 5115 (U.S. 2 July 1982). For a discussion of this case see Z. Smith, "Federal Intervention," and "Stability amid Change."

52 Nebraska Natural Resources Commission, *Policy Issue Study on Property Rights in Groundwater*, January 1983, pp. 1–6.

53 Nebraska Revised Statutes, 46-1001 to 1026.

54 Nebraska Revised Statutes, 2-3201 to 3275.

55 Nebraska Revised Statutes, 46-656 to 674.

56 Nebraska Revised Statutes, 46-658(1).

57 Nebraska Revised Statutes, 46-658(3).

58 Nebraska Revised Statutes, 46-659(1).

59 Nebraska Revised Statutes, 46-666(1)(a) to (3).

60 Johnson and Pederson, "Groundwater Levels in Nebraska 1983," p. 62.

61 *Bamford v. Upper Republican Nat. Resources Dist.*, 245 Nebraska 299, 512 N.W.2d 642 (1994).

62 Steve Gaul, telephone conversation with J. Ashley, 5 April 1996.

63 Nebraska Revised Statutes, 46-673.

64 Nebraska Revised Statutes, 46-673.01.

65 Nebraska Revised Statutes, 46-656.34.

66 Nebraska Revised Statutes, 46-656.66

67 Nebraska Revised Statutes, 46-656.66 and 46-656.67.

68 Nebraska Revised Statutes, 46-656.18.

69 Nebraska Revised Statutes, 46-602 and 66-1101 to 66-1106.

70 Nebraska Revised Statutes, 46-638 and 639; Val Swinton, "Criticism Is Aimed at Ground-Water Act," *Lincoln Journal Star*, 23 August 1981.

71 Aiken, "Nebraska Ground Water Law," pp. 967–68.

72 Nebraska Revised Statutes, 2-1575 to 1582.

73 Nebraska Revised Statutes, 81-1501 to 1533.

74 Nebraska Department of Environmental Control, "Rules and Regulations for the Control of Disposal Wells to Protect Ground-Water and Other Subsurface Resources of the State of Nebraska,"1975. (In 1986 these rules were repealed and

essentially replaced by underground injection regulations. The net outcome in terms of authority over pollution control remains the same).

75 Nebraska Revised Statutes, 71-5301 to 5313; Nebraska Revised Statutes, 57-901 to 922.

76 Nebraska Revised Statutes, 57-901 to 922.

77 This term was brought up in conversation by a professor from one of the state universities in Nebraska at the 1996 Western Social Science Association conference. He stated that the term was coined by a colleague of his and that it has gained popularity among academics who follow water policy in Nebraska. Note, however, that NRD directors are elected officials.

13 North Dakota

1 U.S. Geological Survey, *National Water Summary 1983*, p. 185.

2 <<www.census.gov>>, 15 December 1996.

3 U.S. Bureau of the Census, "Press Release CB 91-07."

4 U.S. Bureau of the Census, *1960 U.S. Census of the Population*, vol. 1, part A.

5 U.S. Bureau of the Census, "1990 Census of Population and Housing, Population and Housing Counts," (1990 cph-2).

6 U.S. Department of Labor, Bureau of Labor Statistics, unpublished data, pp. 150–73.

7 U.S. Bureau of the Census, *U.S. Census of Agriculture: 1964 and 1969*, vol. 2.

8 U.S. Department of Agriculture, "Farm Numbers and Land in Farms."

9 U.S. Department of Commerce, *Survey of Current Business*, p. 55.

10 Solley, Pierce, and Perlman, "Estimated Water Use," pp. 15–17.

11 Solley, Pierce, and Perlman, "Estimated Water Use," pp. 15–17.

12 North Dakota Water Commission, telephone conversation with J. Ashley, 29 December 1995.

13 North Dakota Water Commission, telephone conversation with J. Ashley, 29 December 1995.

14 U.S. Geological Survey, *Guide to North Dakota's Groundwater Resources*, (Washington DC: U.S. Government Printing Office, 1983), p. 15, and North Dakota Water Commission, telephone conversation with J. Ashley, 29 December 1995.

15 Larry Johnson, "They Hope Project No Pipe Dream," *Bismarck Tribune*, 13 March 1979.

16 North Dakota Water Commission, telephone conversation with J. Ashley, 29 December 1995.

17 North Dakota Water Commission, telephone conversation with J. Ashley, 25 March 1996.

18 North Dakota Water Commission, telephone conversation with J. Ashley, 25 March 1996.

19 U.S. Geological Survey, *National Water Summary 1983*, p. 185.

20 Lauren Herdmeyer, "Arsenic Found in Water at Center Mine," *Bismarck Tribune*, 26 June 1980.

21 North Dakota Century Code 61-01-01 (1960).

22 Territory Dakota Civil Code 256 256 (1966).

23 120 N.W.2d 18 (North Dakota 1963).

24 120 N.W.2d 18, 24 (North Dakota 1963).

25 North Dakota Century Code 61-01-01 (1960).

26 Milton O. Lindvig, North Dakota State Water Commission, Water Appropriation Division, letter to J. Ashley, 9 October 1996. Mr. Lindvig is careful to note that the SWC does not have a regulatory authority defined by statute; this power rests with the state engineer. We have seen, however, that the engineer serves at the pleasure of the commission.

27 North Dakota Century Code 61-04-06 (1960).

28 North Dakota Century Code 61-03-13 (1960).

29 North Dakota Century Code 61-04-06.1 (Supp. 1977).

30 U.S. Geological Survey, Guide to North Dakota's Groundwater Resources, p. 20.

31 North Dakota Century Code 61-16.1-03.

32 North Dakota Century Code 61-16.1-15; North Dakota Century Code 61-16.1-09 (2); North Dakota Century Code 61-16.1-09 (8); North Dakota Century Code 61-16.1-09 (20,21).

33 North Dakota state engineer's office, telephone conversation with J. Ashley, 29 December 1995.

34 North Dakota Century Code 61-16.1-13.

35 North Dakota Century Code 61-16-07.

36 North Dakota Century Code 61-16.1-19.

37 North Dakota Century Code 61-05-02 (1960).

38 North Dakota Century Code 61-07 (1960).

39 North Dakota state engineer's office, telephone conversation with J. Ashley, 29 December 1995.

40 Kevin Murphy, "Clark Pledges 'Fresh Look' at Garrison," Fargo Forum, 12 August 1984.

41 Randy Bradbury, "Garrison Study Begins; Fargo Hearing Planned," Fargo Forum, 31 August 1984.

42 North Dakota Water Commission, telephone conversation with J. Ashley, 29 December 1995.

43 North Dakota Water Commission, telephone conversation with J. Ashley, 29 December 1995.

14 South Dakota

1 U.S. Geological Survey, National Water Summary 1983, p. 209.

2 South Dakota, State Legislative Research Council, "Considerations Involving the Use of Ground Water in South Dakota," November 1, 1969, p. 1.

3 <<www.census.gov>>, 15 December 1996.

4 Average growth rate was calculated with 1950 census data provided by U.S. Bureau of the Census, "Press Release CB 91-07," and 1995 census data obtained via the Internet at www.census.gov, 15 December 1996.

5 U.S. Bureau of the Census, 1960 U.S. Census of the Population, vol. 1, part A.

6 U.S. Bureau of the Census, "1990 Census of the Population and Housing, Population and Housing Counts," (1990 cph-2).

7 U.S. Bureau of the Census, County and City Data Book, 1994.

8 U.S. Department of Labor, Bureau of Labor Statistics, unpublished data, pp. 150–73.

9 U.S. Bureau of the Census, U.S. Census of Agriculture: 1964 and 1969, vol. 2.

10 U.S. Department of Agriculture, "Farm Numbers and Land in Farms."

11 U.S. Department of Commerce, *Survey of Current Business*, p. 55.

12 South Dakota, Department of Water and Natural Resources, *South Dakota Water Quality*, 1984, p. 83.

13 Solley, Pierce, and Perlman, "Estimated Water Use," pp. 15–17.

14 Ron Duvall, South Dakota Department of Environment and Natural Resources, letter to J. Ashley, 7 November 1996.

15 Solley, Pierce, and Perlman, "Estimated Water Use," pp. 15–17.

16 South Dakota Department of Environment and Natural Resources, telephone conversation with J. Ashley, 29 December 1995.

17 South Dakota Department of Environment and Natural Resources, telephone conversation with J. Ashley, 29 December 1995.

18 South Dakota Department of Environment and Natural Resources, telephone conversation with J. Ashley, 29 December 1995.

19 South Dakota, Department of Water and Natural Resources, *South Dakota Water Quality*, p. 89.

20 South Dakota Department of Environment and Natural Resources, "1995 Groundwater Quality Assessment" (draft), pp. 139–40.

21 South Dakota Department of Environment and Natural Resources, "1995 Groundwater Quality Assessment," table 8-4 A, Aquifer-Monitoring Data.

22 Darron Busch and Michael Meyer, "A Case of Infantile Methemoglobinemia," *Journal of Environmental Health* 44, no. 6 (May/June 1982), p. 310, and Michael Meyer, "Comment: More on Nitrates," *Water Well Journal* 40, no. 10 (October 1986), p. 31.

23 South Dakota Department of Environment and Natural Resources, "1995 Groundwater Quality Assessment," pp. 140–45. Once petroleum products enter into a groundwater source, they are among the most difficult and most expensive contaminants to clean up (total elimination is practically impossible). Petroleum products such as benzene, toluene, and xylene constitute potential health risks and have been linked to such disorders as cancer (benzene) and organ damage and nervous system disorders (toluene).

24 South Dakota Department of Environment and Natural Resources, "1994 EPA 305 (b) Report," p. 8. The variance between months is also applicable to extreme variance between years. In 1994, for example, 17 percent of the sampled wells failed to meet bacteriological standards, while in 1995 only 2 percent of the wells sampled were below safety standards. As of 1996 it was too early to determine whether the variance was due to improved quality or to changes in monitoring sites or techniques.

25 "Official: Report Distorted Water Problems," *Sioux Falls Argus Leader*, 10 March 1982, p. 3C.

26 South Dakota Department of Environment and Natural Resources, telephone conversation with J. Ashley, 29 December 1995.

27 "The Status of Groundwater in South Dakota," *South Dakota Law Review* 22 (summer 1977), p. 951.

28 *Metzalf v. Nelson*, 8 S.D. 87, 65 N.W. 911, (1895); see also *Dadwood Cent. R.R. v. Barker*, 14 S.D. 558, 86 N.W. 619, (1901).

29 S.D.C.L. sec. 46-6-6.2.

30 S.D.C.L. sec. 46-6-3.1.

31 S.D.C.L. sec. 46-6.
32 Larry Green, "South Dakota Plan to Sell Water for Use in West Sets Off Battle in Midwest," *Los Angeles Times*, 23 October 1982, part 1, p. 20.
33 "Slurry System May Lower Wells," *Sioux Falls Argus Leader*, 11 November 1980.
34 Department of Environment and Natural Resources, telephone conversation with J. Ashely, 29 December 1995.

15 Arizona

1   U.S. Geological Survey, *Annual Summary of Ground Water, Spring 1978 to Spring 1979* (Washington DC, 1980), p. 1.
2   Arizona Underground Water Commission, *The Underground Water Resources of Arizona* (1953), p. 66.
3   Dennis Sundie, Water Resources Program Manager, Chief of Data Management Division, Arizona Department of Water Resources, letter to J. Ashley, 18 November 1996.
4   Dean E. Mann, *The Politics of Water in Arizona* (Tucson: University of Arizona Press, 1963), p. 3.
5   <<www.census.gov>>, 15 December 1996.
6   U.S. Bureau of the Census, "Press Release CB 91-07," and <<www.census.gov>>, 15 December 1996.
7   U.S. Bureau of the Census, *U.S. Census of the Population: 1970*, vol. 1, part A.
8   U.S. Bureau of the Census, "1990 Census of Population and Housing, Population and Housing Counts," (1990 cph-2).
9   U.S. Department of Labor, Bureau of Labor Statistics, unpublished data, pp. 150–73.
10 U.S. Bureau of the Census, *U.S. Census of Agriculture: 1964 and 1969*, vol. 2.
11 U.S. Department of Agriculture, "Farm Numbers and Land in Farms." Note, however, that these numbers include ranch land. The amount of irrigated acreage stood at around 1 million acres as of the mid-1990s. The numbers are provided to illustrate the relative decline of farming and ranching versus other industries over the past several years.
12 Herb Dislip, Arizona Department of Water Resources, telephone conversation with J. Ashley, 4 September 1996.
13 U.S. Department of Commerce, *Survey of Current Business*, p. 56.
14 U.S. Department of Commerce, *County and City Data Book*, 1994.
15 U.S. Geological Survey, *1980 Annual Summary*, p. 1.
16 Arizona Department of Water Resources, *Arizona Water Resources Assessment*, vol. 1, *Inventory and Analysis* (Phoenix: State of Arizona, 1994), p. 9.
17 Susanna Eden and Mary G. Wallace, *Arizona Water: Information and Issues*, (Tucson: University of Arizona Water Resources Research Center, 1992), p. 10. In this report it was estimated that the recharge rate of the aquifers in Arizona is 2 million acre-feet per year, which accounts for natural, incidental, and artificial recharge.
18 U.S. Geological Survey, *Estimated Use of Water in the United States* (Washington DC, 1955).
19 Arizona Water Commission, *Inventory of Resource and Uses: Phase I—Arizona Water Plan Summary* (1975), p. 15.

20 Solley, Pierce, and Perlman, "Estimated Water Use," p. 13.
21 Arizona Department of Water Resources, *Arizona Water Resources Assessment,* p. xxvi.
22 Arizona Department of Water Resources, *Arizona Water Resources Assessment,* pp. 13–17.
23 Arizona Department of Water Resources, *Arizona Water Resources Assessment,* p. xxvi.
24 Arizona Revised Statutes, *Annotated,* 45-473(A).
25 Helen Ingram, William E. Martin, and Nancy K. Laney, "Central Arizona Project Case Study," in *Western Water Institutions in a Changing Environment,* vol. 2 (Napa CA: John Muir Institute, 1980), p. E-35.
26 Frank Barrios, Arizona Department of Water Resources, telephone conversation with J. Ashley, 10 July 1996.
27 Frank Barrios, telephone conversation with J. Ashley, 10 July 1996.
28 *Howard v. Perrin,* 8 Arizona 347, 76 P. 460 (1904).
29 Robert G. Dunbar, "The Arizona Groundwater Controversy at Mid-Century," *Arizona and the West* 19, no. 1 (1977), p. 8.
30 Arizona recognizes four classes of water supply: surface water, water flowing in definite underground channels, percolating groundwater, and nonreturned effluent, which is considered neither surface water nor groundwater. Surface water and waters flowing in definite underground channels are considered public property and are governed by the doctrine of prior appropriation. See *Howard v. Perrin,* 8 Arizona 347, 76 P. 460 (1904).
31 *Bristor v. Cheatham,* 73 Arizona 228, 240 P.2d 185 (1952); *Bristor v. Cheatham,* 75 Arizona 227, 225 P.2d 173 (1953).
32 *Bristor v. Cheatham,* 73 Arizona 228, 240 P.2d 185, 190 (1952).
33 *Bristor v. Cheatham,* 73 Arizona 228, 240 P.2d 185, 190 (1952).
34 Mann, *Politics of Water,* pp. 57–58.
35 Dunbar, "Arizona Groundwater Controversy," p. 21.
36 *Bristor v. Cheatham,* 75 Arizona 227, 255 P.2d 173 (1953).
37 Zachary A. Smith, "Centralized Decisionmaking," p. 641. For a discussion of the federal role in the passage of the Groundwater Management Act, see Zachary A. Smith, *Interest Group Interaction and Groundwater Policy Formation in the Southwest,* (Lanham MD: University Press of America, 1985) and "Federal Intervention," p. 145.
38 Arizona Revised Statutes, *Annotated,* 45-401.
39 Arizona Revised Statutes, *Annotated,* 45-411(A).
40 U.S. Department of Commerce, *County and City Data Book.* Total overdraft in the state is estimated to be 1.2 million acre-feet, of which 1 million occur within the AMA.
41 Arizona Revised Statutes, *Annotated,* 412(A), 413.
42 Arizona Revised Statutes, 45-415.
43 Arizona Revised Statutes, *Annotated,* 45-102-103.
44 Arizona Revised Statutes, *Annotated,* 45-104.
45 Arizona Revised Statutes, *Annotated,* 45-562.
46 Arizona Revised Statutes, *Annotated,* 45-461(5).
47 Arizona Revised Statutes, *Annotated,* 45-562(B).

48 Arizona Revised Statutes, *Annotated*, 45-564-568.
49 Arizona Revised Statutes, *Annotated*, 45-566(A)(6).
50 Arizona Revised Statutes, *Annotated*, 45-462(D).
51 Arizona Revised Statutes, *Annotated*, 45-476(A).
52 Arizona Revised Statutes, *Annotated*, 45-465(A).
53 Arizona Revised Statutes, *Annotated*, 45-473(A).
54 Arizona Revised Statutes, *Annotated*, 45-463(A) (B), 469 (F).
55 Arizona Revised Statutes, *Annotated*, 45-472(C).
56 Arizona Revised Statutes, *Annotated*, 45-469.
57 Arizona Revised Statutes, *Annotated*, 45-464.
58 Arizona Revised Statutes, *Annotated*, 45-474.
59 Arizona Revised Statutes, *Annotated*, 45-471, 474.
60 Arizona Revised Statutes, *Annotated*, 45-402(18).
61 James W. Johnson, *Summary of the 1980 Arizona Groundwater Management Act* (Phoenix: State Bar of Arizona, 1980), p. 3.
62 Arizona Revised Statutes, *Annotated*, 45-467.
63 Arizona Revised Statutes, *Annotated*, 45-431.
64 Arizona Revised Statutes, *Annotated*, 45-467.
65 Arizona Department of Water Resources, *Arizona Water Resources Assessment*, p. 37.
66 Arizona Revised Statutes, *Annotated*, 45-431.
67 Arizona Revised Statutes, *Annotated*, 45-432.
68 Arizona Revised Statutes, *Annotated*, 45-434, 437(A) (B).
69 Arizona Revised Statutes, *Annotated*, 45-437(A).
70 Arizona Revised Statutes, *Annotated*, 45-434.
71 Arizona Revised Statutes, *Annotated*, 45-593-600; Arizona Revised Statutes, *Annotated*, 45-405, 407, 519, 634, 635, 637.
72 *Town of Chino Valley v. City of Prescott*, 131 Arizona at 78, 638 P.2d 1324.
73 Arizona Revised Statutes, 45-2421, and Arizona Department of Water Resources, "Arizona Banking Authority," Executive Summary, 23 October 1996.
74 Arizona Department of Water Resources, *Arizona Water Resources Assessment*, p. 52.
75 Arizona Department of Water Resources, *Arizona Water Resources Assessment*, p. 51.
76 Arizona Water Commission, *Inventory of Resource and Uses* (July 1975), pp. 39; 148.
77 Arizona Water Commission, *Inventory of Resource and Uses*, pp. 39; 148.
78 Herb Dislip, telephone conversation with J. Ashley, 4 September 1996.
79 Arizona Department of Water Resources, *Arizona Water Resources Assessment*, p. 87.
80 U.S. Department of Commerce, *County and City Data Book*. p. 650.
81 Arizona Department of Water Resources, *Arizona Water Resources Assessment*, pp. 104–5.
82 Arizona Department of Water Resources, *Arizona Water Resources Assessment*, pp. 118–19.
83 Arizona Department of Water Resources, *Arizona Water Resources Assessment*, 124.
84 Arizona Department of Water Resources, *Arizona Water Resources Assessment*.

85 Arizona Revised Statutes, *Annotated*, 49-281 to 287.
86 For a discussion of Arizona's groundwater history and the events leading up to the passage of the Arizona Groundwater Management Act, see Z. Smith, *Interest Group Interaction.*
87 Z. Smith, *Interest Group Interaction*, p. 142.

16 Nevada

1   Nevada Department of Conservation and Natural Resources, Division of Water Planning, "Nevada Water Facts" (1992), p. 10.
2   Solley, Pierce, and Perlman, "Estimated Water Use," pp. 15–17.
3   <<www.census.gov>>, 15 December 1996.
4   U.S. Bureau of the Census, "Press Release CB 91-07," and <<www.census.gov>>, 15 December 1996.
5   U.S. Bureau of the Census, *1960 Census of the Population*, vol. 1, part A, and U.S. Bureau of the Census, "1990 Census of Population and Housing, Population and Housing Counts," (1990 cph-2).
6   U.S. Bureau of the Census, *U.S. Census of Agriculture: 1964 and 1969*, vol. 2.
7   U.S. Department of Labor, Bureau of Labor Statistics, unpublished data, pp. 150–73.
8   U.S. Department of Commerce, *Survey of Current Business*, p. 56. Services would include hotel accommodations and the income derived by hotel/casino employees but not the proceeds from gaming itself. While services contribute approximately 33 percent to the gross state product, gaming revenues account for roughly 47 percent of Nevada's annual state budget according to an official with the Nevada Department of Natural Resources who depends on state funding for agency operations.
9   Nevada Department of Conservation, "Nevada Water Facts," pp. 28–31.
10 Randy Pahl, Nevada Department of Conservation and Natural Resources, Division of Water Planning, letter to J. Ashley, 17 September 1996.
11 Nevada Department of Conservation and Natural Resources, "Water Conservation in Nevada," (1979), p. 9.
12 Solley, Pierce, and Perlman, "Estimated Water Use," p. 17.
13 Nevada Department of Conservation, "Water Conservation in Nevada" (1979), p. 10.
14 Solley, Pierce, and Perlman, "Estimated Water Use," p. 17.
15 For a general discussion of the history of the development of groundwater in the West see Z. Smith, *Interest Group Interaction*, chap. 10.
16 Nevada Department of Conservation and Natural Resources, "Water for Nevada" (1971), p. 1, 5, 6. Increased demand has also been met by the conversion of water rights from agricultural to municipal use and, in Las Vegas, by increased use of Nevada's allotment of Colorado River water. Nevada Department of Conservation and Water Resources, letter to Z. Smith, 15 December 1986.
17 Solley, Pierce, and Perlman, "Estimated Water Use," p. 17.
18 Nevada Department of Conservation, "Nevada Water Facts," p. 25, and Department of Conservation, telephone conversation with J. Ashley, 28 December 1995.
19 Nevada Department of Conservation, telephone conversation with J. Ashley, 28 December 1995.
20 Nevada Department of Conservation and Natural Resources, Division of Water Planning, *Water for Southern Nevada* (Carson City: Division of Water Planning,

1982), pp. 98–99. As the U.S. Geological Survey's Water Survey Data Report NV-94-1, "Water Resources Data—Nevada, Water Year 1994" (1995), reveals that groundwater levels have continued to hold to a pattern of steady decline through the mid-1990s, there is no reason to believe that the statement is any less true today than it was fourteen years ago. In fact, conditions have worsened.

21 U.S. Geological Survey, "Water Resources Data—Nevada," pp. 577–80.

22 Nevada Department of Conservation, telephone conversation with J. Ashley, 28 December 1995.

23 Nevada Department of Conservation, telephone conversation with J. Ashley, 28 December 1995.

24 Anthony Mindling and John Blume, "Effects of Groundwater Withdrawal on Freeway and Vicinity," Report Series 33 (Center for Water Resources Research, Desert Research Institute, University of Nevada Project, 1974), p. 32.

25 R. Patt and G. B. Maxey, "Mapping of the Earth Fissures in Las Vegas, Nevada," Pub. No. 41051 (Water Resources Center, Desert Research Institute, University of Nevada, March 1978), p. 1.

26 Donald A. Haselhoff, "Water for Las Vegas Metropolitan Area," *Journal of Environmental Engineering* 109 (1983), p. 702.

27 Nevada Department of Conservation, telephone conversation with J. Ashley, 28 December 1995.

28 Nevada Division of Environmental Protection, "Comprehensive State Groundwater Protection Program Profile," 14 December 1995, p. 19.

29 Nevada Department of Conservation, telephone conversation with J. Ashley, 28 December 1995.

30 Nevada Department of Conservation, "Nevada Water Facts," p. 68.

31 U.S. Geological Survey, *National Water Summary 1983*, p. 167.

32 Nevada Department of Conservation, "Nevada Water Facts," p. 67.

33 Nevada Department of Conservation, "Nevada Water Facts," p. 69.

34 *Mosier v. Caldwell*, 7 Nevada 363, 366–67 (1872). The decision was affirmed in *Strait v. Brown*, 16 Nevada 317, 321 (1881).

35 *Strait v. Brown*, 16 Nevada 317, 321 (1881).

36 Nevada Revised Statutes, sec. 534.020 (1977).

37 Nevada Revised Statutes, sec. 534.010, 534.030, 534.180 (1977).

38 Nevada Revised Statutes, sec. 534.030 (1) (1977).

39 Nevada Revised Statutes, sec. 534.120 (1977).

40 Nevada Department of Conservation, "Nevada Water Facts," pp. 20–25.

41 Nevada Revised Statutes, sec. 534.050 (1) (2) (1977).

42 Nevada Revised Statutes, sec. 534.120 (1977).

43 Nevada Revised Statutes, sec. 534.190 (1977).

44 Nevada Revised Statutes, sec. 534.120 (1977).

45 Nevada Revised Statutes, sec. 534.110 (2) and 533.370 (3) (1977). In 1993 the Nevada legislature amended section 534.110 in order to give domestic well owners more protection from adverse impact from municipal or industrial water users withdrawing water at a rate of 0.5 cubic feet per second or more. As a condition for municipal or industrial permits, pumpage may be limited or prohibited in order to prevent impact on existing domestic wells located within 2,500 feet of the municipal or industrial well—unless there is an agreement between the parties for the mitigation of

the impact. Clark County is exempted from the amendment (presumably because Las Vegas needs more water for municipal use if the city is to continue to grow).

46 Nevada Revised Statutes, sec. 534.035 (1977); Nevada Department of Conservation and Natural Resources, Division of Water Resources, *Special Information Report Water—Legal and Administrative Aspects* (1974), p. 25.

47 Nevada Revised Statutes, sec. 534.060, 534.170, 534.110, 534.120–70 (1977).

48 Despite the fact that many basins are overappropriated, some within the Department of Conservation and Natural Resources believe this is not a sign of mismanagement. It is argued that overappropriation does not lead to overuse. Many agricultural groundwater rights are only exercised to supplement surface water in dry years, and thus withdrawals only exceed recharge rates at certain times (see Randy Pahl, letter to J. Ashley, 17 September 1996.). However, given the "use it or lose it" nature of prior appropriation, it seems to us that wise use and conservation during wet years would be precluded because of concerns over retaining water rights.

49 Nevada Department of Conservation, "Nevada Water Facts," p. 25.

50 Nevada Department of Conservation, *Water for Southern Nevada*, p. 80.

51 Nevada Department of Conservation, "Nevada Water Facts," p. 58.

52 Haselhoff, "Water for Las Vegas," p. 702.

17 New Mexico

1 New Mexico Water Quality Control Commission, "Water Quality and Water Pollution Control in New Mexico 1994," p. 4.

2 Jay Groseclose, engineer, New Mexico Interstate Stream Commission, letter to J. Ashley, 18 January 1997.

3 New Mexico Water Quality Control Commission, *State of New Mexico Water Quality Status Summary* (Santa Fe NM, May 1980), p. 12.

4 <<www.census.gov>>, 15 December 1996.

5 U.S. Bureau of the Census, "Press Release CB 91-07," and <<www.census.gov>>, 15 December 1996.

6 U.S. Bureau of the Census, *1960 U.S. Census of the Population*, vol. 1, part A.

7 U.S. Bureau of the Census, "1990 Census of Population and Housing, Population and Housing Counts," (1990 cph-2).

8 U.S. Department of Commerce, *County and City Data Book.*

9 U.S. Department of Commerce, *Survey of Current Business.*

10 U.S. Department of Commerce, *Survey of Current Business.*

11 U.S. Bureau of the Census, *U.S. Census of Agriculture: 1964 and 1969*, vol. 2.

12 U.S. Department of Agriculture, "Farm Numbers and Land in Farms."

13 Jay Groseclose, letter to J. Ashley, 18 January 1997.

14 Jay Groseclose, letter to J. Ashley, 18 January 1997.

15 New Mexico state engineer's office, letter to J. Ashley, 24 June 1996.

16 New Mexico Water Quality Control Commission, "Water Quality," p. 23.

17 New Mexico Water Quality Control Commission, "Water Quality," p. 23.

18 New Mexico Water Quality Control Commission, "Water Quality," p. 23.

19 S. E. Reynolds, letter to the U.S. General Accounting Office, p. 49.

20 New Mexico state engineer's office, letter to J. Ashley, 24 June 1996.

21 77 New Mexico 239, 421 P.2d 771 (1966).

22 S. E. Reynolds, letter to the U.S. General Accounting Office, p. 6.

23 New Mexico Water Resources Research Institute and University of New Mexico Law School, *State Appropriation of Unappropriated Groundwater* (January 1986), pp. 178–80. In 1985 a forty-year period was declared the maximum amount of time that a municipality could hold water rights (without using the water) for future use. See New Mexico Statutes, *Annotated*, sec. 72-1-9 (1978) as amended in 1985.

24 New Mexico Statutes, *Annotated*, sec., 74-6-4 (B–E).

25 New Mexico Water Quality Control Commission, "Water Quality," pp. 116–17.

26 New Mexico Water Quality Control Commission, *State of New Mexico Water Quality*, p. 59, and New Mexico Water Quality Control Commission, "Water Quality," pp. 118–21.

27 U.S. Geological Survey, "Open File Report 91-231," (Albuquerque NM, 1991), p. 9.

28 New Mexico Water Quality Control Commission, "Water Quality," p. 59.

29 New Mexico Water Quality Control Commission, "Water Quality," p. 59.

30 New Mexico Water Quality Control Commission, "Water Quality," pp. 119–20.

31 New Mexico Water Quality Control Commission, "Water Quality," pp. 118–19.

32 New Mexico Water Quality Control Commission, "Water Quality," pp. 120–21.

33 New Mexico Water Quality Control Commission, "Water Quality," p. 52.

34 New Mexico state engineer's office, letter to J. Ashley, 24 June 1996.

35 New Mexico Water Quality Control Commission, "Water Quality," p. 121.

36 *Vanderwork v. Hewes*, 15 New Mexico 439, 446, 110 P. 567, 569 (1910). It is on the basis of this court decision that the authors concluded that New Mexico initially followed the common law in groundwater. However, given long-standing Spanish and Mexican tradition in the management of surface water, and given the dearth of groundwater cases, the point is arguable. Surface water in New Mexico has never followed the common law. For a discussion of this topic see New Mexico Water Resources Research Institute, *State Appropriation*, chaps. 3 and 4.

37 Robert Emmet Clark, "Ground Water Law: Problem Areas," *Natural Resources Lawyer* 8, no. 377 (1975), p. 171.

38 New Mexico Laws 1927, chap. 182, sec. 1.

39 *Yeo v. Tweedy*, 34 New Mexico 611, 286 P. 970 (1930).

40 New Mexico Laws 1931, chap. 131.

41 *State ex. Rel. Bliss v. Dority*, 55 New Mexico 12, 225 P.2d 1007 (1950).

42 New Mexico Statutes, *Annotated*, sec. 72-12-1.

43 New Mexico Statutes, *Annotated*, sec. 72-12-3 (1978) as amended in 1985.

44 New Mexico State Engineer's Office and New Mexico Department of Environment, "The Rural Homeowner's Water Guide" (June 1991), p. 12.

45 New Mexico Statutes, *Annotated*, sec. 72-12-3(d).

46 New Mexico Statutes, *Annotated*, sec. 72-12-3(e).

47 *McBee v. Reynolds*, 74 New Mexico 783, 399 P.2d 110 (1964); Heine v. Reynolds, 69 New Mexico 398, 367 P.2d 708 (1962).

48 New Mexico Statutes, *Annotated*, sec. 72-12-3(f).

49 New Mexico state engineer, Annual Report, 1979/1980 p.10.

50 New Mexico Constitution, art. 16, sec. 5.

51 *C.M. Kelley v. Carlsbad Irrigation Dist.*, 71 New Mexico 464, 394 P.2d 139 (1964).

52 New Mexico Statutes, *Annotated*, sec. 71-12-1.

53 New Mexico Statutes, *Annotated*, sec. 72-13-2.

54 New Mexico Statutes, *Annotated*, sec. 72-13-4.
55 New Mexico Statutes, *Annotated*, sec. 72-13-5.
56 New Mexico Statutes, *Annotated*, sec. 72-13-8.
57 New Mexico Statutes, *Annotated*, sec. 72-13-9.
58 New Mexico state engineer's office, letter to J. Ashley, 24 June 1996.
59 *Cartwright v. Public Serv. Co.*, 66 New Mexico 64, 343 P.2d 654 (1958).

18 Oklahoma

1 U.S. Geological Survey, *National Water Summary 1984*, p. 347.
2 Oklahoma Water Resources Board, "Oklahoma Comprehensive Water Plan," Publication 94 (1 April 1980), p. 46.
3 Solley, Pierce, and Perlman, "Estimated Water Use," pp. 15–17.
4 <<www.census.gov>>, 15 December 1996.
5 U.S. Bureau of the Census, "Press Release CB 91-07," and <<www.census.gov>>, 15 December 1996.
6 U.S. Bureau of the Census, *1960 Census of the Population*, vol. 1, part A.
7 U.S. Bureau of the Census, "1990 Census of Population and Housing, Population and Housing Counts," (1990 cph-2).
8 U.S. Bureau of the Census, *County and City Data Book.*
9 U.S. Department of Labor, Bureau of Labor Statistics, unpublished data, pp. 150–73.
10 U.S. Bureau of the Census, *U.S. Census of Agriculture: 1964 and 1969*, vol. 2.
11 U.S. Department of Agriculture, "Farm Numbers and Land in Farms."
12 U.S. Department of Commerce, *Survey of Current Business*, p. 56.
13 Oklahoma Water Resources Board, "Oklahoma Comprehensive Water Plan Update 1995," p. 1.
14 Brian Vance, Oklahoma Water Resources Board, telephone conversation with J. Ashley, 24 May 1996.
15 Solley, Pierce, and Perlman, "Estimated Water Use," p. 17.
16 Oklahoma Water Resources Board, "Oklahoma Comprehensive Water Plan Update 1995," p. 25.
17 Oklahoma Water Resources Board, "Oklahoma Comprehensive Water Plan Update 1995," p. 42.
18 Oklahoma Water Resources Board, telephone conversation with J. Ashley, 23 May 1996.
19 Brian Vance, telephone conversation with J. Ashley, 24 May 1996.
20 Oklahoma Department of Environmental Quality, "1994 Oklahoma Water Quality Report to Congress," pp. 99–104.
21 Oklahoma Department of Environmental Quality, "1994 Oklahoma Water Quality Report," pp. 99–100.
22 Oklahoma Department of Environmental Quality, "1994 Oklahoma Water Quality Report," p. 92.
23 Territory Oklahoma Statutes, 4162 (1890). See also Z. Smith, "Centralized Decision-making," p. 641.
24 *Canada v. City of Shawnee*, 64 P.2d 694, 699, (1937).
25 Oklahoma Statutes, *Annotated*, Tit. 82, 10003-1013 (West).
26 Oklahoma Statutes, *Annotated*, Tit. 82, 1010.1-1020.22 (West).

27 Oklahoma Statutes, *Annotated*, Tit. 82, 1020.4 and 1020.5 (West).

28 Oklahoma Statutes, *Annotated*, Tit. 82, 1020.3 (West).

29 Oklahoma Statutes, *Annotated*, Tit. 82, 1020.9 (West).

30 Oklahoma Statutes, *Annotated*, Tit. 82, 1020.10 and 1020.11(C)(West).

31 Oklahoma Statutes, *Annotated*, Tit, 82, 1020.14 (West).

32 Oklahoma Statutes, *Annotated*, Tit. 82, 926.3 and 1020.21 (West).

33 Oklahoma Water Resources Board, "Rules, Regulations and Modes of Procedure 1982," (as amended 1983), Publication 107. Reciprocity applies to the residency requirements.

34 Oklahoma Statutes, *Annotated*, Tit. 82, 277.5 (West).

35 Oklahoma Statutes, *Annotated*, Tit. 82, 277.6 (West).

36 Oklahoma Statutes, *Annotated*, Tit. 82, 541(b) (West).

37 *Oklahoma Water Resources Board, et al. v. Texas County Irrigation and Water Resources Association, Inc.*, 56 OK 355 (1984).

38 Prior to this decision, publici juris was most recently recognized and utilized by the Oklahoma Supreme Court in *State ex. rel. Poulos v. State Board of Equalization*, 522 P.2d 1134, 1137 (Oklahoma 1975).

39 *Oklahoma Water Resources Board, et al. v. Texas County Irrigation and Water Resources Association, Inc.*, p. 9 of the majority opinion.

40 *Oklahoma v. Texas County Irrigation and Water Resources Association*, 818 P.2d 449, 455 (Oklahoma 1991).

41 Oklahoma Water Resources Board, *State-Level Research Results for the Six-State High Plains Ogallala Aquifer Area Study*, (Norman: Oklahoma University Printing Services, 1983), p. 15.

42 Oklahoma Water Resources Board, "Oklahoma Comprehensive Water Plan," p. 206.

43 Board member, Oklahoma Water Resource Board, Planning Division, telephone conversation with J. Ashley, 24 May 1996.

44 Chuck Ervin, "Water Movement Issue Still Boils," *Tulsa World*, 15 January 1978.

45 Ken Jackson, "Water: Can It Keep Up With Soaring Human Needs?" *Tulsa World*, 14 September 1980. See also Kent W. Olson, "Economic Prospects for Interbasin Water Transfer to Southern High Plains Farmers," in *Water and the Future of the Southwest*, ed. Zachary A. Smith (Albuquerque: University of New Mexico Press, 1989).

46 Oklahoma Water Resources Board, "Oklahoma Comprehensive Water Plan Update, 1995," p. 6.

47 Oklahoma Water Resources Board, "Oklahoma Comprehensive Water Plan Update, 1995," p. 8.

19 Texas

1 U.S. Geological Survey, *National Water Summary 1984*, p. 397.

2 Tony Bagwell, director, Water Resources Planning Division, Texas Water Development Board, letter to J. Ashley, 10 October 1996.

3 <<www.census.gov>>, 15 December 1996.

4 U.S. Bureau of the Census, "Press Release CB 91-07," and <<www.census.gov>>, 15 December 1996.

5 U.S. Bureau of the Census, *1960 U.S. Census of the Population*, vol. 1, part A.

6 U.S. Bureau of the Census, "1990 Census of Population and Housing, Population and Housing Counts," (1990 cph-2).

7 U.S. Department of Labor, Bureau of Labor Statistics, unpublished data, pp. 150–73.

8 U.S. Bureau of the Census, *U.S. Census of Agriculture: 1964 and 1969*, vol. 2.

9 U.S. Department of Agriculture, "Farm Numbers and Land in Farms."

10 U.S. Department of Commerce, *Survey of Current Business*, p. 56.

11 Solley, Pierce, and Perlman, "Estimated Water Use," p. 13.

12 Solley, Pierce, and Perlman, "Estimated Water Use," pp. 15–17.

13 Texas Department of Water Resources, Water Planning Division, telephone conversation with J. Ashley, 30 May 1996.

14 Texas Department of Water Planning, Water Planning Division, telephone conversation with J. Ashley.

15 Texas Department of Water Resources, *Water For Texas: A Comprehensive Plan for the Future*, vol. 1 (1984), p. 3.

16 Texas Department of Water Resources, Water Planning Division, telephone conversation with J. Ashley.

17 Tony Bagwell, letter to J. Ashley, 10 October 1996.

18 Garland F. Smith, "The Valley Water Suit and Its Impact on Texas Water Policy," *Texas Tech Law Review* 8 (1977), p. 580, and Otis W. Templer, "Texas Groundwater Law: Inflexible Institutions and Resource Realities," *Ecumene* 10, no. 1, (1978), pp. 6–15.

19 John Teutsch, "Controls and Remedies for Ground-Water-Caused Land Subsidence," *Houston Law Review* 16, no. 2 (1979), pp. 288–92.

20 98 Texas 146, 81 S.W.279 (1904). A subtle yet important distinction needs to be made here. Property owners in Texas are said to have the "undisputed right of capture" and hence, it is argued, technically the landowner does not own the water but has, absent malice, the unlimited right to withdraw the water. The effect, in terms of competition and overdrafting, is the same.

21 208 S.W. 2d 577 (Texas Civil App. 1948).

22 271 S.W. 2d 503 (Texas Civil App.-El Paso 1954).

23 Roger Tyler, "Underground Water Regulation in Texas," *Texas Bar Journal* 39 (June 1976), p. 533.

24 154 Texas 289, 276 S.W.2d 798 (1955).

25 527 S.W.2d 754 (Texas Civil App.-San Antonio 1974).

26 576 S.W.2d 28 (1977).

27 632 S.W.2d 624 (Texas Civil App. 1981).

28 Teutsch, "Controls and Remedies," p. 283.

29 Tony Bagwell, telephone conversation with J. Ashley, 30 May 1996.

30 Tony Bagwell, letter to J. Ashley, 10 October 1996.

31 Texas Water Code *Annotated*, sec. 52.002–52.401 (Vernon 1982).

32 Texas Water Code *Annotated*, sec. 52.117 (Vernon 1982). In a communication with a staff member of the Texas Water Development Board it was noted that there was "not full agreement" on the extent of the UWCDs to regulate well production." The statute cited above, however, includes the delegation of authority.

33 Texas Department of Natural Resource Conservation, telephone conversation with J. Ashley, 30 May 1996.

34 Texas Department of Natural Resource Conservation, telephone conversation with J. Ashley, 30 May 1996.

35 Corwin W. Johnson, "Texas Groundwater Law: A Survey and Some Proposals," *Natural Resources Journal* 22, no. 4 (October, 1982), p. 1020. See also *Beckendoff v. Harris-Galveston Coastal Subsidence District,* 558 S.W.2d 75 (Texas Civil App. 1977) affirmed, 563 S.W.2d 239 (Texas 1978).

36 Texas Department of Water Resources, *Water For Texas,* p. 1–9. These numbers are currently correct as confirmed by the Texas Water Board, telephone conversation with J. Ashley, 30 May 1996.

37 Johnson, "Texas Groundwater Law," p. 1023.

38 Texas Water Board, telephone conversation with J. Ashley, 30 May 1996.

39 Texas Department of Water Resources, *Water For Texas,* pp. 4–16.

40 See Tyler, "Underground Water Regulation," p. 535; and Teutsch, "Controls and Remedies," p. 297.

41 See Z. Smith, "Federal Intervention"; Gina Wickersham, "Groundwater Management"; and Carlos A. Rincon Valdez, "De aguas subterraneas en la region de Juarez-El Paso," *Natural Resources Journal* 22, no. 4 (October 1982), 969–70.

42 Texas Department of Water Resources, *Water For Texas,* p. 1–9.

43 Texas Department of Water Resources, *Water For Texas,* pp. 1–9 and 1–10.

44 Texas Department of Water Resources, *Water For Texas,* 1–9.

45 Texas Department of Water Resources, *Water For Texas,* 1–10.

46 Texas Natural Resource Conservation Commission, "Joint Groundwater Monitoring and Contamination Report 1993" (May 1994), table 1.

47 U.S. Geological Survey, *National Water Summary 1983,* p. 215.

48 Jack T. Dugan and Donald E. Schild, "Water Level Changes in the High Plains Aquifer—Predevelopment to 1990," U.S. Geological Survey Water Resources Investigations Report 91-4165 (1992), p. 47.

49 Tony Bagwell, telephone conversation with J. Ashley, 30 May 1996. Oil companies are encouraged to use low-quality water for their secondary treatment; however, if prices rise and oil production increases there is the possibility that oil companies will also require some supply from potable sources.

50 Tony Bagwell, telephone conversation with J. Ashley, 30 May 1996.

51 Texas Department of Water Resources, *Water For Texas,* pp. 2-10 through 3-2.

52 Tony Bagwell, telephone conversation with J. Ashley, 30 May 1996. Withdrawals have been limited to eliminate adverse effects of groundwater pumping—land subsidence. According to Tony Bagwell, there is still plenty of water in the Houston area, but the adverse consequences of withdrawing the water outweigh the benefits.

53 Tony Bagwell, telephone conversation with J. Ashley, 29 August 1996.

54 Tony Bagwell, telephone conversation with J. Ashley, 29 August 1996.

55 Lonnie L. Jones, "External Costs of Surface Subsidence: Upper Galveston Bay, Texas," Land Subsidence Symposium, Publication No. 121 of the International Association of Hydrological Sciences, Proceedings of the Anaheim Symposium, December 1976.

56 R. K. Gabrysch, "The Impact of Land-Surface Subsidence," *Impact of Science on Society* 1 (1983), pp. 118–20.

57 Teutsch, "Controls and Remedies," p. 331, and Texas Department of Water Re-

sources, Water Planning Division, telephone conversation with J. Ashley, 30 May 1996.
58 Texas Department of Water Resources, *Water For Texas*, p. 3–5.

Conclusion

1   Zachary A. Smith, "Interstate Competition for Water Resources: A Survey and Analysis," *Journal of Land Use and Environmental Law* 2, no. 2 (1986), p. 641.
2   See, e.g., Ryan J. Barilleaux and C. Richard Bath, "The Coming Nationalization of Southwestern Water: A Cautionary Tale," in *Water and the Future of the Southwest*, ed. Zachary A. Smith (Albuquerque: University of New Mexico Press, 1989), and Z. Smith, "Federal Intervention."
3   Z. Smith, "Centralized Decisionmaking."
4   Z. Smith, *Interest Group Interaction*, chap. 11.

Glossary

(Adapted from U.S. Geological Survey, Supply Paper 2275. National Water Summary 1984.)

absorption. Process by which substances (e.g., water) are assimilated or taken up by other substances (e.g., soil).

acre-foot. Volume of water required to cover 1 acre of land (43,560 square feet) to a depth of 1 foot; equivalent to 325,851 gallons.

alluvium. A general term for deposits of clay, silt, sand, gravel, or other particulate rock material in a streambed, on a flood plain, on a delta, or at the base of a mountain.

aquifer. A geologic formation, group of formations, or part of a formation that contains sufficient saturated permeable material to yield significant quantities of water to wells and springs. See also confined aquifer; unconfined aquifer.

aquifer system. A body of intercalated materials that acts as a water-yielding, hydraulic unit.

artesian aquifer. See confined aquifer.

artesian well. A well tapping a confined aquifer in which the static water level is above the bottom of the upper confining unit; a flowing artesian well is a well in which the water level is above the land surface.

basal groundwater or basal lens. A major body of fresh groundwater in contact with underlying saline water in the lowermost part of the flow system.

base flow. Sustained low flow of a stream. In most places, base flow is groundwater inflow to the stream channel.

bolson. An extensive, flat, saucer-shaped, alluvium-floored basin or depression, almost or completely surrounded by mountains, from which drainage has no surface outlet. The term is used primarily in desert regions of the southwestern United States.

brackish. Water that contains from 1,000 to 10,000 milligrams per liter of dissolved solids. *See also* saline water.

brine. Water that contains more than 35,000 milligrams per liter of dissolved solids. *See also* saline water.

commercial withdrawals. Water for use by motels, hotels, restaurants, office buildings, commercial facilities, and civilian and military institutions. The water may be obtained from a public supply or it may be self-supplied.

cone of depression. A depression in the potentiometric surface around a well, or group of wells, from which water is being withdrawn.

confined aquifer. An aquifer in which groundwater is confined under pressure that is significantly greater than atmospheric pressure. Synonym: artesian aquifer. *See also* aquifer; semiconfined aquifer; unconfined aquifer.

confined groundwater. Water in an aquifer that is bounded by confining beds and is under pressure significantly greater than atmospheric pressure.

confining bed. A layer or mass of rock having very low hydraulic conductivity that hampers the movement of water into and out of an adjoining aquifer.

conjunctive use. Combined use or management of groundwater and surface waters.

connate water. Water entrapped in the interstices of sedimentary rock at the time of its deposition.

consumptive use. Water that has been evaporated, transpired, or incorporated into products, plant tissue, or animal tissue and, therefore, is not available for immediate reuse.

discharge area (groundwater). An area in which subsurface water, including groundwater and water in the unsaturated zone, is discharged to the land surface, to surface water, or to the atmosphere.

dissolved solids. Minerals and organic matter dissolved in water.

domestic withdrawals. Water used for normal household purposes, such as drinking, food preparation, bathing, washing clothes and dishes, flushing toilets, and watering lawns and gardens. Also called residential water use. The water may be obtained from a public supply or may be self-supplied.

drawdown. The difference between the water level in a well before pumping and the water level in the well during pumping. Also, for flowing wells, the reduction of the pressure head as a result of the discharge of water.

evapotranspiration. A collective term that includes water discharged to the atmosphere as a result of evaporation from the soil and surface-water bodies and by plant transpiration.

fresh water. Water than contains less than 1,000 milligrams per liter of dissolved solids. Generally more than 500 milligrams per liter is undesirable for drinking and for many industrial uses.

glacial drift. Rock material (clay, silt, sand, gravel, boulders) transported and deposited by a glacier.

groundwater. In the broadest sense, all subsurface water, as distinct from surface water; as more commonly used, that part of the subsurface water in the saturated zone. *See also* underground water.

groundwater reservoir. Permeable rocks in the zone of saturation. *See also* aquifer.

groundwater system. A groundwater reservoir and its contained water. Also, the collective hydrodynamic and geochemical processes at work in the reservoir.

hardness (water). A property of water causing formation of an insoluble residue when the water is used with soap and forming a scale in vessels in which water has been allowed to evaporate. It is due primarily to the presence of ions of calcium and magnesium.

industrial withdrawals. Water withdrawn for or used for thermoelectric power (electric-utility generation) and other industrial uses such as steel, chemical and allied products, paper and allied products, mining, and petroleum refining. The water may be obtained from a public supply or may be self-supplied.

infiltration. The movement of water into soil or porous rock.

instream use. Water use taking place within the stream channel. Examples are hydro-electric power generation, navigation, fish propagation, and recreational activities. Also called nonwithdrawal use and in-channel use.

irrigation return flow. The part of artificially applied water that is not consumed by evapotranspiration and that migrates to an aquifer or surface-water body. *See also* return flow.

irrigation withdrawals. Withdrawal of water for application on land to assist in the growing of crops and pastures or to maintain recreational lands.

mining of groundwater. Groundwater withdrawals in excess of recharge. *See also* overdraft.

nonpoint source of pollution. Pollution from broad areas rather than from discrete points, such as areas of fertilizer and pesticide application and leaking sewer systems.

normal. Average (or mean) conditions over a specific period of time, usually the most recent thirty-year period; for example, 1955 to 1984.

offstream use. Water withdrawn or diverted from a groundwater or surface-water source for use. Also called withdrawal use and off-channel use.

overdraft. Withdrawals of groundwater at rate perceived to be excessive or in excess of recharge. *See also* mining of groundwater.

perched groundwater. Unconfined groundwater separated from an underlying main body of groundwater by an unsaturated zone.

percolation. Slow movement of water through openings within a porous earth material.

permafrost. Any frozen soil, subsoil, surficial deposit, or bedrock in arctic or subarctic regions where below-freezing temperatures have existed continuously from two thousand to tens of thousands of years.

permeability. The capacity of a rock for transmitting a fluid; a measure of the relative ease of fluid flow in a porous medium.

point source of pollution. Pollution originating from any discrete source, such as the outflow from pipe, ditch, tunnel, well, concentrated animal-feeding operation, or floating craft.

potable water. Water that is safe and palatable for human use.

prior appropriation. A concept in water law under which users who demonstrate earlier use of water from a particular source are said to have rights over all later users of water from the same source.

public supply withdrawals. Water withdrawn by public and private water suppliers for use within a general community. Water is used for a variety of purposes such as domestic, commercial, industrial, and public water use.

recharge. The process of addition of water to the zone of saturation. *See also* saturated zone.

recharge area. An area in which water infiltrates the ground and reaches the zone of saturation.

renewable water supply. The rate of supply of water (volume per unit time) potentially or theoretically available for use in a region on an essentially permanent basis.

return flow. The amount of water that reaches a groundwater or surface-water source after release from the point of use and thus becomes available for further use. Also called return water. *See also* irrigation return flow.

riparian rights. A concept of water law under which authorization to use water in a stream is based on ownership of the land adjacent to the stream.

runoff. That part of precipitation or snowmelt that reaches streams or surface-water bodies.

rural withdrawals. Water used in some suburban or farm areas for domestic and livestock needs. The water generally is self-supplied and includes domestic use, drinking water for livestock, and other uses such as dairy sanitation, evaporation from stock-watering ponds, and cleaning and waste disposal.

safe yield (groundwater). Amount of water than can be withdrawn from an aquifer without producing an undesirable effect.

saline water. Water that generally is considered unsuitable for human consumption or for irrigation because of its high content of dissolved solids. Generally expressed as milligrams per liter of dissolved solids, with 35,000 milligrams per liter defined as seawater.

saturated zone. A subsurface zone in which all the interstices or voids are filled with water under pressure greater than that of the atmosphere.

sediment. Particles derived from rocks or biological materials that have been transported by a fluid.

sedimentary rock. Rock resulting from the accumulation of loose sediments into layers. This can be effected either mechanically, by precipitation from solution, or from the remains of secretions of plants and animals. The term includes both consolidated and unconsolidated sediments. Sedimentary rocks constitute one of the three main classes (igneous, metamorphic, and sedimentary) into which all rocks are divided.

semiconfined aquifer. An aquifer that is partially confined by a layer (or layers) of low permeability through which recharge and discharge nevertheless may occur. *See also* aquifer, confined aquifer, unconfined aquifer.

transmissivity. The rate at which water, at the prevailing temperature, is transmitted through a unit width of an aquifer under a unit hydraulic gradient. Transmissivity normally is expressed as foot squared per day or foot squared per second; it can be expressed as the number of cubic feet of water that will move during one day under a hydraulic gradient of one foot per foot through a vertical strip of aquifer one foot wide extending the full saturated height of the aquifer.

transpiration. The process by which water passes through living organisms, primarily plants, and into the atmosphere.

turbidity. The opaqueness or reduced clarity of a fluid due to the presence of suspended matter.

unconfined aquifer. An aquifer whose upper surface is free of the water table and thus able to fluctuate under atmospheric pressure. *See also* aquifer; confined aquifer; semiconfined aquifer.

underground water. Subsurface water in the unsaturated and saturated zones. *See also* groundwater; saturated zone; unsaturated zone.

unsaturated zone. A subsurface zone in which interstices are not all filled with water; includes water held by capillarity and openings containing air or gases generally under atmospheric pressure. Limited above by land surface and below by the water table.

upconing. Process by which saline water underlying fresh water in an aquifer rises upward into the freshwater zone as a result of pumping water from the freshwater zone.

water budget. An accounting of the inflow to, outflow from, and storage changes in a hydrologic unit.

water table. The top water surface of an unconfined aquifer at atmospheric pressure. The water levels in wells that penetrate the uppermost part of an unconfined aquifer mark the position of the water table.

water year. A continuous twelve-month period selected to present data relative to hydrologic or meteorologic phenomena during which a complete annual hydrologic cycle normally occurs. The water year used by the U.S. Geological Survey runs from 1 October through 30 September.

withdrawal. Water removed from the ground or diverted from a surface-water source for use. Also refers to the use itself; for example, public supply withdrawals commonly also refer to public-supply use. *See also* offstream use.

Selected Bibliography

Includes works not cited.

"Administrative Action in the Processing of Ground Water Appropriation Permits: Where is Kansas?" *Washburn Law Journal* 2 (1972).

Aiken, J. David. "Nebraska Ground Water Law and Administration." *Nebraska Law Review* 59, no. 317 (1980).

———. "Nebraska Water Law Update." Cooperative Extension Service, University of Nebraska-Lincoln (January 1986).

Alaska Department of Environmental Conservation. "Water Quality Assessment, 1992." July 1992.

Alaska Department of Environmental Conservation, Water Programs Division. *Alaska Water Quality Management Study—Initial Phase.* Executive Summary. 1979.

Alaska Water Study Committee. *Alaska Water Assessment—Problem Identification.* Juneau: State of Alaska, 1975.

Allen, Preston K., and Gordon L. Elser. "They Said It Couldn't Be Done—The Orange County California Experience." *Desalinization* 30 (1979).

American Institute of Professional Geologists. *Ground Water: Issues and Answers.* Arvada CO: American Institute of Professional Geologists, 1984.

Anderson, Gary S. "Hydrologic Reconnaissance of Tanana Basin, Central Alaska." U.S. Geological Survey Hydrologic Atlas, HA-319, 1970.

Anderson, Gary S., and Chester Zenone, *Summary Appraisals of the Nation's Ground-water Resources—Alaska.* Washington DC: U.S. Government Printing Office, 1984.

Anderson, Terry L. *Water Crisis: Ending the Policy Drought.* Baltimore: Johns Hopkins University Press, 1983.

Anderson, Terry L., ed. *Water Rights: Scarce Resource Allocation, Bureaucracy, and the Environment.* San Francisco: Pacific Institute for Public Policy, 1986.

"The Application of Federal Reserved Water Rights to Groundwater in the Western States." *Creighton Law Review* 16 (1983).

Arizona Department of Water Resources. "Arizona Banking Authority." Executive Summary. 23 October 1996.

———. *Arizona Water Resources Assessment.* Vols. 1–2. Phoenix: State of Arizona, 1994.

Arizona Underground Water Commission. *The Underground Water Resources of Arizona.* 1953.

Arizona Water Commission. *Inventory of Resource and Uses: Phase I—Arizona Water Plan Summary.* 1975.

Arnow, Ted, and Don Price. "Summary Appraisal of the Nation's Groundwater Resources—Upper Colorado Region." Geological Survey Paper No. 813-C. U.S. Government Printing Office: Washington DC, 1974.

Ashworth, William. *Nor Any Drop to Drink.* New York: Summit, 1982.

Balding, G. O. *Water Availability, Quality, and Use in Alaska.* Washington DC: U.S. Department of the Interior, Geological Survey, 1976.

Banks, H. O. "Management of Interstate Aquifer Systems." *Journal of Water Resources Planning and Management Division* 107, no. 2 (1981).

Bard, Carla M. "The California Approach to Ground Water Quality Protection." *Proceedings of the Thirteenth Biennial Conference on Groundwater.* Davis: Water Resource Center, University of California, 1981.

Barilleaux, Ryan J., and C. Richard Bath. "The Coming Nationalization of Southwestern Water: A Cautionary Tale." In *Water and the Future of the Southwest,* ed. Zachary A. Smith. Albuquerque: University of New Mexico Press, 1989.

Bauer, Donald C., et al. *Natural Resources Law Handbook.* Rockville MD: Government Institutes, 1991.

Beattie, Bruce. "Irrigated Agriculture and the Great Plains: Problems and Policy Alternatives." *Western Journal of Agricultural Economics* 6 (December 1981).

Beattie, Bruce R., and H. S. Foster Jr. "Can Prices Tame the Inflationary Tiger?" *Journal of the American Water Works Association* 72 (August 1980).

Beatty, K., H. Doerdsen, and J. Pierce. "Water Resources Politics and Interest Group Tactics." *Water Resources Bulletin* 14, no. 2 (1978).

Beck, Robert E., ed. *Waters and Water Rights.* Charlottesville VA: Michie, 1991.

Bittinger, M. W. "The Ogallala Story—What Have We Learned?" *Ground Water* 19, no. 6 (1981).

———. "Survey of Interstate and International Aquifer Problems." *Ground Water* (March/April 1972).

Botz, H. K., and Ambrey Gartner. *Groundwater Quality and Pollution Assessment for Montana Statewide 208 Area.* Bozeman: Western Technology and Engineering, August 1978.

Boulding, K. *Western Water Resources: Coming Problems and the Policy Alternatives.* Boulder CO: Westview, 1980.

Bouwer, H. "Protecting the Quality of Our Groundwater: What Can We Do?" *Ground-water Monitoring Review* 1, no. 2 (1981).

Bowden, Charles. *Killing the Hidden Waters.* Austin: University of Texas Press, 1977.

Braids, O. C., and N. P. Gillies. "Ground Water. Literature Review of Water Pollution." *Journal of the Water Pollution Control Federation* 49, no. 6 (1977).

Brown, F. Lee, and Helen Ingram. *Water and Poverty in the Southwest.* Tucson: University of Arizona Press, 1986.

Burmaster, D. "Groundwater Contamination: The New Pollution." *Technology Review* 24, no. 2 (March 1982).

Busch, Darron, and Michael Meyer. "A Case of Infantile Methemoglobinemia." *Journal of Environmental Health* 44, no. 6 (May/June 1982).

California Department of Water Resources. "Analysis of Aquifer-Systems Compaction in the Orange County Ground Water Basin." June 1980.

———. "California's Ground Water Bulletin No. 118." September 1975.

———. *California Water Plan Update 1994.* Bulletin 160-83.

———. *Groundwater Basins in California.* January 1980.

———. "Sea-Water Intrusion in California." Bulletin No. 63-5. October 1975.

California Department of Water Resources, Division of Planning. *California Water Plan Update 1994.* Bulletin 160-93. Executive Summary. November 1994.

California Governor's Commission to Review California Water Rights Law. *Final Report* (Sacramento: The Commission, 1978).

California State Water Control Board, Division of Water Quality. "California's Ground Water Profile." April 1994.

Canter, L. W., R. C. Knox, and R. P. Kamat. *Evaluation of Septic Tank System Effects on Ground Water Quality.* Norman OK: National Center for Ground Water Research, May 1982.

"*Cappaert v. United States:* A Dehydration of Private Groundwater Use?" *California Western Law Review* 14 (1978).

Cappock, Raymond H., Robert M. Hagan, and William W. Wood Jr. "The Problem, The Resource, The Competition." In *Competition for California Water,* ed. Ernest A. Englebert. Berkeley: University of California Press, 1982.

Caspar, Lawrence, and Daniel W. Smith. *Groundwater Quality Effects on Domestic Water Utilization.* Fairbanks: Institute of Water Resources, University of Alaska at Fairbanks, March 1974.

Castberg, A. Didrick. "Water and the Future of Energy Development in the Southwest." In *Water and the Future of the Southwest,* ed. Zachary A. Smith. Albuquerque: University of New Mexico Press, 1989.

Caves, Richard E., and Julius Margolis. *Northern California's Water Industry.* Baltimore: Johns Hopkins University Press for Resources for the Future, 1966.

Cederstrom, D. J. "Groundwater Resources of the Fairbanks Area." Water-Supply Paper 1590. Alaska: U.S. Geological Survey, 1963.

Charbeneau, Randall J. "Groundwater Resources of the Texas Rio Grande Basin." *Natural Resources Journal* 22 (October 1982).

Chun, Michael J., H. F. Reginald, Arthur S. Kowatache, and Paul R. Bolduc. "Groundwater Pollution from Sanitary Landfill Leachate." Hawaii Water Resources Research Center, Technical Report No. 87. Honolulu, 1975.

Clark, Robert Emmet. "Ground Water Law: Problem Areas." *Natural Resources Lawyer* 8, no. 377 (1975).

———. "Ground Water Legislation in the Light of Experience in the Western States." *Montana Law Review* 42 (1960).

———. "Institutional Alternatives For Managing Groundwater Resources: Notes For a Proposal." *Natural Resources Journal* 18 (1978).

Colorado Department of Public Health and Environment. "Status of Water Quality in Colorado, 1994." November 1994.

Connall, Desmond D., Jr. "A History of the Arizona Groundwater Management Act." *Arizona State Law Journal* (spring 1982).

Corker, Charles E. "Water Rights and Federalism: The Western Water Rights Settlement Bill of 1957." *California Law Review* 45 (1957).

Dace, Robert W. "Oil and Gas: Water and Watercourses: The Right to Use Fresh Groundwater in Waterflood Operations." *Oklahoma Law Review* (winter 1982).

Davis, G. H., and F. A. Kilpatrick. "Water Supply as a Limiting Factor in Western Energy Development." *Water Resources Bulletin* 1 (February 1981).

Dearborn, C. L., and W. W. Barnwell. "Hydrology of Land-Use Planning—The Hillside Area, Anchorage, Alaska." U.S. Geological Survey open file report 75-105, 1975.

Dennis, Harry. *Water and Power.* San Francisco: Friends of the Earth, 1981.

De Young, Tim. *Preferences for Managing New Mexican Water.* Las Cruces NM: New Mexico Water Resources Research Institute, 1984.

Dregnue, H. E. *Desertification of Arid Lands.* New York: Academic Press, 1983.

Dugan, Jack T., and Donald E. Schild. "Water Level Changes in the High Plains Aquifer—Predevelopment to 1990." U.S. Geological Survey Water Resources Investigations Report 91-4165, 1992.

Du Mars, Charles T. "New Mexico Water Law: An Overview and Discussion of Current Issues." *Natural Resources Journal* 22 (October 1982).

Dunbar, Robert G. "The Arizona Groundwater Controversy at Mid-Century." *Arizona and the West* 19, no. 1 (1977).

———. *Property Rights and Controversies in Montana Completion Report.* Bozeman: Montana University Joint Water Resources Research Center, Montana State University, 1976.

Durant, Robert, and Michelle Deany Holmes. "Thou Shalt Not Covet Thy Neighbor's Water: The Rio Grande Basin Regulatory Experience." *Public Administration Review* 45, no. 6 (November/December 1985).

Dycus, J. S. "Development of a National Groundwater Protection Policy." *Boston College Environmental Affairs Law Review* 11, no. 2 (1984).

Eden, Susanna, and Mary G. Wallace. *Arizona Water: Information and Issues.* Tucson: University of Arizona Water Resources Research Center, 1992.

El-Ashry, Mohamed T., and Gibbons, D. C. *Troubled Waters: New Policies for Managing Water in the American West.* Washington DC: World Resources Institute, 1986.

Englebert, Ernest A. *Water Scarcity: Impacts on Western Agriculture.* Berkeley: University of California Press, 1984.

Erhardt, J. Wayland, and Randolph Lyon. "Alternative Structures for Water Rights Markets." *Water Resources Research* 19, no. 4 (1983).

Everett, L. G. *Ground Water Monitoring.* Schenectady NY: General Electric Co., Technology Marketing Operation, 1980.

Exner, M. E., and R. F. Spalding. "Evolution of Contaminated Ground Water in Holt County, Nebraska." *Water Resources Research* 15, no. 1 (1979).

Fischer, Ward H. "Management of Interstate Ground Water." *Natural Resources Lawyer* 7 (1974).

Fradkin, Phillip L. *A River No More: The Colorado and the West.* New York: Knopf, 1981.

Franco, David A., and Robert G. Wetzel. *To Quench Our Thirst: The Present and Future Status of Freshwater Resources of the United States.* Ann Arbor: University of Michigan Press, 1983.

Frederick, Kenneth D. "The Future of Western Irrigation." *Southwestern Review of Management* 1 (spring 1981).

Frederick, Kenneth D., and James C. Hanson. *Water for Western Agriculture.* Washington DC: Resources for the Future. 1982.

Freeze, R. A., and J. A. Cherry. *Groundwater.* Englewood Cliffs NJ: Prentice Hall, 1979.

Fricke, Carl A. P., and Darryll T. Pederson. "Ground-Water Resource Management in Nebraska." *Ground Water* 17 (November–December 1979).

Gabrysch, R. K. "The Impact of Land-Surface Subsidence." *Impact of Science on Society* 1 (1983).

Gallaher, B. M., and M. S. Goad. *Water Quality Aspects of Uranium Mining and Milling in New Mexico.* Santa Fe: New Mexico Geological Society, 1981.

Gardner, B. Delworth. "Institutional Impediments to Efficient Water Allocation." *Policy Studies Review* 5, no. 2 (1985).

Gardner, B. D., R. Coppock, C. Lynn, D. W. Rains, R. S. Loomis, and J. H. Snyder. "Agriculture." In *California Water,* ed. E. Englebert. Berkeley: University of California Press, 1982.

Gardner, B. Delworth, Richard E. Howitt, and Carole Frank Nucton. "The Case for Regional Groundwater Management." *California Agriculture* 35 (1981).

Geophysics Study Committee. National Research Council. *Groundwater Contamination.* Washington DC, 1984.

Gessaman, Paul H. *Groundwater Rights, Part I—Property Rights, Preferences, and Conflict Resolution.* Lincoln: Cooperative Extension Service, University of Nebraska–Lincoln, 1984.

Getches, David H. *Water Law.* St. Paul MN: West, 1990.

Giambelluca, Thomas W. "Water Balance of the Pearl Harbor—Honolulu Basin 1946–1975." Hawaii Water Resources Research Technical Report No. 115. Honolulu, 1983.

Goodall, Merrill R., John D. Sullivan, and Tim De Young. *Water Districts in California: An Analysis by Type of Enabling Act and Political Decision Process.* Sacramento: California Department of Water Resources, 1977.

Gordon, Wendy. *A Citizen's Handbook on Groundwater Protection.* New York: Natural Resources Defense Council, 1984.

Gordon, Wendy, and Jane Bloom. *Deeper Problems: Limits to Underground Injection as a Hazardous Waste Disposal Method.* New York: Natural Resources Defense Council, 1985.

Gottlieb, Robert, and Margaret Fitzsimmons. *Thirst for Growth: Water Agencies as Hidden Government in California.* Tucson: University of Arizona Press, 1991.

Grainger, Alan. *Desertification.* Washington DC: Earthscan, 1983.

Grant, D. "Reasonable Groundwater Pumping Levels under the Appropriation Doctrine: The Law and Underlying Economic Goals." *Natural Resources Journal* 21 (1981).

Hamilton, Alexander. "The Plight of the Riparian under Texas Water Law." *Harvard Law Review* 21 (1984).

Harrison, David C. "Institutional Barriers to National Water Policy." *Water Spectrum* 2 (1982).

Harrison, David L., and Gustave Sanstrom Jr. "The Groundwater Surface Water Conflict and Recent Colorado Water Legislation." *University Of Colorado Law Review* 43 (1971).

Hartman, L. M., and Don Seastone. *Water Transfers: Economic Efficiency and Alternative Institutions.* Baltimore: Johns Hopkins University Press, 1970.

Haselhoff, Donald A. "Water for Las Vegas Metropolitan Area." *Journal of Environmental Engineering* 109 (1983).

Haveman, Robert H. "Efficiency and Equity in Natural Resource and Environmental Policy." *American Journal of Agricultural Economics* 55 (1973).

Higdon, P., and Thompson, L. "The 1980 Arizona Groundwater Management Code." *Arizona State Legislative Journal* (1980).

High Plains Study Council and Nebraska Natural Resources Commission. "Summary of the Nebraska Research for the Six-State High Plains Ogallala Aquifer Study." December 1981.

Hillhouse, William A. "Integrating Ground and Surface Water in an Appropriation State." *Rocky Mountain Mineral Law Institute* 20 (1975).

Hirshleifer, Jack, James C. DeHaven, and Jerome W. Milliman. *Water Supply: Economics, Technology, Policy.* Chicago: University of Chicago Press, 1960.

Hoag, Stephanie, and Lynne Minton. *Surface Impoundment Assessment—Alaska.* Anchorage: Environmental Services Limited, 1979.

Hopkins, David M., Thor N. V. Karlstrom, Robert F. Black, John R. Williams, Troy L. Péwé, Arthur T. Fernald, Ernest H. Mueller. "Surface Geology of Alaska." U.S. Geological Survey Professional Paper 264-F. Washington DC.

Horne, A. "Groundwater Policy, A Patchwork of Protection." *Environment* 24, no. 3 (April 1982).

Horwitch, Mel. "Coal: Constrained Abundance." In *Energy Future,* 3d ed., ed. Robert Stobaugh and Daniel Yergin. New York: Vintage, 1983.

Hostyk, Aaron H. "Who Controls the Water?" *Tulsa Law Journal* 1 (1982).

Howe, Charles W., Paul K. Alexander, and Raphael J. Moses. "The Performance of Appropriative Water Systems in the Western United States during Drought." *Natural Resources Journal* 22 (April 1982).

Hrezo, Margaret, and William Hrezo. "From Antagonistic to Cooperative Federalism on Water Resources Development: A Model for Reconciling Federal, State and Local Programs, Policies and Planning." *American Journal of Economics and Sociology* 44 (April 1985).

Hundley, Norris, Jr. *Dividing the Waters.* Berkeley: University of California Press, 1966.

Hutchins, Wells A. "Trends in the Statutory Law of Ground Water in the Western States." *Texas Law Review* 34 (1955).

———. *Water Rights Laws in the Nineteen Western States.* Washington DC: U.S. Government Printing Office, 1974.

Idaho Department of Health and Welfare, and Idaho Department of Water Resources. "Annual Ground Water Contamination Report, State Fiscal Year 1991."

Ingram, Helen. "Patterns of Politics in Water Resources Development." *Natural Resources Journal* 11 (January 1971).

———. *Water Politics: Continuity and Change.* Albuquerque: University of New Mexico Press, 1990.

Ingram, Helen, William E. Martin, and Nancy K. Laney. "Central Arizona Project Case Study." In *Western Water Institutions in a Changing Environment.* Vol. 2. Napa CA: John Muir Institute, 1980.

Jacobs, James J. *Hawaii's Water Resources: Sources, Demands, and Issues.* Manoa: Hawaii Institute of Tropical Agriculture and Human Resources, University of Hawaii, 1983.

Jenkins, Edward D. "Ground-Water Management in Western Kansas." *Journal of Hydraulic Engineering* 109 (October 1983).

Johnson, Corwin W. "Texas Groundwater Law: A Survey and Some Proposals." *Natural Resources Journal* 22, no. 4 (October 1982).

Johnson, James W. *Summary of the 1980 Arizona Groundwater Management Act.* Phoenix: State Bar of Arizona, 1980.

Johnson, Martin S., and Darryll T. Pederson. "Groundwater Levels in Nebraska 1983." Nebraska Water Survey Paper Number 57. Conservation and Survey Division, Institute of Agriculture and Natural Resources, University of Nebraska–Lincoln.

Jones, Lonnie L. "External Costs of Surface Subsidence: Upper Galveston Bay, Texas." Land Subsidence Symposium, Publication No. 121 of the International Association of Hydrological Sciences, Proceedings of the Anaheim Symposium, December 1976.

Josephson, J. "Groundwater Strategies." *Environmental Science and Technology* 14, no. 9 (September 1980).

———. "Safeguards for Ground Water." *Environmental Science and Technology* 1 (1980).

Kahrl, William L. *Water and Power.* Berkeley: University of California Press, 1982.

Kansas Department of Health and Environment. "Groundwater Quality Monitoring Network 1992 Annual Report." December 1994.

Kansas Equus Beds Groundwater Management District No. 2. "Management Program." 1 May 1995.

Kansas State Board of Agriculture, Kansas Agriculture Ogallala Task Force. "Report of the Kansas Agriculture Ogallala Task Force." September 1993.

Kansas Water Office. "Irrigation Water Conservation Program for the State of Kansas." November 1993.

King, Jonathan. *Troubled Water.* Emmaus PA: Rodale Press, 1985.

Kneese, Allen E. "Economic Related Problems in Contemporary Water Resources Management." *Natural Resources Journal* 5 (October 1965).

Knight, A. W., and M. A. Simmons. *Water Pollution: A Guide to Information Sources.* Detroit: Gale Research Co., 1980.

Kromm, David E., and Stephen E. White. *Public Perception of Groundwater Depletion in Southwestern Kansas.* Topeka KS: Water Resources Research Institute, 1981.

Lee, Eugene C., and Harrison C. Dunning. "Political Dynamics and Decision Making." *California Western Law Review* 20 (1984).

Legrand, H. E. "Patterns of Contaminated Zones of Water in the Ground." *Water Resources Research* 1 (1965).

Lehr, J. "Groundwater in the Eighties." *Water and Engineering Management* 123, no. 3 (1981).

———. "How Much Ground Water Have We Really Polluted?" *Ground Water Monitoring Review* (winter 1982).

Leshy, John. "Irrigation Districts in a Changing West—An Overview." *Arizona State Law Journal* 2 (1982).

Littleworth, Arthur L. "New Legislation in California and Its Effects." *Proceedings of the Thirteenth Biennial Conference on Groundwater* 46 (1981).

Maas, Arthur, and Ray Anderson. . . . *And the Desert Shall Rejoice: Conflict, Growth and Justice in Arid Environments*. Cambridge MA: MIT Press, 1978.

MacDonald, Gordon A., and Agatin Abbott. *Volcanoes in the Sea: The Geology of Hawaii*. Honolulu: University of Hawaii Press, 1983.

Mann, Dean E. *The Politics of Water in Arizona*. Tucson: University of Arizona Press, 1963.

Mann, John F., Jr. "The San Fernando Case—Its Impact on Future Ground Water Management." *Proceedings of the Tenth Biennial Conference on Ground Water*. Davis: Water Resources Center, University of California, 1975.

Matthess, G. *The Properties of Ground Water*. New York: Wiley, 1982.

McCool, Daniel. *Command of the Waters: Iron Triangles, Federal Water Development, and Indian Water*. Berkeley: University of California Press, 1987.

McGauhey, P. H. "Man-Made Contamination Hazards." *Ground Water* 2 (1976).

Meyer, Michael. "Comment: More on Nitrates." *Water Well Journal* 40, no. 19 (October 1986).

Meyers, Charles J. "Federal Groundwater Rights: A Note on *Cappaert v. United States*." *Land and Water Law Review* 1978.

Miller, G. Tyler, Jr. *Living in the Environment: An Introduction to Environmental Science*. 6th ed. Belmont CA: Wadsworth, 1990.

Mindling, Anthony, and John Blume. "Effects of Groundwater Withdrawal on Freeway and Vicinity." Center For Water Resources Research, Desert Research Institute, University of Nevada Project Report Series 33 (1974).

Montana Department of Health and Environmental Science. "Montana Water Quality 1994."

Morrison, A. "If Your City's Well Water Has Chemical Pollutants, Then What?" *Civil Engineering* 51, no. 9 (September 1981).

Mosher, Lawrence. "Polluted Groundwater Clearly a Problem, but Few Agree on Extent or Solution." *National Journal* 4 (February 1984).

Mumme, Steven, and Helen Ingram. "Community Values in Southwest Water Management." *Policy Studies Review* 5, no. 2 (1985).

Muys, Jerome C. "Interstate Compacts and Regional Water Resources Planning and Management." *Natural Resources Lawyer* 6 (1973).

National Resource Council. *Groundwater Recharge Using Waters of Impaired Quality*. Washington DC: National Academy Press, 1994.

Nebraska Department of Environmental Control, "Rules and Regulations for the Control of Disposal Wells to Protect Ground-Water and Other Subsurface Resources of the State of Nebraska," 1975.

Nebraska Department of Environmental Quality. "1994 Nebraska Ground Water Quality Report."

Nebraska Natural Resources Commission. "Estimated Water Use in Nebraska, 1990." December 1994.

------. *Policy Issue Study On Property Rights in Groundwater.* 1983.

Nevada Department of Conservation and Natural Resources, Division of Water Planning. "Nevada Water Facts." 1992.

------. "Water Conservation in Nevada." 1979.

------. "Water for Nevada." 1971.

------. *Water for Southern Nevada.* (Carson City: Division of Water Planning, 1982).

Nevada Department of Conservation and Natural Resources, Division of Water Resources. *Special Information Report Water—Legal and Administrative Aspects.* 1974.

Nevada Division of Environmental Protection. "Comprehensive State Groundwater Protection Program Profile." 14 December 1995.

New Mexico State Engineer. *Annual Report.* 1979/1980.

New Mexico State Engineer's Office and New Mexico Department of Environment. "The Rural Homeowner's Water Guide." June 1991.

New Mexico Water Quality Control Commission. *State of New Mexico Water Quality Status Summary.* Santa Fe NM, May 1980.

------. "Water Quality and Water Pollution Control in New Mexico, 1994."

New Mexico Water Resources Research Institute and University of New Mexico Law School. *State Appropriation of Unappropriated Groundwater.* 1986.

O'Connor, Howard G., Susan Waldorf, and R. L. Dulas. *Groundwater Pollution.* Topeka: Kansas Geological Survey, 1978.

Oklahoma Department of Environmental Quality. "1994 Oklahoma Water Quality Report to Congress."

Oklahoma Water Resources Board. "Oklahoma Comprehensive Water Plan." Publication 94. 1 April 1980.

------. "Oklahoma Comprehensive Water Plan Update, 1995."

------."Rules, Regulations and Modes of Procedure 1982" (as amended 1983). Publication 107.

------. *State-Level Research Results for the Six-State High Plains Ogallala Aquifer Area Study.* Norman: Oklahoma University Printing Services, 1983.

Olson, Kent W. "Economic Prospects for Interbasin Water Transfer to Southern High Plains Farmers." In *Water and the Future of the Southwest,* ed. Zachary A. Smith. Albuquerque: University of New Mexico Press, 1989.

Oregon Department of Environmental Quality. "Oregon's 1994 Water Quality Status Assessment Report." April 1994.

Oregon Department of Water Resources. "Groundwater Levels 1967–1968." 1970.

------. "Groundwater Resources of Dallas-Monmouth Area, Polk, Benton, and Marion Counties, Oregon." Groundwater Report No. 28. 1983.

------. "Report for January 1981 to December 1982."

Ostrom, Elinor. *Governing the Commons: The Evolution of Institutions for Collective Action.* Cambridge MA: Cambridge University Press, 1990.

Paehlke, Robert, and Douglas Torgerson. *Managing Leviathan: Environmental Politics and the Administrative State.* Lewiston NY: Broadview, 1990.

Parker, Jennie C., Clynn Phillips, and Sherry E. Ferguson. "Water Development in Wyoming: A Study of Resident Attitudes, 1971." Water Resources Research Institute, University of Wyoming.

Patt, R., and G. B. Maxey. "Mapping of the Earth Fissures in Las Vegas, Nevada." Publication 41051. Water Resources Center, Desert Research Institute, University of Nevada, March 1978.

Peck, John C. *Legal Questions and Problems of Kansas Groundwater Management Districts.* Topeka: Kansas Water Resources Research Institute, 1980.

Pojasek, R. J., ed. *Drinking Water Quality Enhancement through Source Protection.* Ann Arbor MI: Ann Arbor Science Publishers 1977.

Pontius, Dale. "Groundwater Management in Arizona: A New Set of Rules." *Arizona Bar Journal* (October 1980).

Postel, Sandra. *Conserving Water: The Untapped Alternative.* Washington DC: Worldwatch Institute, 1985.

———. *Last Oasis: Facing Water Scarcity.* New York: W. W. Norton, 1992.

———. *Water: Rethinking Management in an Age of Scarcity.* Washington DC: Worldwatch Institute, 1984.

Pringle, Laurence. *Water—The Next Great Resource Battle.* New York: Macmillan, 1982.

Pye, Veronica I., Ruth Patrick, and John Quarles. *Groundwater Contamination in the United States.* Philadelphia: University of Pennsylvania Press, 1983.

Quarles, J. *Federal Regulation of Hazardous Waste: A Guide to RCRA.* Washington DC: Environmental Law Institute, October 1982.

Reis, Robert I. "Legal Planning for Ground Water Production." *Southern California Law Review* 38 (1965).

Reisner, Marc, and Sarah Bates, *Overtapped Oasis: Reform or Revolution for Western Water.* Washington DC: Island Press, 1990.

Reynolds, S. E. Letter to the U.S. General Accounting Office, 13 June 1980. Reprinted in "Groundwater Overdrafting Must be Controlled." U.S. General Accounting Office, 1980.

Rubin, Hal. "The Toxic-Chemical Storm Over California." *California Environment and Energy* (Sacramento: California Journal Press, 1980).

Russell, Dick. "Ogallala: Half Full or Half Empty?" *The Amicus Journal* 7, no. 2 (fall 1985).

Saleem, Z. A., ed. *Advances in Groundwater "Mining" in the Southwestern States.* Minneapolis: American Water Resources Association, 1976.

Sanghi, A., and R. Klepper. "The Economic Impact of Diminishing Groundwater Reserves on the Production of Corn Under Center Pivot Irrigation." *Journal of Soil and Water Conservation* 32, no. 6 (1977).

Schad, Theodore M. "Water Resources Planning—Historical Development." *Journal of the Water Resources Planning and Management Division* (March 1979).

Schooler, Dean, and Helen Ingram. "Water Resource Development." *Policy Studies Review* 2 (November 1981).

Seastone, D. A., and L. M. Hartman. "Alternative Institutions for Water Transfers: The Experience in Colorado and New Mexico." *Land Economics* 39 (February 1963).

Sheaffer, John, and Leonard Stevens. *Future Water.* New York: Morrow, 1983.

Sheridan, David. "The Desert Blooms—At A Price." *Environment* 23, no. 3 (April 1981).

Sloan, Richard F. "Groundwater Resource Management in Kansas." *Kansas Water News* 22 nos. 1, 2 (winter 1979).

Smith, Garland F. "The Valley Water Suit and Its Impact on Texas Water Policy." *Texas Tech Law Review* 8 (1977).

Smith, Zachary A. "Centralized Decisionmaking in the Administration of Groundwater Rights: The Experience of Arizona, California and New Mexico and Suggestions for the Future." *Natural Resources Journal* 24 (July 1984).

———. "Federal Intervention in the Management of Groundwater Resources: Past Efforts and Future Prospects." *Publius: The Journal of Federalism* 15 (winter 1985).

———. *Groundwater Policy in the Southwest.* El Paso: Texas Western Press, 1985.

———. *Interest Group Interaction and Groundwater Policy Formation in the Southwest.* Lanham MD: University Press of America, 1985.

———. "Interstate and International Competition for Water Resources." *Water Resources Bulletin* 23, no. 5 (October 1987).

———. "Interstate Competition for Water Resources: A Survey and Analysis." *Journal of land Use and Environmental Law* 2, no. 2 (1986).

———. "Rewriting California Groundwater Law: Past Attempts and Prerequisites to Reform." *California Western Law Review* 20, no. 2 (1984).

———. "Stability amid Change in Federal-State Water Relations." *Capital University Law Review* 15, no. 3 (spring 1986).

———. *Water and the Future of the Southwest.* Albuquerque: University of New Mexico Press, 1989.

Solley, Wayne B., Robert R. Pierce, and Howard A. Perlman. "Estimated Water Use in the United States, 1990." Circular 1081. Washington DC: U.S. Government Printing Office, 1993.

South Dakota Department of Environment and Natural Resources. "1994 EPA 305(b) Report."

———. "1995 Groundwater Quality Assessment." Draft.

South Dakota Department of Water and Natural Resources. *South Dakota Water Quality.* 1984.

South Dakota State Legislative Research Council. "Considerations Involving the Use of Ground Water in South Dakota." 1 November 1969.

Spalding, R. F., J. R. Gormly, B. H. Curtiss, and M. E. Exner. "Nonpoint Nitrate Contamination of Ground Water in Merrick County, Nebraska." *Ground Water* 16, no. 2 (1978).

State of Hawaii, Department of Health. "Updated Groundwater Contamination Maps for the State of Hawaii." October 1993.

"The Status of Groundwater in South Dakota." *South Dakota Law Review* 22 (summer 1977).

Stephenson, B., and A. Utton. "The Challenge of Mine Dewatering to Western Water Laws and the New Mexico Response." *Land and Water Law Review* 15 (1980).

Stokes, Bruce. "Water Shortages: The Next Energy Crisis." *The Futurist* (April 1983).

Stone, Albert W. "Montana Water Rights, a New Opportunity." *Montana Law Review* 32 (winter 1973).

Straughn, R. O. "The Sanitary Landfill in the Sub-Artic." *Arctic* 25, no. 1 (1972).

Sweet, H. R., and R. H. Fetrow. "Groundwater Pollution by Wood Waste Disposal." *Groundwater* (March–April 1975).

Swenson, Robert W. "A Primer of Utah Water Law: Part I." *Journal of Energy Law and Policy* 5 (1984).

Tarlock. "So It's Not 'Ours'—Why Can't We Still Keep It? A First Look at *Sporhase v. Nebraska.*" *Land Water Law Review* 18 (1983).

Templer, Otis W. "Texas Groundwater Law: Inflexible Institutions and Resource Realities." *Ecumene* 10, no. 1 (1978).

Teutsch, John. "Controls and Remedies for Ground-Water-Caused Land Subsidence." *Houston Law Review* 16, no. 2 (1979).

Texas Department of Water Resources. *Water for Texas: A Comprehensive Plan for the Future.* Vol. 1. 1984.

Texas Natural Resources Conservation Commission. "Joint Groundwater Monitoring and Contamination Report 1993." May 1994.

Trelease, Frank J. "Alaska's New Water Use Act." *Land and Water Law Review* 2, no. 1 (1967).

———. "Conjunctive Use of Groundwater and Surface Water." *Rocky Mountain Mineral Institute* 27B (1982).

———. "Federal Non-Reserved Water Rights." *University of Chicago Law Review* 48 (1981).

———. "Federal Non-Reserved Water Rights: Fact or Fiction." *Natural Resources Journal* 22 (1982).

———. "Uneasy Federalism-State Water Laws and National Water Uses." *Washington Law Review* 55 (1980).

———. "Water Rights of Various Levels of Government—States Rights vs. National Powers." *Wyoming Law Journal* 19 (1965).

Tripp, J. T. B., and A. B. Jaffe. "Preventing Ground Water Pollution: Towards a Coordinated Strategy to Protect Critical Recharge Zones." *Harvard Environmental Law Review* 3, no. 1 (1979).

Tyler, Roger. "Underground Water Regulation in Texas." *Texas Bar Journal* 39 (June 1976).

Ulrich, Randolph. "Relative Costs and Benefits of Land Reclamation in the Humid Southeast and the Semi-arid West." *Journal of Farm Economics* 30 (1953).

U.S. Army Corps of Engineers, in conjunction with the Municipality of Anchorage, Alaska. *Metropolitan Anchorage Urban Study—Summary Report.* Vol. 2. Washington DC: U.S. Army Corps of Engineers, 1979.

U.S. Department of Agriculture, National Agricultural Statistics Service. "Farm Numbers, and Land in Farms." July 1994 release.

———. "Rankings of States and Commodities by Cash Receipts." Report SB-848. 1991.

U.S. Department of Commerce. *County and City Data Book.* 1994.

———. *Survey of Current Business.* 1995.

U.S. Department of Labor, Bureau of Labor Statistics. Unpublished data. Quoted in Kathleen O'Leary Morgan, et al. *State Rankings 1993: A Statistical View of the Fifty United States.* Lawrence KS: Morgan Quinto Corp., 1993.

U.S. Environmental Protection Agency. *Ground Water Pollution in Arizona, California, Nevada, and Utah.* Washington DC: Government Printing Office, December 1971.

U.S. Geological Survey. *Annual Summary of Ground Water, Spring 1978 to Spring 1979.* Washington DC, 1980.

———. *Estimated Use of Water in the United States.* Washington DC: U.S. Government Printing Office, 1955.

———. *Guide to North Dakota's Groundwater Resources.* Washington DC: U.S. Government Printing Office, 1983.

———. *National Water Summary 1983: Hydrologic Events and Issues.* Water-Supply Paper 2250. Washington DC: U.S. Government Printing Office, 1984.

———. *National Water Summary 1984.* Washington DC: U.S. Government Printing Office, 1985.

———. *1980 Annual Summary.*

———. "Open File Report 91-231." Albuquerque NM, U.S. Government Printing Office, 1991.

———. "Open File Report 94-9." Washington DC: U.S. Government Printing Office, 1994.

———. "Summary Appraisals of the Nations Groundwater Resources—Hawaii Region." Professional Paper 813-M. By K. J. Takasaki. Washington DC: U.S. Government Printing Office, 1978.

———. "Water Resources Data—Nevada, Water Year 1994." Water Survey Data Report NV-94-1. 1995.

U.S. Geological Survey in cooperation with Hawaii Department of Health. "Elements Needed in Design of a Groundwater-Quality Monitoring Network in the Hawaiian Islands." Report 79-263. By K. J. Takasaki. U.S. Government Printing Office, 1976.

Utah Department of Environmental Quality. "EPA 305(b) Report 1994."

Utah Department of Natural Resources. *State of Utah Water.* 1985.

Utah Department of Natural Resources, and U.S. Geological Survey. "Ground-Water Conditions in Utah." Cooperative Investigations Report No. 34, spring 1994.

Utton, Albert E. "The El Paso Case: Reconciling *Sporhase* and *Vermejo.*" *Natural Resources Journal* 23 (January 1983).

Valdez, Carlos A. Rincon. "De aguas subterraneas en la region de Juarez-El Paso." *Natural Resources Journal* 22, no. 4 (October 1982).

Varhol, Bradley P. "Restoring Wells Is No Gamble in Las Vegas." *The Johnson Drillers Journal* (1980).

Viessman, Warren, Jr., and Claire Welty. *Water Management: Technology and Institutions.* New York: Harper and Row, 1985.

Warner, Donald A. "Ground Water in Wyoming." *Journal of the American Water Works Association* 41, no. 3 (March 1949).

Washington State Department of Ecology. "Hydraulic Continuity Policy." Draft. Olympia: Washington State Department of Ecology, 9 September 1992.

———. "1994 EPA 305(b) Report" (draft).

———. *Washington's Water Resources Program: Sixth Biennial Report to the Legislature.* Olympia: Washington State Department of Ecology, 1983.

Welsh, Frank. *How to Create a Water Crisis.* New York: Johnson, 1985.

Westman, Walter E. "Some Basic Issues in Water Pollution Control Legislation." *American Scientist* (November–December 1972).

Westphal, Joseph W., and James J. Lawler. *Commitments, Priorities, and Organizational Options for Water Resources Planning in Oklahoma.* Stillwater: Oklahoma Water Resources Research Institute, 1979.

Wheatcraft, Stephen, F. Patterson, and D. Heutmaker. "Water Injection into the Hawaiian Ghyben-Herzberg Aquifer." Technical Report No. 96. Honolulu: Hawaii Water Resources Research Center, 1976.

Wickersham, Gina. "Groundwater Management in the High Plains." *Ground Water* 18, no. 3 (May/June 1980).

Wiley, John K. "Eastern Washington May Face New Controls on Water." *Sea Times* 3 February 1995.

Wilkinson, Charles F. "Western Water Law in Transition." *Colorado Law Review* 56 (1985).

Willardson, Anthony. *State-Federal Financing and Western Water Resource Development.* Salt Lake City UT: Western States Water Council, 1984.

Windscheffel, Arno. "Kansas Water Rights: More Recent Developments." *Journal of the Kansas Bar Association* (fall 1978).

Woodfin, Max. "North Part of Edwards Aquifer Targeted for Protection." *American Statesman* (April 1984).

Worster, Donald. *Rivers of Empire: Water, Aridity, and the Growth of the American West.* New York: Pantheon, 1985.

Wyoming Department of Environmental Quality. "Water Quality Rules and Regulations." 1980.

———. "1983 Annual Report."

Wyoming Department of Environmental Quality, Water Quality Division. "1994 Wyoming Water Quality Assessment."

Wyoming State Engineer's Office. "A Water Development Program for Wyoming." October 1974.

Index